# KIND-HEARTED
# TIGER

# KIND-HEARTED TIGER

## by GILBERT STUART
## with ALAN LEVY

LITTLE, BROWN AND COMPANY · BOSTON · TORONTO

Published simultaneously in Canada
by Little, Brown & Company (Canada) Limited

*I dedicate this book to the Chinese*
*who shared their destiny with*
*mine in a desperate effort to*
*serve the cause of China,*
*and to those who still*
*live in desperation*
*and know not*
*the end.*

# Contents

[ vii ]

## Part III: Burma Road (1939–1942)

## Part IV: Chinese Army (1942–1946)

# I

Hong Kong Mines

[ 1938–1939 ]

# The Mouth of the Dragon

THE first thing I did when I saw the Agitator standing on top of a muck pile was to make sure my pistol clip was filled. I stuck the gun into the *front* of my belt; I didn't want anyone to sneak up from behind and slip the weapon out of my holster. I gripped my hose by the rubber end; the other end was solid lead. Then — and only then — did I listen to what the Agitator was saying.

"We are twenty of us down here tonight. Just one white man," he was telling the miners. "We kill him down here. Then we kill Indian guards up above. Then we kill other white men in mining camp. We take everything in camp. Then we cross border into China before nobody realize what happen."

I considered myself a tolerant man at the time, which was 1938. I was a shift boss at the Hong Kong lead mines and I had, after all, hired the Agitator as a miner despite the long criminal record he had amassed in the Malay States. If the management of the Mines had frowned upon criminals, we would have lost many of our best men; in fact, we probably would have had to close up shop. To many coolies, the main advantage of working for us was that the jobs were underground — where the legal authorities could scarcely find them. For some, the mines were a hideout; for others, a headquarters.

The Agitator was a killer, which was not unusual there. What made him a leader of men was his own bigotry: he hated the white man. He hated the white man's law. His crimes, he felt, were none of the white man's business, but the white man kept throwing him into jail. Other Orientals felt just as strongly, of course, and I seldom turned my back on more than two or three of my miners. But, of them all, only the Agitator had a philosophy — and that is what made him more dangerous than a dozen bigger men.

He was saying what I'd expected to hear, so I waited no longer. I was, after all, the first white man he had plans for. Springing out of the shadows and into his audience, I slashed vigorously but indiscriminately with my hose. I battered a face here, dented a head there. I must have clobbered six Chinese before any of them realized what was going on. "Get back to work!" I commanded sharply, as if I had stumbled onto nothing more than a group of idlers.

Most of the mob, retrieving their picks and shovels, obeyed. Even four of the bleeding men staggered instinctively to their posts. But eight of the miners didn't move — two because they were out cold; six others because they were the Agitator's hard core of toughs.

"Kill him!" the Agitator commanded shrilly. "Kill him now!"

I went for the Agitator, since he was the smallest and most influential of the lot. But, when a little man starts from the top of a six-foot-high pile of ore, he can go a long way. The Agitator flung himself at me. The impact knocked me off my feet. I fell to the ground with him swarming all over me. He clawed at my face. My hose slipped from my grasp. The Agitator retrieved it with a triumphant cackle.

That momentary victory of his may have saved my life, for his henchmen thought he had me and so they stood back to watch. But the hose was still attached to my right wrist by a leather thong. Unless the Agitator could manipulate my arm as well as the hose, the weapon was useless to him. While this was dawning on him, I pulled his hair.

Like most overseas Chinese in the 1930's, he had long hair. With my left hand, I got a good grip on his flowing locks and yanked his head back until I could see his wisdom teeth.

He still couldn't bring himself to relinquish his hold on the hose. Meanwhile, his other hand was trying to pry me loose from his hair. While both his hands were still occupied, I brought my knee up hard into his groin.

He rose at least a foot off the ground. When he came down, both his hands were clutching his groin. His mouth was still open, but now it was gasping for breath. While he lay there helplessly — on a mine floor 120 feet below the entrance — I rolled over, stood up, and kicked

[ 4 ]

him in the head. I didn't want any more trouble from him for a while. I knew I would have my hands full. These overseas Chinese (as Chinese who had lived most of their lives outside China were called) knew all the dirty tricks of East and West.

The Agitator's hoodlums had realized that their peerless leader was not going to win in man-to-man combat. Screaming curses, all six of them closed in on me. I pulled my gun and fired low — right into the center of the onslaught. The bullet didn't hit anybody, but it did its work. The Agitator's men backed off. In fact, they were so panicked that one of them began pummeling another of his pals.

My foreman, old Liu, had been powerless to help me when I first arrived, but now he swung into action. With several of the miners behind him — including one of the men I had bashed with the business end of my hose — Liu rushed at the Agitator's men. Brandishing a four-foot steel drill, the old man, bent by several decades below the ground, attacked like a mad musketeer. This comical sight was the finishing touch for the Agitator's forces. They crumpled weakly. I gave a few swishes of my hose. Soon, there was no opposition at all — just a bloody, silent mess on the floor.

I ordered all the other miners to line up facing me. "Down here, I am your master. Down here, I am your law," I told them and they nodded eagerly. "I am your law even when I am not here. Savvy?" They all nodded again. One or two of them bowed.

"Good," I continued. "So long as that's understood, I won't turn you over to the guards this time. I'll forget about this but if I ever catch you standing around listening to troublemakers again, you'll find out what a good memory I have."

When the men had resumed their work, I sent for the Indian guards who served as the mine police force. They took the Agitator and his gang to the mining camp hospital. Although the Agitator was probably the least badly hurt of the lot when he left the mine, he was the last to be released from the hospital. En route, the burly Indians administered a treatment for which they were famous. When the Agitator left the hospital, he was truly a sick man. I had him blacklisted from the mine because I never wanted to see his face again. Before he left, however, he vowed that I would.

The Hong Kong Mines were about thirty-five miles north of Hong

[ 5 ]

Kong — near Ling-Ma-Hang, a little village tucked between two high mountains. Ling-Ma-Hang stood on the border of the British New Territories and China. The Japanese, however, had invaded south China a year earlier and had made heavy gains. They ran the border patrols on the Chinese side. The border was wide open — and smugglers, spies, and adventurers took advantage of this.

The Hong Kong Mines, on the other hand, were sealed off — even from the British territory in which they lay. They were off limits to all Europeans unless they had special passes issued by the Hong Kong Police. Above and below the ground, there was constant danger of robbery and murder at the mines.

The mines themselves were several centuries old. They had changed hands many times — from Chinese to Portuguese to British to American. Although the mines were rich with galena, a high-grade lead and silver property, nobody had made a success of operating them. The early owners had been amateurs at both mining and humanity. Their only objective had been to get the best galena out of the ground at the cheapest cost — measured in money, not lives. If part of a mine caved in and trapped a dozen men, who was to blame? Why, the miners themselves, said the owners. The men were probably all dead already. It would be wasteful and futile to try to dig them out. Instead, the owners would hire twelve new men and start mining a new section — until the next cave-in.

When the Neilsen Mining Company, the American concern for which I worked, took over the mines in the twentieth century, they were already a notorious death trap.

The Americans, like their predecessors, were primarily interested in extracting a profit. But their ambition was tempered by an economic realization: Their properties would never pay off if they couldn't find the laborers to mine them. They solved this problem by initiating an occasional safety measure and by hiring some of the toughest coolies on the China coast — thieves, smugglers, murderers, bandits, army deserters, and even pirates. The police let them alone if they were working for us. After all, what better place for the scum of the earth than in the earth itself?

This comparatively progressive thinking had its weaknesses. For several years before I arrived there, the miners had been running the mines. Below the earth was their empire. They settled their grudges underground — and it was hardly news when we found a coolie with his throat cut. In the past, a few European supervisors had met similar fates. The other white men had virtually abdicated power, for they were either afraid of their miners or totally unaware of how to handle them. No matter how well a man thought he knew Orientals, he was in for a few surprises at the Hong Kong Mines — for these Chinese were outcasts from their own society.

With the twin menaces of cave-ins and one's fellow men always lurking, the mines were no place for weaklings. The three shift bosses — A. Duchet, a mining engineer with a checkered, raffish past; Victor Shamroff, a White Russian; and I, a twenty-six-year-old Australian with a lot of hostility to vent — had learned how to get the most out of our miners.

Our first measure had been brute force. For months, we had whipped discipline into our coolies while training them in the rudiments of mining. If we couldn't bring them around to our way of thinking, we could at least show them what and how we thought. They had to be aware of our code of ethics; eventually, they might come to respect it.

At first, we had to be cruel before we could be kind. By dealing sternly and violently with such men as the Agitator, we clubbed the coolies not into submission, but into a wary truce. As they started to produce, we gradually relaxed our tactics (if not our guard).

I had come to the Hong Kong Mines in early 1938 as a fervent friend of all things Chinese and an enemy of all that was Japanese. As a boy growing up in Australia, I had always considered the Chinese the heroes and the Japs the enemy. My father was a British Indian Army officer (sometimes, an agent for British Intelligence) and his attitudes may have impressed themselves on me. I know that it always hurt me to hear of the Chinese poverty, droughts, famines, and particularly, the frequent wars with the Japanese. "The Chinese must be good," I had told myself in my teens, "for they are more than two thousand years old." Perhaps my vision of the Chinese was childish, but it had helped bring me to the Hong Kong Mines. My hatred for the Japanese also shaped the crucial years of my life. It is, in a way, the story of my life. As my tale unfolds, you may come to understand me better, but this is not the time to explain myself further — for, in 1938 at the Hong Kong Mines, I did not understand myself much better than you do right now.

My blind, undiscriminating love for the Chinese people was assailed soon after I arrived at the mines. Even my relations with such kindly, gentle men as my foreman Liu were disillusioning. When I tendered my personal friendship, they wanted no part of it. When I offered my services to help them and their homeland — too much of which was already in Japanese hands — they responded listlessly. China was over there; they were here. If any of my grandiose schemes happened to possess a commercial side, which would profit my Chinese acquaintances, then they would listen. But even then they would ask one final question and then dismiss my offers. Their question was phrased in many ways, but it invariably came down to this: "What is in it for you, Mr. Stuart?"

The more altruistic my replies became, the more suspicious my listeners became. History had given them many reasons to distrust the foreigner; personal experience had added a few more. And in the twentieth century — East or West — nobody is looked upon with more suspicion than the man who offers something for nothing.

At sunrise one morning — after getting off the night shift — I was sipping bourbon on the porch of my bungalow. From where I sat I could gaze out and watch a narrow road — used for military travel — winding its way toward the mountains of the Chinese mainland. Along the road were small huts in which some of the miners lived with their families. Behind the houses were rice paddies — and the Chinese border, which was far more informal than I had expected it to be. A small river, running almost unseen east and west through the rice paddies, was the frontier.

I was wondering if this was as close as I would ever be to China. I could see across the border, but I could not go. The Japs — the enemies of China — could roam it at will, but China's friends couldn't. Almost opposite my chair — but a nation away — was a small village of ten houses. It stood at the foot of a mountain that rose to a height of at least a thousand feet. The mountain stood like a wall. At the time, I thought of it as another Great Wall of China — designed to keep me out.

[ 8 ]

My own bungalow, which I shared with Duchet, was built on the side of a mountain almost as tall. That was why my view was so encompassing; the distance from the foot of my mountain to the foot of the mountain inside China could not have been more than a few hundred yards.

Looking almost straight down, I could see the various mine buildings — the mill, the main office, and the mine police station, where we kept our Indian guards. Glancing upward past the mill, I could see a small trail snaking its way up the side of my mountain. It wound past my little office and ended abruptly at the mouth of the West Portal — the main entrance —of the Hong Kong Mines.

The sky grew bright and the air fresh and sweet. Nature and bourbon made me rejoice for a moment that I was alive. I even enjoyed being alone with my thoughts, which was uncharacteristic. I also enjoyed being with my good friend, the bottle. This was more like me.

I even felt a recurrence of my foolish benevolent thoughts — such as "All Chinese are good" — as I watched the miners traveling like ants along the trail between mill and mine. I watched the coolie women struggling with heavy burdens of timber as their men passed. Some of the women were slipping and sliding — not from the weight of the timber, but from the added weight of pregnancy. I thought of how all their tomorrows and tomorrows would creep in this petty pace and tried to remember what play that was from. I watched them for a while, glanced again at the Great Wall of China Mountain, downed my morning bourbon, and dozed off feeling remarkably well.

At five P.M., I was climbing the trail to the West Portal and passing many of the miners I had seen ascending in the morning. The day shift miners were half-running, half-stumbling toward me. As they passed, I could feel the ground vibrate with the impact of delayed dynamite charges going off down below. It was as if an underground monster were trying to smash a hole through the side of the mountain.

Each coolie smiled at me as he heard or felt the concussions. Explosions always stirred up a peculiar mixture of excitement and fear in the miners.

[ 9 ]

To give myself a better footing on the steep and narrow path, I pushed some of the coolies aside and cursed them as I brushed past. This made them smile at me again. The Chinese found my arrogance much more understandable and likable than my previous efforts to win friends and influence people. Authority had to be authoritarian.

My office — a field branch of the main office — was two-thirds of the way up the side of the mountain, not far from the mine's main entrance. By the time I reached there, I was soaked with sweat, exhausted, and, as usual, in a bad mood. There was a crowd of coolies assembled outside. The jabber of their dialogues slackened as I approached. Gradually, they stepped away from the door to let me enter. They were a tough-looking bunch — dressed in clothing which had been on their backs for so long that it had totally lost its color. For that matter, so had the men. The dirt from the mines had eaten into their skin and made them blend with the underground rock formations. It was perfect — but unwanted — camouflage.

My outer office was crowded with miners and muckers who were collecting their identification discs before going underground to work the night shift. I heaved and pushed and struck some of them to make way into the center of the room. The timekeeper sat at his desk to the left of the door. He was completely hemmed in by coolies, shouting at the top of their lungs for their identification discs, which they would get in due course. It was perfectly normal bedlam for the Hong Kong Mines.

The timekeeper was chatting with one of my older and more reliable miners, whom I had not seen for two weeks. Since there was a penalty for being absent more than two days without a satisfactory excuse, I made my way toward him. I wanted to hear his reasons.

As I approached, he spotted me. He snatched his identification disc from the timekeeper, thrust it into his pocket, and started for the door.

I grabbed him by the neck and kept him in the room. But he was slippery with sweat and I lost my grip. As he headed for the door again, I hit him with a rabbit punch to the side of the neck. He slumped to the floor in a daze.

There were rumblings behind me. The other coolies didn't appreciate this seemingly unprovoked roughness by me, so I swung on them with my fists. I knocked several of them down. The others rushed to the door. They were shouting that I had gone mad, but they were pushed back in by the men outside, who wanted to see what the commotion was all about. And, just like that, I had a riot on my hands.

Over all the din, I heard the calm but booming voice of Sam Coldron, the mine superintendent: "Just how many times do I have to tell you not to hit the bastards with your fists, Gil?"

The riot stopped abruptly — out of deference not to Sam, but to the Indian guard at his side. The Indian's look of anticipation would have done credit to a tiger waiting to be unleashed.

I decided to give the ferocious Sikh a little exercise. "Clear the place out!" I commanded. The guard threw his 260 pounds behind his nightstick and smashed into the mob. In slightly less than a minute, there was only one miner in the room — the one I had wanted to question. I had kept him from leaving. He was cowering in a corner.

Although I understood enough Chinese to establish my authority and a small reputation for cursing, I had a part-time interpreter named Alex, who was nineteen years old, half-Korean and half-Swedish. He and I dragged the miner to his feet.

"Where have you been for the past two weeks?" I asked and Alex interpreted.

The man hung his head and said nothing.

I slapped him across the face several times. Then I repeated my question.

"I been working, Mr. Stuart," he said. "I been working every day."

"You're a liar," I assured him. Then I turned to Alex and said: "Search him!"

Alex reached into the miner's pocket and came up with *three* identification discs. Two of them belonged to men who had also been missing for two weeks.

I turned to the timekeeper, a little man who was trying to make himself even smaller.

"Let me see the time sheets for the past two weeks," I said.

"Oh, sir," he said, looking positively bereaved. "They down the hill. At main office."

He, too, was lying. I lashed out and struck him on the head. When he picked himself up off the floor, his face wore a foolish grin that let me know his pride as well as his body had been hurt.

"You're going to lose a lot more face," I told him. "But you'd better start talking fast or I'm going to take you apart while your face is getting lost."

His hands began to claw at his desk. His face was twitching where I had slapped him.

"Mr. Stuart," he said, hanging his head. "I did make mistake. The time sheets are in my desk drawer." He reached in and handed them over.

The records showed that all three men had worked every day for the past two weeks.

I asked Alex to look through his own timebook, from which the time sheet records were made. Alex's book showed that none of the men had been working.

"You know," I told the timekeeper, "I don't demand perfection from you. I suppose it's possible for you to make a copying error once in a while. But I can scarcely understand how you'd make the same three errors every day for two weeks."

If I was trying to be funny, I wasn't succeeding. His grin was fading fast.

Alex took it seriously, too. "You're making me look bad, you bastard," he told the timekeeper. Alex grabbed the man's arm and started to bend it back toward the breaking point.

"This business must come to a stop," I told the perspiring timekeeper, "or I'll break every bone in your body. I've been watching you for the past few weeks. There aren't just three men you've been putting on the payroll; there are at least forty. What kind of a cut are you taking — ninety per cent?"

"Seventy-five, sir," he said pleadingly. Alex gave his arm another twist.

"I've been around long enough," I continued, "to know exactly how you bastards operate. And now that I've caught you red-handed, I'm going to fine you three months' pay."

This was, in a way, capital punishment. It hurt him far more than Alex's grip on his arm. I had learned that you could dish out any kind of punishment and a Chinese wouldn't turn a hair — until you docked his pay. Then he'd go to pieces.

[ 12 ]

"I'm sorry, sir," said the timekeeper. "I promise I pay you back. Only please don't fine me."

"You son of a bitch," I said. "I'm letting you keep a good desk job. What I should do is turn you over to that Indian guard for a little character guidance. He's just itching to put his hands on your neck."

I think the Chinese would have preferred this punishment, but I knew that if he were hurt I would then have to break in another time-keeper. Sooner or later, the next one would turn out to be as crooked as this one — but maybe he'd be a little smarter. At least I was aware of this one's tricks. For a while, he would slacken off; or rather, he might not squeeze so hard.

Alex let go, pushed him into a chair, and slapped his face. When I left, he was dictating to Alex a complete list of the participants in his scheme. They could be blacklisted — all except the few I knew to be good workers when they worked. I started for the inner office to check out with Sam Coldron, the mine superintendent.

As I stepped through the doorway, a coolie came flying through the air. He almost hit me in the face, but I sidestepped and he landed at my feet. To put him back on his feet, I gave him a good swift kick. Before he could gather momentum, however, he collided with Vic Shamroff, another shift boss. Vic pushed the coolie back to me, but I wasn't having any part of him. I gave a roundhouse swat that landed him at Vic's feet again.

Sam Coldron said: "When you boys have finished playing soccer, I'd like to ask you a question, Gil."

He leaned back in his swivel chair. His feet were crossed atop his desk. A cigarette dangled from the side of his mouth. His eyebrows had a habit of rising and falling disconcertingly several times a minute. There was a faint grin on his tight thin lips, but it vanished when he looked down at the coolie. Sam pointed his pencil at him and said bitterly:

"Gil, take a good look at that face." Sam hardly moved his lips. When he spoke, he spat out his words. He also had a nervous mannerism of making a spitting sound without actually expectorating. He went through this dry-spitting cycle several times and then said: "Have you ever seen him before?"

The coolie's mouth was bleeding. He had a cut across his cheek. His shirt was ripped open and I could see blood on his hands. It was

[ 13 ]

oozing out beneath a cord that was bound tightly around his wrists. Obviously, Sam and Vic had been giving him more than a casual working-over. But, even allowing for the effects of their beating, I knew I had never seen him before.

"How about those two?" Sam asked. For the first time, I noticed two other coolies sitting on the floor in the corner. Their hands, too, were tied behind their backs.

"I recognize them. They're drillers," I told Sam.

"But you've never seen this first guy before?"

"No."

"I thought as much," Sam said. "Look what we found on the three of them."

On Sam's desk were twenty sticks of dynamite.

"I hear the going price is one Chinese dollar per stick," I remarked, "so business must be booming. Where did you catch these guys?"

Vic Shamroff answered: "Coming out of the East Portal of the mine. As soon as they saw me, they started running. I didn't know what was amiss, but I took after them." Vic glared down at the first coolie, kicked him hard, and continued: "And this one here, believe it or not, pulled a knife on me and wanted to play rough."

Now I knew why Sam and Vic had worked him over so thoroughly: "He did what?"

Vic repeated everything, starting with the kick. "He pulled a knife on me. Didn't you, you bastard?" Vic kicked him again. "Now who's the tough guy? I'll teach you to pull a knife on me."

"Do *you* happen to know him?" I asked Vic.

"Never saw him before in my life," Vic replied.

I studied the man. "He's not a miner," I said. "You can tell that just by looking at him. His skin is weather-beaten and too damn clean. And his trousers are rolled up like a fisherman's." I sniffed the man. "Yes, he's a fisherman. He must be the dynamite buyer."

Sam Coldron lowered his feet from his desk and glared at Vic and me. "It's getting to be a big business when the buyer comes direct to the mine for his stolen dynamite. We've never had that before," Sam said. "Just what the hell is happening to you two guys? Are you getting soft with those Chinese bastards? Are you letting

[ 14 ]

them walk all over you? Do you know how much dynamite they're stealing each week? Last week, it was over three cases — not to mention detonators and fuses. If this keeps up, we'll be out of business in a month. Hell, they're buying dynamite right under your nose. We've got to find a way to stop it."

Sam was asking the impossible. If we caught half the thieves, we'd be doing well. "I'll get the guards to search the miners more carefully," I said.

"Fine," Vic replied, "but who's going to search the guards?"

There was no answer, so Sam dry-spat and then lit a fresh cigarette. From inside a cloud of smoke, his voice issued orders about the prisoners: "Call in the guard and have the one with the knife put in the guardhouse. Have the other two put on the blacklist. Add a note that, if we ever see any of them again, they're to be shot on sight."

The Indian guard was standing near the door. He had been listening to all that was said. He had obviously been hoping that we wouldn't work the coolies over too hard before he took over. At my signal, he fell upon them. He dragged the knife-wielder by the hair to the center of the floor. He forced the man's head between his knees and squeezed them together. I thought the prisoner's eyes would pop out of their sockets. I almost felt sorry for him at that moment.

Then the guard freed the man's head, grabbed him by the ears, and twisted them until the Chinese let out a hideous scream. The sound was music to the guard's ears, for he stopped glowering and began to smirk.

I hate to see anyone becoming smug, even when he's on my side, so I sneaked behind the guard and planted a kick in his rear. It knocked him off balance. Before he could do so much as snarl, I ordered him to stand at attention.

"We are not impressed by your performance," I told him. "You play with him like you would a baby. Now why don't you take him to the guardhouse and tuck him into bed for the night. And, if you don't do better hereafter, I'll beat your guts away and tear out your beard by the roots."

With an expression of despair, the Indian guard kicked all three coolies to their feet. They disappeared, with Vic Shamroff trailing behind the procession and murmuring: "That one there pulled a knife on me. He wanted to play rough."

"Well," Sam said after the door closed, "now we can talk in peace. What are we going to do about the dynamite thieving, Gil?"

"Now, look, Sam," I said, "it's a damn shame, but you know that we'll never be able to do much about it because the biggest stealers are our most reliable Number One's." Foremen were called Number One's in the Hong Kong Mines.

"Hell, yes," Sam agreed. "They're stealing hundreds of sticks a week and selling them to the fishermen at Shatowkok for a dollar a stick — or a dollar-fifty with fuse and cap."

The Chinese dollar was worth about three cents in American money. Ten Chinese dollars were enough to keep a coolie alive for at least a month or two.

I told Sam: "I'll try to work out a system of loading so that one of us is with them at all times. But the trouble is it'll slow down the job. And it'll only be a matter of time before they think up a way to get around it. You know, Sam, while you and I are worrying about a bundle of problems, those bastards are thinking twenty-four hours a day about just one thing: stealing an easy buck. They'll always be one jump ahead of us."

"Well," Sam said resignedly, "just so long as that one jump isn't on your back when you're least expecting it. Now let's get to work."

From outside, I could hear Vic and the Chinese foremen lining the miners into groups. The sun had slipped out of sight. I liked the night shift because I didn't miss any light when I worked. The air had a faint smell of burnt dynamite fuses wafted by the evening breeze.

"What's doing down in hell tonight?" I asked Sam.

"About the same as yesterday. The ore chutes are empty on the upper and lower levels. If it's like the last few nights, we'll be short of men. We've got a couple of Limey tramp foremen who are even worse than the worst overseas Chinese."

"They're always too scared or too drunk to go underground," I remarked.

"Tonight they're both," Sam said. "Anyway, I haven't seen a sign of them."

"Then at least I won't have to keep an eye on them," I said.

[ 16 ]

"The thing for you to watch, Gil, is the stope in Four West." A stope is the underground room where ore is mined.

"What's doing there?"

"It looks too wide. We'll have to fill it before it caves in. You'd better get in there ahead of the muckers and check the back of it for cracks. We don't want to waste any more time digging those thieving bastards out."

On my way to the mine, I caught up with my best Number One, old Liu. Even though he was one of my few Chinese friends, I noticed that, whenever I spoke to him, he swung his miner's lamp nervously from one hand to the other.

Maybe he was afraid I'd found out that he was stealing dynamite. I'd have worried more if he *hadn't* been stealing in moderation.

Or maybe he was afraid I'd take away his lamp. I had given him permission to take his lamp home with him after work. He was one of the few who had this privilege, which gave him much face in his community.

I told him: "Liu, the day shift blasted in Four West and it'll be very dangerous tonight, so I want you to listen to what I say."

"I listen, Mr. Stuart."

"When you get into the stope, keep your men along the sides and the back. Then use your crowbars to pry down all loose rocks and slabs. Have half your men carry in eight-by-eight timbers and put up wooden props wherever they're needed. The other men should be separating as much waste from the ore as they can. They're to put the ore into the chute, as usual. But save as much waste as possible. When all the ore is taken out, you can use the men to fill in the back of the stope with the waste. Maybe that'll hold it together until the finishing touches are done. You savvy what I say, Liu?"

"I savvy everything. We work plenty good. We put plenty ore in chutes. I savvy."

"Liu, there's just one other thing. If I catch you stealing dynamite, God help you! Do you savvy that, too?" As a gentle reminder, I gave his neck a slight but painful squeeze.

Liu laughed and said: "What I do with dynamite, Mr. Stuart? I no take dynamite. But I savvy."

"You savvy all right, Liu, so don't try to tell me you're not stealing it. I haven't caught you at it, but when I do you'll get the same treat-

[ 17 ]

ment as all the others." It was the most tactful way I knew to warn him to go easy because we were cracking down. He swore his loyalty a few more times.

When I thought he had himself believing that he was a pillar of honesty, I gave him an affectionate kick in the stern and sent him on his way. He was clutching the seat of his pants as he hopped along the trail to catch up with his men.

The West Portal of the Hong Kong Mines looked like the open mouth of a dragon. With the flicker of the miners' lights inside, the dragon could have been breathing fire.

An ordinary dragon, however, would be noisy. This one was silent. Even the chatter of the Chinese miners had faded when they entered. I stood right where — not many years earlier — the entrance had caved in and taken several lives. Over the centuries, the dragon had devoured hundreds of men.

The silence filled me with alertness. Every night — in the same ritualistic way that people wish upon a star — I cursed the dragon known as the Hong Kong Mines. "I will blast your guts out and fill you full of muck until I choke you to death, you bastard," I swore nightly, knowing I could never win.

Wisps of powder smoke still floated out of hundreds of holes, drifts, and cross-cuts that honeycombed the mine. I swung my lamp — which had a twenty-foot beam — in an arc from left to right. Then I pointed it up over my head. I was watching out for two dangers: attack by my miners and first signs of potential cave-ins or hanging rocks.

Water was dripping from old cracks thirty feet overhead. Long iron-stained rocks hung down like the teeth of a monster, but the teeth weren't loose. Satisfied that all was well, I moved forward.

Some twenty feet further on and a little to the left was the entrance to an old drift. In a mine, a drift is a man-made passageway that follows the course of a rich vein of ore. This drift dipped down a hundred feet toward an ancient stope that had caved in several months earlier. Ten men had been working inside the stope. It had been impossible to save them without risking the lives of the rescue workers. The stope and the men had been left to rot.

[ 18 ]

Every time I passed the old drift, I fancied that I could smell rotten flesh.

I moved away to the right, where the back slope of a cave met the floor in what seemed like a dead end. But, looking closely, one could perceive a tunnel entrance — about two feet high — barely concealed by a pile of fallen rocks.

The most direct route through the tunnel was on your back. I sat down on the rocks and slipped through the hole. Then I slid down. Whenever I did this, the analogy to a dragon recurred: I was slipping down the monster's throat.

It was some thirty feet to the bottom of the tunnel. When I slid out of it, I rolled over onto my knees. There still wasn't enough room for me to stand up, but I was able to crawl another forty feet through a perfectly horizontal drift until I reached the stope, where some forty of my men were already mining the ore.

We had been working in this particular stope for months — and we were nearly finished. The ore was mined out, except for a few feet near the upper level. It is at such times that the danger of a cave-in is high. To keep the stope standing firm, we had taken care to leave pillars of solid galena; these pillars, we hoped, would prop up the stope as long as possible.

It was time to extract everything of value — and then make our getaway. This was a process that would take several shifts of doing. Right now, we were whittling down the pillars— our most visible means of support — from forty feet in diameter to twenty feet. The element of risk would be magnified a thousand times.

This stope promised to be particularly treacherous. There was an old, caved-in stope somewhere above us, but we had never been able to pinpoint it. All we could be sure of was that thousands of tons of rock and dirt were waiting to come crashing down on our heads. Probably, it would take the mere removal of one key rock to unleash the deluge.

My only consolation was that I had a good shift with me that night. Six jackhammers were drilling away at the pillars, while other men propped timber under loose slabs. About thirty muckers — already coated with slime and sweat — were shoveling as fast as they knew how. This wasn't fast enough for me.

I pushed my way over to where the coolies were working. I climbed up on the muck pile, from which the Agitator had harangued many of the same men. As before, I held a two-foot length of hose with a lead tip. The man who malingered would feel it across his back.

I beckoned to old Liu and said: "Tell them the stope may cave in and crush us all to death any minute now. Tell them to speed it up, and, as soon as they've mucked out all the ore, they can clear out and work another stope until it's quitting time."

This was a calculated risk. It was intended to goad them into a frenzy of efficiency. It could also backfire; they might decide to leave now. At times like this, there were always a few men who would try to sneak out of the stope by slipping past me. I would halt them with my hose and whip them back to the muck pile. There were others who would try to maneuver themselves behind me and bring me down with their picks. There was only one way to defeat them: I never let them sneak behind me. Whenever I suspected an attack, I simply lashed out with the hose — hard, but not hard enough to disable a man. I needed every workman I could get and keep.

Most of the men trusted me as much as they would allow themselves to trust any white man. They had learned that I was always the last man out of a tough spot. Unlike other bosses, I wouldn't leave them to face any horror I wouldn't face myself. So long as I was there, they felt safe. I had saved them before; I would save them again.

I envied them this fragment of security. I had nobody in whom to put my faith. To me, each stope was a tomb and I was its keeper.

My gamble worked that night. The place became alive with action. The sweat began oozing out of the men in new spurts. There was hardly any air down there; what little there was came through one entrance. There was also an ore chute, which led to a drift two hundred feet below the stope. The chute was filling up with ore. Although the stench was terrible, the smell of sweat was heartening at this stage.

I found the rock dust — sprayed by the drills — far more irritating. It filled the air and slashed at my throat, but I couldn't afford to stop yelling at my men.

They worked as if their lives were at stake, which they were. They grew impatient when, every thirty minutes, I would make everybody

[ 20 ]

stop work while I looked and listened for new cracks in the hanging walls. I would also pummel the wooden stalls, which had been propped under the big slabs, to make sure everything was holding firm. The ring of the timber would tell me all that I wanted to know.

Once I was satisfied, I would rap the nearest man with my hose. "Why aren't you working?" I would ask him.

All the miners would grab their picks and their drills and resume work in a new frenzy of fear. Some shouted or prayed or moaned as they worked. And I would shout: "It won't be long now. If we don't get our work done, we'll all be dead men."

The last of the ore was out shortly after midnight. I sent the workmen to another stope — a safe one, for a while — where they could begin a new project. Liu and I remained behind to plant the dynamite charges that would bring down the pillars of galena — and perhaps the whole stope.

If the stope came tumbling down, that would be the end of it. A few tons of lead, but no lives, would be lost.

If the stope remained, it would take another shift of men a whole day to salvage the galena from the blasted pillars. They would have to rely on the solidity of the rock ceiling above them. This was a gamble indeed; the old caved-in, unmapped stope was lurking somewhere above — just waiting for an opening.

Perhaps I should have sent my men back into the same treacherous stope to start the clean-up work, but I couldn't do it to them.

I had promised to liberate them when they extracted the ore — an assignment Sam Coldron scarcely expected to be completed in less than two days. We did it overnight. Let Duchet and the day shift clean up after us!

With a clear conscience and a feeling that the job was well done, I left the West Portal of the mine and trudged to my office, where I lit a cigarette and made out my reports on the night's work. Duchet, who bossed the next shift, was a hard driver. I hoped he would clean up the stope in one day because, if I spent any more time there, I would go out of my mind.

A few minutes after the last of my miners went off duty, the dynamite charges Liu and I had planted went off.

Sitting in my office, I felt — rather than heard — the sharp crackle coming from far away. The vibration grew more severe and then, from the gaping hole of the West Portal, came an ear-splitting roar.

The dragon was digesting his dynamite and letting loose his noise. If Duchet and his men were lucky, there would be no more stope when they arrived there.

But, if its roof had not come tumbling down, then Duchet's men were in for ten or eleven tense hours even worse than the ones we had just spent.

I signed my papers and started down the mountain toward my bungalow.

My amah (the Oriental equivalent of maid, cook, and nurse) and my houseboy were waiting up to serve me. Their smiling faces and affectionate care were invariably the high points of my day.

I tossed the boy my hat and lamp. Without stopping, I loosened my gunbelt and let it slip to the floor. Still moving, I stripped off my clothes. Racing like a sailor en route to a busy whore, I was under the shower less than sixty seconds after I had crossed the threshold. I turned the water on hot and stayed there until I heard my boy come back with a tall glass of bourbon on the rocks.

The amah came in to collect my clothes and give me hell for messing up her floor. She cleaned it so often that she considered it *her* floor, not mine.

I was starting to feel human again, so I wrapped a dry towel around my waist, picked up a soggy towel from the shower floor, and took off after the amah. I whacked her several times on the rump with my wet towel. The boy, who was watching, laughed so hard that he almost dropped my bourbon. I sat down for supper, drank my whiskey, and continued to tease the amah.

"You're a good cook," I told her, "but you're not as good a cook as your husband."

Her husband was a miner who lived with her in the servants' quarters. "He no cook," the amah told me.

"Well," I said, "then maybe you have other qualities that I know nothing about. Perhaps my houseboy knows what they are."

The young boy cackled. The amah blushed and ran into her bedroom to awaken her husband, a good-humored man who came in sleepily to find out in what way we were torturing his wife today.

When we told him, he laughed and remarked that, if we discovered any good qualities in his nagging shrew of a wife, we should let him know. "In twenty-five years," he said, "she no make any babies. She no good." He laughed again. I knew, however, that things said in jest are often meant in earnest. After living together for all those years without bearing children, the amah and her husband had suffered considerable frustration and loss of face. But they learned to share the burden and even to tease each other about it. Now — in middle age — it was almost forgotten and forgiven.

After supper, I settled down with a book and the bottle of bourbon I needed for unwinding before attempting to sleep. Soon, I heard Duchet — who shared my bungalow and my servants — preparing for the day shift. One of the oddities of a household whose members kept totally different hours was that Duchet's breakfast came just an hour or so after my supper.

"What the hell are *you* doing up, Gil?" he asked, as if he didn't find me in the dining room every morning. He looked me over and clucked disapprovingly. "Drunk again?"

"Not yet," I replied. "I can't sleep until I am."

"You don't need the booze," Duchet told me. "All you need is a trip to Hong Kong and one of those White Russian countesses."

"I like Hong Kong just fine," I said, "but after two days there, I'm ready to come back to the mines."

"You dumb bastard!" Duchet exclaimed. "You must be mad!"

"You're the same way. Why are you here?"

"For the money, of course," he said, studying me as if I might know more than that.

Duchet was a conceited, arrogant, insecure drunk with dark hair, bushy mustache, and thin-rimmed eyeglasses that made him look unexpectedly prim. I had neither the patience nor the wisdom even to try to understand him. So I blundered on: "Duchet, let me ask you something. Just out of curiosity, of course." Then I stopped and waited until he asked impatiently what I wanted to know. He was growing edgy.

"Duchet, why did you leave the Philippines in such a hurry?"

I thought he would leap over the table. Instead, he drew himself up and told me: "That's none of your God damn business, you

[ 23 ]

Limey bastard. I'd beat your brains out — if you had any. My advice to you is: Don't get curious. Understand?"

"Sorry, Duchet. No harm meant. Let's just forget the whole thing."

But I had learned everything I needed to know from this seemingly unrevealing conversation. I already knew why Duchet had left the Philippines: the usual sordid, rather dull story of booze and a woman. Over our third bottle of bourbon a few nights earlier, he had told me all.

You can make no worse enemy than a man who knows you share his terrible secret. Thus, the two things I had learned from this conversation were useful to me:

Duchet had been too drunk to remember having told me his story.

And I would be wise never to remind him.

While Duchet ate, he inquired — as casually as he could — about the sturdiness of the Four West stope.

"Well," I told him, "we got through my shift without any injury. And we got all the ore out, except for the clean-up operation."

"That's all?" Duchet remarked ironically.

"That's plenty. In my opinion, we just ought to leave those pillars and stay out of the stope while the staying's good. It could cave in any minute now if it hasn't already."

"I wish it had," Duchet said, "but we'd have heard about it by now."

"I feel like a murderer every time I send my men in there," I remarked.

"I feel like I'm committing suicide every time I go to work," Duchet said.

We both knew, however, that our orders were to mine the stope until the last ton of ore was out of it.

"This stope," said Duchet, "is worse than all the others because there's only one way in and one way out. And what a son of a bitch that exit is, too." He summoned the houseboy and said: "Bring me a glass of tomato juice. I have a hell of a hangover."

Since I had contributed to Duchet's difficult morning, I told him to skip the tomato juice: "I'll make you a prairie oyster."

"The last thing on earth I need right now is fish," Duchet assured me.

When I explained that a prairie oyster is a drink, Duchet handed

[ 24 ]

me an empty glass. "All right," I said, "pass me the Worcestershire sauce. And, boy, bring me a raw egg."

The houseboy disappeared, shouting "low egg! . . . low egg!" at the amah. When he came back with the egg, he stayed around to watch.

"You pour half a glass of Worcestershire sauce," I continued. "Add plenty of pepper and salt and then you break the raw egg like so into the concoction. The egg, you'll notice, kind of floats. Now all you do is drink it. It'll put a lining on your guts and it'll steady your nerves."

Duchet looked warily at the glass and then at me.

"I guess I'm a sucker," he said, "but I can't feel any worse than I do now." He lifted the glass, closed his eyes, and then gulped it down in one swallow.

The houseboy blanched. I was a little nervous, too.

Duchet smacked his lips, belched a few times, and then sat back in his chair with a contented look on his face.

"Not bad, boy. Not bad at all," he complimented me. "Not bad indeed for a boy from a backward country like Australia."

As he donned his gunbelt and set off for work, he said: "What do you call it again? Prairie dog?"

"Prairie oyster," I replied. "You want me to write down the recipe?"

"No," he said. "I won't need it again. I just wanted to try it on for size because I've never had one. I guess we only have to die once."

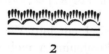

## 2

# The Dragon Strikes

I USED to dream every morning that the mine had caved in. Often, I awoke to find that I was lying on my side and my face was pressed hard against the wall near my bed. I was groping with my hand trying to find a way out. In the dimness of my room I continued to

[ 25 ]

grope for a few seconds. Then I came to my senses and went back to sleep — only to dream that I was beating my fists against the side of the stope.

At ten o'clock in the morning — just three or four hours after Duchet's prairie oyster — I was awakened by a gentle tug on my arm. The amah was there and I said to her: "What the hell are you doing, amah?"

I think I already knew what she would tell me: "Much trouble topside. All mine come down on coolie. Coolie run. Much trouble. So Boy Number One he come to tell you."

I bolted upright in my bed. My first reaction was: *Well, it's happened. Maybe now I won't dream about it any more.*

I asked the amah: "Where's Boy Number One?"

Her answer was more devious than usual: "Your dog."

"My dog? What the hell does my dog have to do with it?"

"Your dog bite Boy Number One, so boy say the hell with waiting for you. He go running back topside before dog bite him again. He say he see you up there."

I laughed. I knew it would probably be the only touch of comedy I could expect all day.

The mine office was empty when I arrived. Hundreds of coolies were running uphill and downhill. They were carrying timber to the disaster area. From their frantic pace, I knew the situation was bad.

I sat just long enough to catch my breath. I was soaked with sweat, although I hadn't even reached the scene of the disaster. I was shaking all over — partly from fatigue, partly from excitement, and mostly from fright.

Near the West Portal, I ran into Vic Shamroff. Armed with a pick handle, he was threatening a mob of confused coolies with death if any of them disobeyed him. I could see he had his hands full.

I pushed forward. A few feet to my right stood a hundred Chinese women and children. They were huddled together, chanting and wailing their grief, on the side of the hill overlooking the portal.

Just inside, the coolie rescue workers were shrieking. And, to add to the din, someone was setting off firecrackers by the hundreds in there. It is a Chinese custom to explode firecrackers in the presence of the dead. This is supposed to frighten away various evil spirits, who would otherwise torment the dead. At the moment, however, the firecrackers weren't helping the rescue any. I ordered the coolies to put away their toys and start to work with picks and shovels.

Farther along in the portal, coolies were stacking timber. Others were carrying baskets of dirt and rock from the disaster area.

A human chain of coolies was passing baskets of dirt along as fast as they could. The smell of sweat and fear was almost overpowering. As I pushed past them, I would occasionally have to clamber over a rescue worker who had passed out from exhaustion. Visibility was poor. The lack of oxygen had almost extinguished the carbide lamps hanging from pillars.

Still farther in, some coolies were digging a tunnel with short-handled shovels, but a good fifteen feet of debris remained between them and the trapped miners. Sam Coldron, the superintendent, was standing just inside the tunnel they were digging. When I joined him, he had to crouch down because there wasn't enough room for two of us to stand there.

"If we can stop these bastards from taking off down the hill and if we can keep them working at this speed, we may save some of the guys inside," Sam told me.

"How many are in the stope?"

"We don't know for sure," Sam said.

"Didn't anyone count them before they went in?"

"Yes," Sam replied, "but we don't know how many came out before we got here. Some of them may have had a chance to escape if they thought fast enough. Those that did get away are probably still running down the hill. The guards managed to stop some of them and march them back up. But we had one hell of a job persuading them to enter the portal again. They say the devil himself is in here."

"I think they're right, for a change," I said. "Where's Duchet?"

"He's O.K.," Sam told me. He pointed into the tunnel that was being dug. "He's up front, making sure they work."

I was relieved. In retrospect, Duchet's words at breakfast had sounded like those of a doomed man.

Sam interrupted my meditation: "Just where did you work last night, Gil?"

"Right where you told us to. And then I slabbed those pillars when we got to them — exactly as you told me to."

Sam knew that I didn't bear any responsibility for the disaster. Neither did he. "It's a good thing," he said, "that we have those orders in writing from the main office."

"They know as well as I do that, if you knock down the props of a stope, the roof's going to cave in sooner or later."

"They always gamble on it happening later, not sooner," Sam said. "I've been warning them, but they said, 'Don't worry about possibilities; your job is to worry about results.'"

"Well," I said, pointing down the tunnel, "these are the results."

Sam said: "I'd like to put some of those front office bastards down here in this hole with a muck stick for just one shift. They'd change their tune."

I changed the subject. I offered to go forward and give Duchet a rest.

"O.K.," Sam said. "Do that. But make sure you keep an eye on the Chinks. They'll kill you if you give them half a chance."

The tunnel was so narrow that each mucker had to stop work to let me squeeze past. I slapped several of the coolies across the face just to let them know I was on the job and every bit as mean as ever. To my surprise, they were happy to see me.

I wormed my way to the side of Duchet, who greeted me with: "So here you are at last, you Limey bastard. This is your mess and if you think I'm going to clean it up for you . . ."

"Hold it right there, Duchet. Are any of my men in there?"

"No," he said, "mine."

"O.K. Then it's your mess, you son of a bitch. But I'll be good to you. I'll help you clean it up."

Duchet relaxed slightly, took off his glasses, and tried to find a dry spot on his shirt to wipe them clean. Giving that up, he said: "Gil, do you have a cigarette on you? Mine are all soaked with sweat."

I gave him my whole pack.

"You didn't by any chance bring a flask of booze down with you?" Duchet asked next.

"No. I thought you had a hangover."

[ 28 ]

"That's exactly why I want it, you dumb Limey. I need either a drink or another of your prairie oysters."

"Stop daydreaming and tell me how it happened."

The stope had caved in a few minutes after the men had entered it — just as Duchet was reaching the main entrance to the mine. The foreman had already arrived in the stope. He was telling the men to stand back while he barred down the hanging rocks. He must have pried loose the keystone — the one rock that was holding everything together.

Down came the roof of the stope — gradually at first. This gave some of the men a chance to run to the sides. Others froze in their tracks.

Duchet had descended through the hole and was crawling along the drift that led to the stope. "Even if I hadn't started out on all fours, I would have ended up that way," he recalled. "The draft that hit me would have knocked me over. I was scared to death. I didn't know whether to get the hell out or take a look. I didn't hear a damn thing. Then the place was filled with dust. Something bumped into me. It knocked my hat off and put out my light."

The "something" was a coolie fleeing the disaster. Every time Duchet tried to get up, he was knocked over by other escapees. He guessed that he was trampled by ten of them.

"Finally," he said, "I lit my lamp, but it was no good to me. The dust was too thick to see through. I crawled along the drift and met my foreman coming the other way. We bumped heads and rolled over. As we picked ourselves up, we heard slabs falling in the entrance to the stope. We started to run — away from the stope. We just reached the end when we heard one hell of a racket behind us. The drift was going, too."

There were men behind Duchet and his foreman, but they didn't escape in time. "I heard them scream," he said.

As Duchet told his story, I beamed my light so that it fell on the debris, which was gradually receding as the men chipped away at it.

"Duchet," I said, "have you noticed the color of the dirt that's mixed in with the caved rock?"

"Yes, it's backfill."

[ 29 ]

"That means only one thing. It's muck from that old stope we never could locate."

"Where do you think it came from? A rice paddy? And you know what this means if we ever get inside? That old stope'll be dangling over our heads, too." I was glad to hear Duchet's sarcasm. It meant he was regaining his composure.

But, since I was fresher than Duchet, I suggested that I take over the men who were digging through the drift. There was room for only one boss in the cramped space. Duchet went back to goose the coolies in the second echelon.

"Dig!" I told the crew. "Dig, you lousy bastards!" I wasn't satisfied with their pace, so I took a shovel from a coolie and began to dig myself. Since I was the healthiest and newest man there, I filled the dirt baskets very rapidly. Then I shouted that this was the pace I expected of them.

The spectacle of a white man working with his hands was a rare one for them. They passed the word down the line of coolies, who reacted with jeers of disbelief and then with the cries I wanted to hear: "Hurry, hurry! . . . White devil, he filling baskets." As they sped up their work, they began to chant in rhythm.

We worked feverishly. As we cut through the drift, we erected a whole new tunnel of wood. The day wore on and the men plowed on, too afraid to quit. If they slackened, I would kill them. They did well. By the time I brought them out, it was well past sundown. Most of them had been working fourteen hours without a break. A new shift had been assembled to relieve them.

Duchet and I weren't knocking off, however. While the shifts changed, we stood inside the main entrance to the mine. The air was so fresh and sweet that you could almost taste it. It tasted rich. We lit cigarettes and just stood, smoking and breathing.

Carbide and oil lamps had been placed here and there inside the portal. They threw strange shadows that danced on the wall. Outside, a few lamps were burning where men were still assembling timber.

My houseboy and the amah brought us food and, while we ate, Duchet and I discussed the outlook.

"One good thing about the old missing stope caving in," I said, "is that it probably was near the surface and now there's some sort of opening. If the men inside weren't killed by the cave-in, they

[ 30 ]

should have plenty of fresh air for a while. They won't smother."

This was no consolation to the families waiting and wailing and exploding firecrackers outside the mine. Duchet and I stepped out to look at them.

"What a happy bunch of bastards!" Duchet remarked. "I bet they're going to love us for this."

"From the number of mourners, I have a horrible feeling that there are more men inside that stope than we think."

Some of the mourners were urging the others to attack us. I called one of the Indian guards over and told them to keep them quiet without getting rough or starting a riot. "If they make any trouble now, we'll never get their people out," I said.

"They're probably still mad because they're not allowed to set off their firecrackers inside the mine," Duchet said.

"Let's get back in our hole before these people get any ideas."

As we entered the mine, I detected a strong smell of opium coming from down below. At any other time, I would have gone after the miners who were smoking it. I didn't object to their chewing opium underground, but smoking it would make the place an opium den.

"Let's overlook it this time," I said to Duchet. "Maybe it'll give them the same kind of Dutch courage that we get from liquor."

"I know what you mean," he said. "A few more days like today and I'll be ready for the pipe myself."

We were almost to the drift when Chan, one of the foremen from my night shift, came hurrying toward us. He grabbed my arm and said, "Mr. Stu! Mr. Stu!" He was too sweaty and exhausted and excited to make any sense. All I could fathom was that there was news. I couldn't tell whether it was bad or good.

Duchet and I pushed on past Chan to the end of the drift. The men were taking a rest period, which gave them time to think over the situation and their surroundings. One quick look at their faces showed me that fear and terror were starting to get the better of them.

"Stay between the new tunnel and the drift," I told Chan. "Don't let anybody out."

The fear I saw on the rescue workers' faces was a reassuring sign. They must have made some kind of contact with the trapped men. They would not be this afraid of their tunnel caving in on them.

[ 31 ]

Now they were worrying about the dead bodies or evil spirits they might soon be recovering.

At the very tip of the tunnel, Vic Shamroff was forcing timbers into place to hold back the dirt. "I broke through the face of the stope at the top right-hand corner," he told us, "with a hole about the size of your head. Then I took a shovel from a mucker and tried to make the hole bigger. But the faster I mucked the dirt out, the faster she came in. So the hole's all filled in again."

I asked: "Did you hear anything? Any noise from inside?"

"Yes," Vic said. "I could hear the men and they must have seen the light shining through the hole. There's a hell of a racket going on in there. If you listen, you can hear."

I told Chan to keep his men quiet behind me. Duchet and I listened. The survivors sounded quite a long way off for men who were just a few feet away.

"I believe they're over on the other side of the stope," Vic said.

"Well," I said, "let's get some more timber in here and keep digging. Remember, though, we'll have to dig with care. We're right in the area where all the caving happened and we're part way into the stope. If we make any false moves, we'll feel the results."

I told Duchet to clear half the coolies out of the tunnel. Thus those who remained had plenty of room for fast work. Although they did work quickly, it took six tedious and nerve-wracking hours to dig away from fifteen feet of dirt and rock.

Finally, a hole appeared right where Vic Shamroff had penetrated more than six hours earlier.

This time, we inserted timber to hold it open. Then we made the hole larger — partly by scraping dirt toward us, partly by pushing dirt in. I could feel a draft coming through the hole. This meant that air was reaching the trapped men.

Soon, the hole was large enough to look through. By then, we were hearing a steady human wail coming from inside the stope. As Duchet stepped forward to see what was going on in there, he remarked, "At least they sound as if their lungs are healthy."

Although the hole wasn't big enough for his shoulders, he was able to poke his head into it.

Suddenly, Duchet staggered back and landed in a heap. Blood was streaming down his face.

[ 32 ]

Through the hole came a naked coolie writhing and punching his way out. In his hand was a rock, with which he had attacked Duchet. We focused our lamps on his face. The glare stopped him momentarily when he was about halfway through. His head was held high, revealing the full expression on his face. His eyes seemed to be protruding from his head. They were staring at the light with a peculiar fixity. Patterns of dried blood ran from his ears, his mouth and his nose. A chill ran down my spine as Duchet shouted up from the floor: "Look out! He's gone mad! He'll kill!"

The coolie slid head first out of the hole, down the muck pile, and right into the open flame of my lamp, which was mounted on my belt. He let out a hideous scream. I was kneeling and his impact knocked me back against a side of the drift.

The coolie's slimy body was all over me — and then there were others, equally mad, crashing out of the hole and landing on top of me like a football team. These men, however, were playing to kill.

I heard two shots and knew that Duchet was back in action. But at the same moment I felt a pain in my right hand as the first coolie chomped down on it like a mad dog. I was bent back with my legs pinioned under me. The full weight of the coolies was on top of me.

The only weapon I had was my one free hand. With it, I reached for the first coolie's eyes; if I got them, maybe he'd loosen his bite on my other hand. I couldn't quite reach eye level. Nevertheless, I did manage to poke one finger up his nostril, which I started to rip out until I heard a crunch and a thud. Then the coolie went limp. He slid to the side. Duchet had hit him on the head with the butt of his pistol.

Duchet pushed the others off me by jabbing them with his pistol. I scrambled to my feet — or, rather, to a crouch, which was all space would permit. Lighting my lamp, which had been smothered in the brawl, I hurried to Duchet's side.

The coolies had regrouped. Now they came at us like yelping beasts. We knocked them out one by one, with our gun butts aimed for their groins.

I have no idea how long the fight lasted. When it was over, Duchet and I fell back exhausted against the pile of naked bodies — the men whose lives we had saved and who tried to kill us for doing so. They were bent and twisted, coated with blood, and so mashed together that it was difficult to guess which head belonged to which body. And the pervading stink was the worst detail of all. Duchet and I were panting for breath. And, from having fought for our lives in a bent-over position, our limbs felt like a ten-century history of arthritis.

We were jolted back into action when we glanced up at the hole we had dug. Terrified by the brawl, one of the coolies was heading back *into* the stope.

The hole had caved a little on him and he was trapped. Duchet and I dug around him and freed him in a few minutes.

When we looked him over closely, we saw that he was an old man. He was conscious, although in a state of shock. He was trying to talk; the words, however, were not coming to his lips. He must have thought we were demons. When at last it dawned on him that we weren't going to kill him, he began to cry. You seldom see Chinese cry. But this old man cried like a baby — or, as one of the foremen said later, like a woman with child.

Vic Shamroff had returned with some of the rescue workers, who were clearing away the pile of half-dead madmen. I turned the old man over to Vic with this suggestion: "Take him out and see if he'll talk. Also, get the doctor to work on some of the others. Try to find out whatever you can: What's going on inside the stope? How many men were in there? How many do they think are still alive? How many are buried under the muck pile?"

Then Duchet and I compared our wounds. His face was gashed where the first mad coolie had struck with his rock. My hand was bleeding steadily. Blood was coming from my lip, too. We considered ourselves lucky not to be in worse shape.

Vic Shamroff came back to tell us that he could get no sense or useful information out of the survivors. He also reported that the rescue workers up above were threatening to defect: "They think these men we're bringing up are the dead coming back to life — and maybe they're right. They won't have anything to do with evil spirits, they say." I told Vic to get back upstairs and quell the insurrection. Our rescue efforts would come to naught without the help of every man on every level.

No more survivors were coming through the hole, so Duchet and some muckers were enlarging it. We worked frantically for about three hours. The smell that emerged from the stope was unbearable. The battle that follows a cave-in is also a fight against death, rocks, dirt, terror, and nausea. When, at last, the hole was big enough for us to crawl through without disturbing the sides, I told Duchet I would go first. "I hope my luck's better than yours," I said. "This time, I'm going hands first — so I don't catch it in the face." I had a club in one of my hands. Even if somebody wrested that away from me, Duchet would be right behind me.

I wriggled through the hole. What I saw as I emerged almost made me take a U-turn.

Ten feet to the right was the side of the stope. To my left was a mountain of dirt and rocks — about forty feet high and seventy feet long. The ceiling of the stope was like an enormous cone. Huge slabs of rock were hanging down loosely from the sides and the back. The least movement could easily bring them down.

Overhead but directly in front of me was a gap about forty feet long. It was where the ancient long-lost stope had been. But now most of the old stope had tumbled into our stope. I held my breath, for it seemed as if merely exhaling would bring all the loose dirt in the world crashing down upon me.

I opened the water jet in my carbide lamp and shook it to get better light. Gently, with the lamp held over my head, I took a step forward.

Partly covered by rocks, three men lay on the floor. Eight others were crouched nearby, clinging to the side of the stope. Their faces were twisted from pain and fear. There was not a stitch of clothing on them. They had ripped off their sweaty garb in their first frenzy of despair.

I called to them: "Come one at a time."

Just like trapped, desperate animals, they stared at the light and then cringed. They began to cling more closely to the rock walls of the stope — as if they were enacting my recurrent nightmare. They were incapable of thought or any real control over their movements. But, from hunting a few wild beasts in Australia, I knew that, if they ever did move, they would pounce.

Duchet was right behind me. For a moment, both of us were frozen by fear. When you are confronted by the terror of violent death, you think many thoughts — and the irrational ones come first. My first reaction was: "That God damn Duchet! If these madmen attack, he'll be blocking off my only exit. He can escape, but I never will." Fortunately, in such a crisis, you think fast and you think of everything and, eventually, you think sanely and well.

Duchet said: "Gil, see if you can edge forward and grab the one nearest you. If he gives you any trouble, knock him cold. Whatever you do, though, don't disturb the muck pile. If you can drag them back to me, I'll carry them the rest of the way and push them through the hole." Vic Shamroff was at the other end with his most reliable and quick-thinking foremen.

"O.K.," I said to Duchet. "Try to keep your light on the eyes of the others. If you do, they may not notice what else is going on."

For a second, I focused my lamp on the mound of caved dirt and the rocks balancing on its side. The rocks would be the first to go, so I'd have at least a second or two in which to yell that the end was near. And maybe I could stop the smaller rocks with my hands. Possibly, this would keep them from rolling and unleashing the bigger rocks. Possibly, but probably not.

I backed through the stope until I reached a pillar that was holding up what remained of the roof. Then I turned and slowly edged my way along the side. When I was within a few feet of the coolies, I hooked my lamp to my belt. I would need both hands. But I kept the light focused on the eyes of the coolie near me.

Reaching out gently, I touched him on the arm. He stiffened like a frightened horse. He closed his eyes tightly. I had my other hand poised with my club. If he drew back and resisted help, I was ready to strike him.

I murmured to him reassuringly. He opened his eyes and then slowly reached out with his hand. He touched my legs. Only when he felt that I was real did he relax his grip on the rock he was clinging to. Then he threw himself at my feet and hugged them.

I almost lost my balance. As I bent down to help him up, I noticed the two coolies nearest him arising and edging toward us.

"Be careful," I called to them in Chinese.

I was not sure what they were up to. Knowing very little about their state of mind, I suspected the worst. If they ran in any direction, I would let them have it with my club and psychoanalyze them later.

[ 36 ]

But when they drew close enough, they, too, threw themselves at my feet. All three coolies started pawing me. Their heads were bent to the ground. They were chanting verses hailing me as a spirit from another world — which I guess I was.

I started to focus my light on my own face. Let them see that it was good old Mr. Stuart and not some spirit.

But then I had another thought: If they saw the look of fright on my face, the jig would really be up.

In Olympian tones, I ordered all three of them to their feet. I showed them how to hold on to each other and move slowly along the side of the stope. I carefully backed along ahead of them. I kept my eyes out for them, the muck pile, and the other coolies, who were still hugging the side of the stope for dear life.

As I backed up, one of my feet sank into something soft. I fell to one knee.

I was kneeling atop the naked body of a miner. He was half-buried in dirt, which was why I hadn't seen him before. I was just thinking that I had one foot literally in the grave when, to my surprise, the man groaned.

I crawled off him and continued back toward the hole, where Duchet was standing. The other coolies walked over the man as if he were a rug. They never even glanced down.

The hole and Duchet were about ten feet above the floor of the stope. I told Duchet: "I'll let them up one by one. When you're able to reach them, steer them through the hole to Vic."

The three coolies were coming to their senses — particularly as they grew accustomed to the light. When they looked up and saw the huge rocks dangling from above, they practically froze. But they offered no resistance when Duchet lifted them and chucked them into the hole.

Once all three were crawling in the right direction, I made my way back to retrieve the others.

As I neared, the five men still clinging to the wall came to life. They had been in the same crouched position for so long that they had to unfold themselves. When they did, I could see that they were all injured. Blood and dirt had caked on their grimy bodies. Some had open wounds that were no longer bleeding. But as they came to life, pain returned and so did sound. They began to scream.

[ 37 ]

I grabbed the nearest one and dragged him a few feet away from the others. One of his arms hung limp, dangling from the elbow. The rest of him jerked frantically as he fought to free himself from my grasp. Then, with one piercing scream, he collapsed.

He was a dead weight as I lifted him to my shoulder and carried him up the slope to Duchet, who passed him through the hole. We had no time to check whether he was dead or alive. If he didn't move, Vic would drag him out from the other end.

When I approached the next coolie, he sprang up and back. For a terrible moment, I thought he was going to start climbing up the loose, caved rocks, which surely would have toppled. He stood sizing me up for what seemed like a decade.

"Shoot him, Gil!" Duchet cried. "Shoot him before he brings down the whole damn stope."

I drew my gun and took careful aim at the berserk coolie's emaciated thigh. If I shot him there, he was likely to crumple where he stood. At all costs, I had to keep him away from the wall.

Suddenly, he stopped seeing me. His eye was caught by the man who had groaned. The fallen man was fully dressed. The berserk coolie pounced on the body and started to remove the coat. I noticed that the fallen man didn't groan this time. The coolie was muttering to himself as he stripped the man's coat and began to put it on.

I waited for the instant when his arms would be completely involved with the coat. Then I sprang forward and hit him on the head with my club. He collapsed. I let him lie there while I retrieved the others, who put up much less resistance. Duchet and I evacuated all of the walking wounded — plus the one I had clubbed — within an hour.

It took several hours more to dig out the four men who were partly buried in rock on the floor of the stope. Two were dead when we reached them. Another died as we were moving him out. The one who had groaned when I'd stepped on him survived. So, incidentally, did the man who had been a dead weight in my arms when I'd passed him on to Duchet.

While Duchet and I had been working inside the stope, Sam Coldron and Vic Shamroff had been putting down a revolution at the other end of the hole. As our grotesque survivors had emerged, the rescue workers had grown as crazy and terrified as the victims. The rescuers had begun to fight their foremen. Then some of the foremen had begun to fight their white chiefs.

"For a while," Sam told us, "Vic and I were fighting for our lives. You had it pretty easy down there in the stope."

Duchet and I were too exhausted to tell him to go to hell.

We left work at eight the next morning. There is no accurate figure on how many Chinese were missing — and presumably dead somewhere in the debris — but I would guess that there were at least a dozen.

We never went back to the stope. It caved in forever a few hours after we cleared out. With it went the hole we had dug and the adjacent drift.

Duchet, Vic, Sam, and I stayed drunk for two days. It was the only time we truly enjoyed each other's company. In addition, although Duchet and I still clashed like two bulls whenever we were together for more than an hour — the way men do when they are cooped up in an intolerable situation — our battles were tempered with mutual admiration and tinged with respect that we had acquired together in the shadow of death at the gateway to hell.

The Chinese people, too, had learned something — about white men. This was the first time in the history of the Hong Kong Mines that anyone had tried to save the lives of coolies trapped inside. All their concepts of the white devil's brutality needed revision to make room for our small but honorable exception.

While we heroes were drunk for two days, the Chinese spent that time burying their dead, honoring the survivors, paying homage to the miracle that had brought them back, and then shooting off enough firecrackers inside the mine to cleanse it of evil spirits. Only then would the miners and their foremen venture back.

I had wondered if the actuality of a cave-in would destroy my recurring nightmare. More than two decades later and many continents away, I still dream that I am clawing the walls of the Hong Kong Mines. But now, when I dream, I also smell the musky odor of death that was there.

# 3

## Margaret

I HAVE always prided myself on the apparent simplicity of my dreams. Awake or asleep, I am a very literal-minded person. If I had hated my father and wished to kill him, I would not have dreamed of a nail file hacking away at an evergreen tree. I would have dreamed that I was killing my father.

When I feared that the mine would cave in, I dreamed that the mine was caving in. And, having lived through a cave-in far worse than any of my dreams, I subsequently dreamed of cave-ins in more vivid detail. It was a painful dream while I was dreaming; it made me watchful when I was awake.

There was another dream afflicting me at that time of my life. This vision, too, was difficult to bear — particularly on waking — for it was both dream and memory. The details were agonizingly true. I would remind myself that I was at the Hong Kong Mines and then I would remember that it was this incident that had helped to bring me here.

It was about a girl.

Two years earlier, when I was twenty-four, I had been engaged to an Australian girl named Margaret. At the time — which was 1936 — I was sailing on an eighty-ton, two-masted ketch, *Yalata*, that carried lumber between Burnie, on the north coast of Tasmania, and Port Victoria, South Australia. There were four of us in the crew. We worked four-hour watches, with two of us standing watch while the other two slept.

We were sailing from Burnie and I had the first watch on the six-hundred-mile journey. My partner, a huge Swede, was too drunk to stand with me. I cursed the big lug a few times, but in a way I was glad to be alone. Tonight I wanted to think. I always thought most clearly at the helm on a calm night.

I was hoping that when we reached Port Victoria I would find a letter from Margaret. She had been in China on a vacation and I had not heard from her. I had disliked the idea of her taking a trip into China alone at a turbulent time when the Japs seemed to be everywhere. But she had made up her mind and so I had argued with her just once. I might exert more authority after we were married, but I was on my best behavior during Margaret's last months of freedom.

Margaret was a girl whose beauty was not her most striking feature. What stopped a man in his tracks were her eyes, which seemed to do much of her talking, and her smile, which drew a man close and embraced him.

I had met Margaret and taken her horseback riding when we were both in our late teens. And I had soon learned that I was just one of three boys who loved her ardently. Because we shared this sublime passion, we three suitors became not only keen rivals, but close friends. By the time Margaret and I became engaged several years later, the other two suitors — John and Felix — were high among our well-wishers. I think that, if the wedding had ever taken place, John would have been my best man.

Port Victoria, a little town of a few hundred people, had one main street, a few shops, two or three hotels, and a post office. When there was no mail for me at the post office, I dashed to the public telephone just outside and placed a call to Margaret's home in Melbourne, five hundred miles away. She should have been back from China by now, but there was no answer. I then placed a call to John, who would surely know if she was back.

A storm was blowing from the north. Rain was peppering the phone booth. There was a flash of lightning and a clap of thunder. Then the skies opened up and the rain pelted the booth's roof like machine-gun bullets. It was not an auspicious moment, but, over the staccato rain, I heard John's voice:

"Where are you, Gil?"

"Port Victoria, South Australia."

John said something I couldn't hear. I shouted: "Is Margaret home?"

"Yes," John said. "She arrived a few days ago. But, Gil, I have bad news: Margaret is in hospital."

"What on earth is wrong with her?" I asked.

[ 41 ]

"She is having her appendix taken out."

I was relieved: "Well, that happens to a lot of people, doesn't it? It's not serious, John, is it?"

"The appendix? No, the appendix is not serious."

From the way he said this, I knew he wasn't finished with the news. He resumed:

"I have spoken to Margaret in the hospital, and I can't get any sense out of her. At least, I'm almost out of my mind by now and I don't know what to think any more."

"What is it, John? Tell me!"

"Margaret said she had met an officer of the British Indian Army. At present he is stationed in Malaya or some such place. She is going to marry him."

A lump formed in my throat. Cramped in the small booth, I felt like a caged animal. I looked around me. I wanted to leap through the glass and into the rain. But then I might miss some of John's words. Perhaps he would tell me that it was a joke or I had heard him all wrong.

But as John repeated the details and added some facts, I sensed that what I heard was both serious and irrevocably true. John's voice sounded most strange — quite matter-of-fact. I realized that this was because he, too, still loved Margaret. He had lost her to me once and now he had been hurt twice. Even at this crucial moment, I marveled that either of us could discuss Margaret's decision with such consideration for each other and such apparent calm. I even wondered silently how my other friendly rival, Felix, would take the news that Margaret had eluded all three of us. As if reading my mind, John added wanly: "I haven't broken the news to Felix yet."

I found my voice and asked numbly: "Do you think this is final?"

"Yes," said John. "They will marry in about three months. In England. The arrangements have been made."

"John, I can't tell you how sick I feel."

John said nothing for a while. He was evidently debating whether to continue. Then he decided:

"There's more Gil. It may explain things, but brace yourself: it's the worst part. When I saw Margaret in hospital, she said that on her trip to China — before she met this Army chap, mind you — she took a trip into Japanese territory."

[ 42 ]

"Oh, the idiot!"

"While she was there," John continued, "the Japanese accused her of having given them false information about herself. They said she was either a war correspondent or a spy. She denied both, but they said that wasn't their question: They wanted to know *which* she was. She kept saying she was neither and they kept saying they would give her a bad time. There were four or five Japs there."

"And what did they do?" I asked.

"Gil, eventually they let her go — but, first, they all raped her."

I vaguely remember letting the receiver slip from my hand and walking slowly in the downpour toward the wharf where my ketch was sitting out the storm.

Apparently, I lay on the dock for hours. I am told that one of the crewmen found me there and, when he took me on deck, I tried to jump overboard and drown.

When I came to my senses, I quit my job and set my sights on China. The Chinese had been at war with the Japs since 1932. I declared my private war on Japan in 1936. I had a personal account to settle. That was when all Chinese became my allies. That was what drove me to the Hong Kong Mines, which were as close to China as I could come without falling into Japanese hands.

Not even my cave-in experiences and my brush with the Agitator could dull the bitter hatred for Japan that was the first element — and perhaps the essence — of my early romance with China.

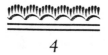

## 4

# The First to Die

THE Hong Kong Mines and the sophisticated city of Hong Kong were worlds apart. Traveling from one to the other required changing not only clothes, but also personality. In the mine, if someone jostled me, I had to respond with instant brutality — kill or be killed. In the city, I would merely say a hypocritical "excuse me" or, at my civilized worst, scowl. When you live by the law of the jungle six days a week, the craft of every-day politeness does not come easily. At noon on my first visit to Hong Kong after the cave-in, I had needed a drink since 11 o'clock.

Inevitably, I went to the Parisienne Grille — the P-G, a fashionable center of Oriental intrigue in the late 1930's. Britons, White Russians, Eurasians, Portuguese *mestizos*, and Chinese mingled easily here. Charm, elegance, and desperation all rubbed elbows. Social barriers seemed provincial in the P-G. Nazi agents dined to the music of a Viennese orchestra composed of Jews who had fled Hitler. Urbanity was the only nationality at the P-G. Service was impeccable, the food among the best in the world, and the prices seventy-five per cent cheaper than Europe's.

The P-G was truly a place to rub shoulders with the famous, for it was always crowded and the tables were close together. Celebrity in the P-G was measured not by wealth, rank, or position, but by what one had done to change the face of Asia. Thus, everyone goggled at such notables as "One-Armed" Sutton, inventor of the grenade and builder of a fabulous arsenal at Mukden, Manchuria; a General Cohen, once the bodyguard of the Chinese statesman Sun Yat-sen; and an Australian known as "Donald of China."

For months, I had been scheming to obtain a minute or two with the elusive Donald. But this noon, I was in the P-G at least a quarter of an hour before I realized that he was there, too.

Donald was Generalissimo Chiang Kai-shek's chief adviser. Once, he had saved Chiang's life, but his deed was already shrouded in legends that varied from province to province and even from café to café. The man himself was wispy, graying at the temples, and — like most living legends — perfectly ordinary-looking.

Donald of China was seated with another white man, a Chinese man, and two pretty young Chinese girls. There seemed to be no way for me to introduce myself until he stood up from the table and left the others. I wasted no time in following him into the men's room.

He was washing his hands when I caught up with him: "Mr. Donald, my name is Gilbert Stuart. I am a fellow Australian."

Donald looked up, smiled uneasily, and said: "How d'you do, Mr. Stuart. Where in Australia are you from?" We then talked home

[ 44 ]

towns, but I was determined not to let my opportunity go down the drain.

"Mr. Donald," I began rather formally, "I deliberately followed you in here . . ."

"Indeed?" he said, looking me over coldly as if I were some kind of masher or pervert.

". . . in the hope that you will grant me an interview at your earliest convenience," I continued rapidly. "I have a problem that is important to me and I need sound advice. I cannot think of anyone who would be more familiar with it than you, sir."

Donald glanced down at his watch. For a moment, I thought I had come to the right place for a brushoff. But then he said: "I can only hope I will be of some assistance. Is it something we could discuss over a cup of coffee at the table?"

"No," I said thinking of the two giggling girls with Donald's party. "It's personal."

"Very well then," he said. He removed a card from his pocket, jotted down a room number, and gave it to me. "I'm at the Gloucester Hotel. Will this problem of yours keep for a week?"

"Yes," I replied gratefully. "There is no immediate hurry."

"Good. Then come to see me a week from Friday. I leave this afternoon for Shanghai, but I expect to be back by then."

We shook hands. His were still wet from washing, mine from perspiration.

When I saw Donald of China again, I was even more tongue-tied. Another week underground had made me that much less articulate. After a stab at polite conversation, I blurted out: "Excuse me, Mr. Donald, if my conversation is a little strange. I seem to have forgotten all human speech."

"Perhaps that's because your problem is so meaningful to you."

"It is, sir. You see, I've come to China in the hope that I may serve in some small way to help the Chinese people defend their country against Japan. I think you can advise me exactly how to get started and whom to approach."

I was watching Donald's face for amusement or boredom, but all I detected was relief that I was at last coming to the point. He said nothing and I continued:

[ 45 ]

"I understand that there's a new group of foreign volunteers flying for the Chinese Government. I can't fly — except for gliders — but, if I can learn, that might be my solution . . ."

Donald halted me by raising a hand and an eyebrow: "Is your heart set on joining the International Volunteer Flying Group, Stuart?"

"Not really. I'm a little suspicious of it because I hear it pays rather handsomely."

Donald chuckled. "You seem to know a great deal for a young man."

"Mind you, sir, I don't sneer at money. But it's not what I'm here for. I'm looking for the opportunity to take part in the fight."

"You *are* young," Donald said, not unkindly. He thought for a long minute and added: "I believe you, Stuart. Therefore I advise you not to join the International Volunteer Group under any circumstances. While I was in Shanghai this trip, I fired fourteen volunteers."

I started to suggest that I might fill a vacancy, but Donald cut me off. "Do you know," he said, "that some of those so-called pilots have never flown in their lives? Yet we have them on the payroll as pilots, living in the lap of luxury at China's expense."

"Sir," I said, growing a bit brash, "I'm cheap and loyal and . . ."

He didn't hear me. He went on: "And most of the pilots who can fly never bother to fly near the enemy. They might get hurt! Why risk their lives in the air when they can live like heroes on the ground? There are a few who'll fight. But they're not effective unless there's a team."

Again I tried to volunteer. Again Donald cut me off.

"We have Russians, Germans, British, French, and one or two Americans. They don't work together well. But I advise you against joining mostly because the group will certainly be abolished before you can learn to fly. And, if you had anything to do with it, you'd be branded as a scoundrel, opportunist, and adventurer."

Donald had no other suggestions, but I told him I would persist. "My big problem," I said, "is to get a foothold. I can't simply walk into a country and say 'I'm here to fight the Japanese.' I have to establish myself in China without obligations to anyone. All I have to decide is how?"

[ 46 ]

"And when. But wait awhile," Donald advised. "First get to know the Chinese and understand them. Feel your way about and your opportunity will come. If I hear of anything, I'll let you know."

I met Donald twice more in Hong Kong. Each time, he warned me to stay away from the International Volunteers, but he was encouraging. He was the only white man (or, for that matter, yellow man) I knew who did not laugh when I avowed my plans.

To his dying day, Donald of China remained a good friend of Generalissimo and Madame Chiang Kai-shek. Although some credit Donald with keeping them in power, his claim to world fame was lost in the sweep of history a few years after I met him. In World War II, he fell into Japanese hands, but they never realized his identity. The Japs held him prisoner and he was a sick man when the war ended. He was given permission to return to Shanghai, where he died in 1947.


Returning to the Hong Kong Mines, I bided my time and kept my eyes open. Once I had clammed up about my devotion to China, I was accepted by my Chinese neighbors and workers — never as an equal, but as a trustworthy big brother.

Gambling was a good common denominator for after-hours mingling. A miner could gain much face when it became known that he had been betting against the boss. And, if the boss kept his eyes open, he could see still another facet of the Chinese personality.

After work one night, I wandered up to the foremen's barracks atop the mountain. Miners of all ranks were there. Some twenty different games were going on. All of them stopped as I entered, but I told the gamblers to resume. Chan, my friendliest and most loyal foreman, offered me a drink of cheap Chinese wine. Every time I drank it, I gasped and just barely overcame vomiting. (Chan later told me that one or two bets were made each time on whether I would vomit.)

Having been made welcome, I was invited to play mah-jongg, the noisiest of the twenty games. Not only did mah-jongg tiles make more noise than cards or beads, but the players were the most violent.

Society ladies of the Western world, who think they invented mah-jongg, would never have recognized it. We sat on wooden bunks that faced each other. The bunks were double deckers, with a player on each level. The aisle between the rows of bunks was just wide enough for a line of card tables. Once the tables were moved in, nobody could come or go. I took a choice spot on a lower bunk. It was within easy reach of the table, but it had strong disadvantages — the foul-smelling feet dangling down from the upper bunk.

We played for more than an hour before a violent argument broke out at the table on my right. In a room where you could not hear yourself think, it took a damn hot argument to attract any attention. But the screaming at the next table grew intolerable. The loudest screamer was within reach, so I nudged him and commanded: "Shut up!"

He ignored me — which was unusual, off-duty or on. I could see by his red cheeks that he had been drinking. "Nothing in the world is going to shut this fellow up," I murmured to nobody in particular. But I was wrong.

One of my hardest-working carpenters was stretched out on an upper bunk nearby. He was not playing. He was a serious man who seldom spoke and never cracked a smile. I was told that he took his tools to bed with him for fear that they might be stolen.

As usual, he said nothing. He merely reached for his tool kit and came up with a short-handled ax. Leaning over the red-cheeked man, he smashed down deftly. He split the man's head open. Then he wiped off the ax and put it away without a word.

The wounded man splattered blood everywhere. As their mah-jongg tiles stained red, other players looked up. There was a general murmur of "Aheeeah, that must have hurt." Several men remarked that he deserved it for making all that noise. The men in his game put him on the table, lifted it aloft like a stretcher, and carried him out. Nothing else changed. The other games went on. I tried to be casual, too, but I wouldn't have bet on myself not to vomit.

When my game was over, I excused myself. On the way out, I noticed that the ax-wielding carpenter was stretched out on his bunk again. Now he was reading a newspaper. What was he looking for — an obituary or an exciting story to enliven his drab existence? Had he silenced the red-cheeked man because it was interfering with *his* rest or *my* mah-jongg? I will never know the answers, but I do know that I never complained about noisy drunks again.

\* \* \*

One moonlit night, I ventured down to Shatowkok, a little Chinese fishing village east of Bias Bay and a four-mile hike from the Hong Kong Mines.

Few white men ventured there, for Chinese toughs were likely to send them back badly beaten and stark naked. Furthermore, the Chinese border ran right through Shatowkok and the British border patrol had installed barbed wire fences.

In Shatowkok, I entered a Chinese store that sold rice, tea, and herbs. The owner, Mr. Wong, spoke some English. (I spoke no Chinese at the time.) He threw his arms up happily, shoved me into a chair, and poured two cups of tea.

He made such a commotion that men, women, and children converged on his shop. I knew most of the men, for every able-bodied male in Shatowkok worked at the mines. They were delighted to see me — and not tense the way they were during even cordial moments at the mine. Here, men whom I had beaten had me at their mercy. But they were proud to be meeting me man-to-man — as equals — on their own soil and in their own home town. No matter what happened, this would be an evening their families would talk about many times.

Mr. Wong was an old man. In his most dignified voice, he announced that my visit was a special occasion and there would be a feast. This unleashed a new commotion.

"What if the Japs see me here?" I asked, making a throat-cutting gesture that caused everyone to laugh.

"Last Jap leave here two days," Mr. Wong assured me. "But let us no speak of Jap. Have big dinner instead."

I shrugged. Everybody cheered. A pretty young Chinese woman raced for the back room and returned with a long, thin knife, which she handed to me. I murmured thanks and, to my surprise, she replied in perfect English, "You're welcome, Mister Gil." Before I could open my mouth, she went to the back room, where the women stayed.

"What do I do with this knife?" I asked the men.

My answer was tugged in by half a dozen laughing and shouting men. It was a balky pig squealing for dear life, as well it might have.

They deposited the pig at my feet. The girl who had brought the knife re-appeared with a huge bowl. "That's to catch the blood," she explained helpfully, again in English. I was too nonplused to ask her whether she had gone to Oxford or Cambridge.

Everyone clustered around to see how well the white devil killed. I knew I could never wield the knife so sharply as their experts. Instead I drew my pistol, aimed between the pig's eyes, and squeezed the trigger. The pig screamed, kicked, lay still briefly, and then thrashed angrily. By then, I was on top of it with the knife. I grabbed its snout with one hand and pulled its head back across my knee. With the knife, I slit its throat. Then I quickly pushed the bowl underneath to catch the blood. I wiped the knife clean on the pig's back. Finally, I slipped the knife in between my gun and my holster. I wanted it as a souvenir and a weapon.

My hosts swung the pig up over a beam and cleaned it. They also slaughtered chickens and ducks. Then the entire meal was carried to a little coolie restaurant next door, where it would be cooked.

While we waited, we sat on the floor of Mr. Wong's shop and talked against the Japanese. My hosts had ample reason to hate them. They stole the farmers' rice and livestock. They conscripted local boys as laborers. People had a habit of disappearing forever when the Japanese were around.

Dinner was ready, so we moved on to the restaurant. After a long argument over what constituted the seat of honor at a round table, I was lifted into it. Ten people were at my table. Mr. Wong, as my personal host, sat opposite me. The others were respected elders of the town, a couple of miners, and the girl who had handed me the knife and bowl.

Her name, she told me in her impeccable English, was Nora Wong. She was no relation to my host. She had been seated next to me because she spoke such good English. I told her that, whatever the reason, I could not have desired a more satisfactory seating plan. (Actually, after one look at Nora, I would gladly have done without the other eight people at our table.) The rest of the village sat at other tables.

The meal started with sweetmeats, wine, and elaborate toasts to everybody's health, long life, and happiness; to the Chinese Government, the Chinese Army, and the downfall of the Japs; to the Hong Kong Mines, to my future, and to an endless list of people, events, organizations, and fantasies. Then came hundred-year-old eggs cured in lime and straw. The egg whites had turned a dark blackish color and a gelatinous consistency; the yolks dark yellow. They tasted smoky and delicious. Excellent, too, were the Yunnan ham, chicken, fish, pork, and soup that followed. As the wine flowed, the villagers lost all their reticence. Their noise would have drowned out a mah-jongg game. How the hell were Nora and I going to become acquainted over this din?

Having seen a carpenter respond with an ax, I was reluctant to ask the others to quiet down. Nora was trying to say something to me. I leaned over her and cupped my ear. Nora shouted that Mr. Wong wished her to convey his apologies.

"Did you say 'apologies'?" I asked.

"Yes," she replied. "He apologizes for the humble dinner and the dirty restaurant."

"The meal is most delicious," I assured her. She translated this instantly to the rest of the gathering, which gave a collective sigh of relief and waited to hear what else I had to say.

I didn't know how to respond to Mr. Wong's apology for the restaurant's being dirty, which nobody could deny. Finally, I said: "I have been here long enough to know that the best food is always prepared in the dirtiest kitchen." My words were greeted with a roar of laughter, another round of wine, and violent backslapping.

Mr. Wong, however, had a question: If I liked everything so much, why wasn't I eating everything they gave me?

"I have not been here long enough to have the capacity of a Chinese," I replied. There were more toasts and then everybody resumed eating.

The restaurant was dimly lit. I could see our huge shadows on the wall. The hands with chopsticks going back and forth looked like giant spider legs reaching out. When I mentioned this to Nora, she laughed.

"Where are you from?" I asked her. "And why haven't I seen you around here before?"

"I live in Kowloon [across the harbor from the island of Hong Kong in the British New Territories] and am visiting an uncle near here," she said. "I am from Canton. I was studying English there. When the Japanese invaded Canton, I moved to Hong Kong, where I have many relatives."

Nora was tall for a Southern Chinese woman. She had a slender figure. Her black hair was smooth and parted in the center. It had a straightforward look, but it formed dark scrolls around her ears. The test of her beauty possessed an alluring sharpness, although she was neither curvaceous nor angular. Her neck was slender and long. Her well-fitted dress split at the knee. When she caught me looking her over, I quickly hoisted my cup and proposed a toast to her. "You have," I remarked, "a great capacity for Chinese wine."

Nora blushed and said: "My father used to make his own wine and he was most proud of it. He never considered it wrong to serve it to us — even when we were at a very young age — and so, perhaps because of this, it never has much effect on me."

"Are you a connoisseur of Chinese wines?" I asked.

She blushed again, but did not deny it.

"One day perhaps," I suggested, "you will do me the honor of dining with me and selecting the wines that you consider the finest in China." My request surprised her, for Chinese wines are made from rice and notoriously unpalatable to outsiders. I added: "You see, I hope one day that I will be forced to change brands and drink only the native wine of China."

I saw a little smile cross Nora's face, but did I also see her nod approvingly? In any event, she piled more food atop the mountain in my bowl. I might have pursued my future in China further if our conversation had not been interrupted.

The restaurant had no door — just an open front now blocked by twenty latecomers who were content just to gawk at me. But an anxious-looking man pushed through them and headed straight for Mr. Wong. He whispered something into Mr. Wong's ear. Both men looked at me.

Mr. Wong's face darkened and he spoke rapidly to Nora. The elders at our table asked the newcomer questions. With each reply, people within earshot stood up abruptly and rushed into the night.

Nora told me: "The Japanese are on their way back into town. You must leave here."

"To hell with the Japs!" I announced, buoyed by wine. "I'm not afraid of them."

"But you must go," Nora said. "You never know what they will do to you or us if they find you here."

"Yes," Mr. Wong chimed in urgently. "Go, go, Mist' Gil. Please go!" The elders and almost everybody else had departed. I was the guest of honor, but I felt like the most unwanted guest in the world. Only a few men — all of the miners — had remained, eating what they could until I made up my mind to go.

When I said all right, they grabbed their plates and told me to follow. They knew a place where we could finish our dinner in peace. As we left, we heard a truck rattling down the road. The miners put out the lights in the restaurant, but, as we passed through the kitchen and into an open yard, we heard the truck brake to a halt at the front gate.

The yard faced the back entrances of a row of houses. We dived into the nearest house, the inside of which was black as pitch. Someone took my hand and led me through a hole in the wall into another house. We crawled through a hole in that house into another house. In our haste, we knocked over furniture and occasionally stepped on people pretending to be asleep.

The holes in the houses had been knocked out by the Japanese. Soldiers could glance inside by using binoculars. They could survey a whole street of houses this way, without having to enter any and risk Chinese hospitality.

When we were a few hundred feet from the restaurant, Mr. Wong said goodbye and melted into the night. Our party now consisted of Nora, myself, and three miners. Nora whispered: "We are on the Chinese side of the border."

"It doesn't make any difference to the Japs if it's the British side or the Chinese side," I whispered back.

"There are three truckloads," Nora told me. "They are dropping off men at different places to take up guard duty."

"Three truckloads just because I'm in town? I'm flattered."

Nora laughed softly and said: "They come and they go. It is part of their training. They do not know you are here."

"Where are we going now?" I asked.

"To a place near the main gate of the barbed wire fence," Nora replied. "Then, if nobody is there, we will finish your party. When it is over, we can both stroll across the border."

"Arm in arm through the front door," I murmured.

First, however, we had to traverse several rice paddy fields. The moon was high and full. Where the terrain was open, we crawled along muddy ground. I noticed that Nora slithered expertly, like an eel. She was in every way a remarkable girl.

We reached the fence and then walked alongside it until we were two hundred feet from the main gate. A shed nestled against the barbed-wire barrier. It had three sections, two of them residential. The largest section was a tea shop with two tables and a few chairs near a counter displaying soda bottles, cigarettes, and fly-specked cookies. A copper pot was simmering atop a little stove. A lone woman tended the shop. At the two tables were a dozen of the party guests, still eating food they had taken with them.

They welcomed us noisily and the party picked up where it had left off, but on a smaller scale. Several men talked simultaneously to Nora, who listened calmly and told me: "They say that the Japanese left their trucks and moved toward the beach. They are maneuvering. First, they assemble machine guns along the beach. Then they dismantle them."

"Then we're safe for a while."

"Not really, Mister Gil," Nora replied. "The Japanese locked up the gate on the border and then sent twelve of their men into town. They are eating at the restaurant where we had our party. After that, some of them may come back here."

"Well, we can enjoy ourselves here until they've finished eating," I said recklessly.

As I spoke, however, I started to shiver. I thought I was suffering an attack of nerves, but then I glanced down and realized I was soaked from the hips down. My hands and shirtsleeves were covered with enough mud to stock a rice paddy.

I looked at Nora. She, too, was coated with mud and was shivering, but I burst out laughing.

"You should see yourself," I told her, although there were no mirrors for miles around.

She gazed down at her stylish dress and said matter-of-factly, almost like a mistress: "Well, Mister Gil, you will have to buy me a new dress."

"You bet I will! And you'll wear it to that dinner when you select the Chinese wines for me."

Nora laughed, then she stood up and went through a door with

[ 54 ]

the woman who operated the little tea shop. While I sat alone and shivering, one of the miners took the pot off the stove and poured me a cup of hot yellow wine. It was as vile as ever, but I enjoyed feeling the alcohol burn all the way down.

Nora returned in dry clothes — black silk coat and baggy pants that almost made her look like a pretty little coolie girl.

No sooner had Nora rejoined me than a man ushered in two young girls — dressed like Nora, but looking very angry. One of the girls slumped into a chair, crossed her legs painfully, and fidgeted with an unlit cigarette. She tapped it on the table and then turned it, end over end, with her fingers.

Everyone, including Nora, crowded around her. She burst forth with an angry stream of words. Whenever she stopped, the other girl picked up the story just as vehemently.

After a while, the men began to talk angrily. Nora came back and I asked her what had happened.

"These two girls had been visiting friends on the other side of the border a little while before we got there. When they came back, they found the gate locked. So they decided to crawl underneath. One of them lifted the bottom strand of barbed wire while the other crawled through. The first girl made it. But when the other girl was halfway under, her clothes caught on the wire. She started to giggle and the other girl giggled, too."

"They don't look as if it's so funny now," I remarked.

"The Japanese were still in the vicinity then. They were just getting ready to go to town. Six of them came running to see what was going on. By the time they reached the gate, the second girl was free. But the Japanese surrounded them."

The vision I had carried with me — of Margaret surrounded by grinning, menacing Japanese — seemed to reappear in the room. I shivered as Nora continued:

"These Japanese had been drinking. One of them was staggering. He walked up to one of the girls and threw his arm around her neck. Then he leaned on her and vomited. She pushed him away. He fell. Then all of the Japanese went wild because much face had been lost. One of the Emperor's soldiers had been struck by a Chinese girl! Four of them jumped on both girls and dragged them into a house. They made the tenants leave . . ."

[ 55 ]

"What about the other two Japs?" I interrupted, fearful that they might still be at the gate.

"One of them helped the sick one to the restaurant in town, where all are now. But the four that took the girls into the house — before they left, they . . ."

Nora hesitated. I felt as if Margaret were in the room as I supplied the missing word: "They raped them?"

"It wasn't exactly rape. The girls knew they would die if they resisted, so they didn't. After the Japanese had finished with them, they let them go."

"The bastards!" I exclaimed, getting myself some more wine from the stove.

I had taken just one sip when a miner rushed in. What he said needed no translating: The Japanese were coming our way. People dived through the doors into the adjoining rooms. I was pushed into one and the door slammed behind me.

There was no light. I stood still for a moment. Someone pulled me through another door into a small lean-to. Then I was pushed to a hole in the wall. I could see moonlight. Someone poked my head through the hole and started pushing the rest of me through it.

I realized that it opened onto a private exit, which had been cut right through the barbed wire fence. My head was dangling over the small military road running along the British side of the border. But I jerked my head back out of British territory and into the lean-to. I wasn't crossing the border tonight without Nora. I could see people's silhouettes by moonlight. Nora wasn't with me.

I whispered her name, but all I heard were more whispers pleading with me to leave. Several hands tried to push me out through the hole. I refused. Instead, I lifted the two girls who had been "not exactly raped" and sent them through the hole. Others followed, until just two miners and I remained.

Loud voices were coming from the tearoom. I groped my way back to the adjoining room, where I could peer into the restaurant through a crack in the door.

The woman who ran the place was standing behind the counter and preparing food. Four Chinese men sat at one table. They were not talking, just sipping tea and making cigarettes out of old tobacco leaf.

[ 56 ]

At the other table sat Nora and two Japanese soldiers.

She had not made it out in time. She sat straight in her chair, which was pushed slightly away from the table. She was poised for a fast getaway. But her face was expressionless. Her eyes seemed focused on nothing in particular.

The two Japs, seated opposite her, were drunk and getting drunker. I surmised that they were the one who had vomited on the girl and the one who had helped him into town. The sick one seemed to have recovered considerably. From what I could gather of their conversation, they were alluding to their chastity thus far tonight. Their comrades had satisfied themselves with women; now it was their turn, they boasted.

They leaned on their elbows and rolled from side to side as they laughed. Making a big show of ignoring Nora, they asked where they could find a suitable woman. But if she stood up to leave there would be trouble.

As I watched, a hand tugged at my arm. Reluctantly, I allowed myself to be led back into the lean-to. Now there was a flashlight as well as moonlight. And, to my surprise, the room was filled with Chinese.

The hand holding the flashlight was cupped over the bulb to keep light from streaming out of the room. I could see that most of the men in the room were my miners. The man holding the flashlight looked especially familiar. I pushed his hand up toward his face. To my delight, the ray illuminated my mine foreman, Chan.

"Where the hell have you been?" I greeted him gruffly, putting my arm around his neck.

"Think you might need little help, Mister Stu," Chan croaked in his froglike voice.

"Do you know Nora?"

"Sure do. We good friends. She other reason we here."

"Good! We have to get her away from those Japs in there. You and three men come with me. Leave this door open. But tell all the others to stand by without making a sound. Whatever happens, we don't want much noise or the rest of the Japs will come running."

Chan and I peered through the crack in the door. Nora and the two Japs had not shifted position. The Chinese at the other table were eating noodles. The woman was cooking more noodles on the stove.

[ 57 ]

Fifteen minutes later, the woman filled two bowls and put them before the Japs. One Jap leaned over, smelled the noodles, dumped them on the floor, and banged his fist on the table. The woman backed away. When the other Jap (the one who had been sick) lunged for her, she dashed out the front door. The Jap took off after her, but he wouldn't have had a chance even in perfect condition.

This left Nora at the table with the healthier of the two Japs. He cackled raucously, but his good humor rattled to a halt when he caught sight of the Chinese men at the other table. Without rising, he leaned forward and slapped them to their feet. Then he stamped his feet and they ran out the door.

He stood up and shut the front door of the tearoom. He flopped into his chair and fumbled in his pockets for cigarettes. He extended one to Nora, who pointed out silently that she was already smoking. Angrily, he snatched her cigarette out of her mouth and pushed his at her. Nora declined.

This was his invitation to rape or murder. He sent the table hurtling across the room. Both he and Nora leaped to their feet. They stood face-to-face with no barriers between them. "Margaret!" I murmured. "Margaret!" Chan looked at me curiously in the darkness.

The Jap studied Nora for a minute. He looked her up and down as if she were naked. Then, without a flicker of warning, he slapped her across the face. Nora fell to the floor with a thud.

I felt Chan quiver beside me. I squeezed his arm and then slowly began to unlatch the door. I edged it open bit by bit. Nora was on her feet, backing away from the Jap. She bumped into the other table, which stood opposite me. For a moment, I feared that she would bolt for my door and collide with it or me. But the Jap jumped forward and pinned her to the table.

With one hand around Nora's throat, he pressed her down. He ran his other hand up and down her body. Nora clawed at him with sharp nails.

Now was the time! The knife I had used to kill the pig was still resting in my holster. I took it out and then threw the door open wide. The Jap had his back to me. He was leaning over Nora. She was tearing chunks of flesh out of his face, but this drove him to further frenzy. Her hands could not reach his eyes, where real damage could be done.

I looked at the knife in my hand. Then I looked at the Jap. Margaret was forgotten. My love for the Chinese was forgotten. Even Nora, right there in his grasp, was forgotten. Individual grudges were forgotten. All my hatred for an entire people took control of me. I leaped forward. While still on the run, I jammed ten inches of steel — right up to the hilt — into the small of his back. Twisting the knife to one side and jerking it up and down twice, I made sure I had cut into his kidneys.

The Jap stiffened slightly, but he never let out so much as a breath of air. A gasp came from deep in his throat.

I wrenched the knife out as he slipped to his knees. Then he fell backwards. His eyes were wide open with horror and surprise. He was dead by the time his head hit the floor.

I knew he was dead. Nevertheless, I stood over his corpse and swore: "Swine. You are the first to die."

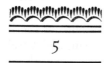

5

# The Tomb of the Miserable Landlord

A MAN never forgets his first woman or his first killing. Each experience involved a certain peculiar detachment. After killing the Jap, I spoke my first thought aloud. My next thoughts were unspoken. Voices within me said: "I don't feel bad. I don't feel bad at all. Matter of fact, I feel pretty damn good." I would kill others in my lifetime, but each killing would seem to have an existence of its own. Sometimes I would feel good. Sometimes I would feel bad. Each time, however, I would feel transformed into a different person forever. Perhaps it was the sensation of playing God. I know that after every killing — first, last, and many in-between — I would feel both nearer to and further from God than ever before.

The room filled up with Chinese, who silently carried the dead Jap to the lean-to, pushed him through the hole, and disappeared with his corpse. The silent procession headed toward the Hong Kong

Mines in the moonlight. I wondered if the Jap would be just another of the secrets buried in the dragon.

Nora trembled all over until her late assailant was out of sight. Then she pulled herself together. It was she who had tasted blood, for the Jap had split the corner of her lip when he slapped her. In *not* crying out for help, she had also bitten her tongue painfully. She walked over to the counter, poured herself a cup of tea, and rinsed out her mouth.

She came over to me and grabbed my right hand. "You are hurt, Gil!" she cried. I didn't feel hurt — just pleased that she no longer called me Mister. Glancing down, however, I saw my hand dripping blood.

"I'm not wounded. That's the Jap's blood," I said, wiping my hand on my wet trousers and turning away so Nora wouldn't see it shake. I turned to Chan and gave orders: "Get the men to stand the chairs and tables right side up. I want this place left as though nothing had happened. Make sure you clean the bloodstains off the floor."

When this was done, we put out the lights and left through the hole in the fence. Nora, Chan, and I walked leisurely in the direction of the mine. We caught up with two dogs walking along the road and licking at something.

"Dead Jap blood," Chan told me.

I shuddered, but all I said was: "Good. Those dogs clean up all the evidence." Chan laughed and Nora looked at me oddly. I told her: "You'll have to get cleaned up sometime before our dinner date."

"Even before then," she said solemnly. "I cannot shop for a new dress if I look like this."

"You look lovely to me," I declared.

The moon was deep in the sky now. Black shadows were enveloping the road when we caught up with the men bearing the body. Were they — God forbid! — delivering the dead Jap to my cottage as a trophy? The men put the body down and engaged in a lengthy conversation with Chan and Nora.

"Anything the matter?" I asked Nora. "I can give them orders, if you want."

"They can't make up their minds where to put the body," she

told me. "They all want to take him to the mine. But Chan says they might run into the Indian guards."

"He's right. It's too risky," I said. I didn't bother to add that it might get me into trouble. I did add, for what it was worth, "We can't stay out here all night with a dead Jap in tow. The British border patrol will be along, y'know."

Chan had thought of an alternative. He said something to the men, who listened intently. Then, jabbering and laughing, they departed with the body. They followed a small trail that skirted halfway up a small mountain and then disappeared over the other side. Chan darted ahead of them, and led the way.

"Where are they going?" I asked Nora as we walked toward the mine.

"Oh," she replied rather vaguely, "to some safe place on the other side of the mountain." She took my arm and we walked on. It was quite dark now and silent. Our stroll was so casual that it was easy to forget I had just killed a man. True, my heart was beating faster than usual. But I could, if I wanted, blame that on Nora. We did not speak until the road made its last bend before leading straight into the mine area.

"I just remembered," I said in my most nonchalant tone, "that I haven't asked you where on earth you're going to stay tonight. There's no way back to Kowloon."

Unfortunately, she had a ready answer: "This weekend, I am staying with an uncle in Ling-Ma-Hang over there." She pointed to a cluster of houses at the foot of the mountain on the China side of the border. Ling-Ma-Hang, I knew, was relatively unmolested by Japs. She would be almost as safe there as in my arms.

"I'm glad to hear you're provided for tonight," I lied. Then I added, a little suggestively: "I was wondering what I was going to do with you for the rest of the night."

She didn't take the hint, but she didn't bristle. She simply said: "I had better leave you here, Gil, and slip across the border. There is a little trail on the other side of the river. I can follow it to my uncle's house. It is not far."

We started to say goodbye. "Nora, in a day or two I'll get in touch with you through Chan. I am looking forward to our dinner engagement."

"I am, too," she said warmly.

She was ready to go, but I turned her around so that her face looked up into mine. "Nora, just where did the men take that Jap tonight?"

She hesitated momentarily. Then she said:

"If you must know, Gil, there used to be a rich landlord. He lived in a village not far from here. That was several years ago. He was very mean. Everyone hated him. The farmers hated him. Even his own family hated him.

"A few years before he died, he built himself a huge tomb on the other side of that mountain. From such a high place, he said, he could keep watch after death. He would watch everyone working on his farms. And he would curse those who were lazy and those who cheated him. And so, when he died, they put him there."

Laughing, I asked if people believed that he watched over them.

"Some do and some do not," Nora replied. "But tonight Chan and the men have taken the dead Japanese to the tomb on the other side of the mountain. They will put him inside to join the miserable old man. If it is so that one can watch from there after death, then it is good to have a sentry there. The old landlord hated the Japanese even more than he hated other men. Almost certainly, the two will quarrel. And they will watch other men enjoy life while they rot together in their stone house."

I came to know Nora much better in subsequent weeks, but I never learned whether or not she believed what she was saying.

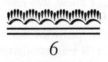

# 6

# A Date with Nora

My taxi slowed to a crawl as it approached a busy section of Aberdeen, a fishing village on Hong Kong Island. Coolies trotted along obliviously. With yokes slung across their shoulders, the coolies looked like dancing oxen. Baskets of fish dangled from some; vegetables, coke, and charcoal from others. The yokes bobbed up and down with the rhythm of feet and the sway of bodies. Rickshaws darted in and out, almost colliding. Pedestrians got where they were going without ever seeming to move forward; they jumped smartly from side to side in a forward direction. There was no keeping right or left. One could possibly describe this anarchic scene as two-way traffic, but it would be more accurate to say that, if a thousand people were on that one street, they were traveling a thousand different ways.

I kept a sharp lookout for Nora. "Pull over to the water's edge," I told the cab driver. Then I paid him and joined the mad procession. Weaving in and out, I craned my neck to look for a Chinese girl in a brand-new dress. After all, I had received and paid the bill. Chan had told me the street, time, and a little more about Nora. I had pestered Chan, but he had assured me that she was asking him just as many questions about me. My date with Nora had sounded so simple. I had not calculated on this swirl of human traffic. I knew the price of Nora's dress, but I would have paid it twice over just to know its color.

She should have been near a cluster of moored sampans a hundred feet ahead. The sampans were there, but Nora wasn't. On the pier, several coolie girls — very businesslike and very, very young — tried to coax me into riding with them in their sampans. They tugged at my sleeves and bounded around me like grasshoppers. "Get away, you little pests, before I throw you into the water," I snapped. The tiny sampans, bobbing up and down, looked as fresh, clean, and perky as their little mistresses.

A few of the more elegant sampans had canopies in the center. Two shapely legs — beautifully but graciously displayed — protruded from beneath one canopy. I followed the legs as far as eyes can travel. "I hope those are Nora's legs," I told myself. "I'll have to become more familiar with them."

Collaring one of the little coolie girls, I pointed at the legs. She protested that they belonged to a visiting lady, not to regular sampan commerce. My argument attracted a middle-aged woman who was peering into the crowd. Upon seeing me, she shouted to the canopied sampan. The legs shifted and Nora peeked out. She smiled up at me and nodded to the woman.

The woman took my arm and led me to the edge of the pier. Then

[ 63 ]

she pressed down on my arm as if to say "wait here." Jumping into the nearest sampan, which was empty, she stepped lithely into and out of several others until she reached Nora's. She paddled Nora's sampan over to the pier. I slipped in, crouching to make my way under the canopy. I eased myself onto a seat facing Nora and apologized for being a little late: "I made rotten connections."

"I waited on the pier," Nora said, "but it was hot in the sun. I asked the woman to watch for you."

I studied Nora because there was something different about her. It wasn't just the daylight or the new dress of stunning dragon-lady green. It was her hair, which was no longer scrolled but gently waved and less severe. I made a mental note to tell her I like it this way.

For now, our conversation was far more reserved. Nora asked me if I had a preference for any particular "boathouse." When I said no, she gave instructions to the woman, who stood behind us and propelled the sampan with an oar toward open water. The sampan swung slightly as the woman brought it around on course. Then the swirl of the oar settled down to a steady rhythm as we cut through the water. After a few minutes, the sampan bumped gently against the gangway of a "boathouse" — one of four floating restaurants in a small inlet.

I hopped out, holding the sampan steady for Nora to follow. We ascended to a room furnished like any other middle-class Chinese restaurant in downtown Hong Kong. Nora led me through without stopping. We climbed to the upper deck, which was also furnished like a restaurant but much more nautically. One felt happily at sea up there.

Mid-afternoon is not a customary dining hour in Hong Kong, so the upper deck was not crowded. And we had service fit for a king and his queen. Several boys followed us to our table unobtrusively. They dusted it and wiped it, although it had sparkled from across the deck. Several others held menus ready for when we wanted them, but not before.

"Would you care for a drink?" I asked Nora.

"Later," she said. "We must first select the fish we will eat."

She stood up and led me to the front of the boat. Gazing over the rail, we looked down at all kinds and all sizes of fish. They were

[ 64 ]

swimming in the water, but trapped there by nets and wire baskets. Crabs, lobsters, and shrimp were crawling all over each other.

"I'm a fiend for shellfish. I'm going to have both shrimp and crab-meat," I told Nora. I stood back, but she tugged at my arm.

"You are not done yet, Gil. The question now is: Which crab?"

"Does it matter?"

"Oh, yes. The fun is in watching the boys catch a particular crab. There are so many to choose from."

"They all look alike to me," I said.

"And to the boys. They never really know which one you are pointing at, so they pick them up one by one. They throw them back until you see one that is to your liking. Then you tell them to stop."

I laughed and said: "Well, let's put them to work."

The first crab looked delicious to me, but Nora said it was against the rules to select the first one.

"This sounds like going shopping with Mother," I remarked.

"If you are fastidious about selecting your crab, then they will be equally fastidious when they prepare it," Nora told me. "It is that way in all of China. Respect and pleasure are rewards for one's will-ingness to engage in lengthy discussion and criticism." Her words awakened me to how brash and superficial my original pleadings of dedication must have sounded to Chinese ears.

"Now I should like that drink," Nora said when we sat down at our table again. "We will have a long wait before we are served."

I ordered a large bottle of beer for the two of us.

"I had a long talk with Chan," I told Nora. "He told me a few things about you . . ."

"I know," she said. "Were you surprised?"

"Not at all. I had noticed your self-control when the Japs were sit-ting with you in the tearoom. When Chan told me that you were a contact for the guerrillas in China, I wasn't at all surprised. You acted as if you'd been through the same situation before."

Nora leaned back in her chair. She gazed out over the water at fishing junks tied side by side. They were airing their nets, which hung down from mastheads to decks. On one deck was seated an old woman, repairing a net by twisting twine with gnarled fingers.

That was the view, but I suspect it was not what Nora saw. When she spoke, her voice came from far away:

[ 65 ]

"Gil, if you had seen the things I have witnessed since the Japanese invaded my country, you would know why Chan and I risk our lives often . . ."

"I do care! I want to understand!" I interjected. But Nora didn't hear. She continued:

"Have you ever seen children bayoneted to death just to amuse a few bored soldiers? Have you ever seen a poor woman following a drunken Japanese soldier? If he vomits, she will be able to pluck out the solid food particles for her children. Have you ever been beaten within an inch of your life simply because you are not Japanese? The worst part of all is seeing the joy of the person doing it to you."

She was facing me now and looking me in the eye.

"Nora," I said, "I have never seen anything like that, but I believe you. In fact, I feel ashamed of the brutality at the mines. But I have a reason. I do not beat the Chinese because I like . . ."

Nora interrupted: "That is the difference. You have a reason." She took my hand gently and continued: "Oh, yes, Gil. I had heard about you before I ever met you. And most of what I heard was good."

"Now I am surprised."

"Do you know what the Chinese call you, Gil? Do you know what *Tz'u-hsin Hu* means?"

"*Tz'u-hsin Hu?*" I said. "I *have* heard the men say something like that when I'm around, so I assume it means bastard."

Nora burst out laughing and three waiters rushed over to ask if anything was the matter. When they went away, Nora said:

"*Tz'u-hsin Hu* means 'kind-hearted tiger,' Gil. That's what the Chinese call you. They say you slap them with one hand and give them a bowl of rice with the other. Most of the miners are considered the lowest of the low by other Chinese. They get far worse punishment every day from their fellow man than they do from you. They cannot understand why you would risk your life to save a thief or a murderer or a deserter, but they are grateful."

"Are you sure you have the right person? Nora, some of them have tried to kill me."

"The few who want to kill you are men you have insulted merely by demanding an honest day's work. Most of the men like you.

[ 66 ]

And ever since that night in Shatowkok, they feel there is an understanding between them and you."

"What kind of understanding?" I asked.

"It is hard to describe, Gil. But take, for example, the men who fled the party. They did not go home to their families. They fetched Chan to help you. They would have saved you themselves if they had known how."

"I'm happy to hear that," I told Nora. "Somehow my real feelings have reached those men. I'd hidden them for so long; even a white man hates to lose face, y'know. And I have a stinking pride. When I got here, I found that the Chinese hated me just because I'm British. I couldn't make them trust me because, for a long while, they were dead sure that all British were alike."

"The Chinese have much to learn," Nora said softly. "And so do you, Gil."

"Agreed," I said. "But when I reached Hong Kong and found I was getting nowhere, I felt like a madman who'd mislaid his soul. I'm sure I turned some of my anger on my miners . . ."

"Perhaps they understand you better than *you* do," said Nora.

"Not any more," I replied. "You saw a turning point the other night. When I killed that Jap, all the hate that was in me went into his back with that knife."

"And you will never hate again?" Nora said dubiously.

"Of course I'll hate again. But all the hatred I had stored up was put where it belongs — where it truly belongs. Since that moment I have felt like a changed man — or, rather, a changing man. For the first time, I feel as if I'm learning the meaning of wisdom. Not the full meaning, mind you, but enough to start to understand the Chinese better."

"And if you could understand yourself better?" Nora asked, but her voice trailed off as if she expected no answer.

Nora could tell me much about myself, I felt. But any answer would be meaningless unless I found it out on my own.

It was the first time I had ever expressed my pent-up emotions to someone Chinese. We talked all afternoon and most of the evening at the Gripps dining room in the Hong Kong Hotel.

Nora complimented me by telling me that I had killed like a professional. And I told her that might have been because I had once been a spectator watching a professional killer in a fight for life.

"And the funny thing was that I had the power to negate the victory, no matter which adversary won."

"Who did win?" Nora asked. Her interest piqued, she lit two cigarettes for us.

While we smoked, I told her the story.

Ever since childhood, I had looked upon hunting not only as an outlet for my savagery, but as a form of toughening up for the struggles ahead. On the last trip I made before leaving Australia for Hong Kong, I was determined to kill the most ferocious animal in the jungle: a wild boar. It weighs anywhere from five hundred to eight hundred pounds. Its tusks are deadlier than knives; they can rip you to shreds in minutes. Like human killers, the wild boar travels with an entourage — a herd of sows piercing the jungle with their screams and squeals.

My guide was an aborigine named Jacko — which was probably not his name, for hunters called all "abbo's" Jacko or Jackie. This Jacko was middle-aged and very talkative. It was, unfortunately, a one-way conversation: His pidgin English was worse than no English at all.

We had tracked several boars, but had lost them in thick foliage. Shortly after four P.M., we headed back for camp. We trudged through an area where small fig trees and bushes interrupted the profusion of mangroves. The ground was swampy; it smelled of decayed vegetation. Some five hundred feet away was the Mitchell River.

I was concentrating on the flies, mosquitoes, and leeches that were hunting me. Jacko was chattering away when the bush resounded with a scream that froze both of us. Then Jacko beckoned me toward the river.

About a hundred and fifty feet from the water was a small clearing. There, the soft bank sloped almost to water level. The landscape, however, was dominated by the backside of an enormous boar. His head was partly submerged in the muddy water.

I cocked my rifle, but something seemed peculiar about this boar. His entire weight — well over six hundred pounds — was straining back, as if he were having trouble lifting his head out of the river.

Suddenly, the boar heaved with all his might and then I saw what was ailing him. A twelve-foot crocodile had clamped its jagged mouth to the boar's snout.

For a moment, the crocodile floated listlessly on the surface. The boar lurched back, dragging his adversary with him a foot at a time. The boar no longer screamed with surprise. Now he made deep, choking grunts that resounded from layers within layers of hide.

Silently, the crocodile let the boar lift part of it out of the water. Then the rest of the crocodile stiffened. Its tail sank to the bottom of the shallow water. More firmly anchored, the crocodile began to drag the boar back into the water. In a few minutes, the crocodile's head was submerged again. The boar's grunts grew high-pitched once more.

The boar buried its weight in the soft bank and held on. The struggle see-sawed for at least ten minutes.

The crocodile thrashed the water with its tail in a desperate effort to knock the boar off balance. The boar didn't budge.

Then the crocodile flipped itself onto its back. The boar's head was twisted so violently that Jacko and I instinctively rubbed our own necks.

The boar seemed to spin in the air. Coming to earth, his entire weight teetered on his hind legs.

The crocodile had won a point. It might have won total victory had it been prepared for success. Caught off balance by the boar's retreat, the crocodile came out of the water with him. A crocodile can fight almost as well out of water as in it. But it has much more confidence in water. As it felt the air, the crocodile released its death grip on the boar.

The boar seized the opportunity. He didn't waste a second, as the crocodile rushed for the water. He sank his straight-razor tusks right through the crocodile's throat. With just a few snarls and slashes, the twelve-foot crocodile became a rag doll. Disdainfully, the boar tossed it farther up the bank.

The boar went to work on his adversary's corpse like a wholesale butcher. He tore the crocodile's soft underbelly to shreds. From where we stood, a hundred feet away, we could smell the filth of the crocodile's guts as the boar gleefully trampled them. With a fanfare of renewed screams, the boar attacked the crocodile's corpse again and ripped it down the middle from throat to tail.

Five minutes earlier, I had been watching a life-and-death struggle so fascinating that I had forgotten my role as a hunter. Now the battle was a massacre. I could scarcely think of this triumphant boar as prey.

Nevertheless, as the great boar turned away from its kill, I raised my .303 rifle. Unless you have a pig dog as decoy, you have just one shot at a boar. The only sure place to wound a boar is between the eyes. If you hit him anywhere else, you have wasted a bullet and perhaps your life. A boar can carry a whole arsenal of lead in his thick flesh. Wounded, he is more dangerous than a stalking tiger.

I had a perfect target as the boar stood facing me. His head was saturated with blood. His mouth hung open. Satisfied with his work, he panted unseeingly in great snorts. He was still a trifle groggy on his feet.

Jacko urged me to shoot now, but I couldn't. To kill this boar after his fight for life would have been sacrilegious. Instead, Jacko and I watched the dazed boar as he slowly wandered off grunting. He was searching for his sows, who had disappeared in the first moment of terror.

"That story is not very flattering to women," Nora said. "Why is it so meaningful to you now?"

"Oh, it doesn't have anything to do with women," I said. "You see, after I spared the boar, I began to wonder if I really had been cut out to kill Japs. I think much of my bravado has to do with these self doubts. I didn't know if, psychologically, I was really the man I was training myself to be. But the other night in Shataukok was outright symbolic: First I killed a pig. Then I killed a man."

"And so," Nora said, "you think you have proved to yourself what kind of man you are. You may find out for yourself that you are both men, Gil. You cannot shed the skin or the soul of a kind-hearted tiger."

"If so," I said, "I must find out for myself on the soil of China."

"That, too, can be arranged — perhaps," Nora said.

[ 70 ]

My flicker of hope became a flame, but no more was said that night. I knew Nora well enough to know that she never spoke idly — whether it was about a dress, a man, or a dream. My expedition to China had been broached in a men's room with Donald the Australian. Now it was being furthered with a woman whose quiet wisdom and beauty made all of China even more personal and meaningful.

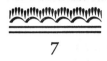

## 7

# The Price Is Dynamite

WITHIN a month, Nora had arranged a meeting with a Mr. Lee in Taipo, a New Territories town on Mirs Bay. "If your request pleases Mr. Lee," Nora said, "he can deliver you to our guerrillas in China." My contact would be my mine foreman, Chan, who was waiting for me when I stepped off the train at Taipo station. He touched his cap in greeting.

Two rickshaw coolies were standing by. Chan beckoned me to one rickshaw. He stepped into the other, which led the way.

It was early morning and Taipo was buzzing with shoppers going to market. Cooking aromas filled the air as food vendors prepared their wares at sidewalk stands. Wisps of blue smoke curled up from cooking pans as the vendors shaped their batter into ornate twisted doughnuts or plain round hotcakes. Then they fried them in fat.

It took fifteen minutes to push through the crowd and onto the road leading along the shoreline. I noticed that Chan's rickshaw had four live ducks hanging from the axle underneath. They swung back and forth as the rickshaw hit every bump in the road. Occasionally, one of the ducks rubbed up against a wheel spoke and quacked angrily. Poor doomed ducks, I thought.

We jounced along until we were fifty feet from the edge of Mirs Bay. Three more coolies were waiting to meet us. They wore well-washed blue coats and trousers rolled up at the knees. One of them limped a little and looked vaguely familiar. He smiled at me, but I could not place him. He carried a yoke with two baskets of vegetables. Another of the coolies carried strips of fresh pork tied together with thin strips of bamboo. Half of the pork dragged along the ground. The third coolie was empty-handed until Chan untied the ducks and handed three to him. Chan bore other parcels, so I offered to carry the fourth duck. My duck eyed the strips of dead pork warily.

The food — dead and alive — was placed aboard a small sampan on the beach. The sampan was pushed into fairly deep water. Then the coolie who limped stooped over. This made him look even more familiar. He gestured to me to climb onto his shoulders, which I did reluctantly. He waded out to the sampan and deposited me aboard. Not a drop of water was on me.

I noticed that Chan received the same treatment. It was not the usual lot of a mine foreman among his fellow Chinese.

We shoved off, with a coolie sculling from each end. "Where are we going?" I asked Chan over the ducks' squawks.

Chan pointed to fishing junks anchored several hundred feet away. "We go board one. It take us to Mister Lee. His junk wait for us. We spend little time only with Mister Lee. He must sail Bias Bay today."

The first junk we boarded was medium-sized. It had a smell of fish that must have been with it since its first day at sea. Its deck was littered with fishing gear. The men hoisted the old square sails, badly in need of repair. With one final creak, the old junk leaned into the sea and glided along like a fish. The master was at the tiller. But the junk didn't seem to need him at all. It knew its way.

I found a spot on deck where I could stretch out without being in anyone's way. I could see the land on both sides of the bay. Around us, junks and sampans tacked back and forth, changing their courses as they navigated their own destinies through little private worlds of their own. After two hours, we pulled into a small cove along the coast of Grass Island.

Mr. Lee's junk was anchored there. When we came alongside, lines were flung aboard and our junk was made secure. It looked like a canoe alongside Mr. Lee's massive vessel, which was low and wide in the beam. Mr. Lee's junk had a tremendous stern and poop deck and sweeping lines that shaped her bow. She was old, but had the strength and dignity of battles won against the waters of the China Sea.

Mr. Lee — a tall, thin man with sparse gray hair — welcomed us aboard in Chinese. He escorted us to a large cabin that was clean but reeking of opium fumes. We sat down at a round table. His wife placed a bowl of tea before each of us. Then Mr. Lee, who impressed me as an amiable yet inscrutable patriarch, spoke in perfect English.

"I wish to thank you for saving Miss Nora Wong from the Japanese," he said. "Her family and ours have been friends for generations. I do not approve of her request that I take you to China . . ." My face fell as Lee continued: "Nor do I approve of you, for you have caused me no end of trouble at the Hong Kong Mines. I have cursed your name every day for months."

"Sir?" I asked uncomprehendingly.

"Not all the dynamite that is stolen by your foremen and miners is sold for profit. I take as much as I can get. Then I ship it to the Chinese guerrillas."

"I should have realized that," I said thoughtfully.

"Thus, Nora's request has its advantages. If it is granted, we can repay the favor you did us by saving her life. And we can get you away from the Hong Kong Mines, where you are preventing us from stealing the dynamite we need . . ."

My hopes lifted again.

"I have just returned from a trip to China," Mr. Lee continued. "There I have seen Chan's cousin. He is a guerrilla leader."

"Ah!" I exclaimed. Now I knew why Chan was treated with such respect around here.

"I told his cousin, Major Chan, about you. The major hesitated. Your desire to join them sounds strange for a Westerner. You could harm them. You could make them easier to find. Or you could be a spy."

My hopes plunged again. Mr. Lee continued:

"Then I took the liberty of referring to you as 'The Source.'"

"Source?"

"Yes. From you we can obtain a large shipment of dynamite. And

Chan's cousin says this: For six cases of dynamite plus detonators and fuses, he will be delighted to accept your services in his guerrillas."

I could not believe my ears. In fact, if Duchet and Sam Coldron and Vic Shamroff had been there, they wouldn't have believed their ears, for my reply was: "All I have to do is steal six cases of dynamite? If Chan will help me — and he damn well better — it's as good as done. How soon do we leave? I can be ready tomorrow."

Mr. Lee smiled: "I am as anxious to be rid of you as you are to be gone. But you must be patient as well as efficient, Mr. Stuart. It will be at least two months before you can be transported there safely."

"Safely!" I exclaimed. "Who cares about safety? That's why I'm joining the guerrillas — because I don't give a damn about my safety!"

"Then you will learn in Major Chan's guerrillas to care for the safety of your comrades and the innocent villagers," Mr. Lee assured me. "The Japanese believe in reprisals. They wipe out whole villages for one raid."

"Well," I said, "I'm ready to wipe out Japanese. I'll try to get you double your order of dynamite. I've never stolen before, but this is not stealing when it is for a good cause."

"It is stealing," he replied in a serene tone that reminded me of Nora, "but I thank you for doing so."

When we left Mr. Lee's junk, I realized where I had seen the limping coolie before. Vic Shamroff and I had kicked him around Sam Coldron's office after he had pulled a knife on Vic. The Indian guard had mauled him there and crippled him later. We had thought he was the "buyer" of dynamite when he was really Mr. Lee's messenger. I was so mortified that, at the end of our trip back to Taipo, I wouldn't let him carry me from the sampan on his shoulders. To everybody's consternation, I waded ashore.

"Listen," I told Chan when we were back in downtown Taipo. "I'm too keyed up to go back to the mine just yet."

"You go Hong Kong and celebrate, Mist' Stu?" he suggested rather eagerly.

"No, I'll only get into trouble with some of my drinking buddies. I might even blurt out my plans. What are you doing tonight, Chan?"

He grew nervous: "Oh, I just go meet friends. Just friends."

[ 74 ]

"Would you mind if I came along?"

Chan shot me a curious look. "You no can come with me. Place much too dirty. Only coolie go there."

"What's wrong with that? After all, I'm going to be a coolie myself pretty soon. So you just lead the way to a place where we can talk and get a little food."

Chan shifted uneasily from foot to foot, so I let on that I knew where he was headed: "It's better, they say, to have some food in your stomach when you're going to smoke opium."

The restaurant was reached only by entering someone's home, exiting through the back door, following a short path, crossing a courtyard, and entering a building that was completely hidden from the street. Inside, coolies and well-dressed Chinese were standing, four and five deep, around a fan-tan game on a straw mat. A sharp-eyed man with a long thin stick was the game-keeper. Spectators were shouting and waving fists filled with money, which they sprinkled onto the mat.

Some forty other games of chance and cards were blocking all passage. By stamping on a foot here and kneeing a groin there, one could reach the restaurant in the rear.

All the tables were occupied, but we didn't form a waiting line. One table for two was crowded with a dozen drunken coolies who had finished eating. Some of them were sprawled across the table; others were arguing in shrill voices. They were not trying to convince, but to drown out, each other. I grabbed one of the sleepers and Chan another. We tossed them out the door without disturbing the debate. When we had disposed of the snoozers, we lifted the debaters out of their chairs and threw them out, too. The owner and two boys were setting the table anew when Chan and I returned from disposing of the last two.

The meal began conventionally with Chinese wines, sunflower seeds, and a plate of highly seasoned hundred-year-old eggs. Then it went on to some dishes that were new to me: snake meat, whitish and something like fish in texture and taste, cooked with hot peppers and bean pods; ducks' heads, fried to a crisp; squid soup; pigs' intestines, cleaned and dried and then cut up and fried in deep fat with vegetables; and cows' nostrils, a gristly dish that tasted like tough

[ 75 ]

oxtail. The names were far more intriguing to me than the food itself. I washed down all I could with heavy doses of cheap Chinese wine.

After dinner, we slipped through the gambling den and the courtyard and into an adjoining building. A flickering light on a small table welcomed us. The air was thick with opium fumes. Distant voices filtered through closed doors. Chan led me up a narrow, unlit staircase. A door opened silently as we approached. Dim amber light came through the opening. We could see the silent figure of a girl awaiting us.

She led us into a room that reeked of opium. Three dim lights burned on little tables in different corners. Tables were almost at floor level. So was a bed, on which I could see two male silhouettes half-sitting and half-lying.

Propped up by cushions and a bolster on his right side, one of the men was poking a long needle into the huge bowl end of an opium pipe. Twisting the needle slightly, he handed the pipe to the other man, who had been watching him closely.

The second man, the smoker, took the pipe from him as gently as a mother holds a newborn baby. The smoker settled down comfortably into the cushions on his left side. Lovingly, he put the pipe to his lips. He deftly tilted the big mushroom-shaped bowl of the pipe over a little tongue of flame burning in an oil lamp. The flame licked upward as he inhaled.

The bowl of the pipe threw a dark shadow, which cut off my view for a moment. I whispered to Chan: "Do you smoke the same brand?" Chan silenced me with a glare that cut through the dimness. I later learned that it is bad manners to make a sound until the smoker exhales. Even an officer making a raid will wait. A moment of bliss is too precious to be interrupted — particularly when it may be one's last.

The smoker's sucking noise became a long, deep, and eminently satisfied sigh. Yes, it had been bought; it was artificial; it was external. But, no matter what the cost of opium, this man was gratifying his life's desire cheaply. I envied him. Behind his aged, drawn face, I caught a glimpse of peace, which flashed and vanished as if he had tried on the mask of a baby for a split second.

Then the girl — as soundless as the shadow of the pipe — slid over to the smoker and bent low. She spoke softly and nervously, as though her very words might make the old man die of shock. The corner of his mouth twitched. He forced his lips apart to make words. His eyes were dry and could not look away from the tiny flame, for it was life itself.

Chan said something and his voice broke the spell. The old man at last turned his head and faced into the dark shadow of the room. He came to life and raised his hand. The girl helped him to a sitting position. For him to have traveled that far from his holiest of all worlds was equal to another man's jumping to his feet and bowing. I felt very welcome indeed.

The smoker was our host, although the servant girl acted for him and performed most of the hostly functions. She showed us to chairs and served tea while Chan and I talked. The old man spoke in a soft, faraway voice that had the melody of a sad song.

When we finished our tea, the girl reappeared with two steaming face towels, which she handed to Chan and me.

"Take off coat, Mist' Stu," Chan said, "and make you comfortable. Old man have sent for daughter who prepare pipe you smoke. Old man say apologize to you. He not feeling well. You can see so. He unable to join us."

"Why, the hypocritical old bastard," I said, beaming insincerely at the old man. "He looks pretty sick, all right, when he isn't smoking his opium. How long does a man like that last, smoking opium night after night?"

"He good for another ten year," Chan said.

"Pretty good! He must be at least seventy."

"He only in early forties," Chan informed me.

"Good God!" I said. "This is going to be the first and last pipe I'll ever smoke."

"In hour, he come to life," Chan said, "and you no recognize him." Chan turned to the old man and said something that made him nod. The nodding motion took control and the old man began to rock back and forth until the servant girl led him back to his bed. The old man's partner, who looked almost his age, was preparing a pipe for himself with great dexterity. Chan whispered to me hastily: "He his son."

[ 77 ]

There was a rustle in the heavy air and a slender figure drifted in. Chan introduced me to our host's daughter. She was in her twenties. She wore a black gown with a high, stiff collar. Her dark hair was drawn back so tautly that her thin ivory face looked naked. Her lips formed a faint smile, but her eyes were as businesslike as a whore's. By far the most expressive parts of her that I could see were her narrow arms, bare to the shoulder. One hand twisted toward an empty bed and I went there. Chan was right behind me.

The three of us stood above the bed for a minute, like worshipers. We gazed down at the small oil light burning softly on the table alongside. It had a warm, evil glow of temptation.

The daughter kneeled before the flame. She adjusted it so its tip burned level with the top of the lamp that surrounded it. Then her inexpressive eyes gazed up at me. One of her eloquent arms motioned me onto the bed.

The bed was draped by curtains coming down from a carved canopy. I crawled through them and took the lying-and-sitting posture that the others had assumed. As I propped myself up with cushions, Chan crawled in to face me on the bed. The girl placed the small table right in the middle of the bed. The hard flat bed was covered with closely woven cane matting, so it took me a few seconds to make myself comfortable.

Chan chided me for being a clumsy Westerner. I was glad that he was so relaxed with me now. But when he tried to give an informative lecture on the art of preparing opium for smoking, I didn't pay much attention. My eyes were riveted to the daughter and every move she made.

From a small silver tray, she removed and examined several long thin steel needles, not unlike knitting needles. She selected one. She placed it on a small slab of marble about six inches square and an inch thick. Once, the marble had been white. Years of use had stained it amber.

Gazing at me with those impassive eyes, she pointed to three pipes on the little table. I chose the most beautifully designed one. It had a long and slender blackwood stem, inlaid with silver. Its dark green jade bowl had eight sides; it looked like the petals of a very flat morning-glory. The center of the pipe's bowl was a hole no wider than an eighth of an inch.

[ 78 ]

The girl lifted my pipe and examined the hole. She probed it with one of the needles from her tray. Then, satisfied that the hole was clear, she lowered the pipe to the table. She selected a small silver container from the tray. The container was about the size of a tiny salt shaker. Like the pipe, it was beautifully carved. She lifted off its lid to reveal a tiny, delicate, dark blue jar inside.

Placing this jar before her, she took up the steel needle. She held it over the little oil lamp and allowed the tip of the flame to lick the needle just once. Then she dipped the needle into the blue jar. The tip of the needle came out coated with a thin amber film of liquid opium.

She held the needle over the flame and twisted it twice. The needle made several similar trips between opium container and flame until a wax-like ball of opium had formed at the tip.

Each time she held it over the flame, the ball of opium sizzled and bubbled and expanded. With an emphatic twist, she signaled that she had toasted the opium to the right consistency. Then she rolled the little ball of precious dope onto the slab of marble until the opium became semi-conical. Satisfied that it would fit the hole in the pipe bowl, she picked up the pipe with her left hand.

With her right hand, she gave the opium one final toasting. She held it in the flame a fraction of a second longer than before. Then, in one quick movement, she stuck the needle into the hole of the pipe. She gave one quick twist of the needle and carefully withdrew it. The needle had left a tiny hole in the center of the glob of opium, which rested in the pipe. She handed the pipe to me.

Steadying my head on the cushions, I held the tip of the pipe stem just inside my lips. With my left hand, I balanced the bowl of the pipe as carefully as I would aim a rifle. Instructed in sign language from the daughter, I poised the pipe bowl over the lamp. Only the tiny ball of opium came near the flame, which reached up like a hungry tongue.

The heat passed through the tiny opening that the needle had made in the ball of opium. Smoke forced its way into my mouth gently — and then it exploded in my throat! I thought I would choke, but instantly the smoke felt strangely soothing. It filled my throat until my lungs opened to embrace it.

There was no waiting. Every pore of me felt the opium. I was soothed, completely relaxed, and, most of all, floating. The sensation lasted for several minutes. I had expected to dream I was the Emperor of China surrounded by a legion of maidens. Instead, I felt only comfort and abstract bliss. (Chan told me later that it takes three to six weeks of sustained daily smoking to become a true addict with lavish dreams.)

I began to feel a small sexual craving for our host's daughter as I handed the pipe back and watched her prepare another for Chan. I almost wanted to make love to those slender skillful hands. Kneeling by my side, she was a Chinese princess dressed in the skin of a viper. But before my imagination could get the better of me, my body did.

Little beads of sweat popped out on my neck and forehead. The skin of my face tightened until I thought it would tear off. My mouth filled up with saliva tasting of opium. A lump grew inside my chest. I kicked my legs over the side of the bed. Rushing forward, I dragged the curtains down all over me. I hurled myself at a spittoon and vomited. I was certain I would leave my heart in the spittoon.

I could hear Chan and the daughter laughing themselves sick — but not as sick as I was. When I could, I lifted my draperies and gave them a baleful look. The daughter disappeared and came back with a hot towel. I buried my head in it.

Chan poured me some tea, but I was too ill to drink it. I crawled back to the bed. Chan suggested I sleep while he smoked a couple of pipes. "*Two* pipes!" I groaned. Then I passed out.

I lapsed into a reverie. Then, in my stupor, I imagined I was floating in the sea not far from Mr. Lee's junk. Mr. Lee leaned over the rail and pointed down at me. I heard him say: "*The price is dynamite*. Six cases or we will let you drown."

When Chan shook me and said a cab was waiting to take us back to the mines, I was still in my trance. I said aloud to an astonished Chan: "Oh, yes. The price is dynamite."

# 8

## The Agitator Returns

THE dynamite was easy to steal. Chan even supplied me with four trusted coolies, who had been in the Shataukok rescue party. They did the stealing. I came along to vouch for them if anyone questioned us. But we never even saw an Indian guard. I delivered a total of fourteen cases of dynamite — plus fuses and detonators to Chan. He notified Mr. Lee, who sent word that perhaps I could be of more use to China if I stayed on at the mines. I sent back an angry retort.

Chan passed only eight of the cases on to Mr. Lee. The others would be delivered only after all promises had been kept and I was with Chan's cousin in China.

"Well, that's over," I told Chan after the last case had been hidden in a shed near Kowloon. "Now I just have to sit back and wait to hear from your cousin and Mr. Lee."

That very night I nearly lost my life.

I took a cab back to the mines. I alighted just before reaching the mine police barracks. Sam Coldron would never equate the dynamite thefts with my nocturnal prowlings, but why should the eternally suspicious Indian guards even know when I came and went? I cut behind the mine police barracks and up a path that led past the tailings dump, a final resting place for the residue that is refined out of ore in the milling process. Tailings come down from the mill as a thick gray liquid mixture of crushed rock, sand, water, and chemicals. Tailings have the dangerous qualities of quicksand, but they dry hard like cement. In liquid form, they smell slightly surgical. Even by the low standards of the Hong Kong Mines, the tailings dump was not a pleasant place.

A night crew of coolies was adjusting the flow of slimy tailings into the dump, which was illuminated by a floodlight. As I sauntered briskly through the floodlight's beam, I gave a cheerful off-duty sort of wave and moved into the blackness beyond.

Halfway around the rim of the dump, someone pushed me from behind.

I went flying down the steep bank. I landed flat on my face in the thick ooze of the tailings. They were, I knew, a good twenty feet deep and as deadly as quicksand.

I righted myself, but as I drew upright, I felt my feet sinking deeper. I pressed my hands down in an effort to push myself up. But my hands simply sank into the muck.

The more I struggled, the faster I was sucked downward. I could hear the coolies working and singing nearby. Nobody had seen the attack on me.

I began to curse — first at the oblivious coolies; then at the ghastly helplessness I felt. Suddenly my pulse quickened as I realized that I was committing suicide. In another minute, I would drown — all because I was too damn heroic to consider crying for help.

It took a painful effort to cry out, for I had trusted only myself for too many years. Finally, I was able to shout quaveringly: "Help! Goddammit! Get me out of here, you silly bastards! Help! Help! Help!"

The coolies on the other side of the dump stopped singing. Several hands grabbed me by the hair and dragged me out — barely in time. I was covered from chin to foot with gray muck. Only my cursing enabled my rescuers to recognize me.

An Indian guard responded to the commotion. I told him I had slipped into the tailings. Had I so much as hinted that I'd been pushed, he would have arrested the whole crew of coolies. The mine police would have beaten hell out of all of the men and obtained a confession from one of them. I suspected, however, that the man who pushed me was no longer around.

I sent the men back to work. Then, after showering for a full hour and donning fresh clothes, I obtained a roster from Vic Shamroff, who was on night duty. I returned to the tailings dump and took attendance.

One man was missing. I didn't recognize his name. I passed it on to Chan the next day.

He reported back that the name was an alias. The man it belonged to was none other than the Agitator — the overseas Chinese killer whose rebellion against the white man had been thwarted, but not ended, by me underground.

The crime had been solved, although the culprit had fled.

"He was blacklisted, all right," I told Chan, "but that doesn't do much good when he takes a new name. He must have been surprised to see me when I came by the tailings dump that night."

"Oh, yes, Gil . . ." Chan began.

I barked at him: "Mister Stuart!" On mine duty, I was still the boss.

"Oh, yes, Mist' *Tz'u-hsin Hu*," he said, using my kind-hearted tiger nickname. "Agitator, he threaten kill any man tell you he back. And when you wave, he figger you spot him."

"Or else he just saw his opportunity."

"He nowhere now. I told he leave Hong Kong. Probably somewhere in China."

"I'll be looking for him when I get there," I said. "The bastard owes me a new suit, a pistol, and a watch. They were all ruined in that slime. If I ever catch up with him, it'll be either his dying day or mine."

My wallow in the opium den with Chan had disappointed me for its lack of opulent dreams. From that standpoint — if no other — my brief swim in the slime of the tailings dump was more meaningful. If I had drowned, I suppose my whole life would have passed in review before me. Fortunately, however, this was merely a brush with death, and I relived only a brief span of my past. One incident stood out with frightening similarity.

When I was five years old in England, my father taught me to ride. Trotting along proudly one day, I slipped out of the saddle and under my pony. Frightened, the pony stepped on my hip and twisted its hoof.

The bone of my left hip was crushed and a tubercular condition developed. Some months later I was placed in a hospital at Seven Oaks, a half-day's trip from home. I spent three lonely years on my back, imprisoned in a huge steel splint which held me rigid. A weight was attached to my left leg in an attempt to cure the condition and it felt as if it were constantly pulling the bones out of joint.

My head was pushed back so that, for the longest while, I could see only the ceiling and the back of my bed.

There was a hollow in the bed for my head to rest — or rather, to sag. My hospital room was small and dark, with just one window. Most of the time, its curtains were drawn. A garden was outside, but I seldom saw it, for my room was slightly below ground level. After I was able to move my head slightly, I could look out. All I saw then was a high bank of lawn and a small slit of sky. What little I did see, I saw upside down.

My father was in India at the time, so he came to see me only once in those three years. My mother came once every six weeks. When I was eight and no longer a child (three years in that lonely prison had robbed me forever of childhood), she came to take me home. I was able to walk on crutches.

In my first year out of hospital, I was cutting across a lonely common during a snowfall. I relished being in snow, which I had barely been able to glimpse through my hospital window. This snow was a foot deep. My crutches slipped and I toppled into a drift that was a good three feet deep.

I lay there flat on my back and I realized I could not get up. I could not move an inch. Nobody was in sight.

I screamed and screamed. Eventually, a big dog — out on other business — discovered me and summoned its master, who rescued me while laughing kindly at my predicament. And I had vowed then, at the age of eight, never to allow myself to be so utterly helpless again.

Almost twenty years later and deep in slime, the same sinking feeling had returned. And I had just barely forced myself to cry out to my fellow man for help.

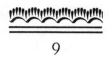

## 9

# Church's Camp

IN between rescues at ages eight and twenty-six, I had dedicated my
life to toughening myself up. I was not merely an ex-cripple trying to
stand erect in a man's world. I was trying to be a man standing alone
in his own world. I devoted myself to toughening my body, although
I was told many times that I would never be fit to lead an active,
strenuous life. Nor could I ever hope to join the Armed Forces. This
was a blow to my father, who had hoped that I would follow in his
footsteps in His Majesty's Army.

By the age of ten, the toy soldiers I played with invariably represented the Chinese Army. I never played with them on the floor of
my room. I would marshal my tiny forces on the garden grass beneath
the shade of a tree. With whatever textbooks and battle histories I
could find, I refought every war — East and West — with the irregular, predatory tactics that are now lumped under the heading of "guerrilla warfare." To my delight, my Chinese toy soldiers won every war,
including the American Revolution, the War of 1812, the Boer War,
and even the Boxer Rebellion.

In 1926, when I was fourteen, my family moved to Australia. I left
my toy soldiers behind, but I was already an accomplished student of
guerrilla warfare.

In my late teens, I virtually disappeared from home — on odd jobs
and hunting trips. The doctors warned me that further damage to my
hip would cripple me for life. It was a sound warning, but somehow
my youthful recklessness equipped me for life. I never felt stronger or
more alive than when I was working as a cattle drover, exploring the
wild and woolly Northern Territories of Australia, or sailing the high
seas.

Every physical experience I had was stored away for future reference. I acquired this file without the formal military training that was
compulsory in Australia then. My history of tubercular hip made me

physically ineligible, sight unseen. For a while, I tagged along unofficially with the Light Horse Guards, but I was just a hanger-on. Even that status was abruptly terminated with a change of commanders.

Over the years, however, I embarked on my own basic training program. While hunting, I became an expert shot with a rifle. On mining jobs, I learned a hundred different ways of using dynamite — with intent to kill, to frighten, to decoy, or to misdirect. I would blast down huge trees just to learn how to destroy bridge piers. I would create small landslides and road blocks by dynamiting loose overhanging rocks. I converted empty jam tins into hand grenades and bombs and tried them out on small alligators sunning themselves on river banks. In short, I was the very model of a modern minor menace.

My friends John and Felix — and even my beloved Margaret — used to advise me that the best route into China was a desk job in export-import. But I knew this would give me precious little freedom to travel within China. I would be doing nothing for the Chinese people other than exploiting their cheap labor. And so I said nothing. They, in turn, never jeered at me — which is perhaps the essence of friendship.

In 1933, I went prospecting for gold. Almost everyone gets the urge after living for a while in Northern Australia. In my case, I hoped to strike it rich and buy my way into China.

Although I never found gold, the experience proved profitable. I learned some lessons that did not seem apparent or important at the time, but they proved vital in later life.

I arrived in Townsville, gateway to the Northern Territories, the last unexplored frontier of Australia. I needed two saddle horses, two pack horses, and plenty of provisions. The man to see was named Church. He ran a lumber company at a place called Harvey's Range, some twenty miles from Townsville. As a sideline, Church traded in horses.

"But be careful with Church," an old codger advised. "Don't let him sell you a stolen horse."

"How in hell can I tell a stolen horse from an unstolen horse?" I asked.

"That's your business, son," the codger replied, spitting a stream of tobacco juice past my left knee. "And another thing: After he's sold you the horses, make sure he doesn't steal them back. Don't hang around Church's camp any longer than you have to. There are some rough characters there."

The next morning, I hitched a ride on an old truck that was delivering provisions to Church's camp. The truck had solid rubber tires. It rattled and shook over a sandy "road" that was really just a bullock trail through the bush.

Near the foot of a mountain range that parallels the coast of Australia, the forest grew thick with giant trees, most of them more than two hundred feet high. These were ironbarks — resembling oaks — with thick white rinds that were smooth on the outside and composed of several hundred corklike, paper-thin layers. You could peel off a layer at a time with your hands. When burned, they exuded thick oily black smoke.

The soil was a mixture of white and red sandy loam in which grew ferns, pandamus trees, and stubble grass. Some grass grew eighteen inches tall. One variety of grass had a fine saw edge on each side. At the slightest touch, it would cut deeply into a man's flesh. Other grasses were shaped like long green darning needles with sharp black points. The slightest prick from one of them would fester within hours.

Northern Australia abounds in strange trees and bizarre plant life. The poison bush is so lethal that nothing will grow within five to ten feet of it. It looks like a cluster of long straight twigs sticking out of the ground. On the side of the "twigs" are long narrow shiny green leaves. If they are eaten, death is inevitable.

Other perils of outdoor life included the stinging tree and stinging bush. If you made contact, the pain would be maddening. Their sting went through your shirt and trousers. The pain lasted for a day — and even longer if you washed the afflicted area or merely perspired. Then it could take ten days for the poison to drain from your system. I have seen horses and cattle gallop away from stinging bushes in such pain that they smashed themselves against trees.

The bullock trail passed right through Church's lumber camp. Hundreds of railroad ties, stacked in neat rows, flanked the makeshift road. An old steam motor hissed away, turning a large circular saw. Several husky men stood around it and fed it logs. Off to one side was an old shed of corrugated tin. It had no door. It looked like a battered crate.

"That's Church's house," the truck driver informed me.

"It's big, but it's not fancy," I observed.

"Nothing here is," the driver said.

Nearby was a corral, where fifty work horses sweated out the noonday sun. A man of about fifty walked over when I climbed out of the truck. He had gray hair and a gray mustache, both of which looked soapy white against his tanned face. His face, neck, and hands were pitted by lifelong exposure to the elements. His cheeks were flushed, with tiny blue and red blood veins crisscrossing near the surface. Tobacco juice worked its way down a trail from a corner of his mouth. His trousers were dirty and his gray flannel shirt sweaty. He weighed a good two hundred pounds, mostly muscle. He stopped six feet from me. I thrust forth my hand.

He responded by hooking his thumbs into his wide leather belt and spitting a gush of tobacco juice six inches from where I stood. Then he looked me up and down several times before asking: "What do you want?"

I looked him in the eye and said: "Are you Church?"

"I asked you a question," he said.

"I want to buy horses, Mr. Church. Two saddle and two pack horses."

"Ain't got none," Church replied. "Just work-horses. And I need them for hauling logs. But if you come back in a few days, I may have what you want." When he said this, I remembered the warning in Townsville about not taking stolen horses from him.

Church walked over to the truck driver, who handed him the mail. They talked in low tones. I could gather that Church was asking about me. After a minute or two, Church spat at me once again and said: "You better follow me over to the house and get something to eat." The prospect of hospitality from this surly man was little short of overwhelming.

Inside the corrugated tin shack was a long table with two benches. Mrs. Church — a dark-haired woman with the physique of a middle-aged fat man — was sizzling steaks in two deep frying pans. A plain but full-breasted young girl of about seventeen was setting the table. She was a cousin of the Churches. There were sixteen places.

Nobody introduced me. I just sat down next to the truck driver. At noon, a bell rang. A dozen men, including those I'd seen around the circular saw, trudged in to lunch. They looked tougher than anyone I'd ever met. Each of them glowered at me, but nothing was said until a thirteenth man came in.

I could tell at one glance that he was Church's son. He was about twenty-five and built like his father. He was quite handsome. There was a perpetual smile on his face. The smile made him seem more cordial and more worrisome than the other twelve men put together. He introduced himself as Jim Church.

"I'm Gil Stuart," I said. I also nodded to the men at the table, who gave me a new round of glares. Their hostility toward me was impersonal. But when they looked at Jim Church, I could see hatred, contempt, and fear.

"Don't introduce yourself to *them*," Jim Church told me arrogantly. "Hell, I don't know their names. Don't care to. Why should *you*?" He spat on the floor. The younger Church had a gift for making you think he had said "scum!" even when he hadn't.

"Are you going to work for my father?" he asked, smiling all the more as he basked in the men's hatred.

"No," I said. "I came out to try to buy horses."

"Are you going prospecting for gold?"

"Well, maybe."

"Listen, Gil, if you want to make some real fast money, that's not the way. We have a big contract with the Government here. We have to deliver twenty-thousand railroad ties in two months. I have twenty men out in the bush cutting trees. Now you look like a bright boy, not like *the others*. If you'd like, I'll subcontract to you. I'll get you a partner. If you and he toe the mark and help us out, you'll make enough to get your horses for free."

Jim's father, Ike Church, sat down at the table and said, "What do you think, boy? Can you wield an ax?"

"Maybe," I said warily. "Not so well as you, I'm sure, but I know how to use one."

"Then how about it?" said Ike Church. "The horse drovers won't be here for another week or so. They're bringing in a hundred head of unbroken horses, so you'd have to stay here a couple of weeks just to break in the ones you buy. In the meantime, you can work."

"Give me time to think it over," I said.

"Good," said Jim Church. "The truck isn't going back to Townsville until tomorrow anyway. This afternoon, why don't you drive out with me to the lumber camp in the bush? You can size up the place and spend the night here. Maybe I'll send my cousin Barbara over to keep you warm. And *everybody* will tell you we're good people to work for."

None of the men at the table said a word, but there were now thirteen glares directed at Jim Church. The added one was from his cousin Barbara, who was serving. We finished the meal in silence. When it was over, I noticed that the men left in pairs.

Jim and I departed for the bush camp soon after. The bullock trail took us five miles into a thick forest of bluegums and ironbarks. The bush camp had a dozen tents, built beside a trickle called Stony Creek. There was also a smaller model of Church's corrugated tin shack. The Churches stayed in this one when they came out to the bush. It had a dining table, but no stove. All the cooking was done on an open fire, which burned constantly twenty feet from the shack.

Nobody was there, but I could hear ax-heads sinking into hardwood not far away. The echoes rang through the forest and bounced back off the blue stone slopes of the Harvey Range.

Periodically, I heard a report — like a shot — as a huge tree snapped. Then there would be a tremendous crash and crunch. It sounded like the death of a dinosaur, for these trees were the ancient monsters of the forest.

Jim Church reached up to a wire hook hanging from a rafter, and offered me a canvas water bag. I gulped the cool water for just a second. Then I felt something in my mouth. Taking the canteen from my lips, I hurled it to the ground and spat violently. I began to cough. Both my hands tore at the inside of my mouth, to which dozens of live ants were clinging by their tweezer-like jaws.

After I had removed them, I glanced down at the one-gallon water bag, which was still spilling out its contents. As the water drained into the parched ground, it left behind hundreds of big black ants struggling to reach dry land. Each ant was a good half-inch long with spindly legs, bulbous body, and a head that was all jaw.

[ 90 ]

Jim Church was doubled up in laughter. Finally, he was able to speak: "That'll teach a city bloke his first lesson: Never drink from a water bag without spilling some out first. Some bastard must have left the cork off."

I glanced up at the rafter, where thousands of ants were milling around.

"You must have seen them when you took it down," I said to Jim Church. "Why the hell didn't you tell me?"

"I have manners," he replied, widening his smile. "I offered you the first drink, didn't I?" Then his whole expression changed — except for the fixed smile — and he faced me with fists clenched in case I wanted to carry the argument further. But I wasn't eager to fight him on his own terrain just yet. When he saw that I wasn't going to answer his challenge, his face rejoined his smile. He liked me better now that he could feel contempt for me.

"No hard feelings?" he said. "I'll make us some billy-tea and then we'll take a walk in the bush. You can meet your new partner." With that, he erupted into laughter again.

"What's so funny?" I inquired.

"I'm thinking that you'll really want to stay when you see your partner. He's exactly like you. Say, you don't happen to have a twin brother?"

I watched carefully while Jim Church made billy-tea. A billy is a water can with a lid; this one held a half gallon. Jim put it on the open fire. When the water boiled, he added the tea. I inspected at every step of the way and, when we were ready for the first sip, I made him swap mugs.

After tea, we walked into the bush for a mile. I made a point of walking behind Jim Church. We passed finches, wild canaries, and gray, pink, and white parrots, but I never took my eye off Jim for more than a second. As we walked, a flock of several thousand black parrots wheeled overhead. They had vermilion-tipped wings and made blood-curdling shrieks that drowned out the axes and even the reports of toppling trees.

We came upon a man swinging his ax hard and true in the distance. "This is your partner," Jim said, as we came up a few feet behind him. "Now do you see what I mean when I said he looked just like you?"

[ 91 ]

I didn't have a chance to look right away. As soon as the man heard Jim's voice, he whirled about. His ax whizzed through the air and planted itself right between Jim Church's feet. Jim didn't move. He seemed anchored to the ground. Even his smile dimmed slightly.

The man spoke in an accent I had never heard before: "Sheeeet, man! Ah thought Ah told you nevuh to come near me agin. Ah'll split you in two, Jim Church, if you ever show your ass out here agin."

The man was an American Negro, Southern division.

He stood six-feet-two. He was twenty-five or twenty-six and very dark. But most impressive of all was the way he spoke — with the air of a craftsman being disturbed at his work by a fool. Or rather, by fools, for he eyed me suspiciously. I hoped he would not judge me by my company. Although I didn't know what his quarrel with Jim Church was about, I was on the Negro's side.

I held out my hand and said: "My name is Gil Stuart. What's yours?"

"Tom Anderson," he replied. But he didn't shake hands. He had a second ax poised in case Jim Church made a move.

"I'm your new partner," I told Tom.

"Ah'd shake," Tom said, "only Ah cain't trust that white man one God damn inch." He glowered at Jim Church, who was trying to restore his toothpaste smile.

"Not that one," I agreed. "I'm glad to be working with you, Tom. You look like a good man with an ax."

"You mean you'll stay?" Jim Church asked with astonishment.

"I'll stay. I'm enjoying myself too much to leave."

"Good," said Jim Church. He began to laugh. I detected a note of menace in his unfunny cackle. He added: "Just wait until the others hear which side you're on."

Turning to Tom Anderson, I asked: "Is it O.K. with you if we work together? After some of the white men around here, maybe you only want to work with a black man."

Tom studied me for a moment. When he saw that I wasn't teasing, he replied: "If a man got a heart, Ah don't mind *who* he is." Now we shook hands. Jim Church didn't make a move toward the ax. He knew when he was in the enemy camp.

Jim didn't say a word all the way back to the lumber camp, where

I borrowed a truck from his father. I drove to Townsville, collected my gear, stayed overnight, and returned to the Church camp. I joined Tom Anderson at the bush camp in mid-afternoon.

"Didn't expect to see y'all agin," Tom greeted me. "If you'd been smart, you wouldn't return to this God damn hell hole."

"What's so bad about this place?" I asked. "Aside from Jim Church and that father of his."

"Y' ain't seen nothin' yet," Tom assured me.

He started to show me to a tent spot, but I told him that he and I would make our camp further up on the bank of Stony Creek: "We're working on a contract basis. It's different from the other men's terms, so we'd best stay away from them. They're getting paid by the day. But Ike Church is going to pay us for each railroad tie we cut. There's no reason why we can't earn a pound a day for each of us."

Tom whistled, for this was good money. But he asked: "What makes you think them Church monkeys'll pay up when the contract is finished?"

"We'll see about that, too," I said, slapping the butt of a .30-30 rifle I had just purchased in Townsville. Affectionately, Tom patted his ax, which was never far away.

After we had pitched camp that evening, Tom and I ate our own supper: salt beef and potatoes, with damper on the side. Damper is the bushman's bread. It is made with no yeast, just cream of tartar, salt, and plain flour baked in a Dutch oven. By baking, I refer to the process of burying the Dutch oven in a shallow hole filled with hot ashes.

As we ate, Tom briefed me on the two dozen men working in our area.

"They some mighty tough hombres," Tom told me. "Most done time in jail. Them that don't got police records, they hiding out from police or someone else."

"How do they find their way here?"

"Oh, Church hires them with no questions asked. He give 'em a place to sleep, plenty food, and liquor once a week. But he don't give them hardly any money. They're like sharecroppers here, but at least they don't get no visits from the police."

"Are the Churches as mean as they look, Tom?"

"Meaner. Old Ike Church, he don't think nothin' of beatin' a man within an inch of his life just to get some little thing he want. And then that son-of-a-bitchin' Jim Church'll try to finish him off. That Ike's a man with brass balls, but Jim's plain chickenshit. Ike'll beat a man because he a mean old man. But Jim'll do it because he enjoy it."

"And because he's scared," I added.

Tom warned me that at least a quarter of the men were stooges for the Churches. They would step in if Ike or Jim ran into any difficulty. That was why the men traveled in pairs. A loner could end up as a human punching bag at the mercy of a small, vicious mob.

"How did you get in with this crowd?" I asked Tom.

"Ah jumped ship," Tom replied. "Ah joined the Navy to get out of Alabama and see the world. The ship turned out to be an indoor Alabama. Then, of all the hellholes, Ah ended up hiding out in Townsville . . ."

"And now here," I remarked. "Out of the boiler room and into the frying pan."

"For three mis'rable months now," Tom said ruefully.

"Has Church paid you any money in that time?"

"Jes' enough to buy tobacco and a few work clothes."

"Well," I said, "we'll see what we can do to get you out of here."

Tom and I worked from dawn to dark every day for two weeks. We made a good team. I learned from Tom about lumberjacking, survival, and the curse of being Negro in America. And I told Tom about Australia, England, survival, and my obsession with China. I was surprised to hear that American Negroes didn't practice cannibalism, even in Mississippi. And Tom was pleased to discover that not all white men in Australia were like the Churches and their employees.

Any two men can tire of each other's company. One Sunday afternoon, we paid a visit to the tent camp. Some of the men were lolling in their tents. Others were washing clothes. Most were playing poker on the dining table in the shack. To a man, they made a point of not seeing us. Finally, I sat down at one end of the table to find out if we were really invisible.

Everything stopped. Every man looked in my direction. Not one was friendly. I heard a faint murmur of "nigger lover" and "cannibal" and the sound of Tom, standing behind me, humming a song and clicking his fingers nervously.

One of the men growled: "If you sit at this table, you got to join the game."

"Suits me fine," I said. I glanced up at my partner and invited him: "Sit down, Tom, and join the game."

Tom's eyes traveled the length of the table, but he made no move to sit down: "Ah think Ah'll just go sightseein'."

The spokesman said: "He can't play. He ain't got no money."

"Tom," I said, "open up your gunny sack and give me a bottle of plunk." Plunk is Australian slang for cheap wine. I'd bought a dozen bottles in Townsville. Tom and I had six of them with us as a peace offering.

Tom handed me a bottle. I drew the cork and raised the bottle to my lips. The wine trickled slowly down my throat and I gargled slightly. Yearning suffused every face at the table. One man drooled passionately. Several necks began to make swallowing motions. I gulped the wine as noisily as I could.

Spontaneously, the men rose slowly from the benches. I lowered the bottle and thumped it on the table like a chairman pounding a gavel. I slid it toward the cluster of men. Anxious eyes followed it like a pool shot.

The smallest and oldest man made a grab for it. The one who served as spokesman slapped him across the face with the back of one hand. With the other, he took the bottle. When he'd had his fill, he gave it to the old man. The bottle passed from one mouth to another. In three minutes, it was drained.

"O.K., Tom," I said. "Give me three more, but let's drink these out of mugs." In a fraction of a second, a dozen tin cups were proffered. And I had established my authority.

"What's your name?" I asked the spokesman.

"Call me Alf," he replied.

"All right, Alf," I said. "And you guys call me Gil. Alf, I'm appointing you bartender." I pushed the three bottles of wine at him. He rationed it out — quite fairly, I noticed.

As he poured Tom and me a shot apiece, Alf said: "If you boys want to join our game, you don't have to pay with money, y' know. You can pay with tobacco, liquor, anything . . ."

"Well, if I win, I won't pay with anything," I said. "But I have

[ 95 ]

money. First, I want to sell two more bottles of plunk. I'm asking five bob a bottle." At five shillings, every man at the table offered to buy.

Alf intervened: "Just a sec, now. I'll do the selling. Half these blokes don't have a penny. I'll take one bottle and Walt here can have the other." He pointed to the old man who had grabbed for the wine. I figured Alf and Walt could put it to good use. Alf handed me ten shillings, which I passed on to Tom.

"Now Tom has money," I told Alf. "How about letting him in the game?"

Alf twisted his gnarled face into his best approximation of a grin. I figured he could stand a few smiling lessons, if not an entire charm course, from Jim Church. "Sure," Alf said. "Now just watch me win my ten bob back — plus a bottle of free wine."

The wine was enough to keep the peace for several games. Since I was the newest arrival, the men pumped me for news from the outside world — mostly from their home towns. They were from Sydney, Brisbane, and various coastal cities. But when I asked questions about themselves, they glanced at each other warily.

Finally, a thuggish-looking kid asked me what was on everybody's mind: "You don't happen to be a pimp for the cops, do you, Gil?"

All eyes were upon me as I leaned back and laughed: "Hell, no. Do you think I'm looking for a broken neck?" I told them a little about my background and there were no further questions. We played poker until suppertime. Tom and I joined them for their evening meal. The conversation was mostly about logging and women. It was dark when Tom and I followed the creek back to our own little camp.

"They're not bad guys," Tom growled. "But today's the first time they ever spoke to me."

We visited the tent camp every Sunday after that. There were often bloody brawls. Tom and I steered clear of those. We made as many good friends as we could — about six of them, starting with Alf and Walt and the punky kid who'd asked if I was a police stooge. All six of our friends had done time in jail. Two of them admitted they were hiding out from the Sydney police. They were wanted for a robbery they'd had nothing to do with, but their long records were against them. I believed their stories. They were the kind of braggarts who would have been proud and boastful if they'd really committed the crime.

After three weeks, Ike Church made good on his promise. He sold me the four horses I needed. I bought two extra horses for Tom because he offered to go prospecting with me when we finished up at Church's camp. I paid cash for the horses. They were good-looking animals. We spent our evenings breaking them in.

A month later, everyone from the lumber camp — including Ike and Jim Church, Ike's wife, and cousin Barbara — moved out to the tent camp. The job was nearly done. The Churches supervised hauling. Tom and I had stacked our ties in neat piles, where we could keep a strict accounting when the Churches were ready to haul them away.

By then we figured the Churches owed us two hundred pounds. "That's eight hundred bucks where Ah'm from," Tom said happily.

One morning, we awoke to find a quarter of our logs missing. We were furious, for two hundred dollars was shot to hell.

"Ain't none of that woulda happened before Jim Church and his shit-eatin' grin got out here," Tom declared.

"Ike must be in on it, too," I said. "It's Saturday. We'll pay a call on old Mr. Church tonight. Maybe he'll tell us that he's credited us with the logs he hauled away."

"Are you kiddin'?" Tom said. We'd see, I replied.

After dark, we strolled down to the tent camp. The moon was bright. The night was filled with the buzzing of crickets and the croaking of tree frogs. Nobody was in the tents. We stood in deep shadows of trees and glanced around for signs of life. Fifty feet away, on the other side of the tin shack, a fire and two hurricane lamps glowed. The small clearing was crowded with lumberjacks plus the surly mill crew.

"From the racket they're making," I told Tom, "this must be liquor night."

"Ole Church done opened his heart, God bless him," Tom said.

"Then let's pay him a call while he's in a benign mood," I said. "I trust you have your knuckle-duster with you."

"Ah have mah *brass knuckles,*" Tom said, correcting me.

"Never the twain shall meet," I murmured. "I've got mine, too. I'll hide my rifle in the hollow of this tree just in case we need it. But before we go celebrate with the Churches, we ought to search each tent for guns. I'm not positive who my friends are around here and I'd hate to be shot in the back for making a mistake about someone."

Tom agreed heartily. We searched each tent and found almost a dozen guns, which we hid near the creek. The only other guns in the vicinity were in the Churches' shack, but we couldn't approach it without being seen. We would have to take our chances.

We strolled into the clearing. The girl cousin, Barbara, had just put a record on a phonograph in the shack. The speaker began to screech "It's a Long Way to Tipperary." One of the mill hands grabbed Barbara and went reeling off with her in his version of a jig. The others cheered them on.

Jim Church spotted us. Grinning broadly, he said: "Well, if it isn't the hermit — and his dark shadow." Tom ignored him and I greeted him curtly.

When she had been to Tipperary and back, Barbara declined another dance and came over to me.

"What brings you down here tonight, Gil?" she asked me. "Can I offer you a cup of tea?"

"Thank you!" I said warmly, sparked by the welcome from a girl to whom I hadn't spoken a dozen words before then. "How about the next dance, Barbara?"

"After you've finished your tea, Gil. There are several dances I've promised first."

I sat down with the two wanted hoodlums from Sydney. Tom took out his harmonica and Barbara danced with a timber-getter to "Red River Valley" instead of that infernal "Tipperary."

The tougher of the two men from Sydney was named Mike. He told me: "May be a spot o' trouble tonight, Gil. A little delegation of us asked Church to pay us off today. He said 'Sorry, lads.' We have to wait until he delivers the railway ties to the Guv'nor."

"The cheating bastard!" I exclaimed. "How long will that take?"

"Another month," Mike said. "If he pays us at all. He told some o' the boys he don't owe them a farthing. Says we're lucky he don't make us pay *him* for keeping us out o' trouble with the bobbies."

"How are the boys taking it?"

"Several blokes are plenty sore. But the old man bought several gallons o' plunk today to make us forget."

"I've got a score to settle with him myself. He's been stealing my logs. How is old Church now? Drunk?"

"Not that chap. Too smart for that. Now Jim Church is having a peg too much — and so are his pals."

I stood up and told Mike: "I think the time has come for a few words with the old man."

I started to walk over to Ike Church, who was standing near the fire and sipping from a mug of wine. Barbara intercepted me.

"It's your turn to dance now, Gil."

"That's good," I said. "I thought you'd forgotten me."

"No," she said. "It's a rare chance to dance with a man who's still sober."

As we danced to Tom's harmonica music (he was playing the wistful "Shenandoah"), I glanced over at old man Church. How was I going to approach him without attracting a crowd?

"Well," Barbara said with a question of her own, "aren't you going to ask me to sleep with you tonight?"

It was the kind of question that can derail any train of thought. "Is that what the other chaps ask you, Barbara?"

"Yes,"

"And what do you tell them?"

"No."

"Then that's why I haven't asked you."

Barbara laughed. Our little dialogue had created an intimacy between us. I felt as if I'd been given a raincheck to be honored if all went well on other fronts.

She leaned closer and drew me away from the center of the crowd.

"Gil," she said confidingly, as we continued to dance, "I'm going to tell you a secret. Do you know that Ike and Jim have been stealing your logs?"

"Yes," I said, pleased to have my suspicions confirmed.

"Well, that's just the beginning, Gil. They're going to steal some more tomorrow. And you were a damn fool to pay cash for your horses. Ike plans to steal them back now that you've broken them in."

"Barbara, why in hell are you telling me this? You're related to the Churches, aren't you?"

"Yes, but I hate them," she replied, practically spitting. "I hate

[ 99 ]

them all. That Jim takes me whenever he feels like it. And when I tell him I can't stand him, he just laughs and takes me again — even when he isn't ready. Sometimes his mother looks on."

We were still dancing. Realizing simultaneously that the music had stopped, we glided to a halt.

"Barbara," I said, leaning over her in a romantic pose, "do you want to do me a favor that might save all of us a little trouble?"

She sighed and murmured: "What more can I do for you, Gil?"

"Collect all the guns in Church's shack," I said, brushing her forehead with my lips, "and hide them. There'll be trouble starting any minute and you'll be saving lives on both sides. Will you do that for me?"

"Yes, Gil," Barbara said in a resigned voice that added years to her age.

"Good. Now be sure nobody sees you. If trouble starts, run down to the creek and hide behind the tents so I'll know where to find you."

We strolled toward the shack, where Barbara left me. About ten men were huddled around Mike, the tough from Sydney. I guessed that in a pinch I could count on their support. They were watching me as I ambled over to old Ike Church.

Ike had downed a few drinks, but I could tell he was nowhere near as drunk as he pretended. He wore his gray felt hat. In his left hand was an old pipe. In his right hand was a half-empty mug of wine. It was tipped and almost — but not quite — spilling wine on the ground. A man's grasp on what's in his hands is often a good measure of how drunk he really is.

His face was red — partly from the wine, but mostly from the fire. He was perched on a chopping block. He stared moodily yet warily into the hot coals of the fire. Someone had just thrown a few dry saplings on. They crackled into flame as Ike Church glared up at me.

"What in hell can I do for you, Stuart?" he asked. Then he looked down. A few feet from the fire, some men with whom I'd never talked edged closer. I could smell liquor on their breaths.

"How are you tonight, Ike?" I began pleasantly.

His piercing eyes were level with my waist now: "I said, what do you want, Stuart?"

"Just a little information, Ike. About some logs you hauled away from my area."

My words took a minute to sink in. Then, without moving his head one inch, Ike Church said: "I don't know what the hell you're talking about, boy. Go see my son Jim. He'll take care of you." He snickered at the thought.

I took several steps backward before turning away from the men loitering near the fire. Then I walked toward the shed, where Jim Church was shadow-boxing in the firelight to the rhythm of Tom's harmonica.

Tom stopped playing as I approached, but Jim Church said: "Play some more, *boy*."

"Man," said Tom, "Ah am dawg-tired of standin'."

"Then sit down and play, *boy!*" Jim said, pointing to a wooden crate. As Tom sat down, Jim Church yanked the crate out from under him. Tom fell sprawling on his back.

If ever a man was all smiles, it was Jim Church. I had never seen him happier. He might have had a jolly evening if he had only resisted the temptation to kick his boot hard into Tom's ribs while the black man was down. There was a thumping sound.

Tom tried to spring to his feet, but Jim aimed another kick at his head.

That was as much as I was willing to watch. I slipped my hand into the rings of the knuckle-duster in my pocket. Then I swung with all my might at Jim's face. The brass rings tore at his smile and laid it open.

Jim fell like a stone on top of poor Tom. My blow was a battle cry. The men standing around Mike overturned the big table, thereby blocking off a crew of Jim Church's stooges rushing to Jim's rescue. Now Mike and his pals were slugging it out with Jim's men.

Tom and I rushed forward to meet the attack from the fireside. Ike Church's bodyguards — about eight of them — were drunk, so the two of us had an advantage. Our brass knucks were zeroed in on their faces. We knew we had them as we felt the short, rough edges of brass tear hunks of flesh from their faces.

Suddenly, there was a shrill, unearthly scream that would have done credit to a banshee. I looked up to see big fat Mrs. Church swinging an ax at Tom's head.

Tom ducked. But, as he did, several of Church's men pounced on him and pinned him down. Mrs. Church stood over him and raised her foot. She was about to bring her heel down in his eye when I tackled her.

It took a while for my knee to find a soft spot in that fat but unflabby woman. When my knee struck home, she dropped her ax and fell back, screaming louder than ever.

I stood up to be confronted by a sight I will never forget. Old Ike Church was hurtling toward me with a flaming sapling held high over his head. He looked like Doom itself.

I jumped aside just as his makeshift torch came whistling by. One of Mike's men leaped forward. With three quick jabs and one knockout punch, he sent the old man toppling right back into the fire.

I had no time to see more. Someone had knocked me off my feet. Two men were tearing at me on the ground. My right hand found a man's face. I groped for the nostrils. When I found them, I stuck two fingers inside. Then I ripped at his nose. With a blood-curdling scream that would have done Mrs. Church credit, he loosened his grip.

But I felt a sharp pain as a knife entered the side of my left leg. The knife was withdrawn quickly. I could see it poised bloodily above me — ready to strike at a more damaging target.

All of a sudden, knife and man vanished. One of Mike's men helped me to my feet. I was in time to see Tom make a parting slash with his brass knucks. His target was once the face of the man who had knifed me.

The lights were out in the shack. The big fire had been momentarily choked by Ike Church's fall into it. Now it flamed back into life. I could see human debris spread all over the campsite. Some men were holding onto various soft spots and moaning. Mike's boys — covered with blood and armed with broken wine bottles — were helping friends to their feet and kicking enemies away.

"Where are the Churches?" I asked.

"I dunno," Mike replied. "Ike and Jim and the old biddy made for the shack. We should ha' heard from their artillery by now."

I laughed. "They won't find them. That's why we're all still alive. You and your chaps follow Tom and me down to the creek."

I felt a stinging pain in my left thigh. By clutching my wound with my hand, I managed to walk to the creek. Barbara was waiting. First, I told Tom: "Give each of Mike's men a gun. But don't let anyone use the guns unless I say so. I want to get us out of this mess with the money those bastards owe us, not with jail terms."

Mike had found a first-aid kit in the Churches' tent. While several men stood sentry duty, Barbara bandaged my knife wound. Then she took care of the other wounded men. If a man was strong enough to make a pass at her while she bent over him, Barbara moved on to another casualty and came back to the lover boy later.

I washed my face and hands in the creek. Then I discussed strategy with Mike. He agreed reluctantly that it would be unwise to leave Barbara out here with this crew of men. Nor would it be right to let the Churches get their hands on her.

"I'll take her into Townsville in one of Church's trucks," I decided, "and see that she makes it back to her family, wherever they are. Then I'll go to the police station and tell them what's happened here. I'll try to have one of them return with me. A little police pressure on Church ought to do it if we can catch up with him."

"I don't think we like the coppers in the picture," Mike grumbled.

"I'll tell them only as much as it's necessary for them to know. I'll tell them what happened out here, not *who's* out here. The only one they'll meet is me and I'm clean."

"But wha' if Church tells 'm who we are?"

"I'll be with them when they see Church. I'll drop a few hints to the old man that, if he lets on about your records, I'll see to it that he's charged with harboring wanted criminals."

"The boys ain't going to cozy to that, Gil. They'll be brooding about whether you'll be coming back — and, if so, with the coppers."

"It's a chance they'll just have to take," I said. "It's a better risk than working for Church, isn't it?"

The truck we found had no lights, but there was a full moon. Once Barbara and I were on the trail, we had no trouble picking out the route to Townsville. As we bounced along, Barbara kept a watchful eye for her nasty relatives. She told me she had enough money with her to pay her fare back to her family's home several hundred miles away: "I found a few pounds while I was hunting for the guns."

"Do you think the Churches will ever try to get back at you?" I asked her.

"Once I've told my folks how I was treated," she said, "the

[ 103 ]

Churches won't dare show their faces within a hundred miles. My family's just as mean as they are."

"Why did they let Church bring you here, then?"

"They didn't want to," she said, "but I thought it would be an adventure." In the moonlight, I could see her smile sadly at herself. I took my hand from the wheel and held hers for a moment.

We arrived in Townsville after midnight. I was unable to awaken the one policeman on night duty there. But I was able to find a late-to-bed landlord, who rented us a room for the night.

Barbara — as I've said before (which was once too often) — was a rather plain girl. I made love to her that morning, however. It was not hard to pretend that she was lovely. When you have seen a disillusioned woman smile sadly in the moonlight, you have seen her at her most seductive.

After I saw Barbara off on a morning train, I visited the Townsville police station. The day people there were most obliging. They asked no further questions as I gave them an account of events at Church's camp.

"Happens twice a year, like clockwork," the chief told me. "If he doesn't pay those crooks, there'll be a small war out there. Or they'll come to town and rob our decent God-fearing civilized folk."

I said I was not admitting that any but the most respectable citizens worked for Ike Church.

The chief gave me a sly wink and said: "Until they make trouble, that's none of my business. Just because they're crooks, neither Church nor any other man has a right to cheat them."

He assigned me a police officer and a "black tracker" — as aborigines were called. This one, inevitably, was named Jacko.

We rode to Church's lumber camp, which was completely ransacked. Several work horses and log wagons were gone. So were all the tents, the Churches' belongings, and food.

"Assuming the Churches did this," the policeman told me, "we'll have no trouble catching up with them. They don't seem to be traveling very light."

Jacko knew the territory even better than the Churches. Before sundown, we caught up with Ike Church, his wife, and a few stooges. They were climbing a steep trail up the Harvey Range. Their wagon

[ 104 ]

had overturned. The horses were still hitched to it in a tangled mess. Jim Church, who was probably with another wagon, was nowhere to be seen.

Ike Church was badly bruised. He had burns on his arms and shoulders. He put up little resistance. Mrs. Church, however, turned loose her unearthly wail when she saw me: "There he is! He's the one who started a riot and beat up a woman! Officer, arrest him!"

The officer remarked flatteringly that, in a fight between her and me, he would have bet on her.

He was less civil to Ike Church, who protested that he was a sick man. "You can get all the care you need in Townsville," the policeman assured him, "but you were going in the wrong direction. On your way to Townsville, you'll stop at your camp and pay your men."

Back at the camp, it was even more difficult to persuade Mike's men to come out of the woods and claim the money that was rightfully theirs.

The policeman, however, asked them no questions. He simply told them he hoped they wouldn't tarry long in Townsville. He added that he'd heard there was work to be had at a sugar plantation on the northeast coast. All of them took the hint and their money.

We said goodbye in Townsville. From Mike and the others I had learned that criminals could be far more decent than the people who exploited them. Even the most vicious criminal has pretty ordinary aspirations until something goads him into breaking the law. Mike and his men could work productively if treated fairly. I remembered this in all my future dealings with that vast man-made legion known as the "scum of the earth."

Tom Anderson and I drifted westward on our prospecting expedition. After a while, we parted and he went back to sea.

From the moment when I had stood between Tom Anderson and Jim Church, I should have known that nothing could be judged in black and white terms.

But if I had been wise enough to apply such mature logic to my thinking about China and Japan, I might never have made my way into the Chinese guerrillas.

# 10

# Blue-eyed Chinese

CHINA was imminent from the day Chan told me, matter-of-factly: "Mist' Stu, you quit job now. Mist' Lee say you leave Hong Kong soon."

I gave Sam Coldron a week's notice. When I told him I was resigning to join the armed forces, he didn't even ask which army. He simply wished me good luck and assured me I'd "meet a more agreeable bunch of bastards in the service."

On the evening I left the mines forever, Chan handed me a note to take to an address in Hong Kong: "Give this to host. I join you around eight after I change your money."

A rickshaw delivered me to a crowded street in the Wanchai district of Hong Kong. It was Sunday. But, at any hour of day or night, you can find something of interest in Wanchai. The most popular attractions were sex, gambling, opium, and morphine. If a stranger appeared, it was assumed he had come there for one or more of the specialties. It was no place, however, for white men or even prosperous Orientals to go "slumming" or for laughs. Neither the best people nor the second best came to Wanchai; it was too tough. It surprised me that Nora had picked this district for our rendezvous.

The address was a noisy restaurant. The plump little proprietor wiped his hands on an apron before taking my note. Reading it, he barked orders. A boy led me up a flight of steps to one of seven or eight private rooms upstairs. He practically pushed me into a chair. He raced out through the room's swinging doors. Before they stopped swinging, he had raced back in with a cup of tea. He served me and disappeared again.

I stared at the swinging doors until they stood still. The barren room gave me the shakes. I guessed that Nora had picked it so that neither Japanese agents nor British authorities would see me conferring with suspicious Chinese. If anybody suspected my intentions, I would find myself on a slow boat to Australia, not China.

Even when you're sitting on the second floor of a noisy restaurant, you can always tell when a woman enters downstairs. There is a shift in the sounds, both masculine and feminine. A few seconds after I heard an appreciative murmur below, I stood up. The swinging doors opened as the roly-poly proprietor ushered Nora in. Then, bowing, he left us alone. Nora kissed me. She was dressed in black trimmed with silver. As I helped her off with her coat, I noticed that she wore more make-up than usual. It was protective coloration in the Wan-chai district.

Nora was excited, so she ate enough dinner for two.

I, too, was excited, so I ate hardly any food at all.

When Nora saw me toying with my meal, she said wisely: "You had better eat as much as you can, Gil. This may be the best meal you'll eat for a long time."

With the help of the Chinese wine, I managed to stuff the rest of the food into me. When we finished, it was after eight. Chan still had not appeared; perhaps he was having trouble exchanging my money for Chinese currency. For almost an hour, Nora and I sat sipping tea, and saying very little. In the small room, we could hear rain beating down outside.

"That mud won't help us sneak across the border tonight," I grumbled disconsolately.

"But the rain will make us harder to see," Nora said.

Conversations about weather seldom accomplish anything.

Noise was coming from a building next door. When I heard English voices, I asked Nora what other Britons were around. She told me that next door was a whorehouse where you could buy anything from a ten-year-old boy to a White Russian beauty. From the shouts I heard, I gathered that two British sailors were picking up a dollar's worth of forbidden fruit on their first night in port. I could not determine on whom or what they were spending their money.

Chan arrived at nine. His money-changer had been delayed, but he had exchanged a large sum of British money without exciting suspicion.

"Four thousand Chinee dollar," Chan said, handing me a bulky package.

"Good, then I'll pay for the dinner and let's go."

The proprietor refused to accept payment from any friend of Nora's.

He was honored by our presence, he said. Putting my money away, I remarked to Nora: "The Chinese are always impossible. My dream of getting into China is coming true, all right. But a simple matter like paying for my last meal in Hong Kong is absolutely impossible."

We took the ferry to Kowloon and then a rickshaw to the small Chinese hotel where I was staying. The owner could be trusted. He knew vaguely that I was going on a long, mysterious journey and had agreed to keep my belongings there. Only Nora, Chan, or I would be allowed to remove or go through them.

"My passport and other possessions are here," I told Nora. I had been instructed to take along no identification. "If I should never return, I want you to go through my bags. Keep whatever you want and send the rest to Australia. There are instructions inside the smaller bag."

I did not mention that a small bottle of perfume was in there for her.

The hotel owner sent for a cab driven by a trusted relative. As we climbed the road over the mountains, I took one last look back at Hong Kong.

The rain had blurred the view. This was appropriate, because I had no vivid emotions about Hong Kong itself. One could lead a playboy's life there — gay and easy, but unrewarding. But who wanted to?

The answer was the large number of foreigners who stayed on there, not the few who left.

It was still raining when we pulled up to the side of the road. We were near the border. On the other side was Ling-Ma-Hang, where Nora's uncle lived.

We stepped down and were ankle deep in mud. The taxi turned and backed around for its lonely return trip to Kowloon. Chan, Nora, and I stood aside to avoid the glare of the headlights. Then, following Chan in the dark, we trudged up one side of a hill and down the other.

"We cross border," Chan whispered. Then he extended his hand and said, "Welcome to China, Gil."

I had expected to feel like a different man once this major transition in my life was accomplished. But, aside from noticing that Chan had stopped calling me Mister, all I felt was wet.

Chan led us down a road and then said good night at a cutoff. Nora would take me to her uncle's house. She and I didn't meet a single soul in our one-mile trot along a winding dirt trail.

Her uncle's house was near the road. It was surrounded by trees. You would have to know it was there before you could find it. We entered a dark room, filled with the comforting aroma of burning charcoal. Nora's uncle arose, lit an oil lamp, threw some more charcoal on the fire, and went back to bed.

In the morning, Nora presented me with a pair of coolie trousers. "This is what you will be wearing from now on, Gil."

I slipped them on and folded the voluminous waistband into a belt. The legs of the baggy trousers ended well above my ankles. Nora and her uncle tried not to laugh at my appearance. They gave way whenever one caught the other's eye.

Visitors came and went all day and the next day. Nora gave me no clues to what was or wasn't happening — except for a tense hour spent under a bed when a Jap patrol passed by.

Late the second afternoon, the pace quickened. Nora made off with my English shoes and gave them to a man headed for Hong Kong: "There must be no evidence that you were here, Gil."

"But I won't travel fifty feet in those Chinese cotton socks you gave me!"

"Gil," Nora said, "you told me once you would walk a thousand miles barefoot over hot nails to get into China."

"I would," I replied, "and I'd complain every step of the way."

At five P.M., Nora's uncle made a fire and prepared the evening meal. While I was plucking husks and other foreign matter from my rice, Chan arrived with two coolies.

Each coolie bore two round baskets dangling from a yoke. One of the men was the limping coolie I'd met in Sam Coldron's office and on my trip to Mr. Lee's yacht. I lost interest in cleaning my rice.

Chan proposed a toast to "our journey."

"*Our* journey?" I repeated. "Who's us?"

Nora and Chan exchanged looks and then admitted that they were coming along to see that Mr. Lee delivered us to the guerrillas.

When we finished our wine, Chan wiped his mouth with the back of his hand. This gesture, I knew, was his way of saying "now let's get down to business."

Soon after supper, he said, we would walk about three miles to Starling Inlet. There a sampan would take us to Mr. Lee's junk, several miles out in the bay. There would be no hurry unless we ran into Japs. If we were not on board by daylight, Mr. Lee would leave without us.

Nora began to rummage through the four baskets the coolies had brought.

"What is this?" I inquired. "A going-away party?"

"Clothes," she replied. "You must have the outfit you will wear in China."

With great glee, Nora and Chan watched me sift through the thin cotton undershorts, one square cotton undershirt, a money belt, and two pairs of cotton socks. The socks had thick cloth sewn on to the instep.

There were also straw sandals; more black trousers; a short black coolie coat with a high collar and small cloth buttons; a straw coolie hat that concealed much of my face; a straw rain cape, and a small mysterious piece of cloth.

"What's this for?" I asked Chan.

"You tie around mouth and neck when cold, Gil. Like scarf."

Nora added: "Any time you feel the least bit cold, Gil, please use it. It will hide your face." Her words made me realize that, while Nora was eager to see me in China, she loved me enough to worry about me. And I would miss her.

The last basket possessed the most exotic contents. There were two or three small red tins of an all-purpose ointment called Tiger Balm — "particularly soothing to kind-hearted tigers," Nora murmured. The basket also contained some tobacco that smelled like old rags — and tasted far worse. With it was the badge of the Chinese coolie class, a bamboo water pipe. It was about fourteen inches long and an inch and a half wide.

When I had donned my new garb, I presented myself for inspection to Chan and Nora. They choked with laughter. Chan assured me, "If not for color and shape of eyes, I swear God you Chinee." When he said this, Nora darkened a little. She warned me to avoid close contact with strangers no matter how well disguised I was.

Nora and her uncle repacked the baskets. They made sure the weights were equal so they would balance easily on shoulders. After supper, as best I could, I thanked Nora's uncle.

In two days as his guest, I had not exchanged a single word with the old man. I suspected that even if I spoke Chinese fluently, we would not have talked much. He was one of those people who don't ask questions and don't listen to whatever people volunteer.

In case the Japanese ever questioned him, his gift of sublime detachment would serve him and us. Because he spoke no English, Nora and I had been free to discuss plans in his presence.

Now, however, as I said my farewells, the old man grew garrulous. Apparently, nobody had bothered to inform him that I was anything but a permanent guest. He had been fully prepared to extend his hospitality to me forever.

He was, in fact, pleading with me not to go. People I have known much better have often said, "Don't go, Gil," or "Come back soon," but I have never heard the invitation extended more warmly than by this old man I hardly knew and never saw again.

Chan and Nora led the way down a steep flight of stone stairs to the trail to Starling Inlet. On the trail, the two coolies traveled a few hundred yards ahead of us. One of them doubled back and halted us whenever danger loomed.

I welcomed such threats because my feet had trouble adjusting to their Chinese sandals. I stubbed my toes five or six times per mile. Even more often, small stones lodged between the sandals and my feet. By the time we reached Starling Inlet shortly after midnight, I had mastered the dancing art of hopping along while flipping out pebbles — without losing step.

The sampan was waiting. As soon as we were underway, I found a place under the canopy and examined my poor feet. The straw sandals had cut into my feet; the space between big toes and second toes were rubbed raw.

Around four A.M., Mr. Lee's junk loomed up in the darkness like a rock. We passed close to her bow. Our oarsmen allowed our sampan to drift back alongside. The big junk and the sampan seemed to come together in a slight swell.

Two lines were passed down to hold us steady.

In five minutes, we and our gear had been loaded aboard. The junk got underway. While Mr. Lee shouted commands, we climbed down to the living quarters beneath the poop deck. Lee's wife and a daughter had prepared tea for us.

Afterwards, we shed our clothes, which had been soaked through during the sampan voyage. The Lees gave us heavy cotton gowns to wear and a small wooden tub with hot water for soaking our feet.

Shortly after dawn, I accompanied Mr. Lee on his next trip to the deck. The cold sea air felt good after four cups of hot tea in the warm, smoky cabin. I could see land not too far off. We were nearing the tip of Mirs Bay. Soon there would be open sea ahead.

To starboard were several huge junks. They were crouched low in the water, like prehistoric sea monsters that had wandered into modern times. As their ancient gray hulls reared out of the sea, I saw they were armed with ancient cannons. These cannons were so old that they had to be loaded through the muzzle.

Glancing around Mr. Lee's junk, I was surprised to see two cannons lashed to the poop deck but concealed by awnings.

"Are you expecting a naval battle with the Japs?" I inquired.

Mr. Lee laughed and said: "No, Mr. Stuart. We have more modern weapons below deck — machine guns and rifles. The cannons give my men a feeling of security. They add to pride, too."

"Don't they worry the Japs?"

"All junks have them. Theoretically, they're for use against pirates. But there are no pirates now, of course," Mr. Lee remarked wistfully. Later, Nora told me that the Lee family's junk had been used — and occasionally was still used — by merchant-pirates to plunder weaker vessels. That was how the Lees had amassed their wealth.

I was proud of the junk's heritage, for I was using it now for high adventure.

There were only a few bunks in the Lees' living quarters, so we took turns sleeping. I was not well rested during our week's trip, partly because my sleeping time too often coincided with the magic hour when Chan and Mr. Lee convened to smoke opium. I would awaken, suffocating from the fumes, to find myself rolling from side to side as the junk bucked choppy seas.

No matter how little I slept, Nora — who was on the same sleeping schedule — slept even less. Whenever I sat up, she would appear by my side with a cup of tea.

Late one night, I arose and wandered up on deck. Mr. Lee was at the helm, where he was receiving word from the lookout in the bow and shouting orders to the helmsman.

I had a feeling that not all was right. Tension seemed to hover in the salt sea air. All hands were on the lookout as if anything or everything might appear there. Ordinarily, Mr. Lee's was a very business-like crew.

Part of the trouble, I knew, was that we were not traveling where we should be. The Japanese occupiers did not authorize sea travel in this area. Thus, we had absolutely no lights on deck. There was no moon.

Still, I could perceive faint lights flickering on the shoreline, about four miles away.

Suddenly, the steady baritone voice of the lookout rose to hysterical soprano. A chorus of shrill screams resounded from all parts of the deck. The wind joined the chant. The surge of the sea pounded like drumbeats.

On the deck, a dark shadow moved from one side to the other. I realized that it was a cluster of panic-stricken coolies, fleeing some invisible monster from the deep.

Mr. Lee stiffened. Then, from out of the darkness a few feet ahead, I heard an echoing chorus of wails.

Another junk was about to cross our path. In the darkness, I saw the junk barely clear our bow.

I exhaled at last. Then I almost choked on my sigh of relief.

There was a new sound of wails and then still another junk crossed our path. We missed it by inches.

Throughout the crisis, Mr. Lee never budged. Nor did he flinch. He stood erect in a heroic pose that was, like most posing, useless.

It took a full minute for the tension to lift. Our coolies found their voices first. They berated the invisible men across the water.

The angry shouts evolved into banter. None of the three junks had lights, so we knew without asking that we were all on the same side.

As we pulled away, the men gathered around Mr. Lee to thank him for saving their lives. He had not moved from the helm. His arm was still outstretched and pointed straight ahead.

By the time his mind realized that danger was past, several coolies were kissing his feet. He began to enjoy the idolatry, although he appeared a little embarrassed.

He should have been. Luckily, the men kissing his feet did not taste clay. But I, who had been standing beside him, knew that Mr. Lee had done absolutely nothing to avoid a collision. He had frozen at the huge tiller. I still liked Mr. Lee, but in my eyes, he had not lost face so much as he had acquired impotence.

The next morning, we anchored in How Lin Bay, the next to last stop before my rendezvous with the guerrillas. I had only fifty miles more to go by sea.

We learned from other junks that the Japs were patrolling the area. Search parties were boarding junks and sampans. Even when nothing suspicious was found, they looted cargoes and kidnapped passengers. If arms were found aboard, the vessels were taken into port, where masters and crews were shot and thrown overboard.

Lee decided to wait a day or two: "Such violent hunts usually subside quickly. While we wait at anchor, we will drink Japanese beer."

"Fine with me, Mr. Lee," I said. "That's the only Japanese thing I can tolerate."

"You are unkind, Mr. Stuart," he said with a shrewd chuckle.

We were anchored in How Lin Bay for three more days. While there, Chan applied the finishing touches to my Chinese coolie disguise. With a pair of hand clippers and then with a home-made Chinese razor about two inches long, he shaved off all my hair.

On our fourth morning in How Lin Bay, we sailed for Tai Shi, a fishing port where our guerrilla contacts would be waiting. Although the distance was only fifty miles, we took a roundabout route — away from the coast — that lasted two days. Finally, at ten o'clock on the second night, we tied up close to a cluster of fishing sampans in Tai Shi harbor.

Around midnight, two small sampans drew alongside. Two men came aboard and were welcomed warmly. They were from the guerrilla forces of Chan's cousin, Major Chan. They thanked me formally but cordially for the dynamite. It had been put to good use already.

Ceremoniously, I told them that more would be forthcoming. I would tell the details to Major Chan in person.

The guerrillas complimented me on my Chinese appearance.

I modestly apologized for my inability to do much about my Western eyes.

One of the men told me that what I was about to see would alter my eyes forever.

Mr. Lee brought out Japanese beer for all. We all drank a toast to "*lan-yen-tsung-kwa-rin*." Only later did I learn that I had toasted myself — "the blue-eyed Chinese."

It was time to leave.

I said goodbye to Chan. He said: "I go with you, Gil. I already quit job at mine. Nora good contact man. She do her work and mine now."

"I was wondering how you got a vacation so easily," I said, "but I'm glad to have you along." I was, in fact, overjoyed. I was starting out my new life as a guerrilla with a friend I could truly trust. Sometimes, it takes years to acquire such a friend.

Nora handed me my Chinese money plus a few belongings, all neatly wrapped in an old cloth. She tinkered with my disguise.

"All right, Nora, this is it. I have you to thank for my being here. You'll never be sorry."

"I am already a little sorry," she said.

"Don't be," I said in vain. "You've made me very happy."

"Then I am happy," she said solemnly. I took her in my arms, kissed her, and held her for the last time. Arm in arm, we walked slowly up on deck.

The others were waiting for us. I thanked Mr. and Mrs. Lee for their kindness. We shook hands all around. Then I followed Chan as he slipped over the side of the junk. We boarded separate sampans.

As both tiny boats glided toward shore, I stood up and waved. I knew Nora couldn't see me. But I knew that she, too, would be waving. I stared after the junk long after darkness had swallowed up everything.

# II

Major Chan's Guerrillas

[ 1939 ]

# 11

## Barefoot to Buddha

OUR sampans followed the shoreline for several miles. We pulled into a beach, where fourteen men were waiting. Chan took command and the men unloaded the provisions and dynamite that had come with us.

"If you'd hustled the men this much at the mine," I told Chan, "our tonnage would have doubled."

"*Their* tonnage," he corrected. "You with them no longer, Gil."

A heavy bundle was thrust into my hands. I was shoved into a line of coolies loading ponies. Having no idea where the horses were, I half ran and half stumbled. Periodically, to keep from getting lost, I bumped into the coolie ahead of me. He and I exchanged Chinese curses; he won. After five hundred feet, I caught a whiff of manure and knew that I had found the horses.

As soon as the pack ponies were loaded, we moved out with them. "Listen, Chan," I said. "I came a long way to be here, so I don't want to get lost now."

Chan tied a line to a pony's saddle: "Hang onto it, Gil, when you march behind. You no can get lost. Pony know way better than we do."

Every little bit helped. I don't think I would have lived through that first strenuous night without the rudiments of survival I had learned in the Australian bush. About all I had to be grateful for was the weather. It was, I remember, the first day of spring, 1939.

My sandals wore out within five miles. They began to drag like lead weights and trip me up, so I kicked them off. I marched on in cotton socks, until they wore through and dangled from my ankles.

The rest of the night, I traveled on bare feet, which grew bruised, then raw, and then numb.

We were still moving at dawn. Our party now numbered twenty men and ten ponies. Our route took no roads or even trails. We marched through wastelands and paddy fields. We were cutting across country and away from the coast. As it grew lighter, we entered a land of mountains and high hills. We never went around them when we could go over them. Every now and then, I caught a glimpse of a house. Our route, however, would take us several miles out of the way just to avoid being seen from it.

We made our first stop at ten A.M. Chan, who had been at the front of the procession, came back to see me. He was all smiles when he saw I had kept the pace. But, when he saw my feet, he swore.

Several other guerrillas clustered around to inspect my feet with mingled shock and admiration.

"Don't worry about them," I said. "They'll be O.K. in a day or two."

"We stop here hour or so," Chan told me. "I sent scout ahead to friend's house two mile away. If safe, we enter village and stay there till dark. Time to tend feet, Gil. Meantime, we unload pony. You ride him."

"Absolutely not, Chan. I want no special treatment. No man and no horse is going to carry my weight."

We argued for most of our hour of rest. I told Chan that I had trained myself for physical punishment. If I couldn't march, how could I be expected to perform more dangerous deeds? It would take a week to toughen me up again for this kind of life, but I had to start now. I clinched my case by telling Chan that it was a matter of face with me.

"Then you finish on feet, Gil," he said with an air of certainty that I wished I felt.

We were resting in a small limbo surrounded by towering mountains. We seemed sealed off from the world.

There was a small stream near where Chan and I sat. Several men were drinking from it while watering the ponies. When I saw this, I remarked; "Damn it, Chan, they'll get dysentery if they don't boil it."

"I know," said Chan, "but impossible explain to them. They no see connection because no get dysentery for hours. All they know is: They thirsty. They drink water. They thirsty no longer. You thirsty, Gil?"

"You bet I am, but I'm not going down there for a drink. This march is bad enough without having the trots, too."

"I have different kind water," Chan said. He unstrapped a parcel from the side of a pony. He produced a half-gallon bottle of Japanese beer. He broke the cap off with his teeth and handed me the bottle. "I steal from Mist' Lee," Chan explained as I took a long swig. I stopped when I had guzzled half the beer. Chan finished it off with several self-satisfied belches.

While we drank, a few of the men pointed at me. I guessed that they were angry because we were drinking beer, but Chan said: "They just discover you foreigner. That how good your disguise."

"Are they going to dislike me or poke fun at me?"

"No. They pleased you with them. You first white man most ever see. They no believe you joining my cousin's army."

"How far before we connect up with your cousin?"

"Not sure. Maybe two, three days. Maybe longer. We find out later. Cousin never stay same place long. Japs too smart."

"Are there many Japs where we are now?"

"Plenty. And many spies. That why we avoid villages. We cannot be sure of own people in houses."

Chan informed me that if we met any Japs now, we would be in real trouble. The coolies with us were not fighting men, but laborers his cousin had hired. The only real guerrillas in our force were the two who had met us at Mr. Lee's junk.

After a while, Chan's scout — one of the two guerrillas — returned from his mission with two villagers. They waved several times. The village was safe, Chan said. He ordered us to move out.

The ponies grunted and swayed a little, for the cool air had chilled their sweaty hides and stiffened their joints. I, too, was stiff as I put my weight on my bare feet. The last two miles into town were the longest ever. Occasionally, I stepped on short grass stubble, which stuck like needles.

We followed the little stream — Dysentery Creek, I called it — to the village, which was not much of a village. It was six buildings. But it was ideal because it was on high ground with only one approach.

Women and children greeted us. There were no young men around. A few had gone off to join the guerrillas; the rest had been taken away by the Japs for forced labor. Nobody knew when and if they would ever be seen again.

Chan put several boys, ages ten or twelve, to work as lookouts. By the way they divided up, I could tell there were professionals.

Several old men were around, but they were too feeble to be of much use. The women ran this village. They unloaded our ponies, watered them, and herded them into a rock formation on a mountain. Nature's corral offered perfect concealment.

The ponies were fed the best beans in town, for horses were hard to replace. Only after the animals were fed did the women prepare a meal for the men. It was our first since leaving the coast around midnight.

One of the guerrillas, Chan, and I adjourned to a house, where we would stay until dark. The others went to other houses. I avoided the villagers and concealed my face with a scarf. Our coolies had been instructed not to mention that a white man was with them. The villagers were reliable, but why should they know of my presence? If a child so much as let a word slip to the Japs about a white devil, a manhunt would be on. As punishment for its hospitality to me, the village might be wiped out.

I asked Chan for hot water. After I had soaked my feet for an hour, Chan doctored them. First, he applied tobacco leaf to my cuts and bruises.

"Are you trying to poison me?" I asked indignantly.

"I cure you."

"It rather looks as if I'm curing the tobacco," I said. But I surrendered to his ministrations.

After the tobacco treatment, Chan bandaged me and said: "I have surprise for you, Gil."

One of the village women had made me a pair of straw sandals that would fit over my bandages. The soles were lined with quarter-inch felt. For added protection, more felt was beneath each toe. I have never worn more welcome footgear. My enthusiasm was such that Chan placed an order for four more pairs to be made for me while we were there.

Then Chan curled up on the hut's dirt floor. I stretched out on

[ 122 ]

an old bed. It was actually a series of boards covered with a thin layer of filthy straw. The bed had been used so often that half of it had been pulverized into dust.

As soon as I lay down, an army of bedbugs attacked. But nothing could bother me now. I slept past six P.M. until Chan awakened me.

"How you now, Gil?"

"Aside from the stiffness in my legs and the bedbug bites around my waist and neck, I feel like a new man." I stepped into my new sandals and added: "It's like walking on air."

My morale was boosted to normal when Chan said I had time to shave. (Even in hiding, I was rarely to go more than a day without shaving. It was essential to my disguise, for Chinese do not have heavy beards.) Dinner was brought in by a smiling woman, who served us rice, pork, herbs, and yellow wine.

I was so hungry that I ate too fast, spilled my food, stuffed too much into my mouth at once, and spat inedible chunks onto my plate or the floor.

Chan watched me approvingly: "You eat just like Chinee."

"Then I'll always eat this way. It'll be part of my disguise."

We left the village around eight P.M. and traveled along a bullock trail for a few miles. Then we cut across country once again. This time, however, I walked with Chan and the two guerrillas at the head of the pony train. It was easier to set the pace than to keep up with it. And Chan could give me directions in his terse English.

Now that we were away from the coast and the heaviest concentration of Japs, we were allowed to stop once an hour for a brief rest. At one rest stop, Chan dispatched a guerrilla and a coolie to a nearby village. There, they would receive our first instructions from the main force of Chan's cousin, Major Chan.

They returned with ten guerrillas. The two guerrillas who had met me were to take ten coolies and the pony train to a guerrilla supply base hundreds of miles north.

The rest of us were to proceed — with caution, but without delay — to join Major Chan some thirty miles away. The ten new guerrillas had been sent out as a fighting escort.

We spent an hour redistributing loads before we split up. Chan reorganized our party, which now numbered eighteen. He divided us into three groups. The first group would lead the way, determine our route, and make the decisions. Chan invited me to march up there with him. The second group consisted of four coolies carrying enough provisions for four days. The third group served as sentries and scouts.

"Why four days' provisions for a thirty-mile hike?" I asked.

"It thirty miles, yes," Chan replied. "But many Japs around. We keep clear all villages, all people. Take roundabout way. If lucky, we see my cousin three, four days soon."

It took three days and nearly a hundred miles. On the second afternoon, we were threading our way high in the mountains when Chan pointed out a Japanese column on the march. The Japs were several miles away and far below. A day's journey, in fact, lay between them and us.

Even so, we all talked in whispers. Nobody took an eye off the Jap column until it had vanished from sight — in the opposite direction.

Distance must have lent enchantment. Like a small boy at a parade, I thrilled to the sight of soldiers in large numbers — even though these were the hated Japanese.

Every now and then, Chan pointed out Japanese garrisons in the distance. They all looked so tiny I felt as if I could destroy them single-handed! My exuberance carried me over the strenuous trail to the temporary headquarters of Major Chan's guerrillas.

I had expected a guerrilla outpost to be a makeshift fortress teeming with tension and activity . . . where every man was on the alert . . . where fighters walked around with guns in hand . . . where others crouched behind embankments . . . poised to fire.

Instead, we arrived at a lush valley that was the most serene place I had seen in Kwangtung Province. I could view sprawling, fertile farms and bustling little communities for miles around. Nobody carried anything more lethal than a bamboo yoke or a hoe.

In single file, we plodded along a narrow path skirting along rice paddy fields. For virtually the first time all trip, we passed people. Nobody seemed surprised to see us.

The path led past small groups of houses. We halted at one cluster of buildings that appeared the same as others. Small trees shaded the cluster and added to its peaceful veneer. Chan instructed our guerrillas to report to one building, the coolies to another.

[ 124 ]

Chan and I stood alone outside the only building that had a court-yard.

"Take good look at this place, Gil. This where my cousin live when we in south China. Our permanent home many miles north. But this be your home for while."

"Then will we go north?"

"No. Not till we drive Jap out of south China."

A heavy wooden door in the wall led into a courtyard. This door was partly concealed by a small mud-brick wall. From my reading on China, I knew that this wall was a "screen" built by religious Chi-nese to keep away evil spirits.

In the courtyard, I remarked to Chan: "This place reminds me of a Buddhist temple."

"That what it is."

"Have we come here to pray?"

"No. It headquarters."

Major Chan's guerrillas, I learned, assembled in peaceful oases like this valley whenever the forces were being reorganized. It gave them a chance to relax after living for weeks and months in combat condi-tions. But, while they relaxed, they were not idle. They found work with farmers in exchange for food and lodging. They were so well dispersed that the Japanese could never guess several dozen guerrillas were there. Yet they could reassemble on fifteen minutes' notice.

At one end of the courtyard, a man was lecturing some twenty men on disassembling and reassembling new rifles. The men sat on stone slabs with the weapon parts before them like jigsaw puzzles. When the instructor saw us, he told a younger man to take over. Then he hurried over and threw his arms around Chan.

I needed no introduction, even though the man complimented me on my disguise. He looked exactly the way Chan would look in ten years — if any man there could be sure of living ten more years. He was Chan's cousin, Major Chan.

He escorted us up a flight of steps to his quarters. We were served tea — my first hot drink in almost four days — and dinner. Several times during the meal, I dozed off.

Shortly before seven P.M., Chan showed me to a room that had been assigned to the two of us. It had two beds. I didn't bother to un-dress. I flopped into bed and fell into a deep sleep.

[ 125 ]

I awoke at 3 A.M. and, for the life of me, couldn't remember where I was. Then I heard a hearty wheezing sound. There was only one man in the world who snored that way — Chan. Reassured, I noticed that someone had covered me with a blanket. I felt warm and relaxed and I dozed off.

An hour later, I awoke with a start. Bells were ringing. A drum was pounding. A gong was clanging. Voices were mumbling and chanting. It sounded like total war.

A haze of smoke drifted in on a beam of light. A smell of incense seeped through the floor. I jumped out of bed and began to look around for a bomb shelter.

Chan awoke, too. He guffawed at my consternation. "It is Buddhist priests at morning prayer."

"Well, they've frightened me out of a year's growth."

"We never need bugler to get up in morning. You and me have choice room. We right above place of worship."

"Amen!" I said. "Let's get the hell out of here, Chan."

"Yes. This go on for long while. We take walk down village. Find place to eat."

When we stepped into the courtyard, I glanced through the open door into the temple. There, Buddha sat grinning. The priests were chanting. Occasionally, they beat on instruments hollowed out of wood and coated with red and black lacquer.

"Chan, aren't you going to pray to Buddha and thank him for our safe journey?" I asked jokingly.

"I do later, Gil."

"Why not now?"

"You want eat now."

"You're the one who suggested eating. If you want to pray, I'll pray with you — if they let me."

"You know how pray to Buddha?"

"I'm not much at praying to anyone. But you go ahead. I'll watch and do whatever you do."

We flung our hats on the ground and entered the temple. Just inside the door, a priest handed us each four joss sticks. A joss stick is a rod of perfumed paste that is burned as incense. (The word *joss* is Pidgin for *deos*, the Portuguese word for God.)

Making sure to keep our right side to Buddha, we approached him. At Buddha's foot were several candles burning yellow. Below them, a thick blue and gray haze emanated from hundreds of joss sticks. They were smoldering in clay and pewter containers.

Watching Chan closely, I did whatever he did. With my two hands clasped together, I raised joss sticks to my forehead and bowed low several times to Buddha. Then I thrust my joss sticks into the flame of a candle. The joss sticks began to smolder.

Holding the joss sticks high with both my hands still clasped, I knelt before Buddha and bowed low — my head almost touching the floor — several times.

Chan and I stood up. We placed our joss sticks with the others in the containers. There was plenty of sand in the containers, I observed with relief. I would not want my new home to catch fire.

We bowed to Buddha a few times on our knees. Then we sat in meditation. Chan prayed to Buddha while I prayed to my God. Back on our knees, we swayed up and down for so long that I wondered if Chan was praying for all of China. The priests near us chanted words that were spoken first by their high priest. Bells and gongs rang sporadically.

Finally, Chan rose to his feet. We headed for the door, but we were not done yet.

The priest at the door handed each of us a long wooden cylinder. It looked like a piece of bamboo a foot long and six inches in diameter. Its inside had been hollowed out. From within, three dozen long thick sticks protruded. Different numbers had been carved into the sides of each stick.

These were prayer sticks. I watched Chan face Buddha and hold the wooden cylinder with both hands. Suddenly, Chan shook it deftly. Just one stick popped out and fell to the floor. Chan picked it up and handed it to the priest. Checking the number on the stick, the priest looked it up in his prayer book. He read aloud a verse and fortune, which Chan summed up for me as: "Do not litter a dust heap."

That struck me as a dim view of life. Still, it wasn't *my* religion. Otherwise, I was impressed by Buddhism as a religion that had everything — even Bingo and fortune telling. I decided to try my luck.

It took several attempts, but I didn't leave until I was able to shake out just one stick at a time. When I succeeded, the priest read my fortune as: "Go ever forward and you will write in the pages of history."

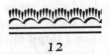

## 12

# The Bandit Guerrillas

HISTORY was in the making then, but the participants had no sense of making history. They merely thought of the day-to-day situation and relied upon various unreliable sources for the "facts." If there existed any "Big Picture," as today's military analysts would say, it was scarcely visible then. Nevertheless, seen from today's perspective, here is how the currents of history were running when I joined Major Chan's guerrillas.

In 1939, the Japanese controlled the key seaports of Canton and Swatow plus most of the China coast, except for Britain's Hong Kong and Portugal's Macao. To reinforce their coastal grip, the Japanese were establishing inland garrisons.

There were hardly any roads. The Japanese therefore had to transport men and equipment by mule and pony trains. They used existing bullock trails and foot paths leading from village to village. The Japs were reluctant to build roads that their enemies might either use against them or destroy. This particular brand of discretion helped to shape Japan's ultimate downfall in Asia.

"In these circumstances, our guerrilla fighting must be strictly ambush," Chan's cousin, Major Chan, explained to me.* "A network of informers works for us — farmers who constantly observe Japanese movements in detail. Not only what they do, but their patterns and habits. When we put together all our information, we can sometimes plot Japanese strategy before the Japs do. You might say we know them better than they do."

---

* To spare readers (and writers) a multitude of middlemen from here onward, readers may assume that when a non-English-speaking person spouts flawless English, some interpreter or other was present.

"Well," I said, "I've often heard that the most difficult command ever uttered was 'Know thyself.' "

Major Chan, who was no philosopher, continued briefing me: "Right now, the Japanese are engaged mainly in the transport of their plunder from Chinese farmers. This is mostly rice stolen to feed the Imperial Japanese Army. This particular area — in the triangle formed by Hong Kong, Canton, and Swatow — is the finest farm country in all of China. It yields three rice crops a year. There is much Japanese movement, but the terrain is mountainous and they do not know it well. They must frequently depend upon directions given by their Chinese forced labor or our own sympathizers. This situation can be a guerrilla's dream . . ."

"Or a Japanese nightmare," I remarked.

Major Chan's guerrillas were one division of a much larger force operating along the China coast. He was directly responsible to a higher command. But he had complete charge of guerrilla actions in several hundred square miles of territory.

He was formerly a Regular Army officer. He had risen to the rank of Major in the Chinese Army, only to be undone by the Army politics that had left China so vulnerable to Japanese attack. Fed up with an intolerable system, he had deserted.

For centuries, the Chinese people — rich and poor — had scorned soldiering as the lowest rung of civilization. As a result, soldiering became little more than legalized banditry and parasitism. Over the years, the Army's lower echelons evolved into the dregs of China.

Every culture, however, had its born fighters. In China, they joined the Army to practice their art. Sadly disillusioned, they had nowhere to turn — until Major Chan and a few other good officers defected. These men followed their trusted leaders out of the Army.

Initially, officers and men formed little groups that turned to organized banditry. To them, their new life was less heinous than the Army's disorganized plunder, corruption, and idleness.

But, in the late 1920's, a Communist librarian named Mao Tsetung organized a revolutionary army. He started with a few hundred followers. Between 1928 and 1930, Mao's ranks were swelled by various fugitive bands like Major Chan's. They joined not for ideological reasons, but because Mao represented a new high in the old art of *guerrilla warfare*.

Chiang Kai-shek took Mao even more seriously than he took the Japanese. Red Army followers were persecuted and massacred. In 1934, Mao undertook one of history's most celebrated retreats, the Long March. His armies marched six thousand miles from Kiangsi in south China to Yenan in Shensi Province to the north.

Major Chan's unit and several others, however, were cut off from the main body of Mao's forces. They remained in the south of China, where they were oppressed first by the Chinese Army and then by the Japanese invaders.

The Chinese Army proved frail when the Japs came. The most effective resistance issued from stray bands like Major Chan's as well as Mao's main army further north. In September, 1937, Mao issued a United Front Manifesto proclaiming his loyalty to China. His armies were reorganized as the Eighth Route Army and an uneasy truce was arranged with the Chinese Central Government. Among many others, Major Chan's bandits were upgraded to guerrillas. Major Chan's military rank was restored. The guerrillas agreed to rob Japs only. They would turn over their surplus loot to the Chinese Army. In return, the Chinese Army ceased stalking them. The Government even gave the guerrillas some financial support.

Thus, in 1939, I had no qualms about entering China under vaguely left-wing auspices. For my selfish purposes, 1939 was a perfect time: It was the beginning of a new era of guerrilla warfare in China. I could not have learned the guerrilla's craft more thoroughly at any other time. These men practiced guerrilla warfare as taught by its master, Mao Tse-tung.

Eventually the Japs drained China of the foods and rice that were the lifeblood of the guerrillas. The Chinese Army retreated deeper into China until its support was worthless.

These setbacks hit not only the guerrillas' morale, but also that of civilians upon whom they depended for support and information. None of these symptoms, however, were as fatal as the lack of experienced replacements.

Major Chan's men, with whom I cast my lot, were guerrillas born to the game. They had lived the nomadic life for so long — as soldiers, deserters, bandits, and revolutionaries — that they possessed the acute cunning of beasts of prey. They knew no better way to survive

[ 130 ]

than to plunder and kill. They had to attack frequently. Staying alive became a twenty-four-hour-a-day obsession. The good earth of China was the campus on which they learned lessons that could not be taught or mastered anywhere else.

At the time I joined them, these men had rare prestige. For the first and last time, their way of life was applauded by the people of China. They were no longer outcasts, but heroes assuming their country's burdens. And they responded by hating the Japanese as they had never been able to hate their own people in their bandit days.

Occasionally, when exposed to the brutal illogic and injustice of the Japanese invasion, they grew heartsick. Sometimes, they even despaired. Mostly, however, they lived their renegade lives with an enviable purity of purpose; they had, after all, scarcely changed their pattern. But the rest of the world suddenly seemed to have sensed the wisdom of their way.

For better or worse, guerrillas were limited in number — and in life expectancy. In battle, mistakes multiply and men die. With each man dies knowledge and experience.

These casualties were supplanted, and although the replacements had the spirit and the will to fight, they lacked the animal instincts of their predecessors. Being civilized cuts a guerrilla's effectiveness in half. It does the same to his chances of survival.

True guerrillas cannot be bred. They are a product of their native land. They must simply dwell uneasily in civilian or military life until fate, injustice, mistaken identity, or their own persistence thrusts them outside the system.

Major Chan suffered from a slight case of mistaken identity in my case. He was convinced that I was an experienced fighter who could teach him some new tricks.

"I am no expert," I told him. "I hope only to be given a chance to learn from you."

He waved this away as a polite protestation of modesty: "I have heard from my cousin that you wiped out an entire Japanese patrol at Shataukok."

"It was only one man."

Major Chan smiled knowingly. I realized that Chan and Nora had performed a masterful selling job in peddling my credentials to him. I therefore tried another tack: "It is important to me that I shed my past. I want no privileges. I want to lose myself among your men as best I can. I want to start exactly where I would have started in my own country's army: at the bottom with a rifle."

He left it at that for the rest of my stay at the Buddhist temple.

I devoted myself to becoming more Chinese than ever. I walked around barefoot to harden my soles and coat them brown with dirt. I seldom washed. After shaving, however, I had the carnation-pink skin that is the clearest evidence of a "white" man. I would smear my face with dirt and soot.

The day sixty of us moved out to the hills came with no advance warning, which spoke well for our security system. That morning, we simply awakened and were told we would leave immediately.

We left the temple in total darkness and followed a path to one of the houses nearby. Three or four men stood outside. They checked us off and let us in.

In a storeroom, boxes of rice and ammunition were stacked nearly to the ceiling. We were each issued a week's rice ration packed in a bandolier (a cartridge belt) of light blue cloth. The bandolier resembled an old-fashioned inner tube. It was worn over the shoulders and around the neck.

Each man was issued four automatic pistol clips and another bandolier. This one was made of gray canvas and loaded with 7.63-millimeter ammunition. It was slung over both shoulders crossed on the chest, and buckled around the waist.

I was also issued a tin rice bowl, a pair of chopsticks, straw sandals, a paper-thin cotton blanket, a 7.63-millimeter German Mauser automatic, and a wooden holster which could be attached as a stock in case I wished to fire the Mauser from my shoulder.

We set out in groups of two or three to avert suspicion. Chan and I were among the last to leave. Late in the afternoon, we joined the other guerrillas, who had reassembled in the mountains.

Some of the men were sleeping. Others were heating water and cooking rice over small fires. They greeted me like an old friend, although none of them had spoken to me at the temple. There was warmth and informality in the field.

I was met less ardently by my field commander, Captain Tung. A

[ 132 ]

small, beady-eyed man, he lectured me that I could expect no special privileges. I would have to carry my own weight. It did no good to assure him that this was exactly what I wanted. He would merely repeat his lecture on the assumption that I had missed his point.

I relished his hostility and respected his aloofness, for I knew that Tung was an able man. If a day had passed without an insult from Captain Tung, I would have felt snubbed. But it never happened.

We set out for higher hills in the morning. In the next four days, we marched on, frequently changing directions and patterns. Sometimes we went hours without resting; at other times, we would take three breaks in one hour.

One morning, we assembled en masse and marched together all day. The next morning, we were divided into little splinter groups. We scattered in every direction and reassembled miraculously at nightfall.

I first thought this was chaotic disorganization. Soon, I realized that it was masterful organization.

If the Japanese ever spotted sixty men heading in a certain direction, it would take a while to send out search parties. By then, we would no longer be a group of sixty men. And we would no longer be headed in the same direction.

The Japanese were notoriously single-minded. Looking for sixty men, they seldom suspected a half dozen or a dozen coolies plodding along with bundles and baskets on their shoulders.

"Many time," Chan told me, "Jap not only catch up with us. They also pass us."

At mid-afternoon on the fourth day, we all assembled high in the mountains. No trails or tracks led to our field base here. It was well shielded. Along the side of the mountain, lookouts stood watch and scanned the terrain with field glasses.

Before we could bed down for the night, Captain Tung gave an hour's lecture. Looking pointedly at me, he repeated his admonition of no special treatment. Then Tung outlined his philosophy of life:

He was a tough guy, he said. He was all business. We would find that out if we didn't know it already. He was a disciplinarian. To disobey his orders was to sign your own death warrant. There was no second chance. You were shot where you stood.

He went on to reprimand us. We had lacked discipline during our trek. We had consumed too much rice. Some of us had eaten a week's ration in four days. Those who had would go hungry for three more days.

We had been instructed to conceal all weapons during the march. Tung read a list of men who had neglected to do this. Most of our names were on it. He also cited times and places.

Our daily ration, he announced, would be cut from three bowls of rice to two.

The men grumbled. Tung reminded all of us that one man's carelessness could doom the whole group. We were getting off lightly. Any man who made the same mistake again was scarcely worth the one bullet Tung would expend on him.

Tung hated to waste bullets. Several men had brought along dogs. Ostensibly, they were companions. Eventually, they would be food. Eating them would be tolerated, Tung said. But no ammunition was to be used in killing dogs. They could be dispatched with sticks or knives.

The dogs had been attending the lecture. When Tung raised this delicate issue, the dogs began to shift uneasily. One of them even performed its tricks.

Its owner patted it reassuringly. But even if the owner decided against killing it, the pet was doomed. Other hungry men would come for it in the night.

Two afternoons later, just before supper, I was sent on my first scouting mission. I was to accompany Chan and two others. "Take automatic with you," Chan instructed.

"Good," I said. "Over supper, explain exactly what we're to do."

"I tell you on way, Gil. We go right now. Without eat."

"But all we've had was a bowl of rice. And that was at five this morning."

"We have little time. We travel fast while still light. It safe for while. Maybe boys have food for us when we get back. Maybe not."

"All right, but if the Japs catch us because they hear my stomach rumbling, don't say I didn't warn you." I was strapping on my ammunition belt as I grumbled.

Our mission was to find out as much as we could from people living along our route. Were there any recent Jap troop movements? Had the Japs penetrated this far off the main travel route to the south? Where was their nearest garrison? If we ran short, what were the chances of buying rice from the villagers?

We also had to make some judgments of our own: Could we trust the headmen of each village? Were they loyal? Were they honest? Above all, were they tight-lipped? How reliable was their information?

If the answers satisfied us, we should tell the headmen what we wanted to know and how to get word to us.

Ours was also a training mission — not only for us, but for the men back at camp. A party would be sent out an hour after we left. They were to try to spot us and report our movements. Our job was to stay out of their sight. Whoever lost the game of hide-and-seek would be disciplined by Captain Tung.

"That least worry," Chan told me. "Other patrol not bright. They go first two, three villages and waste time there."

"But won't they find out which way we went?"

"No. We bypass first couple villages. I know them well. We investigate on way back if need to."

The start of our trip was almost straight downhill. We put miles between us and the camp as well as the men on our trail. On the way down into the farm country, Chan pointed out a spot where we would split up and, after checking on numerous villages, meet again. I was to travel with Chan.

As we said goodbye to the other two guerrillas, we looked back into the setting sun. There were no signs of life behind us.

"Good," said Chan, "we lose 'em already."

Wisps of blue smoke identified each village as Chan and I walked two hundred feet apart. In town, Chan would visit briefly, but I would say nothing. When darkness came, I needed no disguise if I stood in the shadows.

Each trail of smoke reminded me of cooking and my own hunger. In several villages, I could tell we were being invited to stay for supper. Chan, however, begged off. We had miles to go.

In the last village on our list, Chan said something to a headman. As we left, a woman handed Chan a package. When we rejoined the other two guerrillas, we had a picnic: hard-boiled eggs; cold rice wrapped in paper: and peanut candy, about an inch thick, made with soft dark brown sugar.

While we ate, we compared notes. All the headmen had been cordial. They had promised to help us at any time. The Japanese had not bothered the people in this area, but there were plenty of Japs to the south.

Suddenly, I heard a faint noise from the bushes. I pulled my gun and motioned the others to silence.

Chan laughed and told me to put the weapon away. A little boy appeared in the clearing as Chan explained: "Last headman give me names who live three miles from here. They know much more about Jap movement. I suggest we go there tonight. He send son along with us as guide. Boy know all shortcuts."

The boy led us around rice paddies to our destination. Like most shortcuts, this one seemed much longer than the three miles it bypassed. In the village, which was bigger than any we'd seen that night, we were expected. Our guide's brother had carried the word.

A road, about eight feet wide, wound between buildings until it dead-ended at a mud brick wall. A thick wooden door in the wall swung open to admit us. We stepped on to a rock path leading to a house with a door shaped like a half-moon. This door, too, opened as if guided by an electric eye. We walked into the first living room I'd seen in weeks.

A Chinese altar table ran the length of the rear wall. The candles burning on it illuminated the room. Pewter, silver, and brass ornaments on the table flanked the centerpiece — a small Buddha at whose feet were rice, fruit, boiled eggs, and moon cakes. Scrolls and outdated Chinese paper money hung from the walls. The floor was tile. The Chinese blackwood furniture struck my untutored eye as beautiful.

We were led up a flight of stairs and I caught a whiff of opium from above.

"We'll never be able to tear *you* away from here, Chan," I remarked.

"I no smoke on duty," he replied, with a grin.

We were ushered into a room ten times as beautiful as the one below. Its walls were carved blackwood panels. The ceiling, supported by thin black lacquer posts, was covered with paintings, scrolls, and lavish designs.

An enormous opium bed dominated the room. It, too, was carved blackwood. Slabs of marble were inlaid in the headboard. The bed could have slept six, but only three men were there to welcome us.

One was the village headman and this was his home. The other two were a merchant and a landlord. Our host sent for tea and thick hot face towels, with which my companions wiped faces and hands. I declined my towel.

"But you dirtiest of all, Gil," Chan protested.

"That's the way I want it. I'm camouflaging myself with dirt."

Our host was hovering anxiously. Was anything unsatisfactory? When Chan explained my problem, there was laughter all around.

"You among friends, Gil," Chan pleaded. "They say why not take chance being clean?"

"I don't need much persuasion," I said. I buried my face in the hot towel, which came away black.

We talked for half an hour and learned more than we had all night. Two small Japanese garrisons, the only ones for more than twenty miles, could be viewed from the top of the headman's house. These Japs were more policemen than soldiers. Jap mule and horse pack trains occasionally passed through the valley. They stayed overnight at one garrison or the other.

The two men fed us statistics, arms information, routes, and other data. Then our host fed us supper.

I had no qualms about eating a second supper only two hours after my first. In guerrilla warfare, it's either feast or famine. While we ate, we learned one more fact. There was still telephone service in the area. Why, our host himself had one. Did we wish to use it?

Chan said yes. He would leave one of the men in the house for a few days. The man would phone other villages and find out what he could.

Our host assented. He would place the calls himself just in case the Japs listened in.

We apologized to the guerrilla we were leaving behind. He had, of course, no regrets about lingering in the lap of luxury.

Several hours before dawn, we approached our guerrilla camp high in the mountains.

[ 137 ]

"I think I can skip breakfast this morning," I said, still tasting those two meals.

"We lucky if we get back in time for breakfast," Chan said, waving us to a halt. "We rest here till daybreak."

"Why?" I asked. "Nobody's *that* tired."

"No. But I no want to catch bullet from own men in dark."

This sounded unduly cautious. But, when we reached camp in the dawn's early light, I saw the wisdom of Chan.

The patrol assigned to follow us had lost us and lost face. When they reported back, Captain Tung had slapped them on guard duty. They were still standing guard when we returned. Several of them looked surly enough to shoot us "by mistake."

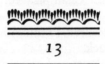

## 13

# Ambush

EARLY the next morning, our encampment was joined by Major Chan, three mounted men, and a dozen pack ponies.

"Well, Gil," Chan said as he saw them approaching in the distance, "all our good information go to waste."

"What do you mean?"

"Those ponies toughest we got. That mean we go deep into mountains, not into valley where villages are."

"At least we ate well," I said. I wasn't disappointed if it meant we would soon see action.

Two days later, we broke camp and moved northwest over rugged terrain. It took four days of strenuous marching before we pitched camp deep in the mountains.

All group leaders were called to a meeting with Major Chan. I was dumfounded to find myself included in the summons. This meant that, despite my protestations and Captain Tung's lectures, I had been promoted to the approximate rank of second lieutenant. Chan was an unofficial first lieutenant in his cousin's band.

"We are going to attack the Japanese within a few days," Major Chan told us. "We will come back to this camp after the ambush. Tomorrow, we move out with bare necessities — just rice and ammunition. A Japanese pack train is about three days away from us. The Japanese will be coming from the east."

Shortly after midnight, two small patrols departed to check security along our route. The rest of us saw them leave, for even the most experienced of us could not sleep.

In my case, I experienced the jitters of any man approaching his first battle. I reminded myself that this was why I had come to China.

The others were excited about the prospect of loot. The Japanese traveled with excellent rations and provisions. The guerrillas talked of making off with boots from dead officers and meat from dead horses. As they talked, they reminisced on previous successes. No man allowed himself to hint that this might be his last battle.

In the morning, we moved out cautiously. There were frequent rest periods. Toward noon, Major Chan halted us. We were less than three miles from the trail used by Jap pack trains. The terrain was ruggedly ideal for concealment.

We were at least a day and a half early. But Major Chan had feared that the Japs might skip their overnight stop.

As we waited, I was astonished by the detailed information flowing in. The Jap column consisted of forty-five men — one first lieutenant, two second lieutenants, two noncommissioned officers and eight men, all on ponies; the rest foot soldiers in three groups.

The first group contained fourteen men equipped with rifles and light machine guns. They marched six to ten feet apart in single file.

About five hundred feet behind them came the main body of the pack train — fifty pack horses, several Mongolian ponies, and a couple of mules. A few ponies were led by foot soldiers; the rest followed in single file. The soldiers leading the ponies were equipped with rifles. Two pack ponies bore heavy water-cooled machine guns. The mounted men flanked the pack train; the first lieutenant appeared particularly active. Sometimes, he led the pack; at other times, he dropped back to check the rest of his column.

[ 139 ]

The rear guard consisted of twelve men armed with rifles, light machine guns, and grenades.

We also had reports on the Japs' behavior patterns. If the trail was rough and steep, the whole column bunched up. If the trail led downhill, the men spread out. The advance guard sometimes slowed down, but it never stopped. The other two groups frequently had to run to close the gaps.

Our own scouts followed the Japs unobtrusively when the enemy was a day away from us. We received further reports on rest habits and security precautions. These Japs might march late into the evening, but they seldom marched all night, we learned.

Much as I detested the Japs, I felt a trifle sorry for them when we received statistics on how often their men urinated per day. Invaders seldom have any privacy in a hostile country, which may be why *all* armies of occupation behave badly.

Our intelligence also marveled at the care the Japs were giving their ponies. In the Japanese Army, horses were treated far better than foot soldiers. The horses were, after all, harder to come by.

When Major Chan decided we had enough information, he studied the terrain for an ambush spot. The site he chose was deep between two mountains. One mountain sloped down for almost three hundred feet to form a 75-degree angle with the trail itself.

The trail was steep at this point. It bent first left and then right. Because of bushes, trees, and massive overhanging rocks, it afforded no more than two hundred feet of visibility. But our lookouts would be able to see the Japs coming for miles.

The Japs were due in mid-afternoon. Undoubtedly, they would be weary from a steep climb preceding their blind date with destiny. But they would not stop to rest, for there was no water in the area. They would continue toward the nearest village, three miles away.

The three parts of the Jap column would be out of each other's sight when we attacked. We could attack the three groups simultaneously. There would be no place for them to hide. Every secluded spot would be staked out with our guerrillas.

All that morning, Major Chan and Captain Tung had us rehearse the ambush. Each man was given a specific location and assignment. Major Chan, Captain Tung, and a Lieutenant Kui impersonated the three parts of the Jap column.

Several of our guerrillas joked about ambushing Captain Tung for real. But Tung was not the kind of officer who is shot by his own men. When combat was near, they depended on him rather than upon the more amiable types.

At lunchtime, Major Chan withdrew all of us. We were fed several miles away. Everyone was excited and alert. A man would rush off in the middle of his meal to inspect his weapon for the thirtieth time that day.

Unfortunately, we had little oil. Mausers are very intricate. When not given proper lubrication, they can grow sluggish or even jam during rapid fire.

I suggested that, as a substitute for oil, we smear lard on the firing bolts. This worked, but we ran out of lard before half the men could apply it.

Suddenly, I remembered Tiger Balm, the all-purpose ointment I had been given at the hut of Nora's uncle in Ling-Ma-Hang. It resembled vaseline. I distributed my tin of it and it, too, worked.

After that, there was no convincing Major Chan or my comrades that I was anything but a seasoned veteran of guerrilla warfare. Even Captain Tung, who considered me a dilettante, remarked grudgingly that I was learning fast.

I was issued two grenades. Ordinarily, no weapon makes me more uneasy than a grenade, for I once stood helplessly as an inept British soldier froze with grenade in hand. He was blown to bits.

This time, however, I found my grenades reassuring. I would keep one of them in case capture were imminent. Then I would use it to blow up my captor and myself.

Major Chan was even more reassuring, for he was taking precautions that I never would have imagined. In the next few hours, the major didn't want anyone wandering out from the village — three miles away — where the Japs were headed for the night. He planted an armed guerrilla behind a tree a mile outside the village. Discreetly but firmly, he was to detain any person venturing eastward.

The major always informed his men of his strategy. Each revelation triggered a buzz of enthusiasm. That afternoon, we were one big happy-go-lucky family. Nobody would have taken us for a band of tough, seasoned guerrillas who knew more about the art of killing than had ever been written.

Not long after two P.M., we were ordered — squad by squad — into battle position. Under Major Chan's watchful eyes, each unit slipped over the mountain and into an assigned spot. Once in position, there was to be no verbal communication. There would be one signal from the lookout when the Jap advance guard was about an hour away. There would be another when it was almost upon us. From then on, we each knew exactly what we were supposed to do.

My squad, commanded by Chan, was the last to move out. Half-crawling and half-running down the side of the hill, I felt dizzy until I realized that I was holding my breath. I exhaled and then inhaled deeply. Having mastered breathing again, I concentrated on my bowels and bladder.

Our squad was posted forty feet from the trail — at the extreme western end of the ambush. Our view to the east — the direction from which the Japs would come — covered 250 feet. The Japs would appear around a sharp bend.

We were concealed behind jagged rocks, some as high as ten feet. Our squad's target was the advance party. When we opened fire, the other two squads would attack the middle and rear guards. Initially, each man was to kill one particular Jap. Mine was the third Jap in the advance party.

For the best firing power, I had to crouch. This pose, however, started my knees and leg muscles twitching so badly that I could scarcely aim. Or perhaps my discomfort was due to nervousness.

As we waited, I reviewed three possible ways to shoot my Jap.

If the Japs were marching in close formation, we were to open fire as soon as the fourteenth man appeared around the bend. This meant that I would open fire on the third Jap when he was approximately a hundred feet to my left.

If they were marching in normal order, my Jap would be directly in front of me and forty feet away when we opened fire. He would be a perfect target.

If they were widely spaced, we would have to hold our fire as long as we could to enable the rear guard to enter the target area. Then I would swing to the right, keep within range of my Jap, and shoot him in the back when the time came. This was the riskiest gamble of all.

Chan was perched slightly above us. With field glasses, he watched his cousin, who was watching the lookout. Shortly after four P.M., Chan whistled and clasped his hand three times. The Japs had been spotted an hour away. They were running late, but it would still be light at five P.M. And they would concentrate on reaching the village before dark.

For the next hour, I shook all over. When Chan signaled that the Japs were entering the ambush area, my heart pounded almost audibly. I barely saw his gesture that the Japs were in normal marching order, which augured well for us.

There would be no more instructions. I crushed myself flat against a rock. I felt like a cornered animal. For a moment, I wanted to rush around frantically and blindly. Then nature took my mind off everything but my bladder. I wanted urgently to wet.

Space was limited, but there was an old Chinese solution to this crisis. I had seen busy coolies do it on the run. Rolling up one trouser leg, I started emptying myself.

When I was done, my shaking had ceased and my fear had vanished. Nature had steadied me as no drink or pill ever could.

I placed my two grenades on a rock ledge. Then I focused on the bend and waited for the Japs to appear.

Two of them came into view. They carried their rifles slung casually across their backs. They should have been one behind the other, but they were practically abreast. They were conversing animatedly like two strolling pedestrians. Impatiently, I itched for the third Jap — my target — to show himself.

He stumbled around the bend seconds later. He was a big man bent by the weight of a machine gun across his shoulders. One hand clutched the grip. The other was twisted around the barrel. Behind him came a smaller man carrying a tripod and ammunition.

I told myself that I had better get my man on the first shot. If he and the next man survived long enough to pool their resources, they could demolish Major Chan's plans.

I fixed my man in my sights and aimed for his guts. The two Japs ahead of him passed opposite me. Then my own Jap stepped into perfect position. I waited impatiently for the first shot that would signal our squad's attack.

Chan fired it when my man was about six paces to my right. I

[ 143 ]

shifted my aim to a few inches below his shoulders and squeezed my trigger. Our entire squad fired simultaneously. Our barrage sounded like one deafening shot.

My Jap keeled forward, still holding his machine gun until he hit the ground. Then he rolled over. He was still alive and his reflexes were working. I fired two rounds into his face. He subsided forever.

There was no sign of life among the fourteen Japs in the advance guard. Like a football team coming out of a huddle, we burst forth whooping and even singing. Each guerrilla was supposed to check the Jap he had killed. Chan, however, was racing the fourth guerrilla to the corpse of the machine gunner's ammunition bearer. He had also been bearing a cigarette. Chan snatched it, still lit, from the dead man's mouth. He puffed contentedly as he hurried over to his own victim.

We stripped the Japs of all clothing and made sure none was playing possum. As we worked, I heard a warning shout.

A frightened pack pony galloped around the bend. Heading toward me, the pony didn't seem to see anything. I leaped forward and grabbed its halter. Three other men held the horse steady.

Other ponies came around the bend at a slower clip. Seeing their leader captured, they put up only token resistance.

Around the bend and up the trail, the firing had ceased — except for an occasional lone shot. To save ammunition, most of the guerrillas finished off wounded Japs by slitting their throats.

The Japanese were well dressed. It took us some time to unwind their puttees and unlace their boots. We stripped them bare. All their equipment was loaded onto the pack ponies.

One of their sixty-odd horses had been killed in the battle. Two others were wounded, so we killed them. The rest were ours.

Chan took a little extra time to cut up the dead ponies. We loaded them onto the eight saddle horses we had captured.

"That keep puppies alive a little longer, Gil," Chan said. "Men prefer horsemeat to dog meat."

Now the doomed dogs back at camp had a little more time to live. This thought comforted me as I walked away from the dead Japs.

Ours had been an almost perfect ambush. Although nothing had gone wrong, there had been one flaw in our intelligence. It was the kind of slip-up that makes a man worry when next he faces battle.

Somewhere along the line, the Japs had impressed ten Chinese coolies into service and forced them to carry sacks of beans for the ponies. None of our reports had mentioned this addition.

"It happen on this morning," Chan told me. "Lookout so busy watching Japs he not notice ten coolies."

Luckily for the coolies, nobody had assigned them as targets. No stray bullets hit them, but they had the scare of their lives.

The Japs had placed them behind the rear group. Once the impetus of the ambush was spent, they were easily recognized. If they had been mixed up in the main body, they would have perished with the Japs.

As it worked out, these coolies were fortunate. If the Japs had not been ambushed, the coolies would have been marched many miles farther from home. Wherever they ended up, they would have been likely candidates for forced labor.

They rejoiced and lent us willing hands as we loaded the ponies. They would rejoin their families by dawn tomorrow. And they would carry the first news of the massacre of forty-five Japanese soldiers.

Not until we were halfway back to camp could I sort out my emotions. I tried to analyze how I had felt when I had the Jap, alive and thinking his own thoughts, trapped in my gun sight. I had felt a chill of unfairness. Wasn't it cheating to shoot a total stranger in cold blood?

The chill had passed, warded off by a strong unconscious force. As I tried to identify it later, I saw a blurry vision of my ex-fiancée Margaret and I heard Nora, who once said: "The Japanese kill for the love of killing. Nothing else."

Now, as I climbed the mountain, I asked myself: "Stuart, are you any better than that?"

I didn't know the answer yet, but I knew I felt no exaltation now that I had killed my second man. I envied both the boar and the crocodile whose death struggle I had witnessed in my youth. The boar had tasted victory after sampling death in a keen struggle. The crocodile had died violently, but it had not died a cowardly death. Even the Jap I had killed today had died creditably.

I was twenty-seven in 1939 and I was caring not only how I lived, but also how I would die.

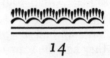

## 14

## Six Go; Two Return

AFTER an encounter with the enemy, marching is no longer drudgery. The greater my distance from the ambush scene, the better I felt.

Looking back, I saw a man toiling up the mountain. He was a good two hours behind us.

"Who's that?" I asked Chan. "A straggler?"

"He sentry my cousin station near village. When ambush over, he go town and tell people evacuate. Japs find out about ambush in day or two. They go crazy for revenge."

"But the Japs know damn well these people are innocent!"

"No matter, Gil. They kill first people they see. Jap no rest until he kill as many as we kill. If we no warn these people, we lose their help. One day those who live betray us to Jap."

"But somewhere forty-five Chinese will die for what we have done for the Chinese cause today?"

"Yes. Maybe more. But we not know who they are."

"And now other Chinese will be bitter at us," I mused aloud. "So hatred spreads like ripples in a pond."

"But Chinese win," Chan assured me.

"How do you know?" I asked him.

"Jap be first to bend. Our people know how to suffer with dignity. Time and numbers on our side. Japs no worse than plague or famine. We no see them. We not know how to fight them. They evil spirits. Strike swiftly. Kill thousands. But we survive. Japs, they men. We see them. We know them. And this is our land, so we win it from them."

It was the most sustained utterance I had ever heard from Chan. He placed his hand on my shoulder as if he needed support after such a long speech. I recognized the comradely gesture, however. I had seen the Chinese use it with one another, but never with an outsider. I was no longer a foreigner to Chan.

Late at night, we reached camp. The sky was cloudless and the moon silver bright. I could see for miles. Far behind us was the place where forty-five Japs had died. Here there was no trace of bloodshed. The air was fresh and crisp. Yet, as I breathed, I wondered why the earth felt as stifling as one enormous tomb.

In the morning, we sorted our loot.

"Most clothes go Chinese Army. Or we sell to buy rice," Chan told me.

"What happens to the guns and the ammo and the ponies?"

"They go north with cousin to main guerrilla group. Headquarters take what need. Send rest to Chinese Army for rice and money."

"But why not keep some of the guns and ammunition here? We could use something better than these God damn Mausers."

"You appreciate Mauser, Gil, when you do more guerrilla war. It most useful weapon. Easy carry. Easy conceal. And most of all, you find plenty ammunition for it."

"You may be right," I said, patting my Mauser. "The best gun in the world is no damn good without a bullet."

Major Chan would be leaving us that night after a festive banquet of horsemeat. Captain Tung made a lengthy after-dinner speech. As usual, he criticized the shortcomings of others. This time, however, the "others" were the Japs, who had paid the only price Tung knew for carelessness.

The Japs' fatal mistake, Tung said, had been not carrying their rifles at the ready. They had slipped the weapons through the cords and straps of their pack saddles.

Yesterday was the first time in Tung's long combat history that he had seen one side wiped out without firing a single shot. This was a revelation to me. I had heard our attacking shots, but I had not listened to the silence from the Japanese side.

A few days after Major Chan had bidden us farewell, we broke camp and pushed westward. We were to pick up new information about Jap movements.

To pass as coolies, each of us carried a bamboo yoke. Two baskets bobbed crazily from it. At first, I found it impossible to attune my yoke to the delicate rhythm of the bouncing baskets. It was an art I had admired from afar when I watched coolies from a rickshaw in Hong Kong. Now I wished I'd taken lessons.

I tried various combinations of walking and trotting to keep in step with the swing of the baskets. For a while, the baskets dominated me. Eventually I found that short springy steps — timed to coincide with each down-bend of the yoke — interspersed with rhythmic shoulder heaves were the best way for me.

This way was also the most exhausting. On level ground it wasn't unduly tiring. On the slightest incline, however, my feet and my shoulders lost synchronization. The baskets would swing into my legs with a roundhouse punch. I would be jerked off balance until I either fell or stopped to begin all over.

This dance of mine amused the others, but not me. After a few hours, the skin of my shoulders began to wear away. My neck and arm and leg muscles tied themselves into knots. Cramps wrenched my legs and guts. On the first night, I couldn't sleep because my pains were so severe. Chan gave me a helpful rubdown.

"Say what you want, Chan, I didn't delay us when we were moving," I declared.

"No. And you keep spirits up, Gil. Many laughs."

The next day, the rhythm came a little more easily. By the third day, I was jouncing along like a veteran coolie. I got more practice, for our march lasted a week. We went a total of a hundred and twenty miles, and ended up some eighty miles from where we had started. We stopped only because we were running out of rice.

Captain Tung sent out a dozen men in three different directions to scout for food. He authorized them to enter villages, but carefully. One prime rule of Tung's was that an enlisted man's entering a

[ 148 ]

village or house without an officer's permission was punishable by death.

"We not worry guerrilla get captured," Chan explained. "That part of game. But we no want his capture involve civilian."

While we waited for the scouts, we camped in a small valley with ample water, trees, and edible grasses. We would not starve here. Each day, we went picking young grass shoots. Chan taught me how to select the best. Our favorite was a long young spear grass. It grew on hills, the banks of streams, and edges of rice paddies.

When enough grass had been collected to feed all the men, it was boiled until it had the consistency of spinach. Then the hot boiling water was poured onto a small quantity of precious rice in each man's rice bowl. This formed a broth, into which we mixed the grass plus dried herbs. It tasted not unlike watercress.

I have eaten this concoction for weeks at a time when the luxuries of guerrilla life, such as dogmeat and horsemeat, were not available.

After we had been on this diet for three days, four of our scouts returned. They had three hundred pounds of rice, vegetables, eggs, fat pork, bean curd, and tobacco — plus good news. In the village that was about to feed us handsomely was a Japanese garrison of one hundred men. The officers lived in the village itself. They had commandeered the residence of a rice merchant.

While we feasted, I asked Chan: "Now that our food problems are over, when do we liberate the village?"

"Captain Tung not sure. He want see for self."

Later that night, Tung organized a mission to explore the village more thoroughly than the scouts. Chan and four other men were to go with him. I wasn't invited.

Tung, Chan, and the other four napped until midnight. When they arose, I helped them prepare. They carried no guns. Each man was equipped with a bamboo yoke and small quantities of charcoal and firewood. If anyone stopped them, they would try to peddle these wares. They would not fool many Chinese, but the Japanese might well mistake them for country people going to market.

The village was a six-hour march from camp, but Tung took along enough food for a full day's trip. He and the others would circle the village to pick out the best attacking approach.

They set out at three A.M. Chan and Tung said their party might be gone for three days. Lieutenant Kui and I were to run the camp.

During the next three days, little happened. The other two sets of scouts, who had been sent out to hunt for food, returned empty-handed. They had observed no Jap troop movements in the area.

By sundown of the third day, I was scanning the east with my binoculars. There was no sign of Tung, Chan, and their party.

On the fourth day, we made no pretense of working. We took turns searching the horizon with our one set of binoculars. There was one false alarm when a caravan passed down a nearby trail. It was hauling roofing tile across China. In the distance, it had looked like a Jap pack train.

On the morning of the fifth day, our lookout sent word that we were being approached from the west. Tung and Chan should be coming from the east, I knew. But, if there had been any difficulty, they would have circled around.

I ran to the lookout's post on a rock ledge. I could tell by the lookout's back that he had seen our men, for he was standing straight and expectant. Had there been any uncertainty about their identity, he would have assumed a more wary posture.

When he heard me coming, he held up two fingers.

"Two!" I exclaimed. "There were six of them."

The lookout spoke no English, but he could sense my incredulity. He held up two fingers again.

My hands struggled to hold the binoculars steady. My heart sank as my eyes confirmed the lookout's report. Captain Tung was not one of the two men. Chan was there and I thanked God for that. But I could see, as he forced himself forward with head and shoulders bent, that his burden of news was heavy indeed.

This is the story Chan told in a husky voice that sounded unfamiliar to me. After leaving our camp five days earlier, the six men had circled around the village. They spent the first night in a smaller village, where they purchased a few pounds of small hot red peppers to add to their wares. If they didn't sell them in town, the men at camp would be happy to devour them.

The next morning, they approached the large village from the southeast. If they were traced, they did not want it known that they had come from the west.

They divided into two groups: Chan and two men, Tung and the other two. Wandering around the village, they took note of Japanese sentry stations and all possible avenues of attack.

Dozens of Japs were swaggering around the village. They took little notice of the strangers in town. All coolies looked alike to them.

The two groups met again on the outskirts of town. This time, Tung said, he and his two men would snoop around Japanese headquarters. Chan and his men should size up the Japanese enlisted men's barracks at the other end of town.

"Everything looks good," Tung told Chan optimistically. "We may be able to attack after all." The two parties arranged to meet near the Jap barracks in early afternoon.

Along the way, Chan talked with a number of villagers. They gave good information and asked him no questions. Chan and his two men even found time to visit a restaurant for half an hour. They interviewed the owner while devouring noodles and tea.

Toward noon, Chan and his men ventured toward the heavily patrolled barracks. Mealtime was the best for reconnoitering without attracting much suspicion.

The barracks looked as if they could hold a hundred men. Nearby were several tents where men were billeted. Chan estimated Jap strength as a hundred and forty men — a hundred in barracks, ten in tents, and thirty in town. This made it the largest garrison for miles around.

On the other side of the barracks was a corral for pack ponies. Harnesses, grains, and beans for the horses were stored in an adjacent shed.

A building that looked like a warehouse stood four hundred feet away. Chan sent one man to look it over.

While Chan prowled, he felt that he was being watched. He whirled around to look into the piggish eyes of the Japanese cook. The man was fat, sweaty, and greasy. But he was not interested in Chan's presence, just his wares.

"I'll buy all your charcoal," he said to Chan and the man with him, whose name was Soong.

Chan was reluctant to sell his props. The Jap named a paltry price, which Chan rejected.

The Jap told him: "If you don't accept, we will take your charcoal and give you nothing for it except a beating. Now deliver it to the galley."

Chan and Soong set out for the galley. Along the way, they were joined by the guerrilla who had checked the warehouse.

He reported that forty Chinese coolies were there as forced laborers. Some were cleaning rice. Others were putting rice into sacks. Still others were building an addition to the warehouse.

"There are just two Japanese guards and they didn't notice me," the guerrilla told Chan. "I talked to the Chinese. They asked for the vegetables I carried. These men were so miserable that I had to give them all my food."

Chan told him he had done the right thing.

"Would you mind if I took your red peppers back to them, too?" the tough guerrilla asked Chan compassionately.

Chan assented, but told him to be careful. The guerrilla disappeared with the peppers.

The cook reappeared: "What's taking so long? You get that charcoal to the galley and wait there for me. I'll bring your payment."

Chan and Soong delivered the charcoal to the bin. They waited in the galley for ten minutes. Then they decided that, at best, the Jap wasn't coming back to pay them. At worst, he would be returning with guards to take them prisoner.

Soong was so angry at being cheated that he didn't want to leave. Chan reminded him that they would be departing unpaid but uncaught. They drifted away from the galley.

Hearing a commotion near the warehouse, they wandered over. Perhaps their generous comrade had been caught red-handed with the peppers. But, when they saw what the disturbance was about, they halted in their tracks.

Prodded by the rifles of two Japanese soldiers, three Chinese prisoners were being brought into camp. Their hands were tied behind their backs. They were Captain Tung and his two guerrillas.

Captain Tung and his party, Chan learned later, had looked over the Japanese headquarters. They were wandering near the officers' living quarters in the town. No sooner had they approached the building than a sentry challenged them.

Tung gave a satisfactory account of himself and his companions. He was almost out of danger when a Japanese officer came along. On the spur of the moment, the officer kicked one of Tung's men and sent him flying.

To show that he, too, was soldiering, the Jap sentry hit Tung across the face with the butt end of his gun. Tung fell in the entrance-way.

Hearing the commotion, several Jap officers emerged from the building. They dragged Tung inside and ordered his companions to come with him.

The Japs worked them over for half an hour. Occasionally, the Japs put out cigarettes in their prisoners' groins. Mostly, the Japs just beat them unimaginatively but steadily. When there was no more fun to be had, the officers turned the three men over to sentries. The prisoners were taken to the warehouse, where they were impressed as forced labor.

Seeing Tung in captivity, Chan and Soong wasted no time in leaving town. The man with the red peppers did not rejoin them. They guessed (correctly, as it turned out) that he had been taken by surprise and captured when the sentries arrived with Tung.

Chan and Soong waited that night and the next night in the small village where they had spent their first night. If Tung were to escape, he would join them there. But nobody came.

On the fourth day, Chan returned to the big village. The friendly restaurant owner assured him that the Japs did not suspect Tung and his companions were guerrillas. They had been taken at face value as out-of-town peddlers. But that had been risky enough. The Japanese seldom molested local people, upon whom they depended for rice and other supplies. Strangers in town, however, were fair game.

The restaurant owner said he had reports that Tung, his two companions, and another man who had been caught smuggling peppers to the laborers were all being worked hard. The pepper smuggler, however, had put up resistance and was badly beaten.

"It would be impossible for two of you to get them out," the restaurant owner told Chan. "Even a hundred men could not rescue them now."

Chan and Soong returned to camp to tell their story. Soong groaned as he heard Chan recall details of the harrowing mission they had shared. Soong was a stolid man whose skinny frame could accommodate only one emotion at a time. It had never been laughter in the time I had known him. Right now, it was pain.

"What we going to do, Gil?" Chan pleaded with me as humbly as he had back in the Hong Kong Mines.

"We'll get them out, of course," I assured him blandly. "First, you have some tea and rice and get settled down. When you've had some rest, you'll be able to think clearly. We'll need all the information and advice you can give us about the village."

Chan slept — crying out occasionally from a bad dream — until late afternoon. He stretched himself in the warm sun. He scarcely saw me as he busied himself with the bugs he had acquired en route. Loosening his pants at the waist, he dislodged — one by one — insects that had secreted themselves in his groin.

As he killed the first few bugs, he squeezed his own blood out of their corpses with his thumbnail. Soon he lost interest in the blood and concentrated on killing the bugs.

I rolled a cigarette and handed it to him: "You look a lot better, Chan. How do you feel?"

"I have sore feet, too," he said, still wrapped up in himself. He was trying to keep out the rest of the world for a while. With Tung gone, Chan was in command. He would not shirk the mantle of leadership, but he needed a few minutes of petty introspection before he began making decisions of life and death.

I had one of the men bring Chan a bucket of hot water to soak his feet in. I made us both some tea. Over our second cup, I said cautiously: "I would like to suggest a plan that may work."

Chan smiled for the first time that day and said: "Ready, Gil."

"The situation is not as hopeless as it appears," I said. "The Japs are short of coolie labor, so they won't kill Tung and the other three if they don't know who they are."

Chan's eyes were half-closed, but I could tell that he saw the same picture I did, thus far.

"Now," I continued, "another resource we have is that there are forty coolies in the same boat with them. It's safe to guess that they'll be on Tung's side when the time comes. The most important thing for us to do now is to plan the attack in split-second detail. Then we must select one man. We brief him thoroughly with our plan and send him to the village. He must get himself captured by the Japs. If he does it without arousing suspicion that he's a guerrilla, he'll be thrown into the coolie labor gang with Tung."

"And then Jap have five guerrilla instead of four," Chan said.

"But Tung will know our plans. He'll be able to coordinate his with ours. That way, we'll hit the Japs from within and without at the same time."

Chan's eyes were bright with interest as I continued . . .

That night, Chan called a war council of squad leaders. As he sketched my plan in Chinese, I could detect a rustle of eager impatience in his audience. With a stick, Chan drew pictures in the dirt. He mapped out the village. He marked the Jap installations and sentry posts. He pointed out the streets the Japanese liked to roam. If the village ever opened up a Chamber of Commerce, Chan should have been its first president.

The weakest link in my plan was attacking the Japanese headquarters. The only guerrillas who had seen it close were now prisoners of the Japs. If we attacked at night, headquarters would probably be fairly deserted. But how could we know for sure?

Although the barracks would be numerically harder to take, Chan and I agreed that we should both lead a small force attacking the headquarters. Lieutenant Kui could head the larger party attacking the barracks, where fewer plans could go astray—particularly with Tung boring from within.

The attack was set for three A.M., three days later. Our envoy to Tung needed enough time to wander into town and be arrested by the Japs.

For this unpromising but vital assignment, we selected a grinning country boy named Lok. He was a clown and practical joker, but trustworthy when the stakes were high. Even the most evil-minded Jap would never guess that Lok was anything more than a husky, well-fed bumpkin coming to town. It was not far from the truth, for he had to be drilled all night to memorize the information he was to relay to Tung.

Chan advised him to act dumb.

[ 155 ]

"How do I do that?" Lok asked innocently.

We tried to teach him a few tricks. Finally Chan told him to be himself. Lok brightened.

I suggested that he hang around the Jap barracks and make a pest of himself. But he was not to ask for information. Any new facts might confuse Lok before he reached Tung.

Hardest of all was convincing Lok not to put up any resistance when the Japs arrested him — even if they beat him. Soon after breakfast, he set out on the most unlikely mission of his life.

Chan sent Soong, his fellow survivor of the ill-fated mission, back to the small village where they had spent their nights. Soong would seek information there. He was to intercept us as we approached the big village.

We set about breaking camp. If we managed to rescue Tung, we would have to flee the area before the Japs came after us in full force.

On the afternoon of the second day, Soong rejoined us with some unexpected good news.

He had been given food and shelter by a farmer in the small village. There was no news of Tung. But the farmer had heard of a silly youth arrested for begging rice from the cook at the Jap barracks. That had been Lok!

There was a market day at the big village. The people of the small village were up for most of the night preparing vegetables for market. They left at daybreak. Soong helped his hosts carry their wares to the outskirts of the big village.

It was well that he did. He had just transferred his yoke and two baskets to the frail shoulders of the farmer's daughter when he heard the clatter of marching troops and the voices of Japanese officers. They were coming along the trail from the village.

The farmer's family and Soong melted back into a rice paddy. There, they watched the Japs pass in single file. The enemy silhouettes were sharply etched in the gray light of dawn. Soong counted thirty men carrying rifles, trench mortars, and machine guns. Several pack ponies carried enough supplies for a week.

The farmer's daughter put down her yoke. She went into town

to find out what she could about the Japanese patrol. Were they hunting for guerrillas? Or going on a long-range mission? She returned with the news that they were going out to meet and escort a Japanese supply caravan headed toward town. They would be gone at least four days.

There was quiet rejoicing in our camp. The odds against us were considerably lower now that the Japs had thirty fewer men to fight us.

At midnight, three hours before the attack, we assembled outside the village.

In Chinese every bit as terse as his English, Chan warned the men that the most crucial area was not the barracks, nor the headquarters, nor the warehouse — but the mile that lay ahead. If any of us was detected, the whole attack would be off. Whether we were there or not, Captain Tung and Lok and their fellow prisoners would push from within at three A.M. If we failed them, they would die horrible deaths.

We re-formed into three groups. Chan and I watched Lieutenant Kui and fifteen men disappear into the deep black night. Their destination was the barracks. Ten men left for the warehouse soon after.

Chan and I led our four men in the opposite direction. We would attack the headquarters from the other side of the village. First, however, we had to kill two sentries guarding the main gate of town.

We had to be silent and deadly, for if a shot were fired by either side before three A.M., all would be lost.

The sentries were in two pillboxes — mud brick emplacements for machine guns — flanking the trail. We had been informed that these two guards had no machine guns, just rifles. But our intelligence had erred before. In case there were machine guns, we could die in their deadly crossfire.

If we made no noise and succeeded, these guards would not be missed for a few hours. They were not due to be relieved until four A.M.

Near the two pillboxes, we split up. Chan took one pair of men; I took the others.

It was so dark that the three of us had to cling to each other's shirt tails to stay together. One of the men with me was Soong.

[ 157 ]

Chan's last words had been whispered: "We see each other again in few minutes, Gil."

I wondered to myself: In this world or the next?

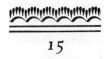

## 15

## Victory without Loot

OUR Jap was droning a tuneless song. We edged toward him on our stomachs. His faint outline was low to the ground. I gathered he was sitting.

The pillbox was built into the ground. Its wall was only three feet tall. A thatched roof kept out the weather. The night was chilly.

A light flashed in the pillbox and I drew my knife.

Our Jap wasn't looking for anybody. He was lighting a cigarette.

The flickering match illuminated the pillbox's entrance for a second. I made an indelible mental note of the layout and congratulated myself on my good luck. Then I crept closer. In thirty seconds, Chan was to attack his man and I mine.

Five seconds before then, I had another stroke of good fortune. The Jap's cigarette had not lit. He struck another match.

He had just lit his cigarette successfully when I plunged through the entranceway. He was still blinded by the glare of his own match. As the light died away, my left hand was on his throat and closing over his mouth.

I heard his tuneless humming stop as his cigarette dropped from his lips. I dug my fingers into his flesh and pulled his head back sharply against my knee. In the same motion, the knife in my right hand ripped open his throat. Just to make certain he died silently, I broke his neck across my knee the way I had once killed sheep in Australia.

His legs jerked straight out from under him as his brain sent its last command.

I dived for the entrance. It was blocked by Soong, who was coming in. I let him past.

As I ducked out, I heard Soong slash the dead Jap to shreds. His butchering took less than a minute. I never saw Soong's handiwork. Having once seen a boar destroy a crocodile, I didn't need to look.

We returned to the trail in total darkness. There was a faint clatter from the other pillbox and then a muffled thump of feet as Chan and his two men rejoined us in silence. We slapped each other, joyously but noiselessly, to indicate success. Then Chan and I hurried into the village with the other four close behind.

We were less than a hundred yards from Jap headquarters. A narrow path led us unobserved to our destination.

We squatted against a building and rested until our heavy breathing quieted. Then we examined the headquarters slowly with our eyes, for we had a tense fifteen minutes of watching and waiting ahead.

The headquarters interior was dark, except for one room on the first floor. This was probably the radio room. Outside, a bright light illuminated the doorway, where a lone guard stood. His rifle was slung carelessly over his shoulder. He was standing there for warmth. The halo of light enveloping him was so glaring that he couldn't possibly see much. As far as we could tell, there were no other sentries.

The doomed guard was kicking one foot against the other. All his energies in his last hour on earth were directed to keeping himself warm.

I pulled out my knife. With telling gestures, I showed Chan that I would cut the guard's throat if Chan would grab his arms.

Chan signaled that *he* would take the leg and throat if *I* would take the arms.

No, I signaled, I would let Chan hold the Jap's arms and legs if he would just leave me the throat.

Chan's final counter-offer was this: I could have the Jap's throat, scalp, arms, and legs later if I would only let Chan kill him. I refused. We both knew to stick to our original plan: I was to kill him while Chan held him.

By then, I had come to think of the Japanese sentry as a corpse. Every time he kicked his own shins, I was jolted back to reality. An unsuspecting man was living out his life before my eyes.

At one minute before three A.M., Chan and I were crouched side by side twenty feet from the Jap sentry.

[ 159 ]

We took three steps forward. Chan threw his arms around the Jap and his rifle.

My left hand reached for the Jap's mouth. I missed and my fingers dug into one of his eyes. However, my right hand aimed true. I buried my knife deep in his throat just as he started a scream for help.

The Jap collapsed in Chan's tight embrace. Our four men poured through the headquarters door. I followed them.

Our initial target was the radio room. It had to be destroyed before the first beep of warning sounded. I entered the only illuminated room just in time to see the radio operator pitch forward from chair to floor. One of our men had shot him between the eyes.

Shots sounded elsewhere in the building. The other guerrillas ran toward the noise. I lingered just long enough to toss a grenade onto the radio.

Seconds later, the building shook. Everything inside, except the people, began to fly.

I met Chan near the entranceway: "Everybody out, Gil. Three Jap on duty. We shoot all."

As the last of us made his exit, Chan hurled another grenade through the doorway. The building heaved and started to waver a little.

From the other end of town, I could hear explosion after explosion. Dazed by the concussion of Chan's grenade, I took a minute to realize what this meant; our attack was taking its toll on barracks and warehouse.

We cut around the rear of the wobbly headquarters, which had caught fire. A side street led directly to the officers' quarters.

The officers came out to meet us. They ran like a pack of schoolboys eager to be spectators at some unknown excitement. They could not imagine what the commotion at headquarters was about.

We stopped dead and flung ourselves to the ground. When the officers were almost on top of us, we opened fire.

Our effect was even more stunning than a meticulously planned ambush. So great was the element of surprise that some of the officers kept running for a few feet even as our bullets slew them.

We were on our feet and away before the last man hit the dirt. We got them all, as a quick run through their silent quarters confirmed. The place was deserted. The occupants would not be back.

The Chinese villagers were staying indoors. Cutting across town, we met only two people — Japs. They must have lived in town.

They offered comic relief as they hurried busily toward us. One was struggling into his trousers and hopping on one foot. The other bore his rifle and his comrade's. His fingers held up his pants until his comrade was ready to relieve him. Never have I seen two more helpless soldiers.

Guerrillas make no provision for prisoners unless information is sought. All we wanted that morning was Captain Tung, so we gunned down the two Japs.

The warehouse was in flames when we reached it. To its right, where once there had been tents, lay fiery canvas and mangled Japs. Some were still alive, though wounded. They groped and writhed dazedly. We put the livelier ones out of their misery. We wasted no bullets on the helpless sufferers.

Shouts emanated from the burning warehouse. We ran to its rear and called inside. The rioters within had to know we weren't Japs.

Several coolies were emerging from the warehouse. Tung and the other guerrillas had already left, but they had told the coolies to arm themselves with Jap weapons.

The barracks, too, was in flames. A few dead ponies lay in the corral outside. Most of the horses had fled in fright, taking half the fence with them.

Our guerrillas were dragging three fallen comrades. Chan checked the bodies hastily and said all three were dead. He ordered the men to look for the living. At least three guerrillas were said to be wounded, though still alive. After storming the barracks, they had come within range of a grenade exploding inside a tent.

Chan ordered everyone to leave within five minutes, whether or not our casualties were found. The firelight made us too good a target for a counterattack, if any Japs were still around.

When we were five hundred feet from the barracks, we were knocked to the ground by a tremendous blast. Picking ourselves up, we fled in haste. The fire must have ignited some stored explosives.

It was now 3:30 A.M.

We had arranged to meet five miles away. Pops and thuds were still resounding from the village when we reached our assembly point. An occasional shot crackled in the distance. The gunfire was so sporadic that any Japs who were left must have been firing at villagers or each other.

I lit a match and looked at Chan. His hands, arms, and face were so coated with blood and dirt that I was sure he had been wounded.

Chan, however, pointed to me and gave a hearty laugh.

As the match flickered, I glanced down at myself. Half-dried blood was caked on me, too. Chan and I might have been looking into mirrors.

I lit a second match. The blood had traveled in a stream from my waist to my knees. My black cotton garb was now stained deep red. From my knees down, the blood was mixing with the heavy dew. It looked as if I were bleeding to death. But I felt no pain.

I lit a third match and saw Captain Tung.

He and Lok, the grinning country boy, and the other three captives and six rescuers had just arrived. Tung, too, was a bloody mess. But the blood on his face was his own.

His face was twice its normal size, but half of his nose was missing. The Japs had pounded Tung's face with a rifle butt. His jaw was broken. He was unable to talk. Nevertheless, his ruin of a face expressed eloquent gratitude.

Fourteen men were missing. Three, we knew, were definitely dead. Tung and Chan decided we must move north immediately and find a camp site with water. We left two guerrillas behind for a day to intercept any stragglers who materialized.

That afternoon, we camped near a wide creek. All of us were exhausted and many were sick.

Whenever I allowed myself to inhale the stench of Jap blood exuding from my clothes, I threw up. So did anyone who ventured close to me. I was the most unpopular man in camp. Still, everyone smiled at me — from a distance.

Thousands of flies swarmed around my head. They were lured by the same blood that repelled my fellow men. Like a cordon of furies, they escorted me to the creek, where I flung off gunbelt and bandolier. I immersed myself in the water, which was dirty. But I was giving it more bacteria than it could give me. Gradually, I stripped off my clothes and wallowed luxuriously in my best bath since leaving Hong Kong.

[ 162 ]

The men were building a fire and boiling rice. This was our first spare moment even to realize we were hungry. None of us had eaten since the night before.

Our place soon resembled a nudist camp. Every man had shed his clothes, washed them, and let them dry in the lukewarm sun of late afternoon.

I was as close to surgically clean as circumstances would allow, so I operated on Tung's fractured jaw.

We had no first aid equipment. I was able to dig up two almost clean undershirts and a pair of Japanese leggings. I cut the undershirts into squares that would fit over Tung's face. I made holes for his eyes, mouth, and nostrils. With the leftover cloth, I made bandages.

I immersed all my materials into a can of water, which I boiled for twenty minutes.

Washing the dirt off Tung's battered face, I quickly covered it with the masklike bandages. Then I wrapped them with the leggings, which I tucked under his chin and tied atop his head. This would hold them in place and give his sagging jaw some support. Until he could receive proper medical attention, his condition would grow no worse.

His most immediate problems were talking and eating. Sign language and passing notes would solve one. A Chinese dish called soojee — a bowl of soupy rice — helped the other.

Thirty-two men had set out to rescue Tung, Lok, and three other prisoners.

In liberating all five, we had definitely sacrificed three lives. Eleven more were unaccounted for.

Subtracting the two couriers we had left behind, we now had twenty-one men in camp.

The next morning, I was awakened soon after sunrise by joyous shouts. The two couriers were back — leading nine survivors out of a possible eleven.

One of the survivors was painfully wounded, but he would live. He had been trapped by the grenade exploding in a tent. The two men who had been with him were definitely dead, he reported.

Statistically, then, we had given up five lives to regain five prisoners. One of the lives regained, however, was Captain Tung's. He would save many hundreds of guerrillas in every year that he survived. Our investment had paid off right there.

True, we had also killed some sixty Japs. And we had immobilized the garrison for at least a week. But at least that many innocent lives would be snuffed out when the Japs retaliated. A thriving village might well be ruined or destroyed.

It was a somber victory for us. This, however, was not the only reason why our men grew gloomy in the ensuing days. All deaths — just and unjust — were accessories to guerrilla warfare. But one essential of guerrilla victory was missing: *There had been no loot.*

Every man likes to be paid for hard work well done. Our earnings were the goods that passed through our hands. They went elsewhere, it was true, but so does money.

Without loot, the men experienced a bad letdown. The mood even infected Lok, the virtually impenetrable country boy. Lok's perpetual grin had often struck me as an innocent Oriental parody of my old Australian lumber camp enemy, Jim Church. When Lok's gleaming good cheer faded to surliness, I knew that hard times lay ahead.

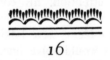

## 16

# A Case of Hara-kiri

TUNG and two wounded men were sent north to Major Chan's guerrilla headquarters, where there was a doctor. A fourth man was detailed to escort them. Our numerical strength dropped to twenty-six and our morale dropped even more perceptibly. In the eyes of men living from day to day, Tung's departure totally negated his rescue.

Chan was our leader now. He could do little about morale. And our food supply was running low again.

Each time we sent men to the villages, they returned empty-handed, but with reports of Japanese reprisals. Our raid was still proving disastrous to Chinese civilians for miles around. Chan knew that when many villagers grow edgy or bitter, a few invariably turn informer.

Our men began talking about stealing rice and vegetables from farmers — an offense punishable by death in Major Chan's guerrillas. Chan, however, lacked the authority of a Captain Tung. If Chan ordered a man shot for stealing, Chan might be shot himself. And I would perish next. That was the way morale stood a week after Tung had left us.

I advised Chan to move the group farther east, away from the swath of Japanese reprisals. Our only prey would be small Jap patrols and an occasional pack train, but a few minor successes might restore the men's morale.

We marched for days through barren land. We camped wherever we found grass — and spent half a day picking it for supper. Never had the term "daily bread" seemed more exotic to me.

One morning, we stumbled into paradise: a mountainside with several varieties of grasses and herbs as well as a rare delicacy, mushrooms!

The men broke ranks and threw themselves upon the fertile land. Each man bore two baskets. For the first time in weeks, both baskets would be full.

Gazing down at several rice paddies in the valley, I asked Chan: "Do you think you and I might hunt for eels and rice snakes down there? A little meat with their grass might do the men a lot of good."

"It be pleasant change," Chan agreed.

We said we were going on a scouting expedition. Then, bypassing the main trail, we ran and slid down the slope like happy truants.

The rice was still green and under irrigation, so no pickers would be around. And the moisture would have attracted other creatures beside us. These others would be edible.

A small paddy lay beneath four inches of water. We smashed down the man-made banks and let the water drain out. Then we rolled up our pants as high as they would go.

Wading into the paddy, we were up to our knees in rice and thick mud. Each grope in the mud netted a handful of slimy eels, eight inches long and about as thick as a finger.

There were hundreds of eels per square foot of mud. If we didn't put them into baskets rapidly, they would squirm away.

When our four baskets were nearly full, we covered over the eels with a layer of green rice. We repaired the damage to the paddy walls and headed back. We had been gone approximately two hours.

We had to take the trail back up the hill. Balancing my baskets with a yoke, I jogged along steadily behind Chan. I had mastered the delicate art of yoke-balancing, but it was still an exhausting uphill climb with a full load.

When we stopped for a rest, Chan spotted our guerrillas two miles ahead.

"Then let's get a move on," I said. "I never want to see these eels again until they're cooked."

We resumed at a faster clip. My sweat-soaked clothes clung to my body. My bandoliers cut into my shoulders. My pistol slapped against my side until I chafed.

We rounded a sharp bend. Suddenly, Chan halted. He signaled me frantically as he threw himself down. I dropped my load and fell flat on my face. I was panting like a horse.

Chan made a hissing noise. Concealed behind a bush twenty feet ahead of me, he was peering through binoculars. He beckoned me to crawl quietly toward him. Unburdened by the baskets, I slithered forward like an eel.

Handing me the binoculars, Chan pointed up our trail. Not more than two hundred feet away were twenty well-armed Chinese guerrillas. Some sat. Others lay flat on their backs, resting. Slightly higher up, four more guerrillas were peering ahead through binoculars.

To my amazement, they were watching our guerrilla group.

Our men were still a mile from them. Eventually, however, our men would be moving toward them. Were they waiting for our band to meet them? Why weren't they making contact with our camp? And why was Chan so cautious with fellow guerrillas?

I studied the strangers more carefully. The glasses made them appear so near that I held my breath. Their clothes were like ours, but cleaner and newer. The men looked fresh and well-fed, but I saw no food and no utensils. Much of the equipment they did have was Japanese.

[ 166 ]

"They follow us long time. That why they so relax now," Chan whispered.

"I guess they didn't see you and me going downhill or they'd be looking our way now."

Chan nodded and said: "We look over carefully. Maybe they bandits pretending guerrillas."

"If those are bandits," I said, "they wouldn't be welcomed by the people around here. They'd be carrying their own food and utensils."

"I almost sure they work for Japs. That only explanation."

"Then what do we do next, Chan?"

"We hunt the hunter. Make sure their intentions. Find out how many men. Make sure no others lying in ambush. Then get word to our men. Now, we wait."

Our men weren't budging until we returned. After a while, the leader of the other guerrilla band ordered his men to their feet. He selected two men. He took their weapons and ammunition away from them. The two men started toward our group.

The rest moved out cautiously. Instead of taking the trail, they took a devious path down the mountain.

Chan and I decided that the two unarmed men, disguised as coolies, were to follow our guerrillas. The others would either attack us down below or, more likely, summon the Japs.

While the two "coolies" took a devious route to get behind our camp, Chan and I plunged straight up the trail. We delivered our eels and told our men what was going on.

Chan instructed our men to arrest the two unarmed "coolies" and question them while he and I and two other men were away tailing the guerrilla band. To fill out our patrol, he selected the humorless Soong and the happy-go-lucky Lok.

Late afternoon found the four of us still trailing the eighteen guerrillas. Soong was dejected about missing out on the feast of eels back at camp. To tease him as we crossed the rice paddy fields, Lok reached down and handed Soong several muddy eels. Soong took umbrage at Lok's thinking he ate his eels raw.

The other guerrillas' route carried them and us very close to farms and villages. Our risk multiplied, for people might spot me as a foreigner. I pulled my straw coolie hat lower over my eyes.

[ 167 ]

Nobody seemed to notice our weapons. Apparently, armed men were a common sight around here. Perhaps we were mistaken for the rear guard of the other guerrillas.

Toward sundown, our quarry stopped. Chan halted us, too.

While we waited, I experimented with a new disguise to conceal my Western eyes.

I still had some Tiger Balm, the yellowish all-purpose menthol salve that had been a going-away present from Nora. This time, I smeared my eyelashes with thick gobs, which started my eyes burning and watering. I had previously used pig lard to simulate mucous of the eyes and disguise them. Tiger Balm was more painful but more realistic.

I was feigning chicoma, a serious eye infection not uncommon in Asia in 1939. It was caused by a parasite that devoured eye tissue. Eventually, the eyes were overrun by a yellow mucous that pasted the eyelide together. Only a small slit remained for the light to penetrate each eye. It was such an unpalatable disease that any chicoma sufferer was likely to squint or hang his head.

The disguise worked, although it had consequences of its own. In China, chicoma sufferers were feared like lepers. As we passed, children and even a few adults threw stones at me. My reflections on human kindness were not very complimentary. But the security that my hideous "eye disease" afforded was worth the price I paid.

The guerrillas we were trailing disbanded. In small groups, they scattered across paddies and disappeared into farms and villages. The leader and two other men continued south on their original trail.

"We stay with them," Chan said. "Follow leader. Know group."

We had been keeping half a mile behind, but as the light dimmed and the population thickened, we closed the gap. The three men we were tailing entered a large village, which was the commercial center for the area. Well inside the village, the three men entered a house.

Chan would have made an excellent private detective. Without slowing his stride, he led us into a house opposite theirs. We swaggered in as if we were old friends expected for dinner.

Two men, both in their sixties, were seated in the front room. Startled by our arrival, they gaped at us and our guns. Chan put them at ease by telling them we were guerrillas from the south. We were headed north, he said, and we needed a place to eat and rest overnight. Would they consider helping us if we paid for food and service?

A woman entered. At the mention of money, she took over the conversation. The two men relaxed. It was clear who cast the deciding vote in this house. First, she said, she wanted to see our cash.

I fished around my waist for my money belt. Extracting two sweaty Chinese dollars, I handed them to Chan. The woman accepted the money. She rubbed the filthy bills in her hand as though they were towels. Chan told her to buy enough food for the four of us and herself and her two men. At this point, our three hosts began tripping over themselves to make us welcome. The men served us tea while the woman prepared supper.

I looked around the room. It was twelve by sixteen feet with a large round table, chairs, stools, a cupboard, drawings of old generals, slogans on the wall, and a false ceiling that did not quite cover the room.

I wandered over to the exposed part and peered up discreetly. There was a second level with sleeping mats on the floor. This was where we would probably spend the night.

Upstairs, there was also a small window covered with rice paper. (One seldom saw glass in China.) The window looked out on the road and the building across the way.

Because of the language barrier, my value would be as a lookout. I caught Chan's eye and whispered to him about the upper level and the window. Chan told our hosts I was tired. Would they mind if I napped on a sleeping mat upstairs? With my "eye condition" so apparent, they were not reluctant to lose my company.

Chan helped me up the bamboo ladder. Upstairs, we could not stand up without bumping heads against the roof. The rice paper was too dirty to allow visibility. With my knife, I made a slit.

We had a perfect view of the other house. It was less than thirty feet to our right. Several trees towered behind it. The tallest tree had a bamboo pole attached. From the pole extended an antenna.

Chan and I looked at each other. I whistled softly and said: "There must be Japs over there with a radio station."

"I go downstairs. Find out what people here know. You keep good watch, Gil."

[ 169 ]

Smells of cooking wafted up to my perch. Trying to take my thoughts off the food downstairs, I merely transferred them to the eels I'd left behind me. Across the street, nobody came and nobody went. I was in my observation tower for two hours.

Chan joined me soon after dinner had been served downstairs. He brought up a bowl of dried squid soup, and a dish piled high with vegetables, pork, meat, egg noodles, and rice. There was enough for three men. I ate it all while Chan took my post at the window.

My mouth was full as I listened to Chan. Two Japs lived across the street, he said. They were in radio contact with a Japanese garrison several hundred miles away.

As far as Chan could learn from the old men, the Japs had several Chinese guerrilla groups in their employ. If the guerrillas helped the Japs, they would receive protection. Their families, homes, and crops would go unmolested.

"Now that we know they have a radio, we've got to knock it out and kill the three guerrillas in there," I said.

"And both Jap, too."

"How do the Japs get power for transmitting from here?" I asked.

"Portable generator. Two month ago, Jap pack train stop here and unload one across street, old man say."

"Then they haven't transmitted the news about us yet," I told Chan.

"How so, Gil?"

"I'd have heard the sound of it transmitting."

"But why no send word to Jap garrison?"

"I don't know," I said, "but we'd better knock it out before they can. Let's go over there and take 'em by surprise. There are four of us. At most, there are two Japs and three guerrillas. And chances are the Japs aren't around right now or they'd have transmitted."

We descended the ladder to the room below, where everyone was belching contentedly. Even Soong and Lok were getting on well in the afterglow of a good meal. Chan apologized to our hosts. I was feeling well again, so we would move on tonight.

As emotionally as if we were her sons, the woman begged us to stay. But, when Chan told her she could keep the money we had paid for the night, she relented. In fact, as she stood in the doorway and checked that the street was empty, she bowed frantically, chanted her humble pleasure, and urged us to go quickly. I didn't know whether she was going to kiss us or kick us as we left.

"Do you think she will talk?" I asked Chan.

"Whatever she do, she talk over with old men first."

"Then it'll take that committee at least a day to reach any decision. We'll be gone by then."

The little street was dark and deserted. Standing in the doorway of the Jap's house, we drew our pistols. I also checked that my knife was handy.

The door opened silently with our first push. We entered a reception room with two chairs, a table, an oil lamp, a teapot, and several cups. A pair of Japanese slippers was neatly aligned on the floor.

This front room led to two others, each curtained off. The one on the left proved to be a bedroom that led nowhere. The other room was to the rear and far more promising. Inside were several rifles, ammunition boxes, rice bags — and a radio.

We tiptoed inside. I put my hand on the radio: "It's cold. Hasn't been used lately."

At the other end of the radio room was a partly open door. Through it came light, voices, and the rattle of dishes. Chan, Soong, and Lok listened briefly.

Without warning, Chan kicked the door open and jumped forward, gun in hand. We all followed.

The three guerrillas we had trailed into town were squatting on the floor in a circle around empty rice bowls and soiled chopsticks. Chan's kick on the door had struck the leader a glancing blow. He had tipped forward in a momentary daze. The other two were too petrified to move.

Soong and Lok searched the three men while Chan pointed his gun.

I stepped forward and kicked each man off balance. Chan made them lie flat on the floor. Soong found cord and old pants to bind their hands and feet. Lok returned to the front door as our lookout.

Chan asked our captives where the Japs were.

They were being entertained in a village two miles away.

When were they expected back?

They usually transmitted around nine P.M., which would be soon. But one could never be sure when they would return.

What were three Chinese doing here — wining and dining in Japanese quarters?

The two men looked at their leader and said nothing.

The leader spoke for the first time. He and his men were setting a trap to kill the Japs. Why didn't we untie them? They would let us help.

Chan kicked out the leader's front teeth. He told the man to speak truth or he would be "excused from talking." In Chinese, this meant his tongue would be cut out.

The leader tried to lie again. Chan kicked an uppercut to his jaw.

We turned our attention to the two subordinates. Chan told them we had been following the guerrillas all day and had captured their two unarmed spies. We knew, he said, that they had told all they had seen to the Japs.

One of the men cried out involuntarily that they had not yet talked to the Japs. His bleeding leader tried to silence him with a glare. But we knew all we needed.

The room we stood in was a kitchen. It opened into a backyard enclosed by three walls and a rear shed. Chan and I went exploring. In the shed, we found several small drums of oil; three dozen five-gallon cans of gasoline; and the portable generator. It, too, was cold.

A door at the back of the shed opened onto a grove of trees and the rice paddy fields beyond.

While Lok watched the front door and Soong the prisoners, Chan and I carried twenty cans of gasoline into the radio room. While we were there, I disabled the radio.

Gagging the prisoners, we dragged them into the radio room. We doused all lights and the fire in the kitchen stove. I made sure no other lamps were burning anywhere on the premises.

We opened the fuel cans and tipped them over. The gasoline spilled out all over the house. We did the same in the shed at the rear.

Making sure our prisoners were firmly bound, we stepped outside and shut all doors. Lok was sent to watch the back shed. Soong, Chan, and I loitered on the street near the front door.

In Lok's absence, Chan assumed the role of practical joker. He asked Soong if he had a match.

Soong fumbled in his pockets. Then, smelling the fumes from inside, he froze and looked at Chan incredulously.

Chan and I burst out laughing. Even in the darkness, I thought I saw Soong blush. I know I heard him curse us under his breath.

That broke the tension and we waited quietly. Each of us had a grenade in hand. I was to throw mine first — as soon as the Japs entered the fuel-soaked building. At the rear of the shed, Lok was poised with another grenade.

An hour later, we heard the thuds of many feet and then heavy panting. Chan said: "That must be Jap with chair coolie."

Four hard-breathing Chinese toiled down the street. They were bearing bamboo chairs filled by two men. The passengers were dressed in Chinese gowns, but they sang Japanese songs.

They sounded a little drunk. When they were lowered to the ground, they arose teetering, and I realized they were very drunk.

They staggered to their front door. One of them kicked it open and walked in.

The other hesitated. Had he smelled gasoline? I doubted that he could smell anything beyond his own breath. But I decided to wait no longer. I unscrewed the safety cap of my grenade and slipped my finger through the little ring. I was about to pull the pin when I saw *why* the Jap was hesitating in the doorway.

He was about to light a cigarette!

"Let's get out of here!" I told Chan and Soong.

We sprang past the four startled coolies and told them to run. We had traveled only forty feet when a deafening blast threw us to the earth.

We could see gas belching out the front door of the house. Then a ball of fire shot skyward as the roof blew off.

No sooner had we regained our feet then we were knocked down again. Another explosion destroyed the rear shed. Lok had done his work.

He caught up with us a few minutes later. We could still hear the popping sound of small arms ammunition exploding in the shed. We congratulated ourselves on a good day's sabotage and tried not to think of the inevitable reprisals.

On the outskirts of town, I saw Lok gazing wide-eyed at something in my hand. I was still holding my grenade.

It was a German "potato masher." The safety cap was removed from the handle of the grenade and the ring attached to the primer cord was around my little finger. I tossed it into the field, thinking, "what a hell of a waste."

Chan laughed. He gazed one last time at the fiery landscape behind us. Then he murmured to me: "What fool Japanese are? They set fire to self."

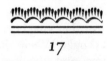

## 17

## Mistaken Identity

WE reached camp early next morning. To our surprise, nobody had tampered with our eels. The guerrillas had saved them for a feast of welcome when and if we returned.

Having dined so well in the village, we weren't overjoyed to see the slimy eels being distributed. But, in the interests of diplomacy, we didn't mention our dinner in town as we recounted our adventure.

The men lit a fire and we dried our clothes.

Shortly before noon, the feast began. It was a do-it-yourself banquet at which each man cooked his own meal. Simply by doing everything Chan did, I compiled this recipe for future use:

ALFRESCO EELS À LA CHINOISE
Cut eels into two-inch sections and place in a cast iron cooking bowl. Mix with finely sliced red hot peppers, mushrooms, onion grass, and frogs. Dice and grate grass and various green

rice shoots. Boil in water for an hour. Serve on heaping bowl of rice.

If it doesn't agree with you, feel free to season to taste, as the cookbooks say.

After dinner, Lieutenant Kui remarked: "We were not idle while you were away." He led us to two graves. They were the last resting place of the unarmed coolie spies our men had captured and questioned.

Anticipating frenzied activity by Japs and treacherous Chinese guerrillas as a result of our sabotage, Chan announced next morning that we would head back toward the China coast. The heaviest Jap concentrations were there. But at least they wouldn't be looking for us.

The men cheered. Food and our foray into the village had restored their morale. They were ready to lick Japs rather than each other.

On the morning we moved out, I arose ahead of Chan. My leader was snoring contentedly on the ground. I kicked him in the behind just the way I had in our mining days.

Chan rolled over, clutching his rear. He rose to his feet with offended dignity, stretched himself slowly, and did his five-minute ritual of ancient calisthenics before asking me: "Why hell you kick me, Gil?"

"God damn it, Chan. My beard is three days old. It's almost as long as my hair."

"Oh, yes," Chan said apologetically. On days when we began long journeys, he shaved me.

This had become a ceremony, which our entire guerrilla force attended religiously. It was better than theatre for suspense and comedy. Speaking in Chinese, Chan would curse me as a white devil and offer to cut my throat while he smiled benignly at me. Every now and then, I was sure he had made good his threat. My face often bled profusely from Chan's close shaves. But everybody insisted that he shave me from ear to ear.

As word spread through the camp, the men arose and gathered round. They encouraged me while I soaked my face with hot water and rubbed Chinese washing soap into my beard.

[ 175 ]

Chan came at me with a home-made razor. Its open blade was two inches long and an inch wide. The soap on my face proved as useful as a bandage at a beheading. Chan dragged and hacked at my whiskers until tears came to my eyes. When the audience inhaled as one man, I knew Chan had drawn first blood.

As we neared the coast, the land grew rich before our eyes. Eels and snakes became staples rather than delicacies. Sometimes we dined on wild duck, rabbit, and quail. There was an abundance of rice birds, about the size of sparrows. We plucked them and cooked them on a spit over hot coals. When crisp, they were eaten — head, bones, and all. From hawk to sparrow, any bird made good eating for guerrillas.

Dog was a special luxury. All our pet dogs had long since disappeared into hungry stomachs. But, near the coast, wild dogs and strays came our way.

The first dog I ate almost turned my stomach when I saw it on the barbecue rack. That night, however, I took a taste. It was delicious. I ate more — and then more. One of many lessons I learned in China was that a hungry man will eat even his favorite pet.

One afternoon, we met a farmer and his family going to market with their wares: pigs' intestines wrapped in paper and tied with string; baskets of vegetables and eggs, and home-made brown sugar. We saved the people a long journey by buying all they had.

That night, we camped at the foot of a hill near a small stream. We ate well.

It was my time to stand watch after dinner. I climbed the side of a hill above camp. I could see all approaches. Our campfire, too, was visible from above.

I could hear a high-pitched voice. One of our men was singing a song from a Chinese opera. He accompanied himself on a one-stringed instrument. From the rhythm, I knew it was a song of despair. Such songs usually tell of a man who has left his beloved to fight a war. But he will never return. Or, if he does return, his woman will have married another.

Deep in night's shadows, I thought of Nora. Standing watch on an unknown mountain, I knew I was serving myself, serving China, and serving Nora.

[ 176 ]

For five more nights, we marched toward the coast. Each day, we ate better than the day before.

The area was crawling with Japs, we knew. Nevertheless, Chan said he had good contacts here.

"How come?" I asked. "We're out of our territory now."

"Yes," Chan conceded. "But you be disappointed, Gil, if you see map."

"Disappointed, hell! So long as I'm deep in the bowels of China, I'm where I want to be."

"You only sixty mile from Hong Kong Mines."

I laughed. Chan had made his contacts here while working for me in the mines.

That night, we pitched camp in the saddle of a mountain range. No trails led to where we were. Our camp covered twenty acres. Water seeped out of the ground to form a small stream halfway down one mountain.

It is amazing what a habitable abode man can forge with what nature provides. We built walls four feet high with stones and rocks. We covered them with underbrush and saplings. We cut sod and placed it like tile over the saplings to form a roof. We covered our floor with grass.

Now we had a home away from the wet ground and the cold wind. And now Chan was ready to leave it.

"You stay, Gil," he said. "I take three men and go village near here. I know headman. He have radio. I tell cousin we here. He tell what to do."

Chan left me in command of the camp. I kept the men busy cleaning their equipment; fighting hand-to-hand combat with each other; and holding shooting matches with empty weapons. I was the referee in the matches. I graded the men on their aim and their technique in "firing" the guns. We called this "dry squeezing."

On the fifth afternoon, Chan returned. His cousin, Major Chan, had ordered us to an area thirty miles closer to the border between China and the British New Territories. Many Japs were there, so various guerrilla groups were converging. We were to hook up with any other guerrilla units that proved trustworthy.

If all went well, there would be dead Japs and loot for all.

We marched only at night. Usually, there was enough moonlight. Occasionally, however, a cloud would smother the moon while we made our way across a rice paddy. Then there would be curses.

Otherwise, nobody talked. Except for an infrequent grunt and the patter of feet, nobody made a sound that could be heard more than a hundred feet away.

One daybreak found us high in the mountains. Before pitching camp, we dispatched a lookout to the top of our mountain to see if all was clear. We sat beside our baskets and waited for word from him.

The man reached the top, took one look, and shouted down to us. Chan and I struggled up the steep slope to join him.

He didn't wait for us. Instead, he clambered downward. In his haste, he almost tumbled off the mountain.

He reported Chinese guerrillas down below. They were marching coastward and in the same general direction that we were headed. Chan and I scrambled up to see for ourselves.

The other side of the mountain dropped almost straight down for two hundred feet. Then it sloped off unevenly until it formed a wedge with the foot of a smaller mountain. In the small gap between mountains, a group of thirty Chinese guerrillas, all well armed, were making their way around the smaller mountain. They were marching in close order. They looked as if they were in a hurry.

"Either they're running from or running after something," I observed. "Do you recognize them, Chan?"

"No. Until find who they are, we no show self."

"It would take us most of a day to get down to them," I said, eying the sharp drop below us.

We watched the morning fog lift from the valley to our east. And then we saw why the Chinese guerrillas had been traveling so rapidly. Snaking along the winding trail came the enemy: a large Japanese pack train with strong infantry support.

"Now we can be pretty sure those guerrillas are on our side," I said.

"Yes. They run from Jap. Or else they hurry ahead to ambush Jap."

"They're damn fools if they do," I said. "The Japs outnumber them ten to one. And the Japs are so close that there won't be enough time to plant an ambush."

"There damn fools in guerrillas, too," Chan assured me.

At the sight of the enemy, my heart began to pound. More Japs passed before my eyes that morning than in all my weeks in China.

When they were directly below, I could see them clearly. Some of the men and all of the officers were mounted on low-slung Mongolian ponies. The Japs' feet almost touched the ground.

Foot soldiers followed. They led pack ponies burdened with small artillery, mortars, machine guns, food, and ammunition. Then came platoon after platoon of armed infantry.

The Japs looked comical in their baggy little britches, thick puttees, and boots — all of which made them waddle. Their heads were hidden beneath thick helmets protecting them like turtles' shells. Their rifles were almost as long as the Japs were tall. From a distance, they looked like children playing at being men.

I knew, however, that within each small frame was stored a dynamo of energy and a fanatical brain, both entirely geared for battle. Once triggered into combat, nothing except death stopped a Jap infantryman.

Chan was staring at me rather than at the Japs. I realized that, unconsciously, I had assumed a posture of prayer.

"You believe God, Gil?" Chan asked me.

I answered thoughtfully: "When you kill and have the power to take away life, you have to feel that what you are doing is right. But you can't always. You need someone to turn to for advice, security, help, and even forgiveness. I'm not positive I believe in God. But I need God."

"You know all this before you come China?" Chan asked me as he focused his binoculars on the Japs below.

"No," I said.

A few hundred feet behind the main procession of Japs came some fifty Chinese coolies, burdened with loads as heavy as those borne by the horses. Some of the coolies were tied together by a long rope around their waists. It spaced them ten to twenty feet apart.

Every now and then, the Japanese guards would jab a coolie with a rifle butt to speed him up. The impact would throw the coolie off balance. Two or three other coolies would be dragged down with him. The guards would slap them back into line.

Two hundred feet behind the coolies came a rear guard of a few mounted officers and foot soldiers.

[ 179 ]

Peering through our binoculars, we witnessed an unusual delay.

In the rear guard, an officer's horse stumbled and then collapsed in a heap. Its rider was thrown to earth. He quickly regained his feet. The horse, too, tried agonizingly to scramble back up. But it could not make it.

The entire column halted. Other officers dismounted and gathered around the fallen horse. An officer, probably a doctor, came racing back from the advance party. He examined the horse's legs and found one to be broken.

The doctor conferred with the horse's rider. Then the others removed the fallen horse's saddle and bridle. The rider took out his handkerchief and blindfolded his horse. He stood a few feet from its head.

A dozen officers formed a circle around the horse. Upon a command, they all snapped to attention and saluted. For a full minute, they stood solemnly paying respects to an injured horse.

A report echoed up the mountainside. The rider stood with a revolver dangling from his hand. The horse died without making another move.

The guards slapped the Chinese coolies into action. With shovels, the coolies dug a big hole beside the dead horse. The animal was rolled in and covered with dirt. The coolies were slapped back into line. The column got under way again.

"The Japs are harder on man than beast," I remarked to Chan.

"No matter," said my favorite Oriental philosopher. "We get down there tonight and feast on barbecue horse steak."

The next day, we took a shortcut toward the coast. At midday, one of our scouts came racing back toward us. Up ahead — near where our shortcut rejoined the main trail — the Chinese guerrillas we had seen yesterday were lying in ambush.

"Where are the Japs?" I asked.

The scout said he didn't know. Our position commanded only a partial view of the winding trail. The other guerrillas had a much better view.

We crept forward for a mile and a half. Chan halted us when we could see the other guerrillas ahead.

"They damn fool," Chan said. "Leave self open for attack from rear. They all bunched together. You and I and five men could wipe them out, Gil."

"So what do we do now?"

"We no help them. They deserve die. If we help, lose our lives and theirs."

"Then let's get the hell out of here."

As I spoke, the advance guard of the Jap column swerved into view. We were trapped by the other guerrillas' folly. Their ambush was on!

As Chan had surmised, the others were classic blunderers. They made almost every mistake in the book. They opened fire while the advance guard was still parallel to them. At best, they would have wiped out the advance guard. The rest of the Jap column was sure to catch up with them.

These guerrillas were poor shots and too far from their target to do much damage. Only a few Japs dropped.

We wasted no more time counting mistakes, but ran back the way we had come. The Japs would be closing in on the ambush site within a few minutes.

We had not traveled far before Jap machine guns started to chatter and then mortars boomed. In between, rifles beat a steady tattoo.

Still on the run, Chan told me: "I take chance. We cross trail half mile from here."

"But we'll be out in the open," I said, panting.

"Yes, but cross now. Within hour, Jap seal off this side of trail. I know how operate after ambush. Much safer on other side — if we get there.

It was a gamble that seemed to pay off. We crossed the trail just behind the Japanese main column and a few hundred feet before the rear echelons.

We were a hundred feet into the safety of a gully between two small hills when a Japanese patrol blundered onto us.

It was a fatal accident. These Japs were not with the infantry column. They were locally garrisoned. Out on a routine patrol, they had heard the noise and come out to help out. They opened fire from above.

We dived for the underbrush. Under ordinary circumstances, we could have evaded them or perhaps wiped them out. Their fire, however, was heard by the main Japanese column.

[ 181 ]

To my dying day, I will curse the memory of those inept guerrillas and their ill-starred ambush. The barrage of Japanese fury they unleashed was turned not on them, but on us. They escaped, virtually unscathed. As mistake compounded mistake, the final joke was played to death. The inept guerrillas had ambushed the Japanese. Neither side won. But we, the innocent bystanders, were the principal victims.

A mortar shell burst sixty feet to our left. Machine-gun fire raked us from right and left. At least half our men toppled in the first splash of bullets. As I crawled for cover, bullets traced my path and marked out my future. Living only in the present, I groped my way into thicker bush. Chan, two other men, and a hail of bullets followed me.

We lay still until the ground shook as mortars exploded nearby. We were showered with dirt and torn bushes. Even when the firing stopped, I could hear no sounds except a ringing in my ears. The mortars had been deafening.

My mouth and nose and eyes were filled with dirt — as if I had been buried alive. I felt more buried than alive. But then my eyes cleared and I could see smooth sky above me. I was alive!

Before the mortar bursts, I had been lying face down. Now I was on my back. The impact had flipped me over like a penny.

My hands roamed my body. I was intact.

Chan was twenty feet away, covered with debris. His eyes were open. They were fixed straight ahead. His automatic was propped up against his shoulder. There were no wounds. But there was no motion.

"Chan?" I whispered fearfully, knowing only that death hovered nearby.

Then I could have shouted for joy! Chan's eyes gave me a warning flicker. Without his moving another part of the body, his alertness told me he was unhurt. And his eyes beckoned me toward the clearing we had just crossed. I rolled over onto my stomach and looked.

The clearing was the last battlefield of our guerrilla comrades. Dead and mangled bodies dotted the grass. One man was no more than fifteen feet from me. His legs were gone from the knees down. Half his clothing had been blown right off his body. He and the others lay still.

Six Japs were advancing cautiously in our direction. They were still two hundred feet away. Two lugged a machine gun while four riflemen gave them cover.

Switching my Mauser to "full automatic" position, I glanced back over my shoulder. We could shoot it out with the Japs from here. If we ran or crawled a few feet, we would be safely out of sight in the underbrush. But we had better open fire on the Japs before they installed their machine gun.

Frantically, Chan signaled me and the other two men to hold our fire.

He was right. Only the first two Japs were good targets for a Mauser, which is a light caliber weapon. Its ideal range is thirty feet; maximum is a hundred feet.

We could kill the machine gunners, but the riflemen would get us.

As the four riflemen advanced, they pumped bullets into the dead and dying bodies of our men. I sweated as I watched the Japanese obliterate the rarest breed of men I have ever met. I tried to tell myself: *Let the Japs waste their bullets on dead men.*

A groan disturbed the sounds of businesslike carnage. It came from a part of the clearing near Chan's position. My eyes swiveled toward the sound. It was the voice of our once cheerful farm boy, Lok.

As we watched, one of Lok's legs twitched with pain. He was still alive.

But not for long. The nearest soldier took careful aim and fired twice. Lok's body rose in the air and came to earth forever.

Fury triggered a burst of gunfire from Chan's Mauser. The Jap who killed Lok fell dead a few feet from his victim. Not all the Japs were in range yet, but the die was cast.

I pointed my gun at the guts of the nearest Jap. Squeezing the trigger, I allowed for two bullets to find their mark. Without even looking to see the result, I fired into the next infantryman.

The two machine gunners dropped their burden and joined the one surviving infantryman in a hasty retreat.

We didn't pursue them. Four of us — Chan, myself, Soong, and a mild-mannered guerrilla named Muy — fled into the underbush. We traveled forty feet before Japanese rifle fire started up again.

The Japs were shooting wildly into the bushes. We pressed forward through the sloping gully. Thick bushes, about ten feet high, made it impossible to see ahead. I guided myself by the sounds of Chan, Soong, and Muy smashing their way forward.

Mortar shells exploded ahead of us. No weapon in the enemy's arsenal is more terrifying. Even when he is far behind, you feel as if he is waiting for you up ahead.

The others recoiled the way I did. But Chan ordered us to keep going. The enemy was firing blindly. If we stood still, we would remain within their range. If we kept going, we had a chance.

Eventually, the mortar shells were behind us and fading. As we fled, it sounded as if they — not us — were retreating.

We continued for another hour before rocky terrain made us rest near an old campfire. My sandals had been torn from my feet. One was missing. The other dangled from my ankle by a frail piece of hemp. Chan, Soong, and Muy were equally or more barefoot.

Chan . . . Soong . . . Muy . . . Me . . . Twenty-six guerrillas had dined on Japanese horsemeat last night. Today, shortly past lunchtime, only four of us were alive.

We all bled from cuts received during the dash through the bushes. Soong was also bleeding from his neck and shoulders. He had been hit by mortar shrapnel.

I asked Soong how he felt. He made a gesture so reassuring that I wondered if his afflictions were imaginary — figments of *my* imagination.

Then I realized Soong didn't even know he was hurt. Fear and shock had completely numbed his pain.

I pointed to his shoulder. Soong responded with the same baleful look he gave any man who teased him.

Chan said something to him in Chinese. Soong looked down at his left shoulder. At the sight of his own blood, his face drained of all color. He weakened with every thought that crossed his mind.

There was little we could do for him. We had dropped all our supplies in the first moment of battle. I still wore my moneybelt, so we would not starve. We could buy food if we found a farmer. But Soong might be beyond hunger by then.

As Chan and I exchanged shrugs, my youthful preparations for China came to Soong's rescue.

Hunting in the outback country of northern Australia ten years earlier, I had seen aborigines cover cuts and wounds with ashes, which halted bleeding.

I asked Chan and Muy to search for spider webs and wild tobacco leaves. I sifted chunks of debris from the powdered ash of the old campfire.

Muy gave me his undershirt. It was not very clean, but it was cleaner than mine. With it I wiped the gash in Soong's neck.

I covered the gash with a spider web. I sprinkled it with powdered ash a quarter of an inch thick. Placing a long clean tobacco leaf on top, I secured this makeshift compress with a bandage made from Muy's undershirt.

Soong's bleeding stopped at once.

I did the same for his left shoulder, which was not so badly hit as his neck.

For what must have been the first time in his life, Soong smiled.

This very serious man must have been saving his lone smile for a monumental occasion — such as being brought back from the dead. For the rest of the afternoon, he strode briskly and kept pace with the rest of us.

Toward nightfall, it began to rain. We were all thoroughly drenched. Muy had a hat, which he gave to Soong. But Soong lost it apparently when gazing up at the sky. As darkness closed in, the cold rain washed down Soong's head and neck. The bandage and ashes were saturated. Soong's neck wound bled again.

We could do nothing for him until we were under cover. Muy and I helped him along at a snail's pace. When we neared a cluster of houses, I told Chan: "We'll have to stay here whether it's safe or not."

Chan went forward to investigate. He returned five minutes later. All was clear.

Through an open door, I saw the flickering of a fire — warm, dry, inviting. As soon as I entered, I sat down as close to the blaze as I could without catching fire myself. Soon, steam rose from my wet clothes. My bare feet, numb with cold, smarted and stung as they thawed.

I stared into the fire and thought no thoughts at all. Someone added more fuel. A bundle of twigs and grass erupted in flame. More charcoal was added. The smoke drifted toward me. It curled my wet clothes, filled my eyes with tears, and seeped down my nose until I thought my lungs would burst. All the opium in China could never grant the searing relief of a warm fire at the right moment.

The firelight brightened a drab room crowded with people. On one side of the fire lay the wounded Soong. He rested on his side and gazed into the fire. Occasionally, his lips twitched with a spasm of pain. A vibrating groan or a mournful chant would emerge.

Chan and Muy sat with a dozen farmers, bemoaning the whims of Buddha that made patriots into hunted men in their own land. Several women were preparing food. One of them had started a second fire — in a little mud stove at the corner of the room. She was heating rice in an enormous cast iron saucepan.

In the center of a table burned a small saucer of oil. A wick, about the size of a match, sprouted over the saucer's side. It burned with a yellow glow. Two farmers huddled close to it as they rolled four cigarettes from coarse paper and fine-cut tobacco.

Ceremoniously, they handed the four home-made cigarettes to Chan. He gave one to me and one to Muy. He took one for himself. We lit them from the burning wick. Chan also lit the fourth cigarette. He stooped over Soong and inserted it between trembling lips.

An old man distributed rice bowls and filled them with wine from a dirty earthenware bottle that had once been white. A younger man, who was our host, lifted his bowl of wine and said: "*Kan-pei!*" This, I knew, was the Chinese way of saying "bottoms up."

I took one large gulp. It was vile stuff. The firewater raced down my throat and into my empty stomach like a torpedo. After fifteen seconds, I emitted a gasp that I made no effort to stifle. I wanted to hear for myself that I was still living.

I smiled wanly at my anxious host and then took my half-filled bowl of wine to the wounded Soong. I placed one hand under his head. Taking the cigarette from his lips, I poured the rest of my wine down his mouth. He gasped as I had. But, after a minute, he began to enjoy it. When he had finished, I stuck the cigarette back between his lips. With my eyes, I apologized for using him as a potted palm for liquor disposal. He didn't seem to mind.

Chan came over with the bottle. Impishly, he offered me a refill.

"God damn it, no!" I whispered desperately. "Soong just saved *my* life. Now let me live to save his."

"After we eat," Chan said, "we go other house for night."

[ 186 ]

"Good," I said. "While we're here, see that he swallows some good hot soup. And then, if you can get it, a pipe of opium. That's the best anesthetic around."

"You have time to work without interrupt. Jap patrol through here today. Ask about us. They back tomorrow. We be gone then."

The ladies were dropping eggs and small Cantonese sausages into a frying pan sizzling with lard. I sat back and watched our hosts fuss over every detail. They were investing the whole village's rations for two weeks in just one supper for us.

It was not a time to enjoy life, but, for an hour or two, I did. Never in my life have I felt more at home than that night in an unknown, unremembered Chinese village.

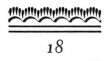

## 18

## In My Own Tomb

I CLEANED Soong's wounds and removed shrapnel fragments from his neck. The next morning, he was on the road to recovery. Although his face was pale and his wounds hurt more than ever, he was eager to start moving as we said our farewells to our hosts in the early dawn. And, when we did move on, he kept forging ahead of us.

Soong had always been an impatient man. Now that he was fighting for his life, he was eager to go where permanent repairs were possible. We took him to a friendly village where Chan made radio contact with his cousin.

Major Chan had already received news of the ill-fated ambush. He had been told there were no survivors at all. We were being mourned at his headquarters, hundreds of miles north, when his radio operator informed him that he had made contact with our "ghosts."

After expressing his jubilation at the latest miracle, Major Chan instructed the head man of the village to nurse Soong back to perfect health. Muy, Chan, and I were dispatched to our original destination near the New Territories.

It took us a week to go a hundred miles. At least twice a day, we barely avoided a Jap patrol or garrison. At last, we reached the rendezvous point — only to find that the three of us were the only guerrillas in town.

"Fifty others were here three days ago, but the Japanese made it so uncomfortable that they went away," the first villager we met told us. We were hungry. The man recommended a coolie restaurant in town. Its food was not special, but its location was off the main street.

A Japanese flag flew from a staff on the highest hill in the village. Its unmolested serenity was ample proof that the Japs had a strong grip in town. Usually, Chinese villagers tore down — or at least damaged — Japanese flags overnight.

We knew that the Japs were hunting high and low for armed men. To throw them off the trail, we hid our guns in a wood pile alongside the restaurant.

The restaurant was a two-story building of mud brick and wood. It had a sunken first floor. Customers stepped down off the street to enter.

The owner lived and worked there. The place had only a few tables and no customers. Two children were playing on the dirt floor. An old woman toiled over a stove that belched clouds of smoke.

Once upon a time, the walls had been white. Now they were covered with soot and stained by water. In a corner of the room was a bed. At one end, a well-worn bolster was propped up at just the right height for an opium smoker. The room smelled strongly of opium.

There was another room in back, which I could not see. A nervous little man emerged from it and showed us to a table. He had a smile that flashed on and off with each lilt of his singsong voice.

Chan asked if he could feed us.

The man glanced at the woman. She said yes, that's what a restaurant is for.

But another female voice — from the back room — said no.

The man hesitated. Then he cast the deciding vote: yes.

Good, said Chan. We would have some noodles.

The man looked to the old woman. She said there were enough noodles.

[ 188 ]

From the back room, however, the woman's voice called out shrilly: There were no noodles.

The man hesitated.

"They ought to get together and decide," I murmured to Chan.

Chan said nothing. He shoved the man aside and entered the back room. A minute later, he emerged — followed by two women and two young men.

"I guess right," Chan explained. "They not have enough food. Just enough to cook for self. But still a restaurant. They lose face when no have food or money to buy."

Chan turned to the little man who had welcomed us. Handing him a bill, Chan told him to go out and buy some food for us.

The man was a stranger to money. He had not seen it for so many months that he stared at it in a trance. To him it was a precious antique.

The old lady made a quicker recovery. She cursed the little man for lingering. He darted out, but her torrent of abuse continued unabated as she went about her chores. Finally, she brought us some hot water to drink. She apologized for being all out of tea.

One of the younger women sat down with us. I recognized her voice as the high-pitched one from the back room. She apologized for the "stupid confusion" about feeding us. She promised that the little man, who was her husband, would prepare his best meal for us when he returned.

We talked for half an hour, which should have been time for several shopping tours of the entire town. The little man's family grew nervous, too. After a while, we abandoned all efforts at conversation.

Fifteen silent minutes passed.

Protesting voices and clattering feet ended the silence. The old woman went to the door. She shielded her eyes with her hands and peered up the street. After a minute, she stiffened.

Without a word, she picked up the children, who were still playing in the dirt, and carried them to the back room.

I ran to the door. Five houses away, a patrol of Japs was kicking open doors.

Around the corner came the little man. He was running. Behind him came two Japs, running with rifles pointed forward.

"Japs!" I shouted.

Chan and Muy rose, knocking over the table. There seemed to be no time to retrieve our weapons, but Muy said he would try. He darted out the back door.

Chan seized a table leg and ripped it off. I ran to the stove. I needed something solid to use as a weapon. The best I could find was a saucepan with boiling water. I took it to one side of the door. Chan stood at the other side.

Seconds later, the little man came flying through the entranceway and into the back.

The two Japs followed. I hurled my boiling water at the first Jap. It missed, but it hit the second Jap full in the face. Chan clubbed the first Jap.

Both soldiers dropped their rifles. Mine was still clutching his scalded face as I retrieved his gun and thrust his own bayonet low into his guts. Withdrawing it, I smashed his head with the butt of his rifle. He joined Chan's Jap on the dirt floor. Chan's victim had died of a bayonet thrust through the head.

The search party reached our house. Chan and I made a dive through the rear door just as the first shots were fired into the front room. We left the house through the rear and entered a house that had already been searched. The house was dark, but it had a familiar smell. Even though the odor was repulsive, its vague familiarity seemed comforting.

"Do you think that little bastard informed on us?" I asked Chan.

"No really," he whispered. "He only tell on us when he hear Japs searching every house on block."

"Then he *did* inform on us."

"He have to protect family. Way he do it, maybe it work."

"For him, not for us," I said.

We were beginning to see our way around the dark room we were in.

On the floor was a human body, partially covered with a white cloth. It was spattered with blood and crawling with flies.

In the center of the room was a large low table. A naked corpse reposed on it. The corpse was almost intact. Around the ears, however, it seemed to have become a skeleton. As we leaned closer, two rats leaped from the table to the floor. One of them still had flesh in its mouth.

"We come to village undertaker," Chan said with a nervous cackle. "Hope not prophetic."

"If I have to die," I said, "I'll let the competition make my funeral arrangements."

We could hear Japanese voices coming from the street and the back alley. We worked our way into the front room, where a huge rack ran the entire length. Inexpensive coffins — made of thin boards and obviously for coolies — were stacked on the floor below the rack. Resting atop the rack were old, expensive, black-and-yellow wood coffins.

"If we've got to go, let's go first class," I told Chan.

Without another word, we climbed onto the expensive coffins. They were arrayed four deep. Sliding over them to the back row, we each selected a coffin with the same care that some travelers give to choosing a hotel.

I pushed up a lid and slid into my coffin. The lid fell shut over me. Inside, the space was almost adequate and the odor of teakwood rather pleasant.

Minutes later, the clatter of military boots and the excited voices of Japanese were with us briefly. Apparently, the smells and sights in the back room did not encourage them to search thoroughly or linger long.

They were back several times that night. Their coffin inspections, however, were most perfunctory. They never opened more than the three of our coffins nearest them. They could hardly have wanted to find anything there.

In between searches, deathly silences started my ears ringing. My new home's musky air and pitch blackness made me feel as if I were falling.

It was easier to concentrate with my eyes closed. If I opened them, I either imagined that I saw light (which seemed to burn my eyes) or I saw the same dense blackness that I "saw" with eyes closed. Was I going blind? No, but I had to take my mind off darkness and silence.

My mind focused on the color blue. I thought of all the shades of blue I had known — the dark blue of a dress Nora once wore; the light blue of Margaret's eyes; the medium blue of my own; sky blue, ah! . . . As I remembered sky blue, I saw white clouds in a blue sky and I drifted off to sleep on one of them.

When I awoke, I was sane again. But I needed air. My temples were thumping.

I pushed at the thick wooden lid with my hands and knees. It lifted by half an inch.

Air rushed in and, with it, the smell of the dead rotting in the next room. Instantly, I heard the slamming of a door and the squeal of a dog. My hands, which could barely hold up the lid anyway, let go quietly.

My hands shook from the exertion. The lack of air became oppressive again.

I drew several bills from my money belt. With one massive effort, I lifted the lid again and jammed the bills under its edge.

There were no further noises of searching. Still, I could hear that we were not always alone. People were below. I could not afford to find out who they were.

Toward daybreak, I heard muffled noise. Perhaps the undertaker had come to work. I had never thought I would look forward to meeting him, but today I did.

I started to lift the lid when I heard a Japanese voice. Back I went. A more immediate crisis kept my mind off the enemy. My bladder was about to burst.

The minute I thought of the only real possibility, it happened. The relief brought me some comfort and a new worry: Was my coffin properly sealed?

It was. If the water had leaked out, it might have given away my bad manners, my hiding place, and my life.

I either fell asleep or fainted. Awakening again, I could not for the life of me remember where I was.

The darkness and smells of my own body were no clues. I had lost all sense of time. Saliva ran from a corner of my mouth. My chin was pressed onto my chest. My throat felt as if it were caught in a noose. I couldn't swallow.

"I'm either strangling or I'm already dead," I told myself.

The mention of death restored my senses. Not long after, I heard a slight thump and a scratching noise. I grew alert. Was Chan emerging? Or were the Japs closing in?

A few minutes passed like a lifetime. Then the lid of my coffin was lifted.

The room was dark again, for it was now the next night. The cool evening air felt like water splashing on my face. Two hands touched my shoulders and eased me up to a sitting position. Each movement made me groan in pain.

I sat there as Chan's two strong hands rubbed at my neck and shoulders for fifteen minutes.

When I had enough strength to climb down off the rack, I followed Chan. A light, but no sounds, could be detected in the rear room.

We pushed the curtain aside and slipped into the back. An oil lamp was burning on a portable altar beside a coffin. The gray ashes of burnt-out joss sticks rested in a small pewter bowl. And in the coffin was the body of the young woman from the restaurant — the wife of the little man who had gone out for our food and come back with the Japs.

"Poor thing," I murmured to Chan. "When the little man informed on us, he signed his wife's death warrant."

"He no 'inform' on us," Chan insisted stubbornly. "He do best he can to save family."

"And look what it got him," I said.

The corpses that had been in the room last night were gone. They had been replaced by the woman's body and another new corpse. The second body was on the table, where it lay unmourned. No joss sticks and no incense were beside it.

I lifted the white cover and looked into the mutilated face of our guerrilla comrade Muy.

His face was his only recognizable feature. His body was a sponge of bayonet thrusts. His stomach had been slit open. His bowels were missing.

I heard a retching sound beside me as Chan added to the filth of the occasion.

We tiptoed out of town in the evening shadows. Nobody noticed us. The whole village was mourning the dead woman.

[ 193 ]

We knew to ask no favors or assistance. I felt lucky to escape without being lynched.

Our route took us back to Shatowkok, where I had killed my first Japanese soldier. There, Chan broke the news to me that my career as a Chinese guerrilla was at an end for now.

"No other guerrilla group take you now, Gil," he informed me reluctantly. "They kill you in sleep first night you with them. Most guerrilla hate all foreigner, not just Jap. And, if I with you, they kill me, too." Now that my usefulness had come to an end, he added, it was better for both of us that he return alone in search of his cousin's guerrillas.

Thus did we part — both expressing vague confidences that fate, which had brought us together once, would do it again some day.

I watched Chan, a lone figure, walk slowly back in the direction whence the two of us had come. When he was out of sight, I turned around and walked out of China.

It was late summer, 1939. I left with mixed emotions. There was defeat: my guerrilla career had ended just five months after it had begun. There was "victory" of sorts: Out of thirty-two guerrillas, I was one of a handful of survivors.

I had witnessed courage, treachery, kindness, and brutality on all levels. "Good" and "evil" were no longer clear choices.

I had seen Chinese spying on other Chinese to betray them to the Japanese.

I had seen all my comrades wiped out by the well-meaning stupidity of other guerrillas fighting the same enemy.

I had brought grief and death to a poor Chinese family — and an eternity of regret to a widowed husband "protecting" his people.

I had killed a dozen Japs. Taking them by surprise, I had seen that they died like other men — humming tunes, telling jokes, coming home from a party.

I had seen Japs slaughter the amiable country boy, Lok, and bury a dead horse with solemn rites.

Many people I never met had died in reprisals for my every "success."

Above all, I had been blessed by on-the-job training with an iron breed of men: the professional bandit-guerrillas of China in the 1930's. If I learned my lessons, I might one day master their craft. If theirs was a doomed destiny, mine might be to relate their glories and their agonies to the civilized world one day. That became my new, long-range mission.

But first I had to use their wisdom in new ways — to win the victories they had died for. This was my old mission. And everything I had seen in those five months reaffirmed my childhood faith in the immortality of the Chinese cause.

III

# III

Burma Road

[ 1939–1942 ]

# III

## Burma Road
### [1939-1941]

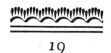

## 19

# Sunrise in Rangoon

NORA was no longer in Hong Kong. I made so many inquiries that her guerrilla contacts grew nervous. Mr. Lee, who had delivered me to China in his junk, appeared unexpectedly one day at the Parisienne Grill. He sat down at my table. While the refugee orchestra played "Vienna, City of My Dreams," Mr. Lee assured me that I would never see Nora again.

"Is she dead?" I asked.

"No, but she has gone back to Canton. She will work against the Japanese there," Mr. Lee confided. "If her new work is successful, then she will stay in Canton. If not, she will die a horrible death there. The Japanese must not even suspect she is there, so please do not call attention to her disappearance from Hong Kong."

I made no further inquiries, particularly because the British authorities in Hong Kong were looking into my own recent travels. On my final morning in Hong Kong, I received my last message from Nora. I went to the hotel in Kowloon to retrieve the luggage I had left behind when I joined Major Chan's guerrillas.

With the instructions to be followed if I should die, I had left a small bottle of perfume to console Nora. It was missing.

It had been replaced by a small silver container inscribed in Chinese: "To my kind-hearted tiger." Inside was a tiny tin of Tiger Balm, the guerrilla's all-purpose ointment.

I never learned Nora's fate, but I know that she left me laughing.

As my boat sailed out of Hong Kong that afternoon, I gazed down at each junk and sampan. I was looking for just one face.

My ultimate destination was the boom town of Rangoon, Burma. Rangoon was the gateway to the Burma Road, which had been opened to truck traffic a few months earlier. The Burma Road threaded its way from Lashio, Burma, to Kunming, the seat of Yunnan Province in China. From Lashio to Kunming by air is 260 miles. By road — winding down one treacherous mountain and then up the next — the distance is 700 miles.

Rangoon was the logical jumping-off place for any adventurer seeking legal entry to China. I arrived there after visiting Singapore, the Malay Peninsula, Kuala Lumpur, and Penang. Night had fallen when, in October, 1939, my ship steamed through the Bay of Bengal into the mouth of the Rangoon River.

I checked into the Strand Hotel and slept until three or four in the morning. The swirling noise of an electric fan made further sleep impossible, so I arose.

A large hotel at an early hour is as unreal as an abandoned city. The Strand in Rangoon was no exception. Three boys, on their knees, were cleaning and dusting the floor of a large reception hall. They eyed me as if I were a ghost, for white guests were seldom up and about before dawn.

I strolled past the main entrance and the terrace. I descended the steps into the black night of Rangoon. On the sidewalk, something brushed against my foot.

Glancing down, I could see nothing for a moment. Then I was touched again. It was the hand of a man squatting beside the steps. He was half-asleep. Being a beggar, however, he had his reflexes working overtime. His voice whined "sahib" over and over. I decided not to let him lose his fine edge of sleep. As I walked on, I wondered how long the Rangoon police would let him camp there.

I had no idea in which direction to turn. When I glimpsed a dim reflection of street lights to my right, I headed that way. Two blocks later, I made another right turn—and stopped with a jolt.

Dim street lamps cast down shafts of light illuminating a hideous spectacle.

The sidewalk was jammed with hundreds of sleeping people — mostly Indian. I had read in books of the "untouchables," reduced to this fate by a caste system and a population surplus. I had never envisoned this sea of people.

There were men and women of all ages — plus children, starting out life in the gutter with the sidewalk their horizon. Some of the adults may have worked as laborers from time to time, but most were beggars. All were without hope.

I stood contemplating naked poverty. Statistics assumed meaning before my eyes.

The first crack of dawn appeared. A few of the street sleepers stretched and adjusted the filthy rags that were their only clothes. They picked themselves free of lice, examined old scurvy scabs, and scratched new mosquito bites. The night was hot and airless. It reeked with stenches of betel nut and human bodies.

What unknown power had sucked the life out of these people's lungs and left them to rot on the streets of Rangoon? I started to walk among the sleepers, around them, and above them. Many who had seemed asleep were lying there with eyes wide open, staring up emptily as in death. Their eyes were mostly white. They must have glimpsed nothing but the horror that life on earth can be.

I felt half dead myself as I wormed my way through these living corpses. I had no business here, I told myself. These were the tenants of the Devil and I was intruding in their home. Sleep was their only privacy. I turned off the street as soon as I could.

I found myself on a main road flanked by shops and office buildings. Apparently, it was off limits to the street dwellers. There were no cars in sight. It was still dark. The only sounds were my own steps and the moaning of the street sleepers around every corner.

Suddenly, as though a switch had been thrown, the whole picture before me was transformed.

My eyes witnessed an explosion, although my ears heard no new sound and my body felt no impact. I was gazing in wonder at my first Burma sunrise.

The darkness belched forth into the blood-red fury of fire. The magnificent golden Shwe Dagon Pagoda materialized in the distance so instantaneously that it might have shot out of the earth. It pierced the dawn like a bolt of fire and light.

The sun was an angry sun. It ate into everything its rays touched. The street sleepers, now visible on every side street, became blood-soaked wretches in a hell on earth. Still plucking themselves free of lice, they now looked tormented by invisible demons. The sun moved on to the buildings, which began to look like walls of fire. In a few minutes, it was all over. The sunrise turned grayish brown, then gold-and-yellow. Another day had begun — my first in Rangoon.

I continued my stroll in a trance. That sunrise had been a religious experience. I felt more than human as I walked upon this sea of human misery. I could see colors within colors. I could see outsides and insides of buildings.

Most remarkably, the street sleepers no longer repelled me. I could see inside them. Deep within their bones, I perceived cleanliness, happiness, and contentment. I saw these wretches clad in rich garments and white silk turbans. I saw the future to which their sufferings entitled them. Perhaps I was merely seeing their dreams. Or my own for them.

I walked on. Nothing vanished from my mind; I simply absorbed more and more. The vivid colors possessed scents of flowers and sweet wood. I drifted up a flight of stone steps shaded by a canopy. It was just a steep hill, but I might have been ascending to heaven.

Buddha brought me back to earth.

No sooner had I emerged from the canopied stairway than a wet, clammy, and powerful hand grasped my wrist and whirled me about. Instinctively, I swung to strike my adversary. As I did, however, he relaxed his grip. When I saw who he was, I lowered my hand apologetically.

He was a Buddhist priest. A yellow gown hung loosely around his small, frail body. His shaved head glistened with sweat. Betel juice dribbled from a corner of his mouth. He chattered rapidly and jerked his head for emphasis.

When he broke the silence, he broke my spell. The colors of the day turned drab, decayed, and sinister. The foul smells enveloped me. I was not in heaven, but at the entrance to the pagoda I had seen in the sunrise.

The little priest was pleading with me to take off my shoes before I approached Buddha.

I removed my shoes and socks. The priest took them from me. He placed them in one of several neat rows of shoes and sandals. As I rolled up the cuffs of my white trousers, he came forward with head bent and both hands outstretched, palms upward. I touched each palm with an anna, worth approximately one and one half cents. The difference between priest and beggar seemed both large and small.

Climbing the stairs, I noticed clusters of chewed betel nut. Over the centuries, worshippers had spat carelessly upon the steps. But no shoes were allowed to defile them.

I was met at the top by four priests. "Do you wish to take a tour of our temple?" one of them asked me in English. I said yes and followed him.

Hundreds of little pagodas surrounded the base of the pagoda I had seen in the distance. My guide told me it was 368 feet high. It was covered with gold leaf from top to bottom.

Some of the smaller pagodas were brilliantly painted and exquisitely designed. The smell of burning incense was everywhere.

My guide led me into the temple. Monks and priests were at prayer. They sang and chanted to the tune of drums, gongs, and bells. A priest turned a prayer wheel, a large-scale version of the prayer stick I had shaken when praying with Chan. Others burned joss sticks.

I came out and wandered from one pagoda to another. I halted before a huge footprint — three feet long and a foot wide — imbedded in a rock.

"Whose foot was that?" I asked my guide.

"It is the footprint of Buddha," he replied, placing my right hand upon it. "You must make a wish. If it is also Buddha's wish, then it will come to pass."

"I was not prepared for this. I cannot think of a single thing to wish."

"Surely there is something you want. You must wish for it now."

I remembered that, while praying with Chan, I had wished only to stay in China. I was out of China now, but I anticipated little difficulty in getting back there in some useful capacity. I thought now of praying to serve the people of China.

My mind seemed empty of those few words. Perhaps it had been drained by the sunrise. After a long moment, however, my voice uttered a prayer that startled even me as I spoke the words:

"Then I wish I could understand."

When I finished my tour, the priest held out his hands the way the first priest had. This time, I crossed each palm with a rupee, which was worth approximately a U.S. quarter.

So generous was my gift that the priest insisted on extending my tour. He led me around the base of the main pagoda. We stopped before a tunnel-shaped entrance that was barred, locked, and chained with heavy steel.

One could, however, gaze down the tunnel. Walls and ceiling were lined with white tile. At the far end sat Buddha in all his glory. Before him, the tile floor was lined with money of all denominations: thousands upon thousands of rupees, more money than all the street sleepers of Rangoon would touch in their lives.

"You must throw some money in as far as you can," the priest said.

My generosity in tipping him was proving costly. I wadded several annas into a rupee bill and tossed it in. It landed at the feet of Buddha.

The priest smiled and led me to a glass building, which looked like a gigantic showcase — and really was. Inside was a crowded but neatly arranged display of gold, silver, precious gems, ivory tusks, ornate cups, and jade. Some of the gold bars were as thick as bricks.

Just seeing such riches and so much poverty in the same day gave me a splitting headache.

My guide said blithely: "All this is Buddha's. These are presents given to him by kings and queens and important people from all over the world for hundreds and hundreds of years."

One sliver of that gold would have kept a thousand street sleepers well fed for life. And yet, did the good fortune of Buddha perhaps offer a straw of comfort for those downtrodden masses on the sidewalks of Rangoon?

Rangoon was awake when I left the temple. The street sleepers had melted from sight like the invisible poor everywhere. Rangoon now resembled the flourishing frontier city I had envisioned.

I saw more trucks than cars. Most of the trucks were brand new. They were creating a hopeless traffic jam.

The worst snarls were near the docks, laden with cargo. Although trucks were loading around the clock, Lend-Lease aid from the

United States and commercial cargo bound for China were coming into Rangoon faster than they were moving out. Occasionally, a wooden pier would groan beneath the weight of hundreds of heavy crates. The docks appeared on the verge of collapse. I vowed to myself that, unlike freight, I would not sit around Rangoon waiting to be transported to China.

I wandered all day. When I returned to my hotel, it was cocktail time. Burma was still part of the British Commonwealth then. The bar and reception hall of the Strand seethed with English people, drinking their pink gin, gimlets, and Singapore gin slings. The Strand in Rangoon, I soon learned, made the best Singapore gin sling to be found anywhere, Singapore included. I drank a few, napped, bathed, and came down for dinner at 9:30 P.M.

The dining room was abuzz with Britons in evening attire. The waiters looked smart and clean in long white coats, dark red sashes, bandoliers, and white turbans trimmed with red and gold.

I ate lightly and wandered into the hotel bar for a drink. There I struck up a conversation with a Greek, who turned out to be the hotel manager.

He was more aware of the Burma Road than any Briton I had met that day. The British colony in Rangoon was so insulated that several members were not even sure there was a Burma Road.

The Greek told me: "So far, the Burma Road is not very successful. The problem is that too many trucks have accidents and robberies on the China side of the border. And the British and Burmese can get no help from the Chinese Government there."

He recommended that I seek out the owner of a night club around the corner, The Silver Grill: "He is an Englishman. A nice chap. If he likes you, he will do anything for you."

The door of the Silver Grill swung open as I approached. Inside was a lavish night spot crowded with British couples, formally dressed. The lighting was subdued, but I could perceive a small cleared space at the far end. It was used for dancing. To the side, a small orchestra was playing Noel Coward's "I'll See You Again." A girl singer slouched against the piano; I couldn't tell whether she was singing badly or just humming. I found an empty table near the band and ordered a drink.

[ 205 ]

A handsome man about twice my size, but well-proportioned, introduced himself to me as Paul Cunningham, the owner. I invited him to join me for a drink.

"No, thank you," he said, "but I would like to ask you some questions." He asked me how long I had been in Rangoon, whether I intended to stay, whom I knew in town, and what business I was in.

I answered tersely and then stood up: "I beg your pardon, but I came here for a drink, not a third degree."

"No offense, old chap," Cunningham said, still eying me warily. "I just like to check on new customers. Ever since this Burma Road opened, all types of foreigners have come into Rangoon. Some of them I do not permit in my club. You know the type, don't you? Too rough, y' know."

My interview was not progressing well at all. I noticed the waiter hovering with my drink, but he would not deliver it until Cunningham gave him the word.

I said curtly: "I hope I meet with your approval. I'm generally a rather peaceable type in public. But if you try to throw me out, then you'll discover the real *me*. I can get pretty rough when I'm insulted."

Cunningham laughed and said: "D'y' know, Mr. Stuart, I think I *will* have that drink with you after all." He signaled the waiter, who served my drink.

"I'm not sure the offer still stands. I made it in the expectation of reasonable courtesy . . ."

"Then it's on the house and I apologize. You see, I . . . well, I thought you were an American."

"That's not the worst crime in the world," I said, "but what gave you that impression?"

"Because you offered to buy me a drink," Cunningham replied sheepishly.

I asked him what he had against Americans.

"Had a couple of them in here last week," Cunningham said ruefully. "Not only weren't they properly dressed, but one of them wasn't even wearing a tie. Just as soon as they entered, I asked them to leave."

"And did they?"

"Not without a terrible fuss. But I refused to serve them, so they had no alternative. They came back on the next night dressed properly."

As I gazed at Cunningham, I marveled at the chasm of misunderstanding among people who spoke the same language. I wondered if my feelings about Japs were any more rational than his about Yanks. I recalled my prayer — "*I wish I could understand*" — and then I changed the subject.

"Who's running the show on the Burma Road?" I asked.

"Mostly the Chinese Government," he said. "A few British and Burmese concerns. They seem to be the ones that run into the most trouble."

"Do any British people actually ride trucks on the road, Paul? I haven't seen one today who looks as if he could survive an hour on the Burma Road."

"There are two, perhaps three, white men who travel with the convoys occasionally. But they're rare. You can't get anyone but Chinese to go out on that road. A good many Chinese go there with a truck and then you never hear of them or your truck again."

"Well, then, would you let it be known that there's a white man who's ready, willing, eager, and able to go out on the Burma Road?"

"It's at your own risk, Mr. Stuart," Cunningham said, but he agreed that he would mention my name. He also gave me some names if I wished to apply.

The few lights in the Silver Grill went out. Colored spotlights went on to illuminate the dance floor. Nobody stood up to dance, however. Every chair turned to face the floor.

The band played a sinuous Hawaiian melody as a girl made her way through the darkness to the center of the dance floor.

She was tall. Dark, wavy hair rippled about her shoulders and framed a lovely face that was delicate ivory. Her eyes flashed beyond the lights and right into a man's heart. She became Nora, Margaret, and every woman for whom I had ever yearned.

Her arms and hands did most of her dancing. They moved with the music and quivered with its rhythm. Her motions excited the music to beauty and shadings it had never before possessed.

I was on fire and, at that moment, there was nothing I would not have done for her love. My eyes wandered over her body, virtually still beneath a tight shimmering dress. All her eloquence was in

[ 207 ]

her hands. Her body stood there as a beautiful but distant shrine.

Cunningham must have sensed my reaction, for he murmured, "She dances rather well, don't y' think?"

"Oh, she could do anything well," I asserted. "Anything!"

"There goes the wicked mind at work again," Cunningham said with an edgy laugh. "Are you sure you're an Australian, Mr. Stuart?"

"Born in England and bred in Australia. I ought to know," I assured him. "But tell me about this dancer. Has she been here long?"

"Off and on. She is from India."

"What's her name?"

"Pauline," he replied. "At least, that's what she calls herself here. She's really a quite famous Indian film star — a serious actress. She comes here three months every year to sing and dance."

"That sounds peculiar. Can't she dance in India?"

"She could dance anywhere," he said proudly, "or act anywhere. But she comes here because she's in love with a man in Rangoon."

"Does he love her?"

"I think so," said Cunningham in a voice drained of emotion.

"Then why don't they get married? Or does he have a wife?"

"No, he doesn't," said Cunningham. "But he is a very stuffy young Englishman. He cannot bring himself to marry an Indian . . ."

I knew there was nothing I could say that Paul Cunningham had not told himself already.

He was silent for a minute or two. Then he stood up and said he had to look after his other customers: "I hope you'll come back often, Mr. Stuart."

"Call me Gil," I said.

He hesitated before clasping my hand and saying warmly: "Well, then, good night, Gilbert."

"All right," I said. "Call me Gilbert, if you must. You've met me halfway."

"Then Gilbert it will be," he said uneasily. "But I find it hard to believe you're Australian. You have a way about you . . ."

"Like an American," I said. "But people are pretty much the same the world over."

"Much the same," he repeated without any conviction at all.

I was reading a newspaper on the hotel terrace next morning

[ 208 ]

when I heard the hotel clerk coping with a middle-aged couple inquiring for "an American named Mr. Gilbert."

Sizing up the situation, I asked the couple: "Did Paul Cunningham send you?"

When they said yes, I introduced myself and assured them that Gilbert Stuart of Australia was the man they sought. My male caller was a tall, thin-featured, and lean English aristocrat. His wife was clearly a lady. Her eyes had a twinkle one didn't see among the pretenders and climbers of Rangoon's British colony.

"My name is Bill Crooks," the man said, "and this is, of course, my wife. We live in Shanghai. I am with Lidell Brothers there."

"Oh, yes. I've heard of them. Old British concern, I believe?"

"Old by British standards, perhaps, but not to the Chinese. We have been in Shanghai for some sixty years. Our business is import and export."

"What do you ship?" I asked.

"Mostly silk and other finery," Crooks replied.

"Also pigs' bristles," his wife added merrily.

"Well," I said, "that's certainly to your credit. They make the best brushes. But do you have a branch here in Rangoon?"

"That is what I've come to see you about, Mr. Gilb—, Mr. Stu—, well, may I call you Gil? We are in the process of establishing a Rangoon branch. The damn Japanese have cut off all communications up the Yangtze River to Chungking, where pigs' bristles come from. We have no way to ship our exports from the interior of China to Shanghai."

"So Rangoon becomes the nearest port of entry and exit," I said.

"We have decided to organize a trucking company on the Burma Road. We'll operate between here and Kunming at first. And then, if we survive, we'll try to get the consent of the Chinese Government to operate between Kunming and Chungking. We'll offer to transport military supplies into China if we can bring our products out."

"That sounds like an excellent solution," I said.

"It's no solution at all right now," Crooks told me. "It's a whole new series of problems. I have just begun to fight my way through Burmese and Chinese paperwork. Our truck parts are starting to arrive, but we haven't assembled them yet. And, even when we do, we won't have drivers. Every Chinese who can drive a truck has a job already. I came to you because Paul Cunningham thought you might have some advice . . ."

"I have more than advice, Mr. Crooks," I said, making my pitch. "I also have some operational experience with trucks. Most important of all, I have excellent knowledge of the Chinese and how they think. I'll train you a crew of Chinese truck drivers from scratch. The ones who don't know how to drive will make the best drivers; the others have learned too many wrong things. And then I'll make every trip into China with them myself."

Crooks stared at me cautiously. His British reserve asserted itself silently but visibly. Ten minutes earlier, we had been strangers. Now I was offering to solve all his problems.

The strained silence was growing stony when Mrs. Crooks unexpectedly patted her husband's arm and said: "Bill, it would be a splendid idea. This whole project is too much for any one man." She turned to me and said: "Mr. Stuart, I would be grateful to you if you could relieve my husband of these burdens, which aren't really his line of work at all."

Bill Crooks gave in: "It had never occurred to me to get assistance, Gil. But my wife's advice is always the best."

I could have hugged Mrs. Crooks, but, of course, I didn't.

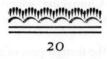

## 20

# The Burma Road

To drive a truck seemed to be the ambition of every Chinese — coolie or educated — in Rangoon around late 1939. It was a way to make money and gain face. Working for me had a guaranteed future, too: I promised to mold each trainee into both driver and mechanic.

This in itself was a drastic innovation. Other companies hired drivers who knew nothing about repairing their trucks. The men simply abandoned them if the slightest thing went wrong. Or, to save face, they "accidentally" damaged them beyond repair.

I recruited forty would-be drivers. If a man claimed experience on the Burma Road, I took him at his word — and rejected him. The "experienced" men had taught themselves driving on their first trips over the Burma Road. If they survived, they became greater menaces on subsequent journeys.

Bill Crooks had purchased ten trucks, all one-and-three-quarter-ton Dodges. But the bodies had to be built before the trucks could take to the road.

The men and I put the trucks together, which is the best way to get to know anything. Then my Chinese recruits would break the trucks in — by learning to drive them. My pupils were so able, quick, and eager that they posed no problem.

My major problem was as yet unseen: the Burma Road.

It has been said, repeatedly but not accurately, that the Burma Road was built by the United States Army Corps of Engineers and won by Errol Flynn. Whoever parrots this misinformation is confusing the Burma Road with the Ledo Road, an access road from the northwest. The Ledo Road ran some three hundred miles from Ledo, India, through jungle to Meiktila, Burma. It was indeed built by the U. S. Army Engineers with all their splendid equipment between 1942 and 1945.

The Burma Road, however, was built entirely by the Chinese in exactly one year — from November, 1937, to November, 1938.

It was carved by hand out of solid rock in the world's highest mountains, the Himalayas. It ran two hundred miles longer than the Ledo Road. No modern machinery was used, for the Chinese engineers had none.

Instead, hundreds of thousands of coolies were hired. They were not slave labor. Each man was paid for the work he produced on a contract — or piecework — basis.

Piecework it was. First, using hand drills and drill rods, they bored holes in the side of a mountain. Their hand drills were two to five feet long. One man held the drill in position while one or more others hammered the drill in. In this manner, they could sink a hole one or two feet deep in an hour.

As thousands of men did this tedious drilling, thousands of others filled their holes with black gunpowder. Then they blasted the rock. More thousands of coolies, bearing hoes and small baskets, scooped up the broken rock. It was used later on to surface the Burma Road.

The road they produced was narrow and dangerous. But it became the lifeline that linked a floundering China with aid from the outside world after Japan cut off all Chinese seaports. Later, it was widened.

The Ledo Road never was so successful as its publicists. It washed out in every wet season. Today, it is once more a jungle.

The Burma Road, however, is still an excellent and well-used road, although it is no superhighway. Ironically, it also endures in the public mind as a monument to "American knowhow."

By the time I reached Rangoon, the Burma Road had been open to traffic for less than a year. Its builders were still surfacing it and cutting down some of the steeper grades. On the China side, it was not always wide enough for two trucks. Every mile or two in such areas, a section of road was carved out to the width of two trucks. In between these safety zones were many fatal arguments over right-of-way.

Bridges on the Burma Road were not always there. When present, they could hold as much as six tons apiece, but they were very narrow. These restrictions limited traffic to light trucks.

Once you entered China, there were no filling stations until the end of the road in Kunming. Gasoline there sold for the outrageous price of three hundred American dollars per drum. Therefore, a considerable portion of our incoming cargo was excess fuel needed to make the round trip from Rangoon, where it sold for a tiny fraction of the Kunming price.

With these considerations in mind, Bill Crooks, the men, and I made our own alterations in the design of the Dodge trucks. We riveted quarter-inch steel fishplates along the full length of the frame. We added two extra leaves to each spring. Thus, we had more space and strength for cargo. Our one-and-three-quarter-ton trucks were able to carry payloads of four tons apiece.

For each truck, we purchased spare parts: generators, starter motors, complete ignition assemblies, plugs, carburetors, brake linings, and springs. Whenever a truck broke down on the road, its defective part could be replaced immediately.

Lidell and Company rented space in the Renault garage at Kunming and set up a small supply depot. All broken parts brought in by our drivers would be repaired there and carried as spares.

Bill Crooks had been wise to buy Dodges. In Asia then, a Dodge sold for as much as three thousand dollars more than other brands. The Dodge truck was built just a little heavier with better, stronger steel. It did not shake apart on rough road, which is more than could be said for many famous makes at that time. Only International and GMC trucks compared with the Dodge. The others barely survived three round trips on the Burma Road.

No matter what brand of vehicle you had, however, you could seldom be sure what kind of parts were inside it. Chinese drivers — particularly those entrusted with Red Cross or Lend-Lease trucks — had a nasty habit of selling brand new engines en route. The price was cash plus a worn-out engine that would take the truck to its destination. If questioned, the driver would blame some honest official hundreds of miles away for the defective motor.

I had never thought of myself as a saint. I had lied, cheated, stolen, and killed. Even so, I was appalled by the corruption and opportunism I first heard of in Rangoon and later saw for myself on the Burma Road. Some of the people I met at Paul Cunningham's Silver Grill wore ties, washed behind their ears, and spoke in cultivated tones. Nevertheless, I had only to hear them making their fast cash and easy deals over cocktails to know that they were the scum of the earth — smugglers, black marketeers, and speculators.

I have never allowed myself to be called a "soldier of fortune." That label was discredited by these adventurers who came to Asia to make money out of chaos and distress.

I was no businessman, but I suspected that these mercenary types weren't either. True, they made twice the money in half the time. But few of them lived to spend it. Sooner or later, vultures and cutthroats prey on one another.

I had too little time to spare. I dared not waste a minute in struggling just to face myself in a mirror or sleep at night. Merely doing what everyone else was doing could never be sufficient rationalization. I was willing to stick a gun in a man's guts to convince him my way was the right way. But it was not the gun that would keep him persuaded; it was the belief behind it.

[ 213 ]

In China, I would be operating where there was hardly any law. What law existed was neither respected nor enforced. I would make my own laws, but they had to be simple ones of which I could feel sure. Otherwise, I would never be able to convey them to my truckers.

Old Biblical laws were the best. "An eye for an eye and a tooth for a tooth," was the first that I taught to Lidell and Company's new crew of drivers.

We would have nothing to hide.

We would do our best to help the defenseless along our route.

We would abide by laws of the land and, when in doubt, by laws of decency.

I could teach this morality to my men, but it would never stick unless I applied it to violators who crossed our path. I would force every Chinese on the road to help others, to cooperate, and to display the courtesy of his forefathers.

The traditional Chinese good manners had been forgotten in the frenzy of Westernization. What laws existed in Yunnan Province, along the Burma Road's route, had been designed for bygone cultures and ideologies. The one that was applied most often — and that has a Western equivalent — was embodied in a two-thousand-year-old Oriental proverb: "Possession is the strongest tenure of law."

Truck drivers, coolies, Army officers, and even Red Cross officials kept as much as they could put their hands on. Occasionally, Chinese military police were sent from Chungking to enforce the law. But not all of them came back. They were hopelessly outnumbered by legions of dishonest men.

The M.P.'s who did not retreat, wringing their hands, were either corrupted or murdered. They had no authority in communities where renegades were kings.

I sometimes found it impossible to believe that, before the Burma Road was opened to the West, the Chinese of Yunnan Province were simple, friendly people with few material demands on life. They depended on nature. The harder they worked, the more nature rewarded them. Stealing from a fellow man was virtually unknown; only hunger could provoke such a heinous deed.

I decided to use ancient Chinese means to achieve my own ends.

As in the Hong Kong Mines, I would have to be cruel to earn the right to be kind. The risk was entirely mine.

If I was wrong, I would certainly die.

If I was right, I might also die — but I would live and die with self-respect.

It would take time.

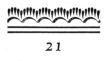

## 21

# On the Road to Mandalay

AFTER our trucks were assembled, I weeded out sixteen of my forty recruits. The two dozen I kept were the ones who had absorbed the most knowledge. The discards were not bitter; they had enough training to latch on elsewhere.

The survivors then began driving lessons. Their only difficulty was that they were all overeager to learn and, like children, they sometimes grew too excited to learn.

I trained two drivers for each truck. Each competed with the other. Eventually, one would be selected as first driver. He would be in charge of the truck on the road. The second would be his relief driver, lookout, guard, and mechanic.

As a campus for our driving lessons, I chose the lake area of Rangoon. Several good blacktop roads wound in and out of the lakeside park. After a few weeks, I took my men out on the highway and taught them how to travel in convoy, keep their spacing in traffic, and pass other trucks without killing anybody.

One noon, I was sitting under an electric fan in the Strand lobby. I was drinking my midday shandy (one part beer; one part lemonade; served ice cold in a quart crystal jug). A shandy must be drunk slowly in Rangoon's noonday heat. Otherwise, the cold beer can shock the system into stomach cramps.

Bill Crooks hurried in, ordered a pink gin, and asked me: "How soon can you leave, Gil? All our papers are in order. I'd like to see you get started before anyone can change his mind."

"Then we'll leave first thing tomorrow morning," I told him. "But don't tell the men we're going. Otherwise, they'll stay up late celebrating and won't be fit to drive."

All the trucks were loaded and gassed for morning practice, anyway. But practice was over now. By the time my truckers reached the Burma Road, which began many miles from Rangoon, they would no longer be novices.

Only the night watchman was at our truck compound when I arrived there in the morning. I inspected all the engines and made sure all cargo was well lashed.

At seven A.M., an hour ahead of the others, my brightest and best educated driver, Dong, came to work. He was wondering why I had summoned him early. When I told him he was to be my second-in-command, he heaved a sigh of relief.

Dong originally came from Shanghai. He was a university graduate who spoke excellent English and adequate Burmese. Since I still had not mastered the Chinese tongue, he would handle my routine dealings with twenty-two customs officials and tax collectors stationed along the Burma Road.

At eight A.M., I assembled the drivers; lectured them on all they had learned; and enumerated their do's and don'ts, which they chanted by heart. Then, almost as an afterthought, I told them to be packed and ready to go within an hour.

They wasted five valuable minutes jumping up and down. At nine-thirty, however, every man was sitting erect in his cab and waiting for me to give the word.

I would drive the lead truck, thereby setting the pace and controlling the speed. No truck was to pass the truck ahead of it. Nobody was to stop for any reason other than engine trouble or an order from me. Dong would ride in the last truck to make sure my orders were obeyed.

Our first stop would be the airport, twelve miles outside of Rangoon. After checking wheel bearings, engine temperature, and cargo, we would drive on — into more than a thousand miles of adventure.

Everybody was keyed up, but nobody more than I. I was on my way back into China.

The road to Mandalay was hard-topped and perfectly flat. If it was less poetic than Kipling's, it was perfect for breaking in green truck drivers. It took us two days to travel some four hundred miles from Rangoon to Mandalay in central Burma, for we stopped often to check our trucks and review our lessons.

As we approached Mandalay, I could see our first major obstacles — mountains to the north and east and the west. Built atop their peaks were tall white pagodas reflecting the late afternoon sun.

British police stopped us at a small bridge a mile from the city. They checked our papers and inspected our trucks rather briskly, asked me a few questions, and waved our convoy through.

We drove down a wide street shaded by high trees. I could glimpse bungalows, made of wood and sheet iron, perched on stilts behind the trees. There was nothing picturesque about them. Like all poverty, they were drab.

So, too, was the boarding house Dong found for us. And so was all of Mandalay. Though the road to Mandalay had been devoid of flying fishes, it was far more interesting than its legendary destination.

There was no external shred of romance, color, or Oriental splendor to be seen in all of Mandalay. It was flat, depressing, and dusty. If the buildings had ever possessed any style, it had decayed. I have always been adept at bringing my imagination to bear on historical landmarks, but Mandalay was beyond redemption.

The huge, walled fortress — once the palace of the Emperor of Mandalay — was the only visible relic of the past. Nothing was stirring within its dull brick wall guarded by a moat. Still, the gleaming rooftops that could be detected within appeared to be the only part of the city that wanted to go on living. But the palace's usefulness had been cut short by the twists of history and the uncertainty of men.

Early next morning, we left Mandalay the way we had come. We rejoined the main road, which rejects Mandalay and sweeps to the northeast. It climbs a wall of mountains until the city below is visible no longer. Then, for hundreds of miles, it writhes around treacherous mountains.

As we gained altitude, the air grew fresh and cool. A clean scent emanated from giant trees. Unlike the Irrawaddy Valley below, where the sun's intense heat suppresses all living things, life up here was blessed with just enough heat and ample rain.

There was no more time to admire the setting. Hairpin bends and steep grades tested the most experienced driver's mettle. Never before had my drivers declutched on a hill or changed from fourth gear to first.

In fact, never before had they been out of my watchful eye for so long. Occasionally, I would catch a glimpse of the truck behind me. Then I would lose it on a sharp, steep bend.

That night, when we arrived in Maymyo, forty miles from Mandalay and four thousand feet higher, my men had passed their first major test.

Maymyo's rich grasslands could grow almost anything. The fresh vegetables were cheap and abundant. The strawberries were the finest in Asia. Maymyo had cows, fat sheep, milk, cream, and quite a few Western businessmen. Maymyo was a white man's agricultural paradise — a bit of northern farm country set down in the tropics.

Beautiful homes were surrounded by well-kept lawns and giant trees. Shoppers bustled in and out of stores. We might have been reluctant to leave next morning if our next stop had not been Lashio, where the Burma Road officially began.

Lashio, like Rangoon six hundred miles away, was a frontier boom town. Lashio, however, was a mixed marriage — half-Asian, half-Western. In the Asian manner, irregular streets crisscrossed on hills and dead-ended mockingly. In between streets were buildings made of wood, sheet iron, and bamboo. They were built with only one concept: to fit into the tight little islands between makeshift streets.

The people of Lashio were decidedly Oriental — Chinese, Burmese, Indian, Malayan, and various mixtures.

What gave Lashio its Western flavor were the trucks. Hundreds of them were parked in every conceivable space and a few inconceivable ones — such as a hitherto well-kept lawn. Some trucks were brand new and looked it. Others, only a couple of months older, were ready for the junk heap. A few trips over the Burma Road had taken their toll.

All sorts of cargoes were being loaded, unloaded, smuggled, and stolen. Lashio was the railhead — the end of the line for freight coming by train from Rangoon. Anything or anyone ticketed for China had to take the Burma Road the rest of the way.

In Lashio, we gave the trucks a complete checkup and fulfilled the paperwork requirements of the Burmese Transportation Commission.

We had planned to spend three days there. We stayed four.

On the morning we were to leave, I discovered that every one of my drivers had turned smuggler.

Checking over cargo, I found fifty to a hundred pounds of unlisted freight in each truck.

I asked my assistant, Dong, what was going on. He replied blandly that this was a local custom known as "pidgin cargo." Everything from opium to bales of shirts could be sold at two thousand per cent profit if smuggled duty-free into China. Why, he even had some "pidgin" himself.

I had heard of "pidgin cargo," but I had also heard myself give my drivers innumerable lectures on honesty. They were all honorable men, but they did not consider "pidgin" smuggling dishonorable. It was a tradition. It was a prerogative of the rank of truck driver. If they did otherwise, they would lose face with the people back home.

All this was truth to them, but I knew that any discovery of "pidgin" incurred delays lasting hours or days at the customs stations. Sometimes, authorities confiscated whole trucks. Certainly, it would be disastrous to let this happen on my very first trip.

When I ordered all "pidgin" unloaded, I thought my men would mutiny. Even my reminders that they were being paid forty U.S. dollars a month, three times as much as other companies paid, fell on deaf ears. I pointed out that they were paid an additional ten dollars a month if they took good care of their trucks. Overburdening their vehicles with "pidgin" would jeopardize their bonus chances. Still, they eyed me with a distrust I had not felt since the Hong Kong Mines.

Only when they had obeyed me and their "pidgin" was stacked on the ground did I suggest an alternative:

"I realize that every driver on the Burma Road carries 'pidgin' and nothing I say will stop you for long. Therefore, if you must be smugglers, I will decide what you will smuggle. Henceforth, you will each give me twenty or thirty rupees before a trip. I will buy small things — atabrine tablets and aspirin — that you can conceal in your pockets."

It worked. For the rest of the day, they disposed of their "pidgin" in Lashio, gave me five or six dollars apiece, and entrusted me with buying their drugs.

I had a little secret that I never let them in on. At each customs station, I planned to (and did) make out a special customs form declaring their hidden cargo. I would pay duty on it myself and swear the customs men to secrecy. It was important that they not discover this "legitimate contraband" when they searched the trucks. It is not cash profit that lures the smuggler, but the thrill of thinking he is getting something for nothing.

The customs men would go back to work and chuckle over our drivers, who thought they were so crafty. The drivers would ride off cackling at the stupidity of customs men. My whole intrigue would create good will all around.

The next morning, I lined up the men in our truck compound, surrounded by the old pagodas of Lashio. The men were cheerful. Their trucks were clean of contraband.

I asked Dong what the men were saying.

"They were angry at first," he admitted. "They said you had no heart at all. Now they say you have a heart, but you are somehow not human . . ."

"*Tz'u-hsin Hu,*" I said. "Sort of a kind-hearted tiger?"

Dong looked at me with amazement. Once again, the name stuck.

Our first 116 miles on the Burma Road — from Lashio to Namhkam, the Burmese border town — were paved and uneventful. We arrived in Namhkam late that afternoon — too late to pass through customs, which closed early.

Namhkam was a one-street town situated on a hill. The hill sloped down to a small river that was the border line. A bridge crossed into China, but traffic was barred by the Burmese customs gate — a thin, guillotine-like structure that dropped from above.

From Namhkam, one could see the customs station across the bridge in the Chinese town of Wanting. China was a quarter of a mile distant, but a day away.

I was not the only impatient man in Namhkam. The town was jammed with trucks waiting to cross. Some had been stuck there for weeks. The drivers had showed up with improper papers. Now the men were waiting around — for further instructions, a change of heart, or the right man to bribe.

Other drivers had been caught with "pidgin." Still others were ensnared in the shifting politics of the Burma Road. Their companies were in disrepute. A few weeks earlier, the British had closed down their end of the Burma Road for several days in an argument with the Chinese Government. Now there were reprisals and harassment.

Fortunately, Lidell and Company had not been involved in the squabble. We were starting with a clean slate.

That night, I toured the town. The principal entertainment was opium-smoking. Opium dens were legal in Burma and illegal in China. Namhkam was the place for that precious last smoke. If you can conceive of smoking your last cigarette, you can well imagine the quiet desperation with which opium was smoked in Namhkam, Burma.

Tough-looking characters prowled Namhkam's only street. I had seen them before in every seaport and border town — weak-willed vagrants who will steal or kill if it's made easy enough for them. I took the precaution of rapping every one of them across the head.

During my wanderings, I also encountered two Anglo-Burmese customs officials dressed in white shirts, shorts, and peaked caps that are the uniform of British customs men in Asia. They invited me to their quarters for a drink.

"I'd be delighted," I said, "but I insist on providing the whiskey myself." From my truck, I produced four bottles I had set aside for this kind of social-business encounter.

I did not believe in paying bribes. A certain amount of public relations was necessary. I wanted to establish my position before they put any squeeze on me or detained me for days at the customs gate with devious hints.

During the evening, I made it clear that I paid no squeeze to anybody. I did, however, like to drink whiskey with men who appreciated good liquor.

On this basis, we became friends. During later trips, I supplied them with up-to-date books and magazines from Rangoon.

While we drank that first night in Namhkam, I confided that I had tricked my drivers into letting me handle their "pidgin" smuggling. We all had a good laugh. They assured me that they would never confiscate so much as an aspirin.

The next morning, we cleared Burmese customs in a matter of minutes. One of the customs men with whom I had been drinking lifted the canvas of one truck (mine), closed it, and sent me into China with a wink and a wave.

We crossed the bridge and stopped at the customs gate in Wanting, China. Customs officials and Chinese military police shared a building here.

As I had instructed my men, the convoy pulled up close together. All drivers stayed inside their cabs. The M.P.'s requested Dong and me to follow them inside. There, an M.P. officer said to me in English: "Your passport, please."

This took me by surprise. Passports were not much in demand in Asia then. Having been passportless during my previous foray into China, I had neglected to bring mine with me this time.

I was carrying a cheap detective novel in my pocket. With perfect aplomb, I handed it to the officer.

His aplomb was as good as mine. He opened the book upside down, thumbed through it attentively, stamped a blank page with a seal, and handed the book back to me. He was not very familiar with British passports or British mysteries. Apparently, "your passport, please" was his only link with the Occident.

I could hear Dong snicker behind me. I flashed him a warning look. He struggled to subside.

On my way out, one of the M.P.'s reached for the revolver slung under my arm. I slapped his hand and marched out the door.

With a manly roar and a cloud of dust, Lidell and Company's convoy was off from Wanting to Lungling. The distance was only a hundred miles. But I was sure our first life-or-death challenge would come before we were fifty miles into China.

Toward noon, the road began its treacherous climb. Endlessly, it twisted one way and then the other. The pavement became too narrow for two trucks. In between safety zones, one would have to pull over to the safe side to let another pass. But nobody ever did this if he could bluff the other fellow off the road.

If you crashed off the road and lived, your adversary would not stop to render aid. If a friend did not come along, you would be left to die. Men with broken legs had lain in agony for days. If villagers were around, they would first steal a truck's cargo. Then they would steal its parts. Then the injured man's clothes . . .

It was survival of the fittest. There was only one guarantee: Your first mistake would be your last.

I was going to be the meanest man on the Burma Road until others respected the rules I laid down for them. My men had been trained to take right-of-way when going from Burma to China, for they could be presumed to be carrying cargo essential to the Chinese war effort. They were to yield right-of-way when traveling in the other direction. Most trucks heading out of China were empty or without vital cargo.

It was early afternoon when we neared the halfway mark between Wanting and Lungling.

"About now," I told Dong, "we should be meeting the first truck that started out from Lungling today."

"This is a bad place to meet him," Dong said. The road was barely a lane-and-a-half wide.

"I couldn't think of a better place to start breaking him in," I said.

As I spoke, I caught a glimpse of a truck threading its way around a bend in the road half a mile ahead. Then it disappeared and came into view around another bend.

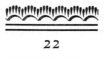

## 22

# Five Uneasy Lessons

I was traveling at twenty miles an hour when the oncoming truck swung into view for the second time and bore down on me. To my right was the side of the mountain, rising almost perpendicular to the road. To my left was a drop of some three hundred feet at a 70-degree angle.

There was absolutely no room for two trucks to pass. Just in case the other driver was overoptimistic, I stuck to the center of the road. (At that time in Asia, one ordinarily hugged the left, British-style.) This move signaled in any language that I was claiming right-of-way.

The other truck came charging at me. Its driver was determined to call my bluff.

I knew I was not going to yield. I braced myself for the crash. He would feel it more because he was hurtling downhill.

At the last moment, he swerved. He leaped from his cab, just as his truck missed mine by inches and careened over the side of the road.

The driver escaped, but he went flying — head first — into the side of the mountain. He was knocked cold.

Two other trucks were behind him. Stopping mine in the center of the road, I jumped to the ground and drew my revolver. I pumped two bullets into the windshield of the first truck. The driver applied his brakes. A front wheel locked and his truck pitched forward, smashing into the side of the mountain.

The next truck stopped on all four wheels. Some Chinese, riding in the back of it, were thrown onto the road. Nobody was badly hurt. The driver of the very first truck was still unconscious, but breathing easily.

The second truck was smashed beyond repair. My drivers pushed it off the road. It rolled down the steep bank and landed in the valley below — a graveyard for trucks and, I suspected, truckers.

The two uninjured drivers and their bruised passengers watched my men work. Several other trucks pulled up behind them. The newly arrived drivers saw trouble was brewing, so they did not budge from their cabs.

I told Dong to wave his gun and assemble all drivers and passengers.

They came forward expecting to be executed. Instead, I lectured them on the rules of the road.

I told them I would be riding the road. I would see that law and order were enforced.

[ 224 ]

Any who disobeyed would die without further questions.

Finally, I ordered them to warn everybody else on the road about me.

They all bowed and apologized for the inconvenience to which I had been put. A few lifted the first driver, who was coming to his senses with moans and wails, and swung him back and forth like a man in a hammock. Others peered over the side of the mountain. When they spotted the two wrecked trucks, they laughed to beat hell.

Brooding on painless education, I climbed back into my truck. Our convoy rolled. I said to Lum, my mechanic and relief driver, "Let this be lesson number one."

At the Government tax office in Lungling, I shed my first cargo. Bill Crooks had given me some $4700 (U.S.) to post as bond for forty cases of indigo dye we were transporting for the Chinese Government. This bond insured that Lidell and Company would deliver the dye to the Government monopoly, not to private parties.

We slept in our truck cabs, had tea at four A.M., and set out for our next stop, Paoshan — only 60 miles away as the crow flies, but 127 by winding road. We were now eight thousand feet above sea level. We would go higher still.

All morning, we wound around curves and between peaks. At no time could we see more than two hundred feet ahead. Toward noon, I rounded what seemed to be the very last bend in the road. A long downhill grade lay before me. Gazing straight ahead, I saw nothing but blue sky. Beneath me were a few scattered clouds.

I pulled over to admire the view. So did the rest of my convoy. To my left, the mountain dropped steeply into some tapering foothills. To my right was a sheer drop of a mile and a half.

This was the Salween Gorge, a chasm with more grandeur than the seven wonders of the world combined.

Our ribbon of a road would lead almost to the bottom, across a bridge, and then up the other side, eight miles away. But getting there would require us to travel more than thirty miles.

In the distance, we could see mountain peaks more than twenty thousand feet high. Their snowy caps sparkled in the sunlight. Up here, a man felt in limbo — a placid limbo.

My men and I loitered as long as we could. We checked bearings, made minor carburetor adjustments, and reviewed our lessons. I reminded the drivers never to coast in neutral. We would descend in second gear and sometimes in first. When we left, we were all prodded by the same thought: A similar view could be had from the other side of the gorge.

In between came lesson number two.

A few miles downhill, an oncoming truck pulled over slightly, but not far enough. I stepped out and asked the driver to pull over another two or three feet: "Otherwise, my convoy cannot pass without slipping over the side."

The three men in the cab grinned at the idea. The driver said in English: "I cannot pull over any farther. But you have plenty of room to pass." Still smiling, he cursed me in Chinese. Then he added in English: "I am coming uphill, so I have right of way."

"Your truck is empty," I reminded him. "It is the general rule for loaded trucks coming into China to have right of way. Our trucks are carrying four tons. It would be impossible for us to pull over any closer to the edge. If we did, our weight would crumble the side of the road and over we'd go."

The driver beamed again, but declined to budge.

"All right," I said, "we have talked enough."

I jumped aboard his truck. The driver swung at me with a wrench. Catching his wrist, I brought his arm down hard. It snapped on the door. The driver cried out in pain. I wrapped an arm around his neck and hauled him out.

My spare drivers had joined me. (First drivers remained with their trucks until summoned.) Dong, Lum, and the others dragged the two riders out of the truck's cab. We tied up all three men and stretched them out alongside the road.

I backed their truck up until the road was clear for my trucks. Before anyone could pass, however, I assembled several drivers whose trucks had arrived during the argument. I made these men stand behind the three prisoners for a fifteen-minute lecture. At the end, I gave an oral test. Each pupil was warned that flunking it could result in his truck's slipping into the gorge. All passed with flying colors. The prisoner with the broken arm was first in his class.

"I know I've made you all a little late," I told my class, "but I'll let

[ 226 ]

you go now. I trust you'll spread the word along the Burma Road."

I never looked back to see if the other drivers tarried long enough to untie the three prisoners.

Our climb up the other side of Salween Gorge was even more dangerous. Our trucks were in excellent shape. But, on the way up, we ran the risk of being rammed by runaway trucks hurtling downhill without brakes. If the road was at all wet, a truck headed uphill could slip backwards even in forward gear. Whenever this happened, my spare drivers knew to leap out and jam wooden blocks under the rear wheels.

We had barely started uphill when it was time for lesson number three.

About half-a-mile ahead, I spotted the tail end of a marathon traffic jam. I immediately halted my convoy. We parked comfortably on the side of the road.

Dong, Lum, and half my men and I walked up to the snarl. Some twenty trucks were facing uphill. An equal number pointed downhill. In most of the cabs, the drivers sat watchfully, smoked, or slept. When we asked what was going on, several men pointed to the center of the jam.

An uphill truck and a downhill truck were poised like battering rams. The downhill truck was perched a little higher. Its front wheels were off the ground. The driver sat on the road. He was smoking.

"I have three flat tires in the rear," he explained, "and nothing to repair them with. In fact, I do not even have a lever to take the tires off the wheels."

"Have you asked any of the other drivers for help?"

No, he hadn't. They could see his problem. But he was a stranger to them. He could not ask. They would not offer. This stalemate had been going on for hours.

"What a dumb bunch of bastards we have here," I remarked to Dong. "Why don't they help each other? Are they too lazy? Or is it the same old business of *face?*"

"A little of everything," Dong said. "They are stubborn and uncooperative. And they say they are truck drivers, not mechanics."

"Well, I will save everyone face."

My biggest audience yet was assembled — at gunpoint — for my lecture, which I knew by heart. Since my hundred listeners included a few women and children, I deleted some profanity and emphasized that this silliness was keeping vital cargo from their country's army.

"While you are sitting here," I concluded, "a Japanese plane could come swooping over here and strafe men, women, children, and trucks. Now, are there any questions?"

An older driver stepped forward to say: "What happens to this man's truck is no business of ours. We are kind not to push it over the side." Behind him, others laughed.

I ignored him. Turning to the two drivers whose trucks surrounded the stalled vehicle, I asked: "Do you carry tire levers and puncture kits for repairing tubes?"

Yes, they said proudly.

"Then go get them," I commanded.

Certainly not! They were smart enough to travel prepared. Why should they encourage stupidity?

Out came my gun.

Out came a whole arsenal of tools.

Everybody went to work. The repairs took thirty minutes. They could have been made in half the time by half the men, but I insisted that every man there take part.

We spent the night in the walled city of Paoshan. The fourth and fifth lessons came the next day.

We left Paoshan at four A.M. I wanted to go 150 miles that day. On the Burma Road, traveling 40 miles by truck in any one day was considered commendable. Hills had 15 to 20 per cent grades for 25 miles at a time. Inexperienced drivers, faulty trucks, and high altitudes made any progress seem formidable.

That morning, we crossed the mighty Mekong River on a rickety bridge. We reached Yungping — the halfway mark on our long day's journey — at eleven A.M. We stopped there for breakfast.

Mostly, we ate two meals a day. We had breakfast at mid-morning or noon. We had dinner upon arrival at our day's destination. I allowed no stopping for tea or snacks.

We gassed the trucks and departed at noon. Five hours later, we were traveling along a precipice that overlooked a small river. Sometimes the road dipped to only twenty feet above the water; five minutes later, we would be several hundred feet above it.

It was almost dark. At that hour of a fatiguing day, I felt like an airsick rider on a roller coaster.

The ups and downs were so monotonous that I cheered aloud when I saw a sharp bend loom above.

Rounding the bend, I saw the back of a truck. I jammed on my brakes. As I stopped, I heard the squeals of my convoy doing the same. "Now I've seen everything," I told Lum. "Parked on a curve on a precipice just when it's getting dark."

Three brand new green Ford trucks were parked there. All bore the imprint of the Chinese Government's Northwest Transportation Company. They were jacked up and most of their wheels were missing. Cargo and empty crates were strewn nearby. Four drivers were sitting in a ditch beside the road. Their hands were tied behind their backs.

When we untied them, they could hardly stand. Someone had worked them over with a wrench. They were covered with blood. Their hands, however, were white from lack of circulation. It took ten minutes and several hefty slugs of Chinese wine before they could tell their story.

With four trucks, they had started out the day in Yungping, where we'd had breakfast. Six Chinese drivers had approached them in search of a ride to Siakwan, where their trucks were. (Siakwan was also our destination for the night.) They offered to pay and the four drivers took them. In early afternoon, the passenger in the first truck received an urgent call from Nature. So did the driver. The small convoy stopped. Each man was caught with his pants down when he received a crushing blow on the head from one or more of his passengers.

The six bandits had loaded whatever cargo they wanted into one truck and driven off with it shortly before we arrived. My men retrieved a few wheels from the river below and added them to spare wheels stored beneath the looted trucks. Thus, we were able to put the three trucks back on the road.

Their drivers were too weak to drive, so I assigned three of my spare drivers to their first Fords.

It was dark when we arrived outside Siakwan. I billeted my men just outside the city. "That way," I told Dong, "you and I and a couple of others can go to town unobtrusively and look for the bandits."

After supper, Dong and I took the healthiest of the four victims for a ride around Siakwan. Twenty or thirty identical Northwest trucks were parked in one long line, but the injured driver went to the stolen one like a homing pigeon.

Cigarettes glowed like embers in some truck cabs. No sign of life was visible in the stolen truck. The three of us tiptoed up. From the cab came a muffled snore.

Dong opened the left door and I reached in. As I had expected, the bandit's head was right there. I brought the butt of my pistol down on his skull. There was a thud — and then another as he fell to the road. He landed face up.

"This is one who robbed us," the injured man told me.

Dong drove the stolen truck back to our billets, where the bandit regained consciousness. He refused to tell where the rest of his gang was. Once I had crushed his fingers with a pair of pliers, he talked fast.

He had been left to guard the truck while his five partners in crime dined. Since there was only one all-night restaurant in town, the bandits would be easy to find. I took fifteen of my men and two of the injured drivers.

The five bandits were all at one table with three other drivers. As we surrounded the table, they all stopped talking and looked up. The owner of the café crashed our cordon long enough to present and collect his bill. Then he and his other customers disappeared.

I pointed my pistol at the eight men and told my drivers to search them. My men found guns, knives, and money. I handed the five bandits' money to their robbery victims: "Here's the first installment on what they owe you." One of the bandits protested. I slapped him across the mouth. All eight men were overseas Chinese from Hong Kong and Singapore.

"Then you all understand English," I said. "You're all coming with us. The first one who makes a break gets shot."

At our billets, we tied up the five bandits and tossed them into the back of a truck with the first man we had captured. I stationed two guards over them. The other three drivers were clearly cronies of the bandits, even though they had not been involved in this robbery. We detained them overnight, but we didn't harm them.

Shortly before dawn, we sent the injured truckers on their way to Kunming. Two of them were still quite weak, so I lent them two of my men to do their driving.

When we were ready to leave Siakwan, we took our six prisoners to the main gate of the city. There, we removed a skid board — fourteen feet long — and propped it up with rocks. It rose to a height about two feet off the ground.

"Now each of you walks the plank," I told the bandits.

As each man reached the top, his arms were unbound. But his thumbs were tied to a rope, which was secured to the top of the open gate. After pulling his arms tight above his head, we kicked the board from beneath his feet.

All six bandits were left hanging by their thumbs. Around their necks were tied notes warning all men against the fate of truck drivers who turned bandit.

It might take two hours before anyone came from that direction. After an hour of their torture, the bandits would be unable to drive for a month.

The remaining two days of our trip were uneventful. I spent part of them pondering the last two lessons:

Lesson number four was almost as old as the first Model T Ford: *No riders.*

The fifth lesson was even older: *Thou shalt not steal.*

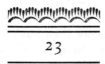

## 23

# Kunming

At four p.m. on a sunny afternoon toward the end of 1939, we wheeled our trucks around the last bend of the Burma Road.

I stopped my truck and jumped down to gaze at the view. To my right was the West Mountain. To my left (due north) were rolling hills, fertile farms, little mud huts, and an occasional large house shaded by bluegum (eucalyptus) trees. Stretching before me was Kunming Lake, reflecting the sky's bright blue. At the north end of the lake was the walled city of Kunming. My future was no more predictable than China's in those turbulent days. But it turned out that I would spend much of the next six years in Kunming.

For the first time since Mandalay, I ordered my convoy into high gear. Soon we were speeding down a narrow strip of asphalt road flanked by bluegum trees. Nine miles later, Chinese soldiers checked us through the west gate of the city.

We rolled down Kunming's main street, Chi Ping Liu, and turned onto a side street, where the French Renault garage stood empty of trucks or cars. It was the size of half a city block. It was fully equipped with tools and overhauling materials. Unfortunately, there were no expert civilian mechanics in Kunming.

I had brought along two of our mechanics from Rangoon. At the Renault garage, they would check over our trucks for the return trip. When the convoy left, the two mechanics would stay on — until they had recruited and trained two able replacements for themselves.

I paid everybody enough money to keep him going, but out of trouble. Then I hailed a rickshaw and told the coolie to take me to a decent hotel where I could have a bath, dinner, a beer, and a good night's rest.

Only two places in Kunming were worthy of the word "hotel." The Hotel de Commerce and the Hotel d'Europe stood at opposite ends of the same street, alongside which ran a small canal. The canal stank. It contained everything — including on occasion, unlucky Chinese.

Kunming's foreign influence then was primarily French. A narrow gauge railway ran the five hundred miles between Kunming and Hanoi, French Indochina. Kunming's French colony lived near the railway station in its own walled community. There was an equally exclusive French club.

I checked in at the Hotel de Commerce, took a hot bath, and sat down to a seven-course French dinner with a bottle of wine. The meal cost forty cents (U.S.).

I had only one complaint: The hotel was out of beer.

The proprietor, a friendly Greek, explained that Chinese were not particularly fond of beer. It was a scarce import. The only place in town that had any was the French club, which did not welcome outsiders.

"I'm sure they'll be glad to see a thirsty new face," I said. I could not have been more wrong.

I wandered through the French club's courtyard and into a cool barroom furnished with tables, cane chairs, and a bar at the far end. Only one table was occupied. I nodded to the people at it, but the best I received was a dirty look. I could, however, feel their eyes following my back right up to the bar.

A Chinese barboy of about forty was polishing a wine glass. He avoided my eye, so I spoke up: "Give me a quart bottle of ice-cold beer, please."

The "boy" continued to polish the glass, which now gleamed blindingly. He wore a white coat and black Chinese trousers, laced at the ankles. His face was pockmarked and clearly Chinese, but it also wore the blasé veneer of the Frenchmen who had just snubbed me.

I repeated my request. When the barboy ignored me again, I thumped my fist.

This time, he replied in perfect English: "You cannot get a drink here. I cannot serve you because you are not a member of the club." He added mockingly, "So sorry!"

In the mirror behind the bar, I could see the customers watching intently. The one who had flashed me a dirty look was gripping his chair with both hands. He was ready to fight for France, for the French club, and even for his barboy.

I had come for a beer, not for an argument.

I whipped out my .45 pistol and slammed it hard on the bar. There was a tinkling moment when the glasses stored below danced. The man behind me sank back into his chair. The Chinese barboy turned white as a Frenchman.

The barboy was so nervous that he poured my beer into the wine glass he had been polishing.

After I had visited the French club this way on each trip to Kunming, I received a cordial letter from the club's secretary. I had just been elected an honorary member.

Apparently, this was their solution to the problem posed by my repeated crashing. Frenchmen can be as devious as Orientals in matters of *face*.

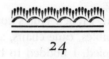

## 24

# Four Hundred Drums to Chungking

EVERY trip was as eventful as my first journey across the Burma Road. For a while, however, our third trip of 1940 had me worried. Hardly anything went wrong. Between Rangoon and Kunming, we had two encounters with bandits and one restaurant brawl with a drunken trucker. But these provided less than routine excitement.

Fortunately, a message from Bill Crooks awaited me in Kunming.

Instead of returning to Rangoon, we were to pick up four hundred drums of aviation gasoline. We would deliver them to the Chinese Air Force in Chungking, some eight hundred miles northeast.

This was the big break for which Bill Crooks had been angling. On our return trip, we could load up our trucks with some of the pigs' bristles and silk that Lidell and Company had been unable to move out of Chungking. Ordinarily, no foreign commercial traffic was allowed between Kunming and Chungking.

Aviation gasoline was a precious commodity in China. It went for as much as five hundred dollars a drum on the black market. If a soldier found some way to remove a dozen drums from the Government's books, he could sell the fuel to black marketeers and retire at once to private life as a wealthy man. Not all Chinese soldiers had patriotic scruples.

Knowing this, I expected trouble when I took my requisition to the Army compound outside Kunming. My papers were processed with surprising ease. The officer in charge served tea and British cigarettes. He told me we could load our trucks immediately.

As we shook hands, the officer added with a smile: "There is, of course, a small matter of paper work."

I sat down again. It looked as if I would be there for the day, after all.

He surprised me again by handing me just one Chinese document for signing.

"What does it say?" I asked Dong.

Dong read it over several times. "It is a bill of lading," he said. "It makes you responsible for any loss or damage to the cargo while in your possession."

Signing it would have invited an ambush one mile down the road. "No, sir," I told the officer. "I'm carrying this fuel free of charge for the Chinese Central Government. I don't want to end up owing the Chinese Government anything."

The officer said he had to account for the cargo.

"That's different," I said. "I'm perfectly willing to sign a receipt that I've taken four hundred drums of gasoline from your warehouse."

We negotiated a little longer. Finally, the officer ordered fresh tea and announced: "It is not necessary for Mr. Stuart to sign anything. But each of his drivers must sign a receipt for the cargo loaded onto his truck."

I agreed to this face-saving compromise, although my men were wary. Finally, I told them: "I intend to get this gasoline to Chungking. Period! Even if I have to take it there myself in ten trips." Since I had never let them down, they assented.

I told them to make sure the cap of each drum was sealed with a wire and a lead clamp. This meant the drum had not been tampered with since it had been filled.

Each man checked and rechecked the seals before signing his receipt. Pulling away from the compound, we proceeded to another Chinese Army station, where each driver was issued three drums and a full tank of truck gasoline for the journey to Chungking.

We parked near the east gate of Kunming to make an early start next morning. Just as a precaution, I posted sentries.

Having put their names to their cargo, my drivers proved to be their own best protection. Several slept on top of the gasoline drums. If anyone lit a match near them, they might perish. But perish forbid that anybody stole their explosive cargo!

\*     \*     \*

The road from Kunming to Chungking winds through the mountains of Szechwan Province like a giant serpent. It was a good road — built by Chinese, of course.

With customary efficiency, not a single inch of the surrounding countryside was wasted. Rich rice paddies were terraced on the slopes of steep mountains. Without any modern equipment, water from low-lying streams and springs was lifted as high as a thousand feet.

How was this done? The device I saw most often was a series of dippers holding a quart of water apiece. A man or woman pumped a foot pedal at the bottom of a wooden structure resembling an elevator shaft. Then the bottom dipper would scoop up a quart of water from a stream and dump it into the lowest rice paddy. Simultaneously, each dipper lifted a quart of water out of each paddy and dumped it into the one above it.

The next pedaling would lift the water one level higher. The operator had to pedal rapidly enough to prevent evaporation, but slowly enough to avert mechanical breakdowns.

The farmers' homes were picturesque and clean. The people were friendly and open. They were not yet corrupted by the Westerner and his implements of progress.

Even then, however, they were doomed by progress. Millions of tons of soft coal were hidden beneath the hard exteriors of their mountains. The farmers were aware of this. But they looked to their lucrative cliffs only for enough fuel to heat their homes. They drove small tunnels twenty feet into the mountains and dug out enough coal for a winter. They made the coal into small briquettes.

Sooner or later, someone would confiscate their wealth of minerals. If their own Chinese Government didn't do it, the Japanese would.

Toward Chungking, the mountains turned into small jagged peaks resembling Oriental landscapes painted on scrolls. The peaks were limestone, but they nurtured green trees. At the base of each mountain nestled villages and farms.

A human spectacle along the way was more unreal than the scenery — a grotesque parade of walking corpses. We passed thousands of military "recruits," young and old, who had been kidnapped from their homes or dragged off streets to fight Japan. Scarcely fed and

[ 236 ]

marching hundreds of miles in bare feet, they were creatures out of Dante's Inferno.

Their presence was more tangible in the distance, when you first smelled them coming, than when they were upon you. They were too weak to make a sound. You heard nothing but the ghostly dragging of their feet in the dust.

Their bare bones poked at cotton uniforms stained by dysentery. Their heads were too large for their frail bodies; their eyes too large for their heads. Most incongruous of all was their presence in any army. They were fit only to die.

They did so in their first encounter with the enemy — if not sooner. Every now and then, one of the walking corpses would stagger away from the wavering line of skeletons. A sentry's gun would echo in the mountains. Something that vaguely resembled a man would drop peacefully into a paddy not unlike the one from which he was kidnapped.

Once upon a time — it seemed very long ago — I had come to Asia to save the Chinese people from the curse of the Japanese. Now, as I witnessed this endless cavalcade of misery, I wondered who would save the Chinese people from themselves.


On our seventh day out of Kunming, my convoy edged its way down the side of South Mountain, which towered over the banks of the Yangtze River and the wartime capital, Chungking.

As we descended slowly, a motorcade of Buicks, Cadillacs, and Packards zoomed toward us. For a moment, I thought I was in America. I pulled over and held my breath until the cars were safely past the rest of my convoy.

"Who the hell was that?" I asked Lum, my relief driver. The answer had to be the Chinese ruler, Generalissimo Chiang Kai-shek.

"It was Generalissimo, all right," Lum assured me. "I see secret servicemen with guns in last two cars."

"And that is the courageous leader," I said, spitting. "Why the hell was he in such a hurry to leave town?"

Lum gazed around. He pointed to a mountaintop nearby. Two huge red balls hung from a mast.

"That a *jimbal*," he said. "Air-raid warning!"

"Spread the trucks out," I commanded my drivers, "and then get the hell away from them!"

Perched on a mountain ledge overlooking our trucks, we had an excellent view of Chungking. Soon, the drone of airplane engines could be heard above us. In a neat formation shaped like an arrowhead, the Japs streaked across the sky.

No Chinese planes came out to fight them. What few planes the Chinese Air Force had were obsolete. One battle would have wiped out China's entire Air Force.

The planes based in Chungking were primarily morale boosters. Just before an air raid, they would take off and circle the city. Civilians watched them as they flew low and then disappeared to a safe base. Their very existence gave the people of Chungking pride, a sense of security, and, above all, hope.

All targets of military value, including the Generalissimo himself, were removed from Chungking before each raid. The Japs simply unloaded their bombs aimlessly over the city. Their mission was to destroy the civilian body and soul.

The Japanese never succeeded.

Hundreds of thousands of people lived through the bombings of Chungking. Each disaster made them more determined than ever to survive. Before the dust had time to settle, the people would be back — sifting debris and reshaping mud brick into homes. These were their roots. Nobody fled Chungking in defeat or panic. People were bombed out of homes and businesses many times, but they never despaired. They turned the other cheek so often that eventually the enemy lost face.

We watched each bomb throw up clouds of dust and smoke. When the last splattering cracks had echoed in the mountains, a deathly quiet swept the valley below. But the silence was turned away at the city, where the swift waters of the Yangtze came alive with sampans. The clatter of instant rebuilding drowned out the first moans of loss and dismay.

Chungking teemed with activity as we drove through it. We reported to an Air Force compound. The officer in charge smiled skeptically when I told him we had a cargo of aviation gasoline. But his interest heightened as we unloaded each truck and he found the seals intact.

[ 238 ]

A Chinese chemist unsealed them. With a long glass tube, he sampled the gasoline for purity.

We watched him go from one drum to the next. Each time, he plunged the tube all the way into the drum. With a finger, he pressed down, drew a small amount of fluid into the tube, and examined its contents.

After the first two or three drums, he cursed. The contents of his tube drained onto the ground. He tested five more drums quickly before turning to me and reporting: "Water! Almost all of it is water!"

My drivers gasped with disbelief. Pushing over several drums, they allowed the contents to flow on the ground. They cupped their hands beneath the liquid and tasted the truth.

I have never seen thirsty men enjoy a drink less.

"But the seals were unbroken," I told the chemist.

"Of course," he said, "but how could you have known what was sealed inside? Those drums may *never* have contained gasoline."

My drivers were raging. They cursed the entire Chinese Army in every dialect. The officer-in-charge and I walked away from the milling mob.

"What are you going to do?" I asked.

"What can anyone do?" the officer replied.

"Then you don't think *we* stole the gas?"

"Oh, no. I am not blaming you. This happens often. When we go to fetch fuel ourselves, we take along a chemist who tests it there. But you have no chemist and no authority to demand a test."

I went back to my men and told them: "Stop bitching. Nobody is holding you responsible. If I did, you'd be dead on the ground right now. Go back to work, you miserable bastards."

They knew me well enough by now to realize I was cursing not them, but human venality. By the time we had loaded up our trucks with commercial cargo for the trip back, my drivers were teasing each other for having slept on their drums every night. They impersonated one another signing receipts and handling the drums ever so gingerly. For weeks, nobody could take a drink of water without provoking laughter.

Our ill-starred journey paid off for Lidell and Company, which now had regular access to and from Chungking. Upon my return to

Rangoon, Bill Crooks insisted on celebrating our "victory." I drank a bitter toast to the defrauded civilians of Chungking.

## 25

# The Day I Closed the Burma Road

ONE dreary day in the wet season of 1940, my convoy crossed from Burma into China after hours. Burmese customs in Namhkam had been closing up when we arrived there. The officer in charge was an old friend by now. He waved us through after reminding me that I had a dinner date with him for that night.

We parked our trucks in the Chinese customs compound at Wanting, China. We would thus be first on line when they opened in the morning.

My men were going to sleep in their trucks. "You can go into Wanting or Namhkam if you wish," I told them, "but half of you must be here at any time. There has to be one man in each truck." Then I slipped back into Burma on foot.

Toward the end of dinner, I was surprised to see Lum, my mechanic and spare driver, standing in the restaurant doorway.

"Sit down and have a beer," I called to him. "What are you doing here?"

He took a long sip of beer before telling me: "The Chinese military police have confiscated one of our trucks."

"What the hell for?"

"Smuggling. The driver, Li, is under arrest."

Lum, Li, and a couple of other night owls had decided to go into Wanting. They had been too lazy to walk a mile to the all-night café there. Instead, they had climbed into Li's truck and driven out of the customs compound. The guard at the gate had not stopped them. But no sooner had they set foot in the restaurant than four M.P.'s entered. They had wanted to know who was driving the truck parked outside. Li had stood up. The M.P.'s had taken him and his truck to their headquarters.

After giving Lum hell for allowing the truck to leave the compound, I turned my wrath on the Chinese M.P.'s. The Burmese customs officer with whom I was dining offered to intervene. He put through a call to the night commandant across the border.

He was on the phone pleading in Chinese for fifteen minutes. When he hung up, he cursed in three languages. When he was coherent, he reported: "Gil, the chap refuses to release your truck. He says you are a smuggler. He says the penalty is loss of the truck."

"He must be new there," I said. "I've never had any trouble before."

"He's new, you bet. And he's the kind of M.P. who likes his cut of everything."

I paced the floor and threatened to wipe the two-bit night commandant off the face of the earth. I would see the day commandant in the morning. The day commandant was an honest man. But I knew he was not brave enough to fight a gangster in uniform.

Another idea occurred to me. "Can your phone reach the Englishman who's in charge of the Burma Road on this side?" I asked my Burmese friend.

"That would be the British Commissioner in Lashio," he replied. "Yes, I can. But it's past midnight, Gil."

"No better time for getting action."

In ten minutes, I was talking to the Commissioner, who acted as if I were part of a bad dream he was having. Only my British accent convinced him I was real.

He listened patiently and yawned audibly as I explained my troubles. Then he proclaimed: "Impossible! They simply can't do that!"

"But they have, sir," I said.

"They can't!" he insisted. "It's so illegal that there's no law to cover it. How on earth can I be expected to solve such a problem in the middle of the night? Those Chinese ought to know better . . ."

Before he became any more muddled, I said: "I have an idea, sir. Remember when you had some trouble with the Chinese Government last year? You closed the Burma Road for three months."

He coughed and then conceded: "We did, but that was a major policy matter."

"If you let them get away with doing this to a British subject now," I said, "you'll be establishing a precedent that will result in a major policy crisis within a month."

"Perhaps you're right, Stuart," he said. "There's entirely too much of this sort of thing happening. Seizing a truck and then waking a fellow in the middle of the night! All right, Stuart. Close up the Burma Road. Keep it closed until you get your truck back. And your driver, too. I don't care if it takes forever. Just see that the Burmese never call me up at home again. Good night."

"Good night, sir," I said, "and thank you."

The next morning at Namhkam, the Burma Road was closed to all traffic in both directions. By the time the Chinese customs officers had contacted their Burmese counterparts, trucks were backed up for several miles.

My friends in Burmese customs told the Chinese that they needed three documents to unsnarl the mess: a release for my truck; a release for my driver; and a written apology from the Chinese night commandant.

Several truce missions came over from the Chinese side with various oral apologies and compromise offers. I rejected them all.

"Aside from the truck and the man, it's none of my business," I pointed out to the Chinese day commandant. "Still, your night commandant has gone far beyond his authority. I don't care how long you take to resolve this, but you're fighting a war. That truck you've seized is carrying Lend-Lease equipment for the Chinese Government in Chungking. You're committing suicide when you allow seizures like this."

Toward nightfall, I had the three documents I required. I also had a fourth that I hadn't solicited. It was an official inquiry form to be forwarded to the Central Government in Chungking. It requested a full account of the incident.

"I'll deliver it in person," I said. "With a little bit of luck, the night commandant may get himself shot for this."

My friend in Burmese customs said: "You may think you're joking, Gil, but you're not."

In the wet season, the red dust of the Burma Road turned into thick mud. No culverts and no ditches were there to hold torrents of water that poured down from the skies and the mountainsides. When we left Wanting the next morning, we encountered whole convoys bogged down in the center of the road.

There were still many drivers — old and new — on the Burma Road who had not been exposed to my sermons on lending a helping hand. If a Chinese driver saw a truck bog down ahead of him, he would seldom stop his own truck on solid ground and then go forward on foot.

Instead, he would drive right on. If he didn't slip off the road while trying to pass the bogged truck, he would stick in the mud right behind it.

I have seen as many as forty trucks in a row bogged down like this. The figure might have been even higher if my men and I had not come along and, often at gunpoint, organized a team rescue operation.

My men were trained to stop and render aid unless the situation smacked of ambush. Each of my trucks carried tire chains, a tow chain, and two planks that served as ramps for bogged trucks. (The planks could also be used to strengthen a bridge or prop up an overturned truck.)

The marooned drivers spun their wheels and sank more deeply into the mud. Even then, they continued spinning until their tires tore to shreds or their axles broke. When we arrived, we sometimes found trucks so close to the ground that it was impossible to insert jacks underneath.

In the wet season, drivers who didn't bog down sometimes met worse fates. Trucks frequently careened hundreds of feet down slopes.

To conserve gas, many Chinese drivers rode their brakes on downhill stretches. Mud would throw these trucks completely out of control.

A typical sight on the Burma Road in the wet season was a truck charging down a steep hill, barreling into another truck or jumping the road at the last second, and smashing to pieces far below. There were many variations. Once a truck left the road at a sharp bend.

Traveling between sixty and eighty miles an hour, it soared through the air with the driver frozen at the wheel. Sometimes, on a winding mountain, a truck would plummet from above and splatter before my eyes like a dead bird.

Every wet season, I became an expert first aid man. I carried a complete kit with extra splints for broken arms and legs. After doing what I could, I would deliver an injured man to a mission hospital — if one was within a hundred miles of our route. If not, I would leave the man to fend for himself. My attitude was more Chinese than cruel.

In China, being sick, wounded, or helpless was even worse than being poor. Animals were put out of their misery, but people were not helped to live or die.

Many times and in many ways, I have heard a Westerner grumble on an Asian street:

"Why the hell don't these people help each other? Why do they ignore the sick and let them die in the gutter? Why don't they take them somewhere and look after them?"

The Westerner usually answers his own question by calling the Chinese "inhuman" or "heathen."

The Chinese, I discovered, are neither. Their feelings are as sensitive as ours. They, however, are as practical as we claim we are. The Chinese masses' prime concern is self-survival. It takes all of a man's energy, ability, and wits just to keep himself alive from day to day. There is nothing to share.

But what about "fortunate" people like truck drivers? There is a Chinese custom that a man is indebted to his rescuer for life. Invariably, all that he has to offer to his rescuer is himself. He offers his services, however limited they may be. Thus — indirectly, but as irrevocably as man's innate humanity — the rescuer becomes responsible not only for a stranger's future, but also for his daily room and board.

A gesture of kindness can become a lifetime burden. As even the most dedicated philanthropist will tell you, there is a limit to how much any man can give.

Man is often forced to impersonate God. I helped people who, in my judgment, stood a chance to survive on their own initiative. To help a badly injured man was merely to extend his time of suffering.

[ 244 ]

I have seen my own drivers stroll past an injured man or step blithely over the sick lying on a street or sidewalk. I have also seen their eagerness to help when a tragedy could be averted or a man was in danger. They were more humane than any other people I have known. And I don't mean to be damning them with faint praise when I say so.

Near Paoshan, a truck loaded with gasoline left the road and nose-dived into thick timber underneath. The door of the cab was forced open. The engine was pushed back, pinning the driver beneath the steering wheel.

My men and I arrived on the scene ten minutes after the accident happened. A dozen spectators were standing around admiring the wreck. Three or four others were trying vainly to pull the driver out.

The man was bent at the hips. The top half of him hung out of his cab; the rest could not be budged without an acetylene torch to cut through steel.

While I stood sizing up the situation, a spectator lit a cigarette. As several of us cried out in horror, the man flicked his match into the gasoline that had drenched the ground.

The wreckage was engulfed in flames. Fire licked at the sides of his truck while the trapped man screamed with fear and pain. Soon, the drums of gasoline would ignite. The whole area would become a ball of flame like the house Chan, Lok, Soong, and I had once destroyed in my guerrilla days.

There was no chance to rescue the poor driver. My first impulse was to shoot him and put him out of his misery. I was not sure, how-ever, that this crowd would approve of such intervention.

I told my drivers to shove the crowd back. While they did, I made a dash for the cab of the burning truck. The trapped man reached for me with a final surge of hope. But there was no hope and no time.

I thrust my pistol into his hand. He gave me a look that had more hatred than anguish. The bearer of fatal tidings is often more reviled than the killer. This man's doom was pronounced to him by the look in my eyes and the gun I handed him, not by the careless flick of a match into gasoline.

I said nothing and he said nothing. Our eyes held a terse conversation. His hand clutched my pistol tighter. He could have killed me and then himself.

We looked at each other for a long fifteen seconds. Then I withdrew. I ordered my drivers into their trucks.

As we pulled away, I heard the report of a pistol. Lum, who was driving, turned to me and said: "Nobody would have thought of helping him in such a way."

I lit a cigarette and said: "Maybe not. But it cost me my pistol."

Lum grinned. He said: "You are not so tough, Mr. Kind-Hearted Tiger."

The Burma Road, as I have noted, was not a limited-access superhighway. It was open to all kinds of pedestrians.

A pack train of ponies would appear from nowhere. Seeing a truck for the first time, some of them would stampede. Packs, cargo, and angry drovers were flung all over the road.

Sometimes we saw coolies — old men, old women, and young children included — carrying one hundred pounds of rice or rock salt on their backs. Each coolie's only support was a strap that was fastened under the load, over the shoulders, and around the forehead. The weight of the load rested between shoulder blades. The body stooped forward and the head had to be held well down.

Even so, the strain was on the forehead. The coolies appeared to be stumbling forward. They could see only a couple of yards ahead.

It was the most agonizing labor I have ever seen. Each step must have made their heads vibrate with pain. I know I developed a headache watching.

Driving close to them was dangerous. I never knew when a coolie, swayed by sudden pressure or a momentary blackout, would stagger into my truck's path.

Another traffic hazard was a superstition that evil spirits were forever following people around. When the opportune time came to rid oneself of evil spirits, no man would hesitate to dart in front of a speeding truck. If it missed a coolie by inches, he could hope that his evil spirits — chasing behind him — had not been so lucky.

Coolies, however, were bad judges of truck speeds. Their mangled bodies lay on the road while their evil spirits went away unharmed and looking for other mortals to afflict.

[ 246 ]

Women with babies were frequent offenders, so the evil spirits often had multiple cause for rejoicing. With four tons of cargo, a split second for thinking, and a few feet for maneuvering, a truck driver sometimes found it impossible to miss.

In some places, superstitious coolies lay in ambush. A dozen would jump across my bow from both sides of the road. Once, two collided in midair and knocked each other cold. On another occasion, when I had halted my truck in the nick of time, ten coolies cursed me because I had spared the evil spirits they were eluding.

In two instances, I was unable to stop in time and I felt like an evil spirit myself. My men and I knew not to stop and render aid on such occasions. If you went on, nobody chased you or blamed you. But, if you stopped, you were admitting guilt. You could be burdened with a lifetime responsibility.

Later, when the American Army reached Burma and China, this practice was put on a paying basis. People threw themselves and their relatives in front of trucks the way farmers used to dispose of sick chickens. Then they filed claims.

Since truck traffic between Kunming and Chungking was limited, ambitious coolies formed small syndicates and went into business. Each syndicate's "fleet" consisted of a small, two-wheeled rubber-tired cart that could hold a ton. Its axle was taken from a wrecked truck. Instead of a steering wheel, it had two shafts. Instead of an engine, it had six men to draw it.

One man was strapped in the shafts like a horse. A rope was tied to each shaft and looped around his neck. Another rope was hitched to the cart, around his shoulders, and across his chest. He used the first rope to balance his load and bear its weight; the second to pull it forward. He steered by shifting his own weight from one shaft to the other. Each time he did so, he dug his feet into the ground with all his force.

Since his job was the roughest, all six coolies took turns in the shafts. The other five hooked themselves to the cart, with two flanking the man in the shafts and three along the sides and back.

Usually, the carts traveled in convoys of six or more. Going up a steep hill, all thirty-six men would push one cart at a time. Going down, they massed in back as human brakes that kept each cart from running amok. The man in the shafts would lean back, leap in the air, and swing his body frantically to steady his load.

Approaching a steep hill not far past Kunming, I saw two carts speeding downhill at high speed. "Poor bastards," I said to Lum. I pulled over to give the carts all the room they needed.

It was well that I did. A dozen coolies were hitched to each cart. They were straining to keep from losing their carts.

The first cart made it. With the second cart, however, one of the men fell down. He rolled under the feet of several others, who toppled like tenpins.

The cart gathered speed. Men were flung in several directions. Two, strapped in tightly, were whipped and dragged until, mercifully, their ropes snapped.

Now there was just one man — in the shafts — careening downhill with a ton on his back. There was no way out, but he fought for every second of life. He was an old man, I saw.

With all his cunning, he threw his weight from one side to the other. The cart stayed on a straight course a little longer. His legs seldom touched the ground. They spun in the air. He leaped like a feather. For a moment, he was a thing of beauty.

His load was moving forward. Two thousand pounds was shifting onto his frail shoulders. His leaps continued, but his feet did not go so high. Death seemed to hammer them to the ground as soon as they left it.

The cart neared the bottom of the steep grade at tremendous speed. The old man gave one last spring. Then the shafts whipped back at him. They brought the full ton down upon his shoulders. The shafts dug into the road and the old man came to earth flat on his face.

The shafts snapped like twigs. The heavy cart dug almost gently into the mangled wreckage of the old coolie. His frame gave one agonized heave. The cart reared in the air. It spilled its load and spun off into the trees.

Lum and I jumped from our cab. We ran over to one of the most gallant men I'd ever seen. He was not dead, but beyond repair. His eyes were open. They stared at a trail of rice leading to the wrecked cart. The dying coolie's eyes were bemoaning the loss of cart and rice, not of man.

"For Christ's sake," I hissed at Lum, "tell him nothing is lost. Tell him Buddha has instructed me to replace his property."

Lum spoke hastily in Chinese to the dying man. He cocked his head and looked squarely at me. I nodded silently. Once again, my eyes conversed with a dying man's.

He opened his mouth to talk, but a spasm of pain stiffened his neck. His lips closed on one side of his mouth. The other side stayed open like a harelip. He died a few minutes later.

We placed him under a tree and covered him with a sleeping mat. His family and friends — themselves battered by their trip downhill — mourned not only him. They bewailed the end of the happy, secure existence his cart had brought them. Their only chance to better themselves had been wiped out by tragedy.

I took up a collection from my men. "I expect each man to give at least eight rupees," I told them. They gave more than double. I added thirty rupees ($7.50 U.S.) of my own. Lum handed the money to the dead man's family and told them to make sure the old man received a dignified burial.

His survivors took a new lease on life. The dazed, stunned expressions of hopelessness left their faces. All their grief and emotion shifted away from themselves and back to their noble patriarch.

We left soon after. For all I know, the old man's family left him beneath the tree to feed the buzzards. But, if our money put his survivors back on their feet, they would thank the old man, not my men and me. He richly deserved whatever immortality our money could buy for him.

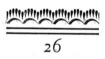

## 26

# Rendezvous at Annan

ANNAN was a little town on the road from Kunming to Chungking. It perched on a mountain pass ten thousand feet above sea level. Annan was a bleak community absolutely unprotected from the wind, but I rejoiced every time I arrived there from Kunming. I had survived the Twenty-Two Bends, one of the most difficult stretches of road in all China.

Approaching Annan from Kunming, one confronted the Twenty-Two Bends at the base of a cliff more than a thousand feet high. Gazing straight up, one could see all but two or three of the Twenty-Two Bends.

More than one of the Twenty-Two Bends required a driver to make five maneuvers — three forward and two backing up — before he could possibly clear it. Some grades were so steep that wheels bounded off the ground; men on foot had to block them.

Whenever I rounded the twenty-second bend, I had completed a day's work — even if the time was noon. And I was less than two miles from Annan.

The people of Annan were largely from the Miao tribe, hill people who had emigrated from the foothills of Tibet. Unlike female Chinese coolies, Miao women wore pleated blue skirts, blouses, headgear, silver ornaments, and semiprecious stones. These women earned their wardrobe. They were hard-working. Their men took it easy, sat around, and accepted only the softest jobs. Anti-Government agitators could always depend on them for an audience in Annan.

A few of Annan's buildings were of stone; the rest were wood. Neither kind looked very clean. The few restaurants in town were not recommended by anybody who lived to tell of them. There was one passable hotel: a converted two-story temple managed by the China Travel Service.

Late one afternoon in 1941, we were unable to park within a block of the hotel.

"What are all those trucks doing in town?" I asked my assistant, Dong.

He asked a few questions on the street and reported: "The bridge on the other side of town is out. The Japanese bombed it two days ago."

The bridge had crossed the Pepan River. Without it, the alternative was to double back over the Twenty-Two Bends and take a much less direct route. I cursed the Japs more heartily than ever.

The hotel manager greeted me happily. Business was booming. He was a little man who wore a long black gown, lined with fur, in all weather. It doubled his size and gave the illusion of his being in mourning even as he rubbed his hands with glee.

He poured me a cup of tea and inquired craftily: "Mr. Stuart, do you think they will take their time rebuilding the bridge?"

"Who can tell?" I said. "Anyway, who can build a bridge?"

"There is a General Mah and thirty of his staff staying here," he said. "They are on their way to Chungking."

I took this as a good sign. If the general and his staff were remaining, then there was hope that the bridge could be restored. If I should want to restore it myself, I could probably count on their support.

"My hotel is full for the first time in history," the manager told me proudly, "but I have a room for you, Mr. Stuart."

"Good," I said. "I could stand a bath, too. And a bottle of brandy."

After tea, I walked along a courtyard corridor to my room. The bitter dampness of Annan ate into my bones. I was pleased to find a boy preparing a steaming bath for me. An earthenware stove stood in the center of my room.

The stove resembled a huge flowerpot. On top of it was a copper tray shaped like a dinner plate. The tray held a small pyramid of charcoal briquettes, glowing cherry-red.

My bathtub was shaped like a bucket. It was made of wood and coated with shiny black lacquer. I stood naked and drinking brandy in the tub while my boy and another coolie doused me with buckets of hot water.

Later, I dined in my room. In Annan, cows' nostrils were prepared in a thick soup with mushrooms, vegetables, and a few mystery ingredients. Pigs' intestines were fried with hot peppers and chopped vegetables. The pigeon-egg soup was a trifle too sweet. The wine smelled like a week-old corpse, but it had a kick like a mule's.

When I stepped outside to belch in the courtyard's fresh air, I encountered a small, thickset Chinese officer. On the collar of his uniform was a general's insignia with two gold stars. "You must be General Mah," I said. "I am Gilbert Stuart."

"Good evening," he said, holding out his hand and bowing slightly without demeaning his rank. "Won't you come in for a few minutes and talk with us?"

"I had planned to in the morning, but why not now!" I told him.

His accent had what I took to be a trace of Oxford. Later, I learned that he was a graduate of Sandhurst, the British Royal Military Academy.

"I will get the boy to make some good hot coffee," he said. "We have S & W." He was naming one of the only two or three brands of American coffee to be bought in Asia. Men had fought and died for those precious green tins with the capital letters "S & W" on the label.

Several officers were lounging in General Mah's room. They jumped to their feet as we entered. The general introduced me. One of them was a Captain Mar who, even before I knew more about him, struck me as an old friend. Scars of battle burned in his face, which had, in fact, been disfigured by flames. His right eyelid was so distended that it forced the eye to stay open. The corner of his mouth curled up like paper in a blaze. There was no red lip on one side. His mouth had been rebuilt, but somehow you could see firmness of character all over his distorted face.

It would take two weeks to spring loose a unit of engineers from Chungking or Kunming, the general told me. There were, however, two Chinese engineers on the other side of the river. But not enough to build a bridge.

The general had been all for doubling back to Kunming and taking another route to Chungking. Captain Mar, however, had pointed out that the town of Annan — for all its temporary prosperity — would wither and die without the Chungking-Kunming traffic.

General Mah had given Captain Mar until tomorrow noon to come up with a solution. "Let's have one last drink and sleep on it," I said. "We'll attack the problem fresh in the morning."

Attack came from an unexpected quarter that night. My bed was a good one — no spring mattress, to be sure, but plain boards covered with thick eiderdown. The fire in my stove had nearly burned out, but it was enough to take the chill out of the room. As I had expected, I fell asleep in seconds.

I awoke a minute later. I found myself clawing at my neck. I itched all over. My neck and waist were afire. I could feel huge welts all over me. My lip was swelling. It half stung and half itched.

It took me a minute to realize what was happening: *My bed was teeming with bedbugs.*

Bedbugs are accessories to any life of adventure. Still, I had never

[ 252 ]

been so savagely attacked before. I switched on my flashlight and lit the oil lamp, but in vain. I searched every inch of bedding, to no avail. I shook out my bedding. I pulled my bed away from the wall. And I mused over the expression "crazy as a bedbug." How many times, I wondered, had bedbugs driven men insane?

With one last curse, I went back to bed. In an instant, the bedbugs were all over me again.

I snapped on my flashlight just in time to see the last two stragglers disappear over my pillow. From the size of them, I could tell that they would be back for blood next time.

Shifting to the two plain wooden chairs in my room, I sat in one, put my feet up on the other, and kept the light on.

Two columns of bedbugs marched out of my pillow and attacked my chairs. Surely this was the end of the world!

I swallowed two slugs of brandy and poured the rest of the bottle over my swollen body. Then I retreated to the stone slab courtyard of the hotel. It was cold, dark, and raining a little. I found a place on some stone steps and leaned back against a pillar. A balcony overhead protected me somewhat, although an occasional fine spray of rain cooled my face.

No sooner had I dozed than I heard the scamper of tiny feet.

I turned on my flashlight. This time, I confronted several large gray rats, each the size of a full-grown cat. Their hair was coarse and long. Their skin was pink streaked with brown and black. Their heads were ugly and fierce. They didn't retreat at the sight of me. Instead, they studied me as a tasty morsel.

I was damned if I was going to go down in history as the man who stayed to be dinner.

I retreated again — to the cab of my truck. There I had two hours of sleep undisturbed by anything more than nightmares.

Rested and refreshed after a fashion, I was up early to look at what had been a bridge. Captain Mar joined me. The welts on his face indicated that bedbugs had no respect for rank. Every now and then, he yawned.

Thirty trucks were lined up at the bridge site. Another twenty were arrayed across the river, only a few hundred feet away. Nobody was surrendering his place in line. Everybody was waiting patiently for the bridge to reappear. Most of the drivers were slumbering in their cabs.

Two stone slab piers were all that remained of a steel A-frame bridge that had been just wide enough to take one truck at a time. A bomb had hit the dead center of the bridge, which collapsed. Its A became a V and then two neat pieces that slid into the raging river and vanished downstream.

Two Chinese stood on the other bank. They were the engineers General Mah had mentioned. Conferring in shouts, Captain Mar and I told them to forage for steel cable and heavy timber at their end. We would meet at noon with work forces assembled on both sides. The engineers would manage the technical details. On our side, I would supervise the men and Captain Mar would keep order.

My task proved the most difficult on the lot. Truck drivers refused to help out. Working as laborers would involve loss of face. I assigned my armed truckers to do more persuasive recruiting.

The local people could not have cared less. I pointed out to the merchants of Annan that, if the bridge was not restored soon, trucks would take another road. Their town would be consigned to oblivion. They shrugged. At the moment, they were thriving.

The tribal headmen were only a little more helpful. They would provide cooks and food if I would find the laborers to eat it.

Finally, I went directly to the pampered males of the Miao tribe. Why should they work for their city's sake when they would not even work for their own families?

I was getting nowhere until, half-facetiously, I offered them free transportation to the bridge site. Suddenly, I was overwhelmed with volunteers. This was their first ride ever on a truck. Like children on the first day of school, they climbed aboard with stiff upper lips and quivering lower lips. After riding the first mile unharmed, they relaxed.

By noon, the local civilians and a few soldiers were all lined up for work. My men, however, had not yet appeared with the other truck drivers in tow.

While we waited, I stood on the bridge pier and gazed down at the roaring river. The bridge site was well below the town of Annan. Mighty mountains towered behind me and before me. Standing in the gorge, I felt like an ant. I could feel a downdraft of air trying to suck me into the turbulent waters of the Pepan.

The two Chinese engineers appeared on the other side. The mountains echoed every sound, so we talked slowly across the swirling water. The engineers had lined up cables, timber, and seventy workers. The two men dictated a blueprint in hoarse shouts. We were ready to start. But where were my own men?

Dong arrived with somber tidings: "Even with pistols, we can't get the truck drivers to come. They say they'll come, but they don't. There's a man there who keeps talking them out of it."

They were on a precipice above us. I pushed my way through a throng of more than a hundred surly truckers. Men who knew me hung their heads sheepishly or giggled as I passed. Strangers looked me straight in the eye, and remained seated in their cabs or on their running boards. They were spoiling for trouble, though waiting for somebody else to start it.

I was gunning for that somebody else.

I found him in the center of the throng. He was small, slick-looking, and about thirty. His pasty face must not have been outdoors much. It looked vaguely familiar.

Stopping a few feet away, I eyed him up and down silently. The men around him flinched, but they stood ready to defend him in a showdown. My men were scattered around the crowd, where they could do me little good in a melee. They might end up shooting each other. The battle would have to be between the pasty-faced man and me.

Staring contemptuously at a man usually takes its toll. It makes him bristle. This one, however, reveled in my gaze. His voice grew stronger. He was a professional.

The first time he paused for breath, I said crisply: "I want these men down at the river bank. Right now!"

He replied to me in English: "Who you? Why you order us about? Do we work for you, Stuart?"

He turned to the crowd, but he still spoke English for my benefit: "Tell foreign devil we wait until trucks have wings. Then we fly over river. Better than working for him."

The mob began to roar with ugly laughter. First, those who understood English cackled. Then they translated the little man's words into Chinese. He was so pleased with himself that he repeated his insult several times in English and Chinese. The crowd of truckers started to cheer him.

"The only wings I can see," I declared, "are the wings of an evil spirit attached to the back of this talkative one. Listen carefully, men! This road is the lifeline to Chungking. Without it, the people of free China cannot resist their enemy. Do you really believe the talkative one? Do you think the bridge will grow back? Or will you just sit here making woman talk until the Japanese come?"

There were a few sniggers, but nothing like the response that the pale little man had excited. I could never beat him at his specialty of sarcasm.

"There is no more time for nonsense," I announced. "I will repeat once more: This is your last chance!"

Everyone looked to the little man. For a minute, he did not respond. The truckers began to discuss my ultimatum seriously. The tightly packed mob loosened slightly.

Suddenly, the pasty-faced little man gave a piercing shriek. He held up both hands. The crowd froze.

"Stuart, you cannot order us about," he said in Chinese, not to me but to them. "We will move only when we are ready to cross the river. Stuart, you are trying to trick us. Why do you want us to build your bridge for you? So your trucks can be the first across. We will stay where we are, Stuart. We will never give in to a foreign devil."

The mob drew together again. The little man pointed his finger at me and said in English: "I know this foreign devil. I know Stuart. But we are all alike to him. He does not remember me." Then he lapsed into Chinese curses.

I watched him turn to the mob and leap up and down, frothing with hatred. It was his madness — not anything he said — that put this crowd under his spell. The mob surged forward. The scene seemed familiar. So did the man. But it was all wrong in broad daylight . . .

The whole picture flashed through my mind. As the little man's high-pitched voice cursed the white man for the ten millionth time, I recalled my encounters with this maniac.

In a stope hundreds of feet below ground at the Hong Kong Mines, he had urged my miners to kill me and escape across the Chinese border. I could see the miners crouching low in the hot, airless stope. I could see their picks and shovels poised to kill. I could almost feel the little man's greasy, sweaty body throttling my life away.

In the tailings dump, he had materialized behind me and nearly drowned me in slime. Now I once again felt my body flailing and my throat struggling for help as death drew me to its embrace.

Ever since then, the Agitator and I had been destined for this rendezvous in Annan. Both of us knew our third encounter would be fatal.

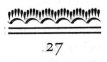

## 27

# He Who Lives by the Mob

THE Agitator was inciting the mob to action. Never taking my eyes off him, I told the crowd:

"The little man with the woman's tongue is right. We have met before. I have a good memory for evil spirits. Then, as now, he spoke well of his hate for man. Let us see if he fights with his hands — or only with his woman's tongue."

The Agitator leaned back against his henchmen, who caught him as he fell. Then they and he backed into the mob. They made a dent, but bounced right out. The Agitator pulled, dragged, and tugged at his stooges. He gave the impression that he was trying to fight me, and they were holding him back. As he struggled forward, he brought the mob with him. It was a demagogue's tactic of committing a crowd to his cause.

When he was good and ready, his henchmen would unleash him. The whole mob would be propelled forward as one. Then only bullets would stop them.

My wish was father to the deed. A half dozen bullets blasted out behind me. Their noise bounced from mountain to mountain like a trapped echo. The mob froze.

The Agitator and his henchmen gazed about wildly. They and I and the others were all trapped on a precipice. A stone mountain lay behind them. Before them was the churning river — and me. On either side were Captain Mar's troops, firing warning shots over the mob's head.

I nodded to Captain Mar in acknowledgment of his help. When I looked back, the Agitator was nowhere to be seen. He had melted into the mob.

It was my turn for oratory. "Give me the great leader," I pleaded. "I will accept no help. You will see for yourselves that it is just him against me. Let him have his wish to tear me to shreds."

Nobody moved. All eyes were upon me. Hatred and ridicule no longer hovered in the air. There was fear.

I drew my gun and fired one shot into the air. Half the mob crumbled. The men flung themselves to the ground.

"I will not waste another bullet on the sky," I said. "Give me the man with the woman's tongue."

The mob churned — a shapeless mass, staggering over itself and regrouping blindly. But when its paroxysm ended, the Agitator had been thrust forward.

He stood all alone ten yards from me. He crouched like a cornered animal. His face was wet. His thick black hair — once neatly combed and held in place by a thin steel loop — hung long over his face.

He looked as pitiful as a woman scorned. He was, however, far more dangerous. He had lived his life by the mob. Now even they had betrayed him. His mouth was drawn back in utter hate. He clutched something in his right hand.

Nevertheless, I tossed my pistol to Dong and stalked the Agitator slowly. He edged along the side of the road with his back hugging the cliff. As I moved closer, I saw what was clasped in his hand: the long, thin, sharp end of a rat-tail file.

We stood eight feet apart. For a minute, we stared at each other like total strangers. Each of us seemed surprised that, face-to-face, the other was only a man. Then, with a shrill scream that his clenched teeth could scarcely muffle, he sprang at me. The rat-tail file was pointed directly at my throat.

I crouched, turned, and caught hold of his right wrist. I held on firmly and used his forward motion to swing him completely around. I brought his arm over my shoulder with a sharp downward swoop. Then I let go.

The Agitator flew straight over me. The tips of his toes barely riffled my hair. He sailed straight through the air with the grace of an angel. His screams ricocheted off the mountains. For a moment, however, it looked as if he might glide to the other side. But then he started down — tumbling end over end until the river below sucked him out of sight.

The mob gasped as it surged to the edge of the precipice. A hundred men looked in vain for a last glimpse of their screaming demagogue.

"He is gone, like the bridge that was here a few days ago," I reminded them. "Did I not tell you that I saw the wings of an evil spirit sticking out of his back? Who would like to join him?"

The answer was nobody. At last, we were ready to build the bridge at Annan.

I appointed several of my men and Annan's headmen as foremen. I drew a simple sketch of the cable bridge we would build. I outlined each foreman's duties and enumerated the men he could have. I organized four shifts to work around the clock.

On the other side of the Pepan River, the two Chinese Army engineers were doing the same — with fewer men but more technical knowledge.

Small wire cables were strung across the river from their end. We fastened them to immovable boulders on our side. Then, at their end, they tied hardwood blocks (about fourteen feet long) to the cables and dropped them into the water. The current swept the blocks over to our side.

We fished them out and dragged them up to the bridge site. There, we formed them into anchor blocks. They would hold long steel cables that were now being strung across the river.

When anchor blocks and steel cables were in place and the cables were pulled as tautly as possible by hand, we had the skeleton of the bridge. Then we strapped wooden deck planks to it.

Hundred of planks were required to form a bridge only twelve feet wide and a hundred feet long. To cross it, a trucker would have to drive an unerring course. But any man who had negotiated the Twenty-Two Bends could manage this. The big question was: Would our makeshift bridge hold the weight of a truck?

Our work lasted three days and three nights. For most of the time, the sky was overcast. At night, it rained.

The weather hampered work, but it proved a blessing. On the third afternoon, we had a few hours of sunshine — and a Jap plane appeared.

Nobody made any effort to hide. I asked Captain Mar why.

"They know him," he explained. "He is Photo Joe. He only takes pictures. The next day, his brothers come back with bombs. Then you will see everybody hide."

"I hope to hell I'm not around for that," I said.

Captain Mar studied the darkening skies and said: "Well, they can't come back today. Tomorrow, you will either be on your way to Chungking or, if the bridge doesn't hold . . ."

He finished his thought by glancing down at the swirling waters of the Pepan.

The bridge was completed at nine o'clock that night. The workers put finishing touches on the deck and reluctantly abandoned their handiwork. Farmers, laborers, and even status-conscious truckers took pride in the reality they had created. They discussed bridges authoritatively. They argued heatedly about engineering techniques they had learned by doing. For the past twenty-four hours, I had not needed to stand over them and guide their every move.

In spite of themselves, they had grown interested, confident, and then proud. I knew now that no matter how often the Japs demolished the bridge, Annan would rebuild it.

There was a formal ceremony, illuminated by truck headlights. General Mah and I walked halfway across the bridge. We shook hands with the two engineers there. I tried not to notice how the bridge swayed beneath our footsteps. In addition, it sagged in the middle because we had not been able to tighten it properly.

One of the engineers accompanied me to our side. An Army truck had been donated for the first crucial test run. I had insisted on driving it.

The engineer made a few adjustments while I organized the truckers, who were now jockeying to cross early. I assigned first priority to Chinese Army trucks. Then would come a convoy of Bank of China trucks, loaded with armed guards and currency. (Chinese money was printed in England and Singapore.) Private truckers, operating with requisitions from the Chinese Central Government, would comprise the rear echelon. All mutinies ended when I announced that my own trucks would be the very last.

Then I climbed into the cab of the Army truck at the head of the line. If the bridge went down, I would go down with it and join the Agitator at the bottom of the Pepan.

Never had I realized how narrow a width of twelve feet can be. Until that night, twelve feet had meant two good-sized men placed end to end. Now every inch was the difference between life and death.

Because of the sag in the bridge, my headlights illuminated not what was directly before me, but the upward slope of the second half. As I approached midpoint, I knew this would be the most dangerous milestone of all. Would the cables hold when the weight of the truck was dead center? And would the bridge be too steep and too slippery for the truck to climb to the other side? I slipped the transmission into second gear.

Passing the center and starting uphill, I stepped on the gas for the first time. As the truck climbed the ramp. I pushed the pedal harder. The headlights pointed up at the sky. I could no longer see the bridge. If it had looked like a ramp before, it felt like a ladder now.

After an eternity of seconds, the truck shot off the bridge and onto level ground. A crowd hugged me as I emerged shakily from the cab. Tearing myself away, I was surprised to see that the bridge was still standing.

It took all night to keep order and move all traffic across the bridge. Heavy cargoes had to be unloaded and carried across by work gangs. The bridge swayed ominously, but there were no mishaps upon it. There was, however, one fatality on the Annan side, when one

Northwest truck attempted to sneak ahead of another. The road was too narrow. The impatient driver's wheels slipped off the side of the cliff. Truck and driver plunged silently into the darkness of the river.

Dawn was breaking as I drove my own truck, the caboose of the convoy, across the bridge. The last crossing was as shaky and perilous as the first.

All morning, we worked our way up a steep mountain. Toward noon, we heard airplanes. A rocky ledge above us afforded concealment for our trucks and a good view of Annan and the bridge seven thousand feet below.

"I hear the planes, but I'm damned if I can see them," I complained to Dong as I scanned the skies above me.

Dong pointed downward. I realized that the planes were below us — in the corridor between mountains.

Six Japanese planes were flying in tight formation and following the river. Their target was clearly the bridge. Photo Joe had done his work well.

Approaching the bridge, the planes formed a small circle. One at a time would peel off, dive at the bridge, drop its load, and vanish from view.

The first plane came in low. The bombardier dropped his bombs too soon. Most of them fell into the river. A few landed on the road. We could see tiny specks that were trucks explode, burst into small blobs of flame, and disappear. The bridge was unhurt.

The second plane came in right on target. It scored direct hits with two bombs. But the bombs smashed right through the bridge decking and exploded just a few feet above the water.

Most of the decking catapulted into the air. From where we crouched, it looked as though the bridge had been destroyed.

The Japs must have left with the same impression. The other four planes dropped their bombs at random upon Annan and trucks along the road.

We turned away sadly and drove on to Anshun. We were certain our bridge had burned behind us.

A week later, when we were preparing to leave Chungking, we learned that our bridge had not been obliterated. True, the decking was lost. But the cables sprang right back into position, none the worse for their battering. Within a day, the Chinese Engineers replaced the decking. We could use the bridge on our way back.

By the time Photo Joe discovered the bridge again, a battalion of engineers was erecting a new bridge three miles away in an unassailable location. I used it many times. At the only hotel in Annan, I was always an honored guest. No matter what the hour of arrival, the manager would come out to meet me. And so would the bedbugs.

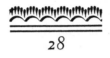

## 28

## New Friends and Old

EVERY time I returned to Rangoon, there were more Americans milling about the lobby of the Strand Hotel. Pearl Harbor had yet to happen, but it was definitely going to. Everybody in Asia who knew the Japs also knew that the attack was imminent. Only two questions — *when?* and *where?* — remained to be answered the hard way.

My room boy mixed me a drink while a hotel boy unpacked my luggage for me. While they worked, they filled me in on the latest news of Rangoon.

"Americans call self Burma Road Technical Group," the room boy said.

The hotel boy laughed and said: "They spend whole day working in Silver Grill."

"They get drunk and spend plenty money," the room boy contributed.

"They fight much. But they pay many times too much for damage," the hotel boy added.

"Do they fight all the time in America, sahib?" the room boy asked me.

"I've never been there," I replied. "I should think that, if they did, they'd be slapped into jail."

"So why they do it here?"

"I don't know," I said. "Let's wait and see if they work and fight as hard as they play. They're here to help your people."

The room boy shook his head and said: "They say nothing about helping Chinese or helping Burmese. They say they kill Japanese."

All this sounded familiar. I said: "Maybe they will be helping all of us soon."

On my way out to lunch, I walked down the steps of the Strand and, as was my custom, almost stumbled over an outstretched hand. It belonged to the lame beggar who had reached out to me on my very first morning in Rangoon.

He and I knew each other well now. If there was such a thing as an official begging concession, he had it. Nobody challenged his right to be there. Nobody tried to compete with him for his lucrative site. The regular customers of the Strand could depend upon him to transmit messages, keep secrets, and give advice.

"Good afternoon, sahib," he greeted me with genuine pleasure.

"Good afternoon. Have the Americans brought prosperity to you, my old friend?"

"Yes," he replied, "but costs have gone up."

"It is the same everywhere, old friend. Have you something to tell me?"

"I do. There is much you should know about yourself, sahib."

"I have no time."

"Then you will never learn," he said wearily.

I dropped a rupee note into his lap. "Here, old man," I said. "You have a kind face and you look thin. Buy yourself a good meal."

To my amazement, the ancient beggar handed back my money and said: "No, sahib. With the Americans here, I no longer need this. Now we can afford to be friends."

I started to walk away, making a mental note never again to think of beggars as beggars if it were at all possible to think of them as men. But my friend called after me:

"One minute more, sahib. I have a message for you. After lunch, you will kindly go see the other Mister Stewart. Do you know who I mean?"

[ 264 ]

I did indeed. The Mr. Stewart who spelled his name differently from mine was a "casual" acquaintance. His job was top secret.

In addition to living high on the Yankee dollar, my venerable beggar friend was, I realized, delivering messages for British Intelligence.

I lunched at Paul Cunningham's Silver Grill with my boss, Bill Crooks. We had been in business together for two years. The Lidell Brothers Company operation was the most successful on the Burma Road. We had not lost a single truck or very much cargo. We now had a fleet of forty Dodge trucks. With full cargo, we averaged six days between Lashio and Kunming. With lighter loads and a little luck, we could traverse the Burma Road in three days.

After lunch, I strolled a few blocks and then took a cab. I changed cabs three times. The last cab left me a few blocks from some small neat bungalows belonging to the British Government.

Inside one bungalow was an elderly Englishman. He was well dressed, well built, and gray at the temples. Mr. Stewart was a very distinguished looking namesake.

Without a word, I placed four rolls of film on his desk. For several months, I had been photographing detours and new faces along the Burma Road for British Intelligence. I also reported on politics and military strength. Mr. Stewart had met me once at the Strand Hotel. Almost without his asking, I had agreed to do a little work for him.

"Very few new faces this trip," I told him. "And what few there are belong mostly to the American Army. You probably know more about them than I do."

"Perhaps not," Stewart said dryly. "Matter of fact, I asked you to come here because I'd like you to keep a careful eye on the Americans while you're out on the Burma Road."

"Good God!" I exclaimed. "You're not planning to declare war on *them*, I hope!"

Stewart chuckled. "No," he said, "but they'll be in it on our side very soon. I'd like to know everything they're doing wrong. Once they're in it, we can straighten them out."

"Maybe they'll have some ideas you can use if you keep your eyes open," I remarked.

[ 265 ]

"Perhaps," Stewart said dubiously.

Refreshed if debauched, I led my convoy out of Rangoon on what turned out to be my last journey to Chungking for Lidell and Company.

Pyu . . . Toungoo . . . Mandalay . . . Maymyo . . . Lashio . . . We reached the Burma Road smoothly. We spent a night in Namhkam, cleared Burmese customs, cleared Chinese customs in Wanting, and headed for Lungling. We planned to spend that night there.

The rains had stopped altogether. The road was dusty. The sun glowed angrily. Not a breath of air stirred the trees.

Sweat washed out of my every pore as I fought the sharp mountain bends along the Burma Road. The afternoon heat bore down on my steel cab. I felt as if I were riding in an oven.

I knew my drivers behind me felt much the same. I was determined, however, not to stop for a break. Any pause would mean more minutes in the scorching sun.

In low gear, my truck negotiated a steep grade at five or six miles an hour. After riding out a sharp bend, I glanced into my mirror. The rest of my convoy was struggling uphill. Uncharacteristically, the trucks were spaced out for several miles. I would have to give the men a refresher lecture when we reached Lungling. Stragglers are sitting ducks for bandits.

I must have had bandits on my mind when six rough-looking, but somewhat forlorn, coolies appeared in the middle of the road. They were trying to thumb a ride. Nobody was stricter than I about not taking riders. I told Lum, sitting beside me, to signal the trucks behind us. They should make haste in passing these coolies.

I gunned my motor as I neared them. They gave way. When we rounded the next bend, I could see at least a dozen more coolies lurking in the bushes.

"Thank God we didn't stop back there," I remarked to Lum.

I heard a shout from the road. One of the first six coolies was running alongside my truck as it labored up the steep mountain. He had snatched an old felt cap from his head. He waved his hands like a madman. As if the uphill climb wasn't strenuous enough, he jumped up and down as he traveled forward. I slowed down to watch him and he threw himself against the side of my plodding truck.

[ 266 ]

I pulled my pistol. Just then, I heard the mad coolie say: "Stop, Gil! Gil Stuart! *Tz'u-hsin Hu!*"

I screeched to a halt. It was a voice I had not heard in more than two years. There — battered but undented by his encounter with my truck — was my mine foreman and guerrilla comrade, Chan!

I leaped from my cab and embraced him. He was panting, spitting, and sweating as he clasped wet hands together in a prayer of thanks. Then he put his arms around my waist and clung to me like a child.

The other coolies came out of the bushes. Two of them were the men who had escorted me from Mr. Lee's junk to Major Chan's guerrillas and later gone off to headquarters.

The Japanese had driven Major Chan's forces out of south China. Almost all the units had gone farther inland, north of Swatow. Chan, however, had heard that war was imminent. He headed for the Burma Road, where his men could find work as laborers until they were needed to fight.

He had also heard a rumor that the "kind-hearted tiger" was prowling the Burma Road.

My drivers bunched up behind me. They sat tensely in their cabs. They watched incredulously as I let ragged bandits embrace me. My newest drivers, who had been lectured incessantly on never stopping for strangers, were goggle-eyed.

"Where were you headed?" I asked Chan.

"We going Lungling," he replied in his customary English. "We inquire there about you. If no find you, go Kunming next."

"I'll ride you and the boys into Lungling," I told him. "I'll treat you all to the best hotel in town until we come back through Lungling end of next week. Then I'm taking you all back to Burma with me. If British Intelligence can't find good use for you, I'll have work for you."

"Driving truck?" Chan asked dubiously.

"No. Training guerrillas. When the Yanks and the British get into war with Japan, they're going to be in for some surprises. Their usual techniques won't do them much good in the jungle."

"You have word when war going start?" Chan asked me.

"No, but it won't be long," I assured him.

It was the last week in November, 1941.

# 29

# Scorched Earth

AFTER December 7, 1941, the Americans flooded Rangoon with thousands of tons of Lend-Lease equipment that the docks occasionally gave way beneath its weight.

The Japanese invaded Singapore and advanced up the Malay Peninsula toward Rangoon. All private enterprise had to cease if the Allies were to evacuate their equipment before it fell into Japanese hands. The supplies had to be transported out of Burma and into China.

General Magruder of the American Army asked me to help organize a project to move 225,000 tons of Lend-Lease cargo out of Burma in six weeks. I asked the Chinese Minister of Transportation for permission to seize all Chinese commercial trucks and drivers on Burmese soil. They would be used only to move vital military cargo. The Minister of Transportation gave me free rein.

By then, I had a small private army of my own to enforce my authority. It consisted of three hundred Chinese camped twelve miles outside Rangoon on the road to Mandalay.

There were Chan's guerrillas, sixty of my drivers, and more than a hundred Chinese Army deserters and other volunteers. I financed my Army myself — by purchasing and pilfering as much equipment as I needed from the Rangoon docks. With skillful bartering, I was able to keep my army fed, too.

Our first formal mission was to stop all commercial truck traffic in Burma. We took the trucks to Rangoon, loaded them with equipment, and dispatched them to China. Balky drivers were threatened with our own martial law. To make sure there were no betrayals en route, I sent Chan out with a "flying squad" that set up surprise roadblocks, made spot-checks, and vanished just as erratically.

Hundreds of trucks traveled the Burma Road with supplies that the Japanese would never see until used against them. Gasoline and other fuels were shipped by river boat and barge up the Irrawaddy

River from Rangoon to Mandalay. There, they were loaded onto trucks just in from China. A new crew would leave immediately with each truck, while the incoming drivers took a one-day layover. By land and sea, more than 225,000 tons of Lend-Lease cargo left Rangoon within the allotted six weeks.

My best contact and closest friend among the Americans was a U. S. Army major named Jim Wilson, who supervised construction of a series of filling stations from Rangoon to the Chinese border. Jim staffed them with forty American technicians who knew all there was to know about how to keep trucks running no matter what was missing.

Despite our best efforts, we couldn't keep pace with the clock. Time was running out. In early 1942, the Japanese were nearing Rangoon. And, just as Mr. Stewart of British Intelligence had hinted, the American and British strategists found themselves at odds. To my own surprise, I sided with the Yanks.

General Magruder wanted to destroy all equipment that could not be moved out before the Japanese moved in. The British, however, would not concede that defeat in Burma was possible. Insisting that they — if nobody else — would hold out against the Japs, the British refused the Americans permission to destroy anything in Burma.

The Americans subscribed to a "scorched-earth policy" — destroying all crops, equipment, and anything else of use before an advancing enemy. They did not, however, want to give the appearance of running out on their British allies. Like Orientals, Americans revered *face*.

Major Jim Wilson conferred with General Magruder and came to me. As a Briton, I could effect the Americans' scorched-earth policy without making it an American operation.

"Gil, we'd like you to paint the town red," Jim told me, "but not the way you and Sammy Yuan usually do it."

"I'm damned if I'm going to be an American puppet," I said, spitting.

"But you know what's right, Gil. You know damn well that fifth columnists have driven Lend-Lease trucks off the road and into the jungle. As soon as the Japs reach here, they'll be completely supplied with transportation — unless somebody does something now."

I gave in toughly: "I'll do it for a price — a hundred bags of rice to feed my little army. And forty of those scout cars you have sitting in Rangoon and just waiting for the Japs to get behind the wheels."

"You can have them, Gil. Nobody wants those scout cars. They don't have machine guns."

"I'll take my chances on that, Jim. Somewhere there must be forty machine guns that nobody wants because there's no way to move them. And I'll need one more thing, Jim: An American who's willing to die for his country."

Wilson sent me an American civilian named Smitty. If he had a first name, I never heard it. Smitty was a six-footer weighing more than two hundred pounds. He was muscular, although he also had a belly that concealed his belt. In all the time I knew Smitty, I was constantly expecting his pants to fall down.

Smitty was belligerent and foul-mouthed, but, like many Americans I met in wartime, he had a heart of gold. Every time I see the late actor Wallace Beery in an old movie on television nowadays, I remember Smitty.

"I'd like to have you with me, Smitty," I told him. "First, though, I want to be sure you're a volunteer. There's a chance you'll be shot — maybe by the Japs, maybe by the British, maybe by mistake. There's no reward. If we're caught, everybody will disown us. We'll be on our own."

"I'm going with you," Smitty said bluntly.

Then I pushed my luck. I asked Major Wilson for one more American volunteer: a fast jeep driver to deliver a message from Rangoon to the first American filling station in Pyu, about a hundred miles to the north.

The second volunteer was a shifty-eyed young fellow who reminded me of a trapped rat.

"At Pyu," I instructed him, "you are to tell the American technicians to halt all southbound trucks. They're to gas them up and send them back toward China."

Smitty and I would be destroying everything valuable between Rangoon and Pyu.

As the second volunteer readied his jeep, Smitty took me aside and warned: "Don't send that dumb son of a bitch. If he don't kill himself with his jeep, he'll louse up the whole God damn maneuver. He don't have a f——ing brain in his head, Gil."

[ 270 ]

I was inclined to trust Smitty's judgment. When we broached the matter to Jim Wilson, however, he glared at Smitty and said: "That's enough out of you, Smitty. Just do your work and don't worry about anyone else."

"All right," Smitty grumbled. "Don't say I didn't warn you."

"What the hell?" I said. "It's just a courier's job."

"There's no job too small for that punk to f—— up," Smitty assured me. I let the matter drop. It was time to assemble our own equipment — two jeeps, each outfitted with a fifty-gallon drum of gasoline; a bucket; a ten-foot hose for siphoning gasoline; a case of .45 ammunition; an ax; a sledgehammer; and four bottles of bourbon. We were armed with both our .45 pistols and two tommyguns.

"You're in charge," I told Chan. "I'll be gone for a week. Man the roadblocks and help out with the evacuation of Rangoon. If the city falls before I return, I'll meet you somewhere on the road to Mandalay."

Smitty and I set out at one A.M. We were not far out of Rangoon when either side of the road became a cemetery for trucks. Some of the trucks were perfectly healthy, but had been hidden there by fifth columnists. Others had been abandoned because of engine or mechanical trouble. In those desperate days, nobody stopped for repairs. And we had no time to salvage or even examine. Shortly before three in the morning, Smitty and I instigated the scorched-earth policy in Burma. We destroyed every empty truck we found.

It is not easy to burn a truck and its cargo, particularly if the latter is fireproof. Nor does fire always destroy an engine. We smashed the engine block and fire-resistant cargo with our sledgehammers. Then we doused engine, tires, cab, and cargo with gasoline. Igniting the truck, we drove on to the next. Our victims were never more than two miles apart.

Despite our haste, we couldn't help noticing that several trucks were in perfect repair and stocked with rice and gasoline for the Japanese invaders. These "wrecks" were the easiest to destroy, for their contents were highly inflammable.

Smitty and I blazed our destructive swath through the night. Occasionally, we heard a truck tearing down the road to Rangoon.

"Sounds to me as if Rat Face didn't get through with his message," I remarked.

"You can count on that bastard for f——ing up," Smitty said.

By firing into the air, we halted most of the trucks. No, the drivers told us, they had not been intercepted at Pyu. We sent them back. Any that we missed would be turned back or confiscated by Chan on the outskirts of Rangoon.

By eleven A.M., we were better than halfway to Pyu. We had destroyed more than fifty trucks. Nobody asked us any questions. British staff cars and other traffic heading toward Pyu simply sped up when they neared us.

Toward noon, however, somebody started gunning for us.

We were finishing off truck number fifty-six when a black Buick roared by. A Thompson machine gun was spraying bullets from its rear window.

I hit the dirt. Bullets tore through the truck's canvas awning. Smitty, shielded by the truck, had whipped out his .45 and was firing back. The Buick disappeared.

Smitty cocked an elbow at the retreating Buick and shouted: "They got no right using an American car!"

"Is this what Chicago is like?" I asked.

"Dunno," said Smitty who was, I think, from Detroit. "Never been there. But I think they do it better."

"Well, anyway. That was a nice compliment for our handiwork. The fifth columnists must be getting nervous about us."

"Just let them pay us another compliment and I'll shoot their balls off," Smitty muttered.

They returned four times that day — always at such high speed that neither they nor we had any chance of drawing blood. Still, they made us jumpy and trigger-happy enough to slow down our operation a little.

We approached Pyu toward dusk. Billows of smoke blackened the sky above the town. The filling station was nothing but smoldering debris. The whole town was on fire. Burmese residents were scampering around frantically. When I asked what had happened, they hid. I could not understand who had done this to a peaceful community through which I had passed many a time.

Finally, a bland and impervious-looking Englishman accosted us: "Now see what you American chaps have started. We'll never have these people under control again."

"I say, old man," I said, startling him slightly, "d'y' happen to know what became of those Yanks in the filling station here?"

"They left hours ago. They started all these fireworks, y' know."

"What the hell d'you mean?"

"Around midnight, a little American doughboy came by in a jeep. Said the Japs were in Rangoon. Said they were on their way here, don't y' know. In that event the Yanks had instructions to destroy the filling station and go north. When they blew it up, this awoke the fifth columnists. They set fire to the rest of Pyu."

"What happened to the soldier in the jeep?" I asked.

"Never budged from his jeep. Hardly slowed down, you might say. Just continued north once he'd given the word."

"That silly little fart," Smitty said.

All I could add was an inconclusive: "If I ever catch up with him . . ."

I never did. Many months later, however, Smitty did in India. Both he and Rat Face were in a depot and awaiting transportation back to the States. Smitty tried to kill him. He didn't succeed. He did cut his face so badly with a broken beer bottle that — for the rest of his life — Rat Face had only to glance into his mirror when he shaved and the flames of Pyu would burn deeply and shamefully.

Smitty and I blazed our way to Mandalay. Then alone we doubled back on the Rome Road. In daylight hours, we found and destroyed whole convoys of trucks parked a few dozen feet off the road.

On the way back, we learned that Rangoon still had not fallen. But it was being bombed and the evacuation was on.

Class distinction was forgotten as rich and poor, white and yellow, took to the road together. All were equally forlorn in the race for survival. On the road, Smitty and I saw pedestrians who had sailed all over the world. We also saw others who had never been out of Rangoon. Now all were en route to China and India. Suddenly, the unknown represented safety to them. Places they had known all their lives now offered them nothing but chaos and destruction.

Watching them stagger toward the jungles and mountains they would have to traverse, I wondered how many would survive — and just which ones they would be.

Their gods were on their lips as they stumbled forward. But, I asked myself, would an almighty power permit this scene of misery? Was this an exodus or a day of reckoning? Smitty and I honked our horns to clear a path through the throng of refugees. Although they parted meekly, they did not look blessed to me.

I saw an old Indian man, carrying his bony wife on his back. I wondered if he and his beloved burden would ever make it? As I slowed down to watch them, a Westerner placed his hand on my wheel.

The tears in his eyes, the sweat on his clothes, and the blood oozing from his shoes rendered his nationality unrecognizable to me. He carried two heavy leather bags crammed with Burmese currency.

"I will give you half my wealth, young man, if you will turn your jeep around and drive me to Mandalay," he said in a tone that had seldom anticipated or tolerated refusal.

"I can't," I said.

"Then take it all! Just get me out of here, for God's sake! I won't make it otherwise! Do you understand what I'm saying?"

I understood. However, there was nothing I could do. He knew and I knew that he would never make it. The old Indian and his wife had disappeared from view, but I suddenly knew they were likely to make it — because they were devoted to each other. This man had nothing except the moneybags beside him. And they were worthless to him.

His blistered hands clung to my wheel. He pleaded, shouted, ranted, and cursed at me. Before my eyes, he lost his mind and crossed the thin line that separates man from beast. If my teeth had been tearing at his throat, there could not have been more horror in his face.

I could not look him in the eye. I looked instead at the impassive sea of Oriental faces surging past and asking nothing. I felt more kinship there than with my fellow white man. The Japanese victories early in World War II were a sorry lesson for the white man in Asia. For many years, he had fattened on the "weakness" of the yellow man. Now he lacked the Oriental's most precious strength: endurance.

I tried to free the man's grip from my wheel, but rigor mortis had set in even as this living corpse wailed for his life.

I drew my .45 and pointed it at him. If he saw it, he didn't react.

Finally, I brought the butt of the gun down on his knuckles — not quite hard enough to break them. He released his grip and fell to his knees. Then he sobbed like a child. His head was held back looking straight up at the darkening sky.

I engaged the clutch of my jeep. I lurched forward. I had to escape from there. I was afraid of what I would do if he persisted. And I was afraid of what I wouldn't do, of what I hadn't done, and, above all, of what I had seen.

It is far easier to face an enemy with a gun in his hand than a lone man with terror and misery in his body.

Rangoon was virtually abandoned, although the Japanese were still a day or more away. Their bombs had taken their toll.

I arrived the morning after the last air raid. What I saw reminded me of my first sunrise in Rangoon. The sky was again blood-red. The horrors it reflected now were man-made. The fire and heat of the grisly day were the work of bombs, not Nature.

The smells of human filth and betel nut were still there. Now there were also new smells that tested the strength of my bowels.

The street sleepers were still there. Some were, as always, too weak to move. Others were dead and dying, soaked in their own blood. Vultures dived at them from the sky. Heads, limbs, and chunks of flesh were strewn about the roads.

Every now and then, I saw an armless, legless man staring wide-eyed as a vulture ripped at his guts. I could never hope to extinguish vultures. Still, I could draw a merciful curtain between a man and his fate. As I fired a bullet into each dying man whose eyes begged me for death, I trembled and thought "Where is God?"

As on my first dawn in Rangoon, I gazed up and glimpsed the golden pagoda in the distance. It no longer gleamed. It was half-hidden and gray in the smoke's shadow. I remembered why God was nowhere to be found. I was in the home of the Devil.

My Army was waiting in Yedashe, Burma. It had picked up recruits along the way. Now it numbered four hundred men and a hundred and fifty vehicles. But we had only a few rifles, hardly any tommy-guns, and rations that would last no more than a week. For all its vehicles, an Army still travels on its stomach.

I had to take my Army into somebody's camp before it starved to death. I rejected the Americans and British, for several reasons.

First of all, I would rather not go where I'm not wanted. Both the British and American armies openly disapproved of my ragged band, even though they used us on occasion to do their unofficial dirty work. They were likely to reject my offer or accept it on such ungracious terms that we would all feel like prisoners of war.

Secondly, I was unwilling to sacrifice my men in the tragic lessons that the white armies were about to learn. The British and Americans arrived in Asia thoroughly prepared to fight the white man's war — the war of the trenches. They could erect superb defenses in minutes. But the coming struggle, I knew, would have to be fought in Asian jungles on Asian terms. There is no such thing as defense in jungle warfare. An Army must keep moving, spread out in small groups like Major Chan's guerrillas. Banding together in one large fighting unit is fatal. Guerrilla tactics are all offensive and all hit-and-run. You attack the enemy's flanks and its rear. You break down the enemy's morale. You create confusion. If possible, you put the enemy on the defensive — and then he is doomed.

Finally, my men might not have followed me into the Anglo-American camp. Even they — who hated the Japanese as only victims can — took malicious delight in the comeuppance the white man was receiving in Asia. It was happening before the astonished eyes of the entire world. He was losing face.

The choice I made seemed particularly incredible to my American friends. I decided to throw in my lot with General Tu Yu Ming, commander of the Chinese Fifth and Sixth Armies.

Of all the Chinese generals around, none was more offensive to "Vinegar Joe" Stilwell, the American general who had Chiang Kaishek's ear in Chungking. One would have thought that Stilwell was at war with Tu Yu Ming, not with Japan. The Chinese general disobeyed or ignored many of Stilwell's decisions. Months later Stilwell was pressuring Generalissimo Chiang Kai-shek to put Tu Yu Ming before a firing squad.

I had met neither Stilwell nor Tu Yu Ming. Nevertheless, I had seen enough of Stilwell's subordinates to form a favorable opinion of their Chinese whipping boy. Stilwell and a few of his staff officers had been stationed in Peking some years earlier. They had mastered

Chinese at the Army Language School there. And because they "knew the country" and "spoke the language," they assumed that they understood the Chinese.

This is the type of misunderstanding that persists all over the world today. A man who speaks the language but does not read the soul can be far more offensive than a bumptious, arrogant, and (thank God!) inarticulate tourist.

Stilwell's officers lacked even the most shallow grounding in Chinese psychology and philosophy.

I led my Army to Chinese Fifth Army field headquarters in Pyawbwe, Burma. General Tu Yu Ming welcomed me warmly. He was a round-faced, jolly man in his forties. He stood about five feet nine. I handed him a letter of introduction from the Chinese Consul in Rangoon. General Tu Yu Ming stuck it in his drawer without reading it.

"I know you quite well, Mr. Stuart," he said in English. "You have a great and talkative admirer in my Special Battalion commander. Perhaps you remember him. He has an ugly face that says much silently of his own heroism. . . ."

"Captain Mar!" I exclaimed.

"He is Major Mar now. He has told me of how you and he built the bridge at Annan. I do not need to consult him now. I know he will approve of what I am going to do. I will accept your Army as a motorized unit. Your men will receive all Chinese Army benefits — pay, food, and enlisted men's rank. They will serve in the Special Battalion under Major Mar's command."

He paused. I was about to ask if I could come along as a sergeant, when General Tu Yu Ming added:

"You will be assigned to Major Mar's battalion, too."

General Tu Yu Ming's legions moved even more swiftly than the toy Chinese soldiers of my childhood. Fifteen minutes later, I had a commission in the Chinese Fifth Army as a major with command of my own unit.

# IV

Chinese Army

[ 1942–1946 ]

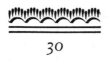

## 30

# Opium to the Rescue

MAJOR Mar was not around to welcome me to his ranks. On my third day in the Chinese Army, I learned that he was missing in action.

General Tu Yu Ming had just received the report. The scarfaced major, eight armored scout cars, and twenty men had disappeared east of Toungoo, Burma, the Japs' first major target after the conquest of Rangoon.

Mar's chances and Tu Yu Ming's manpower were so slim that no rescue operation would be attempted. But I volunteered: "You haven't really put me to work yet, sir, so you're not losing anybody. May I request three days to look for him?" The general gave me permission, a jeep, and a driver — my Burma Road mechanic, Lum.

We left Pyawbwe in the afternoon and drove all night. Two hundred miles later, a wounded foot-soldier told us of Mar's last whereabouts: He and his men were trapped with their scout cars in the bed of a dried-up creek encircled by Japs.

It was early morning by then. The heat was stifling. Lum and I were choking on the red dust of Burma. Our lips were parched. We had not eaten since leaving Pyawbwe. We knew, however, that Mar and his men — if they were still alive — had been without food for almost three days.

After another half-mile, we ran into a barrage of Japanese machine-gun and mortar fire. This did not faze us, because the rugged terrain offered concealment for a while. Lum maneuvered the jeep in irregular patterns. We never stayed in view long enough for the Japs to take an accurate fix on us.

[ 281 ]

Abandoning our jeep two miles later, we walked the remaining mile. On foot, the creek bed was not impossible to enter — and perhaps exit. Major Mar, I gathered, was determined to save his eight scout cars, which were just about all he thought he had. Equipment was dearer than men in the Chinese Army. Mar didn't know that his battalion was now more than a hundred scout cars richer — thanks to the absorption of my private Army.

The Japanese did not seem to know exactly what was in the creek bed. Rather than venture close and see for themselves, they had been drawing a gradually shrinking circle around it. The steep banks of the creek would hide its contents from the Japs for another day or two, at the most.

The creek was thirty feet wide, fifteen feet deep, and bone dry. Trees and thick bushes grew out of its banks. It was a miracle that Major Mar and his men had driven the cars down without flipping them over.

When Lum and I arrived, Major Mar was out scouting for a hole in the Japanese trap. His men were hungry and virtually unarmed. True, they had rifles and grenades, but they had hardly any ammunition. My own tommygun was the only automatic weapon in the whole crowd. Like the scout cars I had secured from Major Jim Wilson in the last days of Rangoon, Major Mar's were naked of guns.

Dead Chinese soldiers and Burmese civilians lay in the dry creek with the cars. They were victims of mortar shells. Several of the soldiers were wounded. Others were weak from dysentery. The few water holes nearby were contaminated.

When Lum explained in Chinese that the new major was the legendary "kind-hearted tiger" of the Burma Road, the men's morale rose slightly. This was not the case, however, with two young lieutenants whom Major Mar had left in command of the men.

They had never heard of me. They had never seen a "white devil" in a Chinese Fifth Army major's uniform. All I meant to them was a threat to their authority. Even in a fatal trap, they had been savoring their first (and perhaps last) taste of power.

Neither was more than twenty. One of them didn't look as if he'd ever needed to shave.

"I have an idea," I told them. "We can start the preparations now

[ 282 ]

and, when Major Mar returns, we'll see what he thinks of them. . . ."

Both lieutenants refused to listen. The swarthier one piped up in shrill Chinese: "We are surrounded. We cannot get the cars back up the creek banks. When we try, the cars fall back and nearly turn over."

"My idea is to drive the cars along the creek beds," I said.

"Too many obstacles!" he shrieked. "Fallen trees! The cars will never make it!"

"You ought to have more faith in American cars," I told him. "They can do almost anything if you treat them kindly. Now I want you to listen to me very carefully. The first man who argues with me or disobeys me will be shot. By me, personally."

I stared straight at the swarthier lieutenant as I added: "Do you understand me?"

The same sullen look crossed both young faces. It was the first time I had pulled rank in the Chinese Army. It was also the first time these lieutenants had ever been given orders by a Westerner.

They said nothing. In eloquent Chinese, Lum began telling them stories of the "kind-hearted tiger," my various escapades on the Burma Road, and even of the time Major Mar and I (all by ourselves, Lum insisted) rebuilt the bridge at Annan. He pleaded with them to heed me before their corpses became part of my legend.

The two lieutenants hung their heads and tried not to hear.

"These are my orders," I said. "You will station several men above the banks of the creek. One or two will climb trees and observe the terrain. The way things are now, we could be wiped out by a Jap patrol. Hell, I walked right in here without being challenged." Pointing to the shrill-voiced lieutenant, I commanded: "You! Get busy selecting the lookouts!"

He did not budge. He said: "We will do nothing until Major Mar returns. We do not take orders from a foreign devil."

Lum moaned. I told the lieutenant: "I have warned you that if you do not carry out my orders I will shoot you."

He took several paces backwards. He voice rose as he spoke his last words: "I am in charge here!"

I swung my tommygun toward him and fired a burst into his guts. He was dead when he hit the ground.

The other lieutenant started to weep, but chills of fright stopped his tears. Lum told him: "I warned you that the kind-hearted tiger makes no idle talk." I pointed my gun at the young officer and said sympathetically: "You don't want to join him, do you, son?"

He chose life. Motioning four men to follow him, he and they departed on the double. He stumbled over his fallen friend's body, but he didn't even look down.

When he and his lookouts reached the top of the bank, I held my breath. No shots from the lieutenant were forthcoming. I had answered the first challenge to my authority by the only means of expression respected in the Chinese Army: *violence*.

I detailed the rest of the men to clear a trail through the creek bed. Each scout car came equipped with a two-man crosscut saw, an ax, and shovels. One of Major Mar's vehicles had a steel cable winch attachment, enabling us to move trees and boulders when necessary.

Progress was slow. Still, we gained a few yards every hour. When Major Mar returned at nightfall, he would have had trouble locating his men without our sentries to direct him.

We had not seen each other since Annan, but Mar greeted me as casually as a man meeting his whist partner at a British club: "Why, Stuart! Good to see you! What an excellent disguise!"

I saluted him formally and announced: "Major Stuart, Chinese Fifth Army, here to get you the hell out of this mess you're in!"

Mar and I brought each other up to date on our careers. Then he told me: "I have had no luck in finding a way out of here, but I see that you're inventing one."

"We have a mile and a half to go," I told him. "It'll take another day if the Japs leave us alone!"

I apologized for costing him a lieutenant while he was away. "Think no more of it," Mar assured me. "Life is cheap in this Army. Anyway, I found that young man difficult to get along with. I would have missed the other lieutenant more. He is promising."

Mar's words sounded even more callous than my killing. I knew, however, that the most livid scars in his face had been earned shielding two panicky recruits from a sputtering grenade one of them had dropped.

The surviving lieutenant — the "promising" one — grew up before my eyes the next day. He assumed my role, in fact. I was immobilized (if that is the proper word!) by dysentery.

[ 284 ]

There was a case of crème de menthe in one of the scout cars. I rationed it to the men with their water. Even a heavy dose of spirits could not kill the devils in my system.

By ten A.M., I was too weak to stand. As I befouled myself repeatedly, my skin tightened and my entire body turned a deathly gray.

The young lieutenant took over my job of pushing the men while Major Mar directed the earthmoving operation, checked our security, and hovered over me. Every half hour, I was carried to the newest landmark that had been attained in the creek bed.

As the men cleared away stones, snakes crawled out. I was obliged to decline some of the best white snake meat in all Burma. The most I could take was a delicious hot snake broth. But my body held it for less than five minutes.

Late that afternoon, we were only five hundred feet from the end of the creek. Japanese mortar was falling all around us, though haphazardly. The enemy had no idea yet of our intentions.

We would have to suspend work for the night. If we used our lights, they would give us away.

"We should be able to make a dash for it some time tomorrow morning," I told Mar. "I wish I could be more useful to you." My dysentery was as bad as ever.

Several times that day, the young lieutenant had glowered at me. He took morbid delight in my sufferings. Every time I was forced to make a pig of myself, I would look up to catch his eye.

In the evening, he must have decided that I had endured my penance for taking his friend's life. He whispered something to Major Mar, who told me: "The lieutenant says he knows of a medicine that will cure your dysentery."

"Then let me have it, sir!" I cried.

"But he says it might also kill you. And I am reluctant to give it to you."

"What the hell is it? Arsenic?"

"Opium — in crystal form."

"I've had opium before," I assured him.

"But you are not an addict, Stuart. You have no tolerance for it. This quantity may kill you."

"I have no tolerance for diarrhea. It may kill me, too. I'll try anything now."

I was suspicious, however. Perhaps the lieutenant had found a way to kill me at my own behest. Nevertheless, I was a desperate man.

One of Mar's men donated his own opium. Kneeling beside me, he removed from his breast pocket a small tin no wider than an American twenty-five cent piece. Sliding back the lid, he emptied the contents into the palm of his hand.

For a lingering moment, the man studied what was in his palm: a piece of opium the size of a jellybean and the color of brown coral.

He broke off a piece the size of a matchhead. Placing it in the palm of my left hand, he gave me instructions:

"Crush it with your thumbnail, Major. Then swallow it."

As I took the opium, I was surprised that it smelled more like molasses. Nor did it have the cloying taste of opium. It was bitter as gall.

Two hours later, I felt better than I had all day. My stomach cramps vanished. My bowels let me alone for an hour at a time.

The next morning, I was back on my feet — a trifle wobbly, perhaps, but unwavering in my gratitude to the wonders that opium can work.

At midmorning, we reached creek's end. We carved out a small dirt ramp. The cars lined up for their perilous journey up and over the grassy bank. As at Annan, I would make the first exploratory trip.

Edging to the top, I was greeted by a curtain of machine-gun fire and then a rain of mortar shells. I eased up on the brake and rolled back. I was trembling when I emerged.

"They're on to us now," I told Mar. "We have to make our move right away. The machine-gunner must be directly ahead — maybe a hundred and fifty yards away. I'm going to charge up there and try to run him down. If he gets me before I get him, we've all had it. But it's our only chance.

"While I'm doing that, you move the other cars out of here. Make a dash for the road with them. The mortars will still be zeroed in on the creek exit."

Mar gave me two men, armed with grenades. I instructed them: "When I give you the word, get rid of those grenades. We have to take that machine gun out of action."

Saying a prayer, I raced my engine, engaged my clutch, put the car into low gear, and crept up the ramp again.

We climbed at a steep angle. Through a small slit in the armor plate protecting the windshield, I could see nothing except sky. It was the bridge at Annan all over again, but now the danger was above, not below.

The car lurched forward on level ground. Machine-gun bullets ricocheted off the armor plating, but I could feel the car wince. A few more rounds and our shield would melt.

I slowed down for an endless second — just long enough to shift into second gear and pinpoint the Jap machine gun. It was vaguely camouflaged by a few bushes.

At full throttle, I aimed straight for the fiery mouth of the machine gun, almost four hundred feet away. The journey seemed to last longer than my first trip along the Burma Road.

We were doing forty-five miles an hour when we rammed the machine gun. Of the four Japs manning it, only one managed to jump aside. Frantically, he was stuffing a rifle grenade onto a rifle. I felt the pounding of my wheels as they rolled over the other three Japs.

"Now!" I cried. My men dropped their grenades over the side. The Jap who had leaped clear was shattered. The impact was so great that my foot was jolted from the gas pedal.

Our "bulletproof" tires blew out. One wheel dug deeply into the ground. Our car tilted at a crazy angle. The two men and I ran for cover in the bushes.

The other scout cars had made their getaway, although two of Major Mar's men had been badly wounded by shrapnel. (They died that night.) Major Mar was waiting for us at the wheel of his car. We drove two miles down a dirt trail. We rounded a bend and were on the road Lum and I had come in on two days earlier. We had broken through the Japanese encirclement.

On our way back to Chinese Fifth Army headquarters at Pyawbwe, Mar and I saw three hundred people milling about a small clearing before a pagoda. Almost all were Chinese Sixth Army soldiers. The rest were Burmese civilians.

At the foot of the pagoda, three naked men were bound to posts. Their heads had been shaved. Their bodies glistened with sweat and blood. As Mar and I pushed through the crowd, we saw that the crowd was stoning the naked men sporadically. At the prisoners' feet, three yellow robes were turning red from dirt that had been trampled into them.

"Three Buddhist priests!" I exclaimed to Mar.

A Sixth Army captain and a sergeant were strangling one of the priests with copper wire. When the priest turned blue and his eyes were about to pop from their sockets, the sergeant nudged the captain, who loosened the wire.

Both soldiers waited for the priest to regain consciousness. As soon as he did, the torture resumed.

An enlisted man was starting to work on the priest's testicles. Mar caught his eye and told him to ask his captain to join us.

The captain lit up with smiles when he saw he had two majors in his audience. He saluted us and bowed several times. He even invited us to take a turn at strangling the prisoners.

We declined and Major Mar asked: "Why have you arrested these priests?"

"Priests!" the captain snorted. "They are Japanese officers. They are spies. Somebody heard them speaking Japanese to each other. When we arrested them, we found pistols tied about their waists under their gowns. Have you ever seen Japanese before, major?"

"A great many," Mar replied. "Dead and alive."

Mar and I walked over to the prisoners, who were more dead than alive. The captain showed me their weapons. Mar looked the prisoners over closely. They were Japanese, all right. But somehow their identities were irrelevant to me.

"Why are you torturing these poor bastards?" I shouted at the sadistic captain.

"I am trying to get them to talk," he replied.

"By choking them to death?" I asked, almost hysterical with rage.

Major Mar added quietly: "If they do talk, captain, who here can understand Japanese?"

"You ought to be up with . . ." I said, but Major Mar silenced me with his eyes. He was determined that the despicable captain should not lose face before his own men.

"There are more than three hundred people gathered here," Mar told the captain solemnly. "If a Japanese plane should fly low, it could strafe you all. Now why don't you strangle this Jap just once more — gently, though. Then shoot all three of them and disperse the crowd. Leave the rest of the work for the buzzards and the vultures."

The captain liked the idea. After one more demonstration, he had the sergeant throw water over the Jap's face to bring him to his senses.

Then the captain, the sergeant, and the testicle twister all drew their guns. The crowd behind the three Japs was cleared away. It was time for the execution.

After looking into his audience and making sure that he was the "hero" of this spectacle, the captain shouted a command. In unison, he and the other two executioners fired into each Jap's right foot. The left foot was the next target. Then they worked up to knees, arms, and shoulders. The captain was saving heads and bodies for last.

With each volley, the crowd cheered. Civilians fought for better views. I reached for my pistol, but Major Mar restrained me. "It will all be over in a minute," he reminded me.

"All right," I said. "But we don't have to stay around to watch it. Then we're as bad as the rest of these people."

Everyone was making noise — screams, cheers, and a few curses — except the doomed Japanese, who were awaiting the end stoically. Some of the spectators were so engrossed that Mar and I had to pistol-whip them to make our way through the throng.

As we entered our car, I caught a glimpse of the pagoda as the sunset reflected on its gold-leaf spirals. The little prayer bells, hanging in clusters, moved slightly. But their sound was drowned out by people crying for more bloodshed. In the name of whose decency was our war being fought?

What did names and nations mean now to me? In my first week in the Chinese Army, I had killed a Chinese officer and cried out my compassion for three Japanese spies.

# 31

# Mission to Mandalay

MAJOR Mar's narrow escape convinced General Tu Yu Ming that our scout cars were useless without weapons: "What good is being fireproof if you cannot fire back?"

"No good at all," I admitted. "Just live targets for the Japanese to practice on."

Mandalay was about to fall to the Japanese. Hundreds of Bren guns sat unused in British warehouses there. General Tu dispatched me — with a jeep, three scout cars, and three drivers — to beg, borrow, or steal at least a hundred guns from my fellow Englishmen.

On the road to Mandalay, I was transformed into the yellowest man in Asia.

A coolie was jogging along the edge of the road. Two baskets of eggs swung gently from a crosspiece on his shoulders. Recalling my own coolie days with the guerrillas, I paid silent tribute to the man's grace and serenity.

Unfortunately, in 1942, people were more nervous than they looked. Hearing my jeep, the coolie glanced around to see who was behind him. As he swiveled, one of his baskets swung into my open-topped jeep's path.

A hailstorm of eggs splattered upon me. My face, lap, and jeep turned a ghastly yellow. The coolie was unhurt, although most of his wares perished. While I cleaned myself off as best I could, dozens of eggs fried on the road beneath the scorching Burmese sun.

I was still a mess when I reached British General Headquarters in the old palace at Mandalay. Nevertheless, I presented myself to the commanding officer there.

Any British headquarters a mile or more from the front lines is as sedate and placid as in peacetime. The colonel in charge wore all the red trimmings of a staff officer. His hair was close-cropped and his mouth slightly ajar. His eyebrows rose skeptically and fell slowly in a regular rhythm. He was clearly a desk soldier who had spent years looking people up and down as if they were less than human. All he lacked was a monocle.

He did not look up as I reported: "Major Stuart, Special Armored Car Battalion, Fifth Chinese Army, sir!"

Then he smelled rotten eggs.

He leaned back in his swivel chair to obtain a better view. When he saw Humpty Dumpty in a Chinese uniform, he had to grip his desk to keep from falling.

He lost all his dignity as his exclamations stumbled over each other: "Who the hell? . . . What the dickens? . . . Where did you? . . . I say! . . . Amazing! Absolutely amazing!"

After a long pause, he summarized: "What the hell are you doing here?"

I stated my mission succinctly.

He pinched himself until he and I winced. "I must be dreaming," he insisted. "An English omelet in a Chinese uniform appears before my desk and demands a hundred Bren guns. . . ."

"Plus ammunition, sir," I added.

"For the Chinese Army? Even in a dream, that is too much. What nonsense!"

"No more nonsensical, sir, than keeping the guns idle in an ammunition depot."

"I have Bren guns to spare and Bren guns to waste," he said, "But General Tu Yu Ming's troops — and you in particular — are the last people in the world I would give them to." He turned to a captain, who had been watching the comic opera with great relish. "Show this man out!" the colonel barked.

Saluting smartly, I said: "Beg pardon, sir. One other thing. I've had a difficult journey, don't y' know. And I have a long trip ahead of me. Would you mind if I dropped in at the Officers Club for *tiffin?*" ("Tiffin" is an Anglo-Indian word for lunch.)

A new series of splutters came from behind the desk: "Officers Club? Tiffin? Drop in? Get this man out of here before I wake up! Give him whatever the hell he wants, but — get — him — out of my sight!"

When we were out of sight and earshot, the captain remarked: "You do look a bit of a sketch, old chap."

[ 291 ]

"No harm done," I said. "And I trust you heard what he said just before we left."

"You mean about giving you tiffin?"

"Well, what he did say was 'Give him whatever the hell he wants.'"

"But he meant . . ."

"It could be taken to mean, 'Give him those Bren guns if it'll get rid of him.'"

"Now really, old man! . . ."

"Let me put it this way," I improvised. "If I took that liberal interpretation, I'd be in a terrible hurry. And I'd spare you the social embarrassment of introducing me around the club."

Nothing could have appealed to him more. I knew he was hooked when, after a moment of thought, he murmured: "Well, he could have meant anything — in his condition."

"You know as well as I do that, in a day or two, you'll have to destroy those guns and blow up the ammunition anyway."

"You're right, of course," he said. "I can't authorize you to take those guns, but I *can* tell you exactly where they're stored. If anybody should stop you, which I doubt, you can mention my name. If they ever check back, however, I'll call you a liar." Without further ado, he drew me a map of the ordnance "godowns," — a British version of the Malayan word *godon*, meaning "warehouse."

The main gate to the godowns was wide open and unguarded. As my little convoy drove in, a British truck lumbered toward us. Rather than act evasive, I flagged the driver down.

"Mind telling me where the godown for Bren guns is, soldier?"

He pointed out the building and went on his way. Nobody else was around. The godown was locked, but I opened it with an ax.

Inside, the Bren guns were neatly stacked in boxes. They were brand new and still smeared with factory grease. We loaded as many aboard as we could without blowing our tires. With an assist from the British, my private army was about to become one of the more fearsome fighting units of the Chinese Army.

On the outskirts of Mandalay, I almost collided with Major Jim Wilson of the U. S. Army. He was the man who had unleashed Smitty and me upon the "scorched earth" of Burma. Jim was usually a very low-pressure American. This time, however, he was so agitated that he noticed neither my Chinese uniform nor its egg stains.

"What's the matter, Jim?" I asked.

"Some of our Lend-Lease equipment has been disappearing," he replied. "I've just learned that a few of our own technicians here are stealing it. They sell it to the Chinese and Burmese. Do you know anything about it, Gil?"

"Only that everybody knows it's going on. Personally, I don't like to deal with American black-marketeers. I steal from the British instead."

"But not for private gain," Jim growled. "I'm going into Mandalay to question some of those bastards now. They're a well-organized ring, I gather."

"Watch your step with them, Jim. They can be dangerous," I cautioned him as his jeep lurched forward. He scowled angrily and waved goodbye.

Jim Wilson died the next afternoon in Mandalay. According to the official report, he was unloading gasoline from a barge on the banks of the Irrawaddy River. The fuel blew up, apparently when a bomb hit.

I still have my own suspicions of who killed Jim Wilson.

I revisited Mandalay a few days later when the entire city was in flames. Bombings and sabotage had destroyed the city. Europeans had fled. Shops had been abandoned. Now the looters were finishing up the job. Armed with knives, swords, and sticks, they traveled in packs of fifty or more. They drifted from shop to shop. They seized precious gems, ivory, jade, silver, and gold. They ransacked all that was worthless to them. They killed everybody who chanced to be in their way. Others went crazy hunting for liquor.

The doors of the leper colony had been flung open. Some of the inmates had stayed there. They huddled together, awaiting destruction. To them, their destroyers would have no nationality: just citizenship in the outside world.

Other poor, hideous lepers wandered the streets of Mandalay. They were lost souls, free at last to roam in the "civilized" world that scorned them. And they were repelled by the hell that they saw.

[ 293 ]

I was searching in vain for information about Jim Wilson's death. Just on an off chance, I visited British Police Headquarters — a large red brick building sitting back off the road. When I saw that it was virtually deserted, I knew I would learn nothing more about Jim.

A small black car was parked in the driveway. At the main door stood a handsome Englishman in his late fifties. He introduced himself as the deputy commissioner of Burmese Police.

"Are you the last man out of the building?" I asked.

"I'm the last Englishman left in Mandalay," he boasted. He was preparing to leave, so I didn't bother to challenge his statement.

Here was the Burmese Police Department's second-in-command prowling around an empty headquarters that still flew the Union Jack. Everything was in perfect order. I could smell faint odors of ink and tobacco from the deserted offices.

Reluctant to depart, the deputy commissioner offered to show me around. The headquarters had also served as a club for British officials in Mandalay. The larger rooms were adorned with expensive trophies and gifts handed down by generations of British policemen in colonial Burma. Lovely jade, ivory, silver, and jewelry mingled with swords and flags symbolizing key events in Anglo-Burmese history, which was ending all around us.

The deputy commissioner explained each object in a calm, proud voice that nevertheless possessed a ghostly ring. A British civil servant was living out the past all alone in these historic rooms, still pervaded by the pride of an empire. But the strength of the empire remained only in richly carved, exquisitely molded symbols adorning the walls. Outside, the Kipling era was ending. The white man's Asia — with its evils and its blessings — was being eradicated.

The deputy commissioner and I finished our tour. He took a long, careful look at the room we were in. I am sure he was photographing every detail in his mind. Mandalay would remain this way as long as he lived.

Finally, he turned to me and said:

"I must leave all this just as it is. What a pity it won't last! After I'm out of sight, help yourself to anything you want. I'd rather a Britisher — or whatever you are, young man — took what he could instead of those looters. They'll destroy it all."

"I can't sir," I said. "I would if I thought I could protect anything. But my future is just as uncertain as this building's."

"Well, then, will you lock up when you go?"

We shook hands. He drove off toward Maymyo. He never looked back at the place that would always be his home, no matter where destiny took him.

A slight breeze brushed gently against the Union Jack. How much longer would it remain on its mast? Within hours, it would be torn down, spat upon, jeered, and cursed — by Japanese and Burmese alike.

I resisted an urge to lower it and take it with me. A flag is like a soldier. Its duty is to stand until defeated and cut down.

As I left Mandalay for the last time, smoke was billowing in the sky and casting a black pall across the sun. Mandalay became a huge shadow into which only vultures dared to fly. The fire, the vultures, and the looters would leave few of the treasures of Mandalay to the "victorious" Japanese.

The loss of Mandalay was obscured by news that awaited me at head-quarters in Pyawbwe. Chan had perished in the battle of Toungoo. He and a small patrol of my men had been trapped in the same sort of encirclement from which I had helped to rescue Major Mar. Their luck had not been so good as mine.

Chan had lasted less than a month in the Chinese Army. Perhaps this was symbolic of a true guerrilla's fate in any formal kind of warfare.

I did not, however, think of Chan symbolically. I thought of his husky voice, perpetual smile, noisy breathing, stooped shoulders, and the old felt hat that he wore on his head, slept in, and even used as a dinner pail. He had kept it on even when dressed in the uniform of a Chinese soldier. I am sure that he died in it.

It never would have occurred to anybody who knew him, but Chan was a truly great man. In the right circumstances, his swiftness, his precision, his anticipation, and even his sense of humor might have coalesced in a great peasant leader.

Any military career for Chan, however, would have been hampered by the innate mischievousness that marks the true guerrilla. Chan never spoke of any higher purpose than to bedevil the Japanese. He aspired only to see their faces when his next deadly plot had been perpetrated.

Chan was so dependable that I had not thought much about him while he was alive. When he was dead, I realized that one of the best friends I had ever had was gone.

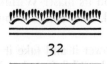

## 32

# A Fatal Case of Gin

THE rest of Burma fell rapidly to the Japanese. As General Tu Yu Ming retreated toward India, he dispatched me on a mission to Kunming because I knew the Burma Road. After delivering his messages, I was to wait in Kunming for the general and his Army to join me there.

I had crossed into China many times before, though never as a Chinese soldier. I looked around for my Burmese and Chinese acquaintances, but they were gone from the Namhkam-Wanting area. The first familiar face I saw in China belonged to a young American.

I will call him Franklin. I had known him in my trucking days. He was in his twenties. He was the son of an American missionary. He had been working in Lashio, Burma, as the representative of an American oil company. Although I had gone drinking with Franklin once or twice, I had not come to know him well because he stopped drinking after the first round. I never heard him curse. In his presence, I always felt that I was a trifle foul-mouthed — even when I wasn't at all. I considered Franklin a very decent young fellow — more of a gentleman than most Americans abroad.

All traffic on the Burma Road was heading north in an interminable traffic jam until young Franklin came bounding toward me in an open jeep, the only southbound traffic I'd seen all day.

An Anglo-Burmese girl sat beside him. She was pretty, but very much out of place in a jeep on the Burma Road. Her silk dress was covered with dust and dirt.

Franklin looked very irritable and disheveled. His face was red from the sun. His hair, once smartly brushed, was loaded with dust.

"What the — What are you doing here?" I barked at him.

"I'm going to Wanting," he said.

"What for? The place is a shambles. And the Japs are headed there from Lashio."

"But this is important," Franklin explained.

In the next few minutes, I learned a great deal about my fellow man. Franklin, who didn't drink much, had made a terrific "buy" on forty cases of British gin in Lashio.

"I had the gin put aboard an American Embassy truck bound for Kunming, where I'm living now," he said. The girl giggled.

"What happened to it?" I inquired.

Franklin explained that at Chinese customs in Wanting the truck's U. S. Marine drivers had been "stupid" enough to follow regulations and declare their cargo. Ordinarily, customs never searched Embassy trucks.

"So the customs men are holding my gin until I pay duty on it." Franklin concluded. "You'd think they had better things to do in the middle of a war."

The same might well have been said of him, but I simply warned him: "You'd better turn right around. Even if customs is still there the inspectors probably drank it. They're not expecting you to drop in for it. Anyway, suppose it's still there. How are you going to carry forty cases of gin in one jeep?"

"I'll worry about that when I get there," said Franklin, racing his engine impatiently. "I can always hire a truck."

Before I could assure him that the Chinese Army was confiscating all trucks, he and the girl were roaring south in a cloud of dust.

Franklin's entire life had become wrapped up in forty cases of gin. Since it sold on the Asian black market for thirty or forty dollars a bottle in those days, I suppose he could have made a small fortune. I still think of him as a basically good man, whose slightly pious shell must have been his protection from himself as well as others. War peels away many shells and leaves man to the guidance of his own frail conscience. In Franklin's case, his paper-thin morality had allowed him to smuggle during a national disaster, use his own Embassy as fronts, and expose a silly girl as well as himself to the perils of death. All for forty cases of gin.

He never regained his lost treasure. The next day, I learned that Franklin and the girl had been shot to death in a brawl along the road.

Years later, I met Franklin's parents, "old China hands" of considerable repute up north. His missionary father asked me about his death. All I said was that I had heard he died on the Burma Road for his country.

They were not the kind of people who conceive of anybody — particularly their own son — dying for forty cases of gin, even when it was worth thirty or forty dollars a bottle.

I still had Franklin on my mind two days later as my jeep wormed its way down the side of Salween Gorge. As with Franklin, all signals were off in wartime here: The morality lessons I had preached on this cliff to truckers at gunpoint were now obsolete. The Burma Road had been made a one-way street. The lonely mountain had become a giant anthill of trucks jammed bumper-to-bumper and pedestrians threading along the side of the road.

The bridge across the Salween River was eight miles away and far below. Viewed from the top, the road appeared and disappeared like a gigantic ladder in a high wind.

There was no wind, however. But suddenly there was the deadly staccato sound of machine-gun fire above us.

Pedestrians ran for cover. Some sought protection under trucks that were still moving. In a minute, all traffic froze. People were still running — some forward, some backwards. By then, the gunfire was coming from all directions.

A Chinese lieutenant dashed by, shouting: "The Japanese! We are all ambushed!"

I jogged alongside him for a moment and asked: "What are they doing here?"

"Riding in civilian trucks . . . Dressed as Chinese . . . Take off your uniform . . . Throw away . . ." I heard him say as he disappeared down the road. He was heading right into more gunfire.

I doubled back to my jeep, found an old pair of civilian trousers, and shed my Chinese uniform. My Army knee boots, however, were glued by sweat to my legs. I slipped the trousers on and trusted them to hide my identity.

I ran as far away from my jeep as I could. Within five minutes, the Japanese appeared above the road. They were in perfect position. Nobody on the congested road made any further effort to move or fight. The Japanese fired a few rounds into the crowd and drew blood. From then on, they simply held us at bay by pointing their rifles.

A patrol of Japanese soldiers came marching down the road. There were no more than a dozen of them. I cursed the fear and panic that had rendered hundreds of Chinese helpless against so few enemies.

The Japanese patrol pumped bullets into any man who carried a gun or looked like a soldier. Then they herded us into groups of twenty and thirty. For half an hour, our captors unearthed more men wearing fragments of uniform. These Chinese were bayoneted on the spot.

Apart from one kick in the groin and several slaps with rifle butts, I did not suffer greatly during my brief captivity. This was the first time I had ever been at a total disadvantage with the hated Japanese. In a numb, almost detached way, I was appalled by what they were doing. But, even then, their swift, ruthless manner of conquest and carnage struck me as more merciful than the vengeance I had seen a Chinese captain wreak upon three Japanese disguised as priests.

I found myself in a tight cluster of thirty civilian prisoners. The Japs were tying the hands of the people on the outside of the circle to form a human fence. The same was happening in other clusters.

Above us, some Japanese soldiers scanned the countryside with binoculars. Others were poised with hand grenades — a German type known as "potato mashers."

The soldiers who were tormenting us withdrew. As they backed off, an officer up above fired one shot into a cluster. This was the signal for a rain of grenades.

The most I could do was wrench around and push myself to the ground, where I had the best chance of absorbing the impact.

The last sound I heard was muffled human voices chorusing the same death rattle as mine. It was neither a gasp nor a scream, but a choked cry of total despair. Death was only a split second away.

I do not remember hearing an explosion. I felt intense heat and a choking sensation. Then I was tossed into the air. I was either blown or pushed over the steep mountainside. I tumbled downhill amidst an avalanche of people, stones, and rocks. As I did, I lost consciousness.

The next thing I remember was pain. My body ached all over. The throbbing behind my eyes and ears was more than I could bear. I started to put my hands to my head, but I couldn't move either arm.

I lay where I was, hoping death or a miracle would end my misery. Nearby, a man yelled in pain. Then he stood up cursing. A burst of machine-gun fire dropped him forever. A new slide of rocks came tumbling down. I closed my eyes.

The rocks jolted me to my senses. I opened my eyes. Then I shut them. The Japs might be watching the scene through their field glasses.

My face was buried in loose dirt. My head was pressed against a boulder. I was lying flat on my stomach. My arms were pinned beneath me. My legs were resting against another boulder. And I was in clear view of the Japanese.

I lay with my eyes closed until nightfall. Having spent twenty-four hours of my life in a Chinese coffin, I did not find this difficult. When I was sure nobody could see me from above, I rolled over on my back.

As life returned to my arms, twinges of pain stabbed below my left shoulder. I was cut and bruised from rolling over jagged ground. A small chunk of shrapnel had lodged in my back, but it had done almost no damage.

Above me, I could see fires burning peacefully. Probably, they were warming Japanese soldiers. But I heard no voices. I decided not to climb a mountain merely to stumble into a Japanese bullet. Anyway, I had been headed downhill when I'd been parted from my jeep. I could make up some time by continuing in that direction on foot.

My descent was treacherous. Whenever I slipped, loose dirt rolled down noisily. I would sit down and dig my feet into the ground. Then I would wait to make sure nobody above took any interest in the noise I had made.

With my undamaged arm, I eased myself down the steeper grades of the slope. Fifteen minutes later, I reached more level ground. I could stand and even walk without losing my footing.

A cigarette glowed behind some rocks. Two Chinese soldiers and a civilian had survived the massacre the same way I had; they had been blown safely over the mountain. One of them handed me a cigarette. We all smoked in silence.

Like me, they were badly bruised and cut. One of them had lost all his front teeth. The corner of his mouth was split and swollen like Colonel Mar's.

Nobody noticed that I was a Westerner. We all belonged to the same race — the aching.

We set out for the bridge that crossed the Salween River. It was pitch dark now. We spent an hour groping our way down the slope until we reached the road.

We walked all night. Other survivors joined our procession. I led the way because I knew every bend in the Salween Gorge. By the absence of traffic, I could tell that the Burma Road had been closed off in this area after the Japanese ambush. Whether or not the Japs were still around, we stood an excellent chance of being shot by Chinese search parties.

As dawn broke, I led my ragged band off the road. We slid down a steep slope and found concealment behind rocks. No traffic passed by all day. We heard trucks and occasional gunfire above us. Toward noon, some planes strafed the road near the bridge. Whose side were they on?

(Days later in Kunming, I learned that the planes belonged to the American Volunteer Group — the "Flying Tigers" — a worthy successor to the discredited International Volunteer Flying Group that I had once been talked out of joining.)

Safety lay across the river, I gathered. I was reluctant to cross the bridge itself, since it was still somebody's target.

Toward dusk, we chose our routes. Several of my group decided to stay put. Others said they would take their chances on the bridge. Five of us decided to swim the turbulent river.

The river was two miles away by road. There was still a sliver of daylight as we stripped off our clothes, tied them around our waists, and waded in.

We were welcomed by a swift current, which carried us most of the way to the other side of the Salween. The first three of us strode out of the water, refreshed by our swim.

The other two men were having trouble reaching shore. I waded in and dragged them out by the scruffs of their necks. There was little else to grip, for they had lost all their clothes in the water.

I was amused when their eyes thanked me as eloquently as those of two drowning puppies I had once rescued.

Later, I found out why. The two men did not know how to swim.

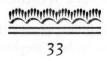

# 33

# Black Dragon Temple

In Kunming, I delivered General Tu Yu Ming's messages and then was left absolutely alone. Nobody there seemed to know of my commission. After all, where was my uniform? People were most polite. They hardly snickered when they addressed me as "major." But I was given no men, no budget, and no pay.

General Tu Yu Ming, Major Mar, and the fighting units of the Chinese Fifth Army had retreated from Burma into India. They would set out for Kunming soon. The general's subordinates in Kunming seemed certain that when Tu Yu Ming arrived, he would unmask me as a messenger boy with delusions of grandeur.

Despite the apathy toward me, I reorganized my armored car unit by stealing a few vehicles that were going to waste. I had no scarcity of recruits. Former truckers of mine found me and joined up. Chinese soldiers deserted from other units to enlist with the "kind-hearted tiger."

While waiting for General Tu, I decided to search for a headquarters outside Kunming — away from the backbiting desk officers there. I found the ideal place by accident.

My men and I were duck hunting forty-six miles east of Kunming. We were near the ancient city of Sungming, built in the days of Confucius. Twice a year, ducks by the thousands settled in the rice paddies outside Sungming. I organized the hunt for target practice and food procurement. My men did not know a proverb about killing two birds with one stone.

Our quest for ducks led us to the Black Dragon Temple, one of the oldest Buddhist places of worship in Yunnan Province. It was on the outskirts of Sungming and a quarter of a mile off a dirt road that ran north to the foothills of Tibet. A hill, called Black Dragon Mound, and a small but thick forest of pine trees shielded the temple from prying eyes.

Black Dragon Temple was a square two-story building with high walls, stone slabs, and wooden beams. It had only one entrance — a thick double door leading into a large courtyard lush with trees, bushes, and plants. There were also ancient rubbing stones, beautifully carved.

The inner walls of the courtyard, the temple rooms, and even the rafters were covered with art — paintings of many hues, gilded and gaudy idols, sinister carved figures, and a bigger-than-life-size Buddha.

Black Dragon Temple had been abandoned by its worshipers. They had built smaller shrines in their own communities. Also abandoned was its annex, closer to the road. This was a large two-story building that could billet four hundred men.

The whole set-up reminded me of my days with Major Chan's guerrillas. Without further ado, Black Dragon Temple became head-quarters of the Chinese Fifth Army's Armored Car Detachment.

For my office, I selected an upstairs room. It looked out on the prayer area, where Buddha sat grinning, and on the whole court-yard. Gazing by day over the gray roof, I could see treetops beyond. My view was serene and reassuring.

The roof of Black Dragon Temple was decorated — almost littered — with carved figures that glistened in the sun. They were supposed to protect the temple from demons.

But when the moon struck them, they had a life of their own. Sometimes, when all was quiet and the moon was full, I sat in the courtyard and watched the frightful little figures on the roof. How could the demons they frightened away be more terrifying? And what strange sights had these Oriental gargoyles witnessed in the thousand years of the Black Dragon Temple?

In the valley and the rice paddies near us, the land was rich

[ 303 ]

and yielding. The people were happy and laughing whenever I visited their villages by day. But at night — brooding in the courtyard — I occasionally heard the screams and wails of some unfortunate woman cast out of her home by her husband.

This fate could befall a woman not only if she betrayed her husband, but also if he betrayed *her*.

Her sound pierced the night, echoed across the valley, and struck terror into my heart. At such moments, even the wind, was afraid to stir. I could sense the woman drifting alone into the night. Cast aside by an unforgiving or unfaithful husband, the woman would have to wander away — begging for food, sick in body, and bereft of soul. And I wondered if hell could ever compare with earth.

Education might one day cure such a barbaric custom. I allocated one large room of the barracks building for a school. I detailed several of my men as teachers. Children were invited from the surrounding villages. At first, they came to see the soldiers drill. Later, they came to learn.

There were other arrivals. In the early summer of 1942, one of the drivers from my main unit reported in. He was ragged, barefoot, and filthy. I knew that he had been missing in action since the fall of Mandalay — back when I was still with Tu Yu Ming.

He dragged himself to within a foot of my desk, stood smartly to attention, and saluted. I took one whiff of him and ordered him to take five paces back. Then I let him tell his tale of how he had walked almost a thousand miles from Maymyo, Burma.

I had instructed my men that if their armored cars should fall into danger of capture by the enemy, they were to destroy the vehicles completely. Somewhere between Mandalay and Maymyo, this driver had learned that Japanese troops were both ahead of him and behind him.

Without waiting to hear more, he drove his car off the road and part way up a steep mountain. There, he took an ax and systematically smashed engine block, engine head, carburetor, spark plugs, radiator, oil sump, electrical equipment, ignition, and steering wheel.

He cut the bullet-proof tires. He doused engine and tires with his remaining gasoline. Then he released the brake.

As the car rolled forward, he lit a match and tossed it into the gas tank.

[ 304 ]

The car burst into flames. It rolled over the edge of the mountain and plunged like a flaming torch for hundreds of feet into the jungle below.

"Did the Japs ever come?" I asked the hero.

"No, Major Stu," he replied in his best English. "Some say I scare Jap off with big fire. Other say Jap nowhere near. I never see Jap whole trip, but I famous far and wide, sir."

"If you're so famous," I said, "how come it took you almost half a year to reach here?"

"I so famous for setting fire to car that everybody afraid to give me lift."


So scant were the rewards for loyalty in the Chinese Army that I encouraged my men to treat courage with respect. We kept their brave deeds alive by holding a big dinner or a formal Day of the Brave every so often. On such occasions, rank meant nothing. Individuals were honored for their heroism. Every time, the man who had set fire to his car and half of Burma (for the legend grew with retelling) was a guest of honor.

I was not able to attend all the festivals. I was busy hunting equipment to bolster the Bren guns on my vehicles. General Claire Chennault of the American "Flying Tigers" obliged me with fifteen dozen 7.92-millimeter machine guns and twelve brand new .30-caliber water-cooled Browning machine guns. The Brownings came off an old American gunboat marooned on the Yangtze near Chungking. The gunboat no longer figured in the white man's diplomacy in Asia.

Chennault took a liking to me, for we were both adventurers. He was a Texas high-school teacher who won an Army commission in World War I and went on to pioneer the cause of military air power. Later, however, his views and those of General Billy Mitchell's were "discredited" by the Army. Both men became martyrs to their cause, which later accredited itself in action. In 1937, Chennault had gone to China on his own to organize Chiang Kai-shek's air defenses. In 1941, he had formed the "Flying Tigers." He possessed the same faith in aerial combat tactics that I had in guerrilla warfare. I used to think of Chennault as an aerial guerrilla.

When Chennault gave me two million rounds of ammunition, my

armored car detachment was the most modern in all the armies of China.

The greatest gift of all from Chennault to me was access to American technicians, to whom I could bring my own specialized problems and tentative suggestions.

I take some of the credit for designing or innovating:

. . . A mount with four 7.92-millimeter machine guns that could be fired individually or simultaneously. One two-second burst from this arsenal would (and did) cut a truck in half.

. . . The first successful .50-caliber heavy-barrel machine-gun mount for a jeep. Ordnance later adopted the principle for the U. S. Army.

. . . Mounts on jeeps for rocket launchers. We used rocket projectors that had been designed for American pursuit planes. Fired in clusters they were devastating. Having been up a creek in Burma with armored but unarmed vehicles, I could never possess too much firepower.

General Tu Yu Ming returned to China via India, the Himalaya Mountains, and the jungle of southeastern Asia. He was a sick man when he reached Kunming in the summer of 1942.

He had lived with the daily problem of feeding and caring for a huge, hungry family — thousands of Chinese troops — in territory seldom penetrated by outsiders. Britain's Royal Air Force had tried its best to drop provisions to Tu Yu Ming's troops, but aerial supplying was still limited. The proper flying equipment was not available. Slender rations had to be stretched across miles and days.

Physically, General Tu was exhausted. Spiritually, he was heartsick. Verbal sniping, by Western advisers, who had Generalissimo Chiang Kai-shek's ear, was taking its toll. Thus far, Chiang had rejected all proposals to depose General Tu. But how much more time did General Tu have?

What kept General Tu afloat was his comparatively sound financial position. Like all the other armies of China, the Fifth Army was poor — but better off than most. General Tu was not rich. He had spent all his savings on his Army. The Chinese Fifth Army may have seemed poor to Americans, but — as late as 1942 — it was the only mechanized Army in China.

Tu had taken help wherever he could find it cheaply. His acceptance of my private army was merely one small example. In the 1930's, he had sent many of his officers abroad for training. Ironically, many of his bravest and most brilliant soldiers, who distinguished themselves fighting the Axis powers, had been trained and equipped by Nazi Germany.

Like all heads of armies, Tu Yu Ming received funds from the Chinese Central Government to maintain his own Army. The funds, however, were insufficient.

To look after his troops, Tu Yu Ming had built and bought several factories. There, his Army manufactured its own uniforms, blankets, towels, tobacco, and even machinery. In addition, General Tu's industrial empire manufactured products for the civilian market. All profits went to the Chinese Fifth Army.

This farsighted planning was Tu Yu Ming's greatest strength. Chiang Kai-shek's American advisers, however, thought this was a hell of a way to run an Army.

They spread rumors that Tu Yu Ming was diverting Chinese and British funds to his own private treasury. To this day, there are Americans who will respond with "that crook!" whenever Tu Yu Ming's name is mentioned. Nevertheless, his Army was scrupulously run. My men and I were paid — not always on time, but invariably in full. No other Chinese Army could make that claim.

General Tu Yu Ming convened his staff officers less than a week after his arrival in Kunming.

One of his first announcements was to clarify my status. My official commission and my command in the Chinese Army were being processed by the War Department in Chungking. They had been approved.

The general notified those present that I had all powers and responsibilities of any Chinese major. Then he added that I would be responsible only to him. He alone would give me orders. I saw several colonels and lesser generals flush with disappointment. They had anticipated having a white lackey.

I asked General Tu Yu Ming for permission to speak a few words:

"Inasmuch as I am a foreigner in the Chinese Army, I neither expect nor desire any special privileges. I will respect all the codes of the Chinese Army.

"I do not want anything I do wrong excused because you think I am ignorant. I have now been in our Army long enough to master its rules and regulations.

"If I do not live up to them, I expect the same consequences that any man in this room can expect."

I quickly found out what the consequences were.

General Tu reviewed the disastrous Burma campaign. One by one, we were questioned, cross-questioned, occasionally praised, and often criticized severely.

One general was accused of showing more concern for a convoy of loot than for his men. General Tu addressed him with biting contempt. The accused officer said nothing. Almost casually, General Tu Yu Ming told him: "You will die."

General Tu ignored him for the rest of the meeting. The man sat silently through the remaining four hours of the meeting.

At the end of the session, General Tu Yu Ming stripped him of his command and turned him over to a sentry. The disgraced general was shot to death in the courtyard. He was being buried when I left Kunming to rejoin my men.

In Chinese justice, an unprotesting silence is taken as an admission of guilt.

Back at Black Dragon Temple, there had been a shortage of meat. My subordinates had organized a wolf-hunt.

Just outside our parade grounds, green hills sloped back into craggy mountains beyond. There, packs of wild wolves preyed.

My men were encouraged to hunt in squads equipped with tommyguns. It was not an easy sport. Sometimes a wolf pack numbered fifty or more. Then it became a battle between two armies — one armed with guns, the other with deadly fangs. Men and beast hunted each other with skill, cunning, and instinct.

Often, the wolves would split up and encircle us with the stealth of Japanese. Then they would close in. Their first attack came from whichever direction afforded them the best advantage in the moonlight.

We would spray them with bullets and they would withdraw. Once, their signals were crossed. As the first few wolves retreated, the rest of their group attacked *them*. The wolves on the other side of us thought

[ 308 ]

their brothers were vanquishing *us*. They burst forth from hiding in a state of mad exultation.

In less than a minute, ten wolves became the prey of their very own. My men and I ended the nightmarish civil war by destroying the whole pack with our bullets.

It was seldom that easy, however. Sometimes, wolves attacked us in small packs of four or six at a time. Our attention would focus on the first small pack or two. Meanwhile, the rest of the pack would sneak in from the side or the rear.

They charged forth at great speed. Some bounded forward. Others kept close to the ground. Even in bright moonlight, they were hard to see.

I was mystified by how the wolves knew when to retreat. As soon as the numerical odds turned against them, the survivors all slunk off into the night. I envied their battlefield communications, whatever they were.

We knew the remaining wolves were watching us as we hauled in our catch. Occasionally, we glimpsed a semicircle of them trailing us at a safe distance. If we should let down our guard for a minute, they would make one final attack.

There would be great rejoicing back at camp. The cook would be awakened. We would all help him skin and dress the wolves. At breakfast, we devoured wolf meat while the story of the hunt was repeated at least a dozen times — with greater color each time.

The men swore that wolf meat not only assuaged their hunger, but also served as a tonic to their blood, hunger, and virility. It was reputed to cure fever, ailments, and impotence.

To me, it was just strong veal. It was tough, but I knew that wolves were not the toughest creatures in Yunnan Province.

## 34

# Yunnanese Bandits

KUNMING was the seat of Yunnan-Fu Province. *Yunnan-Fu* means "South of the Clouds." From the Ming dynasty (1368-1644) until the Burma Road was built, Yunnan had existed as China's remote Siberia. It was a place where political exiles lived out shattered lives. It was a place where criminals and warlords made the local laws to serve themselves.

For centuries, the fierce Yunnanese people had considered themselves self-ruling and independent of the rest of China. They refused to acknowledge the laws of the Republic of China. They paid homage only to the provincial governor.

By 1942, Yunnan had been governed for many years by General Lung, a venerable, stubborn, and fearless warlord. He ran the province to suit his own private interests: lead, silver, tin, coal, and above all, opium.

Yunnan was rich agriculturally, but its country folk were backward, primitive, and poor. They were content with their meager lot because they knew of nothing better.

The Yunnanese had always been proud of their province. With the opening of the Burma Road, they came to detest the Burmese and Europeans who poured into Yunnan. Most of all, however, they detested their own "foreign devils" — the Chinese from other provinces who came to exploit or protect the Yannanese.

The people of Yunnan didn't want any protection. One of General Tu Yu Ming's major problems was protecting strangers from natives. Another was Governor Lung, who had to be handled with tact.

Yunnan was vital to the Chinese cause. If the Japanese captured the province, they would overrun China.

While China was at war with Japan, Yunnan wasn't.

Governor Lung had never officially declared war. He tolerated our presence. He also remained on fairly friendly terms with the Japanese. It was well known that his emissaries stayed friendly with them in south China. He would certainly grow more cordial to the Japanese if General Tu Yu Ming menaced his administration or his flourishing opium trade.

Several times, the question of deposing Governor Lung was raised at General Tu Yu Ming's staff meetings. Each time it was dismissed. "His power over his people is far greater than ours," General Tu declared sadly. "If we interfere with him, his people will sabotage what is left of the Burma Road. They will do everything to bring the Japanese right into Kunming."

My first personal contact with the power of Governor Lung came early in 1943. My battalion received orders to pick up two prisoners in Tsuyung, 118 miles west of Kunming. The prisoners were local bandits who enjoyed the protection of Governor Lung himself. We were to deliver them to Fifth Army headquarters.

I sent a lieutenant and a driver ahead in a jeep. We would have to stay overnight in Kunming on our way to Tsuyung. They were to arrange for billeting.

At the end of a day's work in Black Dragon Temple, I headed for Kunming and Tsuyung. I took along six men, a jeep with two machine guns, and a scout car with nine machine guns. That should have been enough to cope with two Yunnanese bandits.

We had not reckoned upon Governor Lung's intervention. Apparently, he had intercepted my orders. At the east gate of Kunming, our advance driver was waiting sheepishly. Governor Lung's own military police had halted the jeep, seized it, and taken my lieutenant into custody.

The lieutenant was waiting for us when we reached our Army billets. His uniform was torn. His face was badly bruised. His jeep was still in custody.

He had been taken to Governor Lung's police headquarters in the heart of Kunming. There, he had been beaten and questioned about my plans. He gave them no information, but they gave him a message for me. If I took the prisoners into Fifth Army custody, my life would be in danger. If I turned them over to Governor Lung's M.P.'s, my jeep would be returned.

"Are the bastards who told you this still there?" I asked the lieutenant.

"No," he said. "They went off duty after beating me. One of them gave me a ride here on his way home. He said it was nothing personal."

"Well, I'm taking it personally," I said. "We'll wait until morning, when the same people are back there. Then we'll take it up with them — personally."

To brighten up a dismal day, I invited my men out to dinner. We went to an expensive new restaurant, one of several symbols of Kunming's wartime prosperity. I suspect that world history has always had its hamburger stands and get-rich-quick opportunities. This place was a little of both.

The Yunnanese food, always quite spicy, was excellent. We ate toasted flying ants, fried snake meat, bean pods and hot peppers and mushrooms with elephant's trunk.

We followed this with sugared potatoes and pigeon eggs. I sent my lieutenant back to the kitchen with my compliments to the chef, who was also the owner. My officer returned with the owner's gracious acknowledgment.

Our waiter appeared with the check. It was for five times the prices listed on the menu. I sent my lieutenant on another mission to the kitchen. He came back sweating.

"I cannot reason with that fool," he reported. "He says you are an American. You can afford to pay."

My men watched me. They were wondering if I would burn the place down or merely wreck it. Instead, I smiled and told the lieutenant: "Go back once more. Tell the proprietor that, despite his high prices, I think his food is remarkable."

My docility astonished everybody. My men could scarcely believe their eyes as I produced a wad of Chinese bills and paid the check. The owner came forth to bow us out courteously. Nevertheless, I could detect his thinly veiled contempt. I had lost face like a meek kitten.

It was eleven P.M. The café owner was closing up as we drove away. My men were still indignant at him and at me.

"Cheer up, boys!" I said. "The night is young. We've only started to paint the town red."

First, however, we doubled back to our Army hostel in Kunming,

[ 312 ]

where one of my men relieved the sentry who was guarding our scout car.

"You must be very hungry," I remarked to the man going off duty.

His eyes admitted that he could eat half a cavalry.

"I know of a fine new restaurant," I told him, "where they make the best Yunnanese dishes. The rest of us have eaten well, but we will join you. We will drink your health while you eat."

We set out on foot. The restaurant was at the other end of Kunming's main street, Chi Ping Liu. As we strolled, I suggested to the hungry man: "Along the way, we may meet a few of our comrades. If they are hungry, perhaps they would like to come to dinner with you."

Soon, we encountered several half-starved Chinese soldiers. They were wandering the street like beggars and picking over the contents of garbage cans.

They were not an unusual sight in a Chinese Army with low budgets and frequent bad management. When a soldier was too sick or too weak to be useful, his unit turned him loose — unofficially. He was to fend for himself. He was not to wander far, however. His unit was drawing funds proportionate to the number of men on its books. He might be needed as evidence.

Otherwise, these men did not exist. Their weakness and total despair made it certain they would never desert.

It was not long before we had fifty of these wretches in tow. "March them to our favorite restaurant in a column of two's," I commanded.

The place was shuttered. I pounded on the door until the owner opened up. Then I shouted: "The rich American has returned! I am feeling sorry for the poor, underfed soldiers of China. I wish to do my part for their cause. I wish to buy them a meal they will never forget." I waved a fistful of money at the proprietor, and he welcomed us and put his waiters to work.

Some sixty men filed in. I directed them to tables. When the main floor was filled, I led the rest to the balcony. I stayed up there with them and gazed down upon my own benevolence.

The beggars sat like scared children. They were unable to believe what had happened to them. Most had never seen the inside of a grand restaurant. They were sons of the land. Taken hundreds and thousands of miles from their farms, they would never return from the shadows of the city. They would die in Kunming, where they were unwanted as anything but items on a ledger.

Foraging in garbage cans and back alleys after dark caused them to blink at the unaccustomed light of the restaurant. I, too, blinked when my eyes examined them closely.

Their arms and legs had wasted away. The shape of each bone was visible beneath the skin. Their filthy cotton uniforms, last vestige of a role in the human race, dangled from their backs like coats on hangers. The men's heads had shrunk and their caps had fallen down over their ears. Their faces were drawn and hollow. Their eyes resembled glass beads sinking deep into their skulls.

Despite their joy, they hardly made a sound all evening. Their entire systems were numbed by the perpetual shock of a living death.

I ordered food for all. It was enough to clean out the restaurant. My well-fed soldiers attacked the expensive delicacies. The beggars went for the plainer dishes like chicken and duck stuffed with rice. Some had been hungry for so long that all they could hold was soup. Others made pigs of themselves. They would look up guiltily only to find me exhorting them to eat more.

After dinner, we toasted General Tu Yu Ming, Generalissimo Chiang Kai-shek, and each other with hot tea and wine. Then we paired off and played finger games. These are guessing contests in which both men throw out hands with various numbers of fingers extended. The first man who predicts the total number of fingers is the winner. Every time a man loses, he must down a drink. I bought the wine for winners and losers alike. I also bought cigarettes for all.

The party lasted until three in the morning. Tired but happy, the owner totaled up my bill. It was enormous even before he padded it. When his computing was finished, he heaved a long sigh and handed me the check.

I was a little drunk, but mostly tired. Swaying back and forth, I pretended to check the bill carefully. The owner watched me with anxiety. My men rustled with curiosity. The beggar soldiers sensed the tension and slunk out. Some of them murmured thanks. None of them could afford to be involved in trouble.

Finally, I spoke: "Yes, the total is correct."

The owner gave another sigh.

I added: "I have done my duty for the cause of China by bringing these poor, starved soldiers here."

The owner assented. He said he was grateful to me for letting him feed them. I must do it more often.

Looking the owner in the eye, I said: "Now here is your chance to do *your* duty." With those words, I tore up his masterpiece: the artfully contrived bill. I threw the pieces of paper into his face.

He could have used the paper to dry himself. Tears gushed from his piggish eyes. Sweat trickled down his face and onto his white jacket. Saliva drooled from his gaping mouth. Then his voice spouted a stream of abuse that woke the neighborhood.

I slapped his wet face a couple of times and spat at his feet. Turning to my men, I said:

"This revolting fat pig must think twice before cheating Chinese soldiers. If not for us, he would be cooking for the Japanese today."

As I turned on my heel and strode out the door, I knew the café owner would like nothing better than to serve the Japanese a banquet of *me* — exquisitely cooked and carved.

I remarked to my lieutenant: "Those prisoners we're picking up tomorrow aren't the only Yunnanese bandits around."


The next morning, we rode in our scout car to General Lung's M.P. headquarters. The compound had only one narrow entrance, into which I backed the scout car. Its nine machine guns covered the entire area.

Our surprise attack in broad daylight caught the M.P.'s off balance. I ordered my men to flush out every man from the headquarters.

The last to emerge, still buttoning his green tunic, was the general who commanded the Yunnanese M.P. units in Kunming. He was a surly little man whom I had seen before. I addressed my remarks to him:

"I am a commanding officer in the Chinese Fifth Army. You have no jurisdiction over us.

"I have come for a jeep that was stolen yesterday by your subordinates. The officer in charge of it was kidnapped and mistreated.

"I wish to notify you that any future attempts to sabotage our carrying out our duties will result in swift, effective, and personal retaliation by me. I am holding you responsible."

He opened his mouth to protest, but I continued:

"You and every man here are within seconds of sudden death. I will not hesitate to give the order if you interfere with me. Later, would you please relay my message to whoever authorized the stealing of my jeep."

I knew of no better way to send word to Governor Lung.

I walked across the compound and retrieved my jeep. Then, as we were ready to leave, I asked my lieutenant if he knew who had given the order for him to be beaten.

He pointed to an M.P. captain. I told the general: "I am taking this officer with me. He will ride with us while we escort our two bandit prisoners from Tsuyung to Kunming. He will tell you how properly we treated them. He will stay healthy so long as we encounter no trouble from any bandits — either in or out of uniform."

We ushered the M.P. captain to the scout car. He rode all the way to Tsuyung and back seated beside my lieutenant, who never stopped grinning at him.

We didn't harm a hair on the captain's head, but at least a dozen of his hairs turned gray by themselves. He was such a nervous wreck that one of our two prisoners asked us what was the matter. When we told, both prisoners laughed all the way to jail.

On this happy note, my career at Black Dragon Temple was ended. My mission to Tsuyung was my last assignment with the Special Armored Car Battalion, although it would figure in the activities of my subsequent commands. It was now a well-equipped, well-trained fighting force. I had groomed subordinates who were ready and eager to take it over. My old battalion went on to distinguish itself in the defense of China and the second Burma campaign, for which I rejoined it.

"You have done so well with the Yunnanese bandits," General Tu Yu Ming told me, "that you are going to see more of them. I am placing you in my own Special Battalion. You will replace Major Mar, who has been transferred to Chungking. And I am promoting you to lieutenant colonel."

The general's Special Battalion served as his bodyguard, his M.P.'s,

[ 316 ]

his spies, his counterspies, his intelligence network, and his customs authority. Smuggling and opium were its most frequent concerns.

General Tu thought I should work in cooperation with the U. S. Army Criminal Investigation Division on crimes involving Chinese and Americans. In one way or another, hundreds of American soldiers were involved with Chinese in opium trade and other smuggling. Prosecutions often involved two governments. And because of American criticism of Tu Yu Ming, I was to keep an eye on all Chinese officials, civilian or military, who came in contact with Americans in Yunnan Province. If any Chinese so much as hinted at favors from the Yanks, General Tu was to know at once. Stung by the innuendo leveled at him, he did not want to let any of it come true.

Although I had more power than many generals, my new job was not an enviable one. It involved treading on toes and poking into neglected corners. It had many perils, but the thousand deaths I risked were ignominious ones — death in a back alley of Kunming or at the hands of my own comrades in arms. I tried to hew to the determination with which Major Jim Wilson had gone to his doom in Mandalay.

I set up new headquarters in Yanglin, a walled town about forty miles east of Kunming on the road to Chungking. After a few weeks on the job, I knew I was succeeding. I had a new name that was heard even more often than "kind-hearted tiger." It was "the son of a bitch in Yanglin."

General Joseph Warren Stilwell, U. S. Army, visited Yunnan Province occasionally from his base in Ramgarh, India, where he was building up the First Chinese Army for the counterattack on Burma. Stilwell was Chiang Kai-shek's Chief of Staff. Since I would be working with (and, when necessary, against) his men, I decided to reacquaint him with me. I had met him once before — back in Burma, soon after his arrival there.

I had entered a small hut that was his field command post. The place was very quiet. Two men were inside, seated at tables. Each wore dirty khaki trousers and shirts opened at the collar. Neither wore Army insignia. Both were damp with sweat.

"My name's Gil Stuart," I said informally. "I'm with the Chinese Fifth Army. Do you know where I can find the Old Man?"

"Who?" said the man nearest me.

"Stilwell," I replied. "Old 'Vinegar Joe.' " It always paid, I knew, to be casual with the Americans.

The man at the other end of the room looked up: "I wonder who the hell the old bastard is that this young fellow is talking about."

The man near me chuckled and said: "I think he means you, General Stilwell."

Apologizing, I stammered that I had been sure I was talking to a couple of G.I.'s.

"Forget it, son," said Stilwell. "You should hear what some people call me."

We shook hands and became fast friends. Although I didn't always agree with Stilwell, I liked him. Soon, I was one of the few channels of communication between him and Tu Yu Ming, whom he despised.

Stilwell radiated great energy. He was one of the last soldier generals — a breed that gave way to generals who were half diplomats. Stilwell was concerned only with military strategy, direct results, and destruction of the enemy. He tried to leave political ramifications to the State Department experts. (At this, he failed. Late in 1944, he was recalled to the United States because of friction with Chiang Kai-shek.)

No matter how busy Stilwell was, he found time to see me. One day, a few weeks after I had met him, he asked me if I would join the American Army to work under his command.

"I'm honored, sir," I said. But I declined. I had devoted too many years and too many dreams to getting where I was.

General Stilwell had then suggested that I might spend three weeks at his training camp in India, where I could observe training methods. I said I was too busy to go now, but I would take him up on it in a few weeks.

When I met Stilwell again in Kunming, he greeted me by barking: "I thought I ordered you to India. What the hell do you mean by disobeying me, Stuart? Now get your ass on the next plane out of here! That's an order!"

I boarded a C-47 to fly over the Hump (as the Himalayas were called) to India. It was December 24, 1942.

[ 318 ]

The C-47 arrived at Dum Dum Airport, outside Calcutta, at nine o'clock on Christmas Eve. There was a bright moon.

No sooner had the plane come to a standstill than sirens wailed. The Japanese were making their first air raid on Calcutta. All lights went out on the air field, which would be a prime target.

Nobody told me where to go, so I hopped into an empty jeep and raced down the road to Calcutta with my lights off.

My entrance to Calcutta was an abridgment of my first sunrise in Rangoon. First there was total darkness. Then there was a bomb burst from the direction of the air field. Scattered flashes of light illuminated other targets, but our own progress was uneventful.

The lobby of the Great Eastern Hotel was packed with refugees from the street. The lowest of Indian untouchables were almost — but not quite — rubbing elbows with middle-class Indians, soldiers, and Europeans who had taken cover. There was no segregation in the crowded lobby — except at the far end, where a private party was rolling along merrily.

A wooden street barricade set it off from the rest of the lobby. I saw men in tuxedos, women in evening gowns, and Army and Navy officers in uniform. All were British. I also saw champagne. Above all, I saw beer.

All the way across the Hump, I had been dreaming about my first glass of beer since leaving Burma. Without further ado, I crashed the party.

Naturally, an Englishman in a Chinese colonel's uniform does not go unnoticed. But the party had been pretty dull before I arrived. Even the air raid had not enlivened it sufficiently. I became the center of attraction.

Toward midnight, somebody tapped me on the shoulder. I turned to face a tall British colonel with a flowing black mustache. He inquired: "Do you remember me, Colonel Stuart?"

I looked him over carefully and said: "No. Never saw you before in my life."

"Are you sure?" he said.

"Perfectly."

"Well, then permit me to introduce myself. I was almost the last man you ever saw in your life."

[ 319 ]

"You must have me confused with someone else," I said.

"I know you've led an adventurous life, Stuart old boy, but I'm dashed if you could have forgotten a big black Buick in Burma."

I did recall Smitty and me, digging into the scorched earth of Burma as a speeding Buick sprayed gunfire all around us. "I'll never forget it," I said, "but it was the Japs — or else the Burmese fifth column."

"Wrong again," the colonel declared. "It was British Intelligence. We took a dim view of the scorched-earth policy. Burma was still our territory, y' know."

"I'll be damned!" I exclaimed. "To think my own people would try to kill me! . . ."

"Fortunes of war, old chap! Didn't know it was you until we gave up trying. Would have been deucedly sorry if we'd killed you off."

"Even sorrier than I would have been if I'd killed an Englishman."

"I know what you mean, Stuart. One of your bullets singed my ear." He lifted his glass and proposed a toast: "To old times on the road to Mandalay!"

I had a very profitable three-week stay in India, but that is no tribute to Stilwell's training camp at Ramgarh. I was not impressed by what I saw there. Stilwell suffered from a lack of seasoned combat veterans. Many of his instructors were civilians fresh out of training camps in the United States. They were good and often dedicated men, but their Chinese pupils sensed their inexperience. This lack of confidence impaired morale and willingness to learn. Even an inarticulate teacher can prove inspirational if his pupils know that he has already put his knowledge to good practical use.

Stilwell's school also operated on the assembly-line principles of American boot camps. Men were trained by the thousands and sent into action when they had completed a specified program. This may work in a country where the trainees have all passed the same preliminary tests and possess approximately the same level of military experience. In China, however, men were not that easily molded.

I profited later from the mistakes I observed in Stilwell's camp. And while I was in India, I had three brand-new Chinese uniforms tailored for me. Chinese uniforms, like American uniforms, came in two shades of brown. We also had a third for winter — blue, padded, and bulky. As a lieutenant colonel of "cavalry" (as armored troops were called), I wore two gold bars and two gold stars against a silver background on my collar. The Chinese uniforms, incidentally, had been designed in Germany. At the end of my stay in India, I returned to Dum Dum Airport and boarded the C-47 for Kunming. As I strapped myself into a bucket seat, I looked up to see the colonel from British Intelligence next to me.

"Fancy meeting you here," I said.

With a loquaciousness typical only of Intelligence agents, he immediately told me exactly why he was flying to Kunming: "Hello, there, Stuart. Thought I might run into you today. I'm delivering portable radio transmitters to a hush-hush outfit we've planted in the Salween Gorge. Dandy little surprise! Keep it under your hat, though, won't you?"

I was grateful for his consistent level of bumbling. If he hadn't conducted his mobile assassinations at such high speeds, Smitty and I might have died in Burma. Still, I wanted a little revenge.

My chance came after we crossed the Hump and were preparing to land. I could see the beautiful Kunming Lake — all blue, but surrounded by shades of green looking as neatly laid out as if they were flagstones.

"Ever been to Kunming?" I asked the colonel.

"No," he replied.

"Don't you think it looks beautiful from the air?"

"Indeed it does," he said.

"Well, colonel. That is where *I* live. That is *my* home ground. That is where *I* do all the shooting."

He coughed and spluttered like a dying engine.

"Yes, of course, of course, Stuart," he said. "I didn't have any other impression. . . . I mean — after all — what I'm saying is — All I'm here for is to deliver those radios and take off on the next plane back."

"Take your time, colonel," I said reassuringly. "Kunming's an exciting place to visit."

He was in and out of Kunming in record time, I was told. He had originally planned to lay over in Kunming for a few days.

He had a young wife whom I'd met at the party. I trust she was pleasantly surprised by his premature return.

# 35

# Festival of the Harvest Moon

EACH day in General Tu Yu Ming's Special Battalion began like any other day — with a bugle call at four A.M.

The officers and men dressed, washed, tidied their quarters, exercised, drilled, and ran four miles on the open road. We returned to headquarters for a flag-raising ceremony; a speech by an officer on "Principles of Chinese Republicanism" or some other worthwhile subject; and a briefing on the assignments for the day.

By then, it was nine A.M. Then and only then did we eat breakfast. Somehow, we always had hearty appetites.

At each table in the mess hall, a small eggshell porcelain bowl was the center of attention. It contained the main course for each meal. If we were lucky, it would be pork or eggs. More often, it was cabbage and herbs. (I might add that enlisted men received the same menu and rations as officers.) We supplemented it with rice, hot water, tea, and wine — even at breakfast. Only the delicacy in the center bowl changed from meal to meal.

One morning in September, 1943, I arrived at breakfast to find three of my officers eyeing the center bowl hungrily. Each officer stood to attention until I snapped: "Be seated!" Our orderly served the wine, rice, and hot water.

The officers waited for me to eat first. Lifting my chopsticks, I dipped into the bowl of mystery. What I pulled out resembled meat. It was about an inch square and quite black. It had been seasoned with turnips and herbs. When I sniffed, I caught a whiff of anise.

I looked up to find my officers watching me intently. Slipping the mystery delicacy into my mouth, I chewed it gingerly. It was meat, all right, though it tasted mostly of its seasonings. If anything, it was not so tough as most mess-hall delicacies.

I turned to Lieutenant Colonel Lu, a dour, dependable man who had just been assigned as my executive officer, or right-hand man.

"Colonel Lu, what is the name of this tasty dish?" I asked casually.

"Dog meat," he grunted with his mouth full.

I had eaten dog meat before, so I wondered all the more why my officers were so concerned with my reaction.

Another officer, Captain Fong, added: "But this is dead dog meat, sir."

"Of course it is," I said. "I would hate to be eating the dog alive."

Everyone laughed except the roly-poly Colonel Lu, who believed in clarifying everything. "I don't think you understand, Colonel Stuart," he insisted. "One of the men found the dog this morning. It was dead on the side of the road. No doubt it was run over. . . ."

"But who knows when?" Captain Fong interjected.

Colonel Lu continued: "The man took it to the cook and asked if it was edible. The cook never turns down anything. He said he would season it so well that *you* would not know what it was."

"And we made bets on whether you would," said Captain Fong.

"Who told you the story of how the dog was found?" I asked.

"The cook," said Colonel Lu. "He was going to serve it to the men only if you liked it. Now that you have, all the men will like it, too."

I swallowed hard. I envisioned my troops dropping like flies — from rotten dog meat. But all I said was: "An excellent dish! Eat hearty, everyone!"

We did. Nobody reported any ill effects. The dog meat, however, made me thirst for a small sip of revenge.

"Did anybody happen to hear a noise coming from my room last night? Like gunshots?" I inquired.

Captain Fong replied: "Yes, we did, sir. We thought perhaps you were dissatisfied with your bed companion." The others laughed.

"You're not too far from the truth, Fong," I said. "I was killing my bed companions: rats!"

"Oh, we all have rats in our rooms," Colonel Lu observed.

"I'm not one to grumble about a few rats in my room," I said. "Nevertheless, I do object when the little bastards chase each other across my bed. They were squealing and fighting like husband and wife. I grew a little peeved, so I switched on my flashlight and shot two of them."

"Ah, that is a good explanation," said Colonel Lu, helping himself to the last piece of meat in the center bowl.

"But a funny thing happened this morning," I continued. "When I woke up, I saw no sign of the dead rats anywhere."

"That *is* strange," said Captain Fong. "Maybe the other rats took them away and buried them."

"Rats don't do that," Colonel Lu declared succinctly.

"Maybe they ate them," Captain Fong suggested.

"Rats don't do that, either," Colonel Lu said knowledgeably.

"I have a theory," I said. "Perhaps someone heard the shooting. While I was sleeping, maybe he picked up the dead rats and took them to the galley. Our noble cook, after all, could make them taste like almost any delicacy."

Colonel Lu was still holding a piece of black meat in his chopsticks. His hand, however, was frozen in midair.


Having breakfasted, we went to work. A long red envelope was on my desk. It contained an invitation to a wedding.

The date was tomorrow; the time, noon; the place, a village near my old headquarters at Black Dragon Temple.

A young brother of the village chief would be the groom. I was quite honored to be remembered almost a year after transferring to Yanglin.

"How about it?" I asked Colonel Lu. "Tomorrow is a holiday, I believe."

"Yes, the Festival of the Harvest Moon."

I decided to take Colonel Lu, Captain Fong, and two lieutenants as my retinue.

The next morning, we drove to Black Dragon Temple. There, we left our car and hiked along a narrow bullock trail that twisted through paddy fields to the village.

Along the way, Colonel Lu asked me how well I knew the village chief.

"Met him only once or twice," I said. "We got on nicely enough." I added that, like all village headmen, he was the most prominent landowner and respected elder. This one, however, was a very young elder. He was in his thirties. He owed his position to being a relative of one of Governor Lung's high provincial officials.

[ 324 ]

"Then we must be careful what we do or say," said Colonel Lu, who had a suspicious nature.

"There's nothing to worry about, Lu. The chief is a kindly family man who lives in harmony with his four wives."

"Then I will be careful for all of us."

Our host and the village elders greeted us as we entered their town. We shook hands formally in Western fashion. Crowds were milling around. Everyone was dressed in the gaudy picture-postcard colors of country folk the world over.

The mud-brick, gray-tile, and blackwood buildings, with rice-paper windows, were built close together and were connected by narrow dirt paths. The shrill cries of children could be heard everywhere. Ancient water buffalo took the day off and feasted on grass near the rice paddies. Small birds lolled on their backs and plucked out ticks. Everybody and everything knew this was a holiday.

It was a joyous scene that would not have been very different a thousand years earlier.

I remarked to Colonel Lu: "You'd never know a war was going on. The outside world just hasn't penetrated this far."

"The world is always with us," said Colonel Lu.

The village chief led us through a large gate in the wall around his house. Taking me by the hand (a sign of close friendship in China), he walked me through the courtyard and into the largest, most lavishly decorated house in town.

All shutters had been removed from the main reception room opening on to the courtyard. Indoors and outdoors blended picturesquely to make the entire scene look larger than life.

In the courtyard, fifteen round tables — each with a dozen seats — were piled high with beautiful dishes and utensils. In the reception room, opium smells mixed with those of joss sticks burning on an altar that ran the width of the room.

While joss smoke curled about him, a Buddha sat smiling on the altar. Before the Buddha stood small bowls of fresh fruit and newly-cooked rice. The statue was flanked by bronze, pewter, and silver ornaments.

Miniature houses were fixed high on the wall above the altar table. They resembled doll houses. In each dwelt the spirit of an ancestor

[ 325 ]

plus a tiny bowl of rice. Strings of paper, painted gold and silver, dangled from the rafters above every little house. The rice was food; the paper represented money. Spirits had to be fed and paid on this day of days.

The walls were painted with clean white lime. They were covered with scrolls. There were also prints of Chiang Kai-shek, Sun Yat-sen, and old, bald, pious-looking Governor Lung.

The furniture was made of heavy blackwood and rosewood. The table tops were green marble. Everything was immaculate.

After all introductions were made, I was shown to the seat of honor. I put up violent resistance for ten minutes until I was physically put there. My tantrum was good manners in China. The guest of honor must demonstrate that he is not truly worthy of the distinction. He must offer his position to everyone else. In the course of this argument, everyone expresses his deep respect for everyone else. Thus flattered, all are amicable when the serious drinking starts.

We were served hot tea followed by tumblers of French brandy.

"*Kan-pei,*" said our host — "bottoms up."

It was a challenge dear to my heart, but I caught a warning look from Colonel Lu. "Not now," I said. "I will gladly *kan-pei* at dinner."

Our host said he would remember. All the guests had heard I was an excellent drinker. I would have the chance to prove myself later.

We chatted about families, etiquette, and weddings until we were silenced by a gong and some cymbals outside the courtyard wall.

Through the open gate, I glimpsed a large, ornate, completely enclosed sedan chair passing by. It was transported by four coolies and trailed by a mob of hysterical little girls.

"There goes the bride," Captain Fong explained. For three days before the wedding, bride and groom traveled together about the countryside in separate sedan chairs.

A few minutes later, gong and cymbals rang out again. Another chair came by, followed by a mob of overwrought little boys. This chair stopped near the courtyard gate. A young man alighted. The village chief introduced me to his brother, the bridegroom.

The groom was seventeen and boyishly handsome. He bowed several times and offered me his hand, which was frail and trembling.

I said a few kind words. The other men teased the boy with some bawdy jokes. Even without understanding much Chinese, I knew I had heard them all in English. The groom's face flushed and he backed out on the run. A stream of wisecracks followed him to his sedan chair.

"What is the bride like?" I inquired. "Is she good-looking, too?" My host and the others burst out laughing.

"What's so funny?"

My host placed his hand on my arm and said: "Our father is dead. Therefore, as oldest son, it becomes my duty to choose a wife for my brother. I have chosen a girl from a very rich family. They own many acres of rich rice land."

"But all I asked was how she looked. . . ."

"Ah, you should see her, my friend!" my host shouted with glee. "You must see the prize I have chosen for my brother!"

Again, everybody was convulsed — even the bride's father, who was drinking heavily.

"If so," I said, a trifle peevishly, "then why don't I go see her?"

This time, I thought every man there — including Colonel Lu — was going to wet his pants.

"It is not usually done," said my host when he had collected himself. "But since you are a foreigner, you may see her."

I was led to a completely shuttered house. The bride's empty sedan chair stood outside. The entrance was guarded by two husky women, who stood warily with arms folded. At a word from the chief, they opened the door and stood back.

Without another word, I was lifted from behind and tossed straight through the entrance. Behind me, I could hear the men yelling with laughter as the door slammed shut.

Some twenty screaming, jabbering women fell upon me. They attacked me so violently that I almost hollered "Rape!" Their attack took the form of tearing at my clothes with desert-island passion. Only their unfamiliarity with my uniform slowed them down and saved me from total nudity in a matter of seconds.

As it was, my hat went sailing across the room and several buttons popped from my tunic.

My fate might have been worse if one of the female doorkeepers had not made her way in from outside. She folded her arms about me and barked something at the ugly seraglio. They promptly backed off.

The woman dragged me to a staircase, handed me a small oil lamp, and pointed upward.

"Well," I said to myself, "if I have to leave by the roof, it's worth it."

The stairs led to a small trap door. I pushed it up and climbed into a small closet of a room. It smelled of stale tobacco smoke. I closed the trap door behind me and discovered the huddled form of a woman at my feet. She squatted with her head buried in her hands. She said nothing.

Her most salient feature was her size. By any standard, she was large. For a Chinese woman, she was huge.

I bent down and touched her on the shoulder. I held the oil lamp close to her face. She raised her head only slightly.

Kneeling, I put my arms under hers. I wished to raise her to her feet. She understood my intention and stood up. She still kept her hands over her face.

I brought the lamp very close. She dropped her hands for one second and exposed her face. She was about eighteen. Her face was big, round and puffy.

That was not all. Her face was completely disfigured by hideous red pockmarks. Now I knew what the men's laughter had been about.

"Poor kid!" I said aloud. Feeling very ashamed of myself, I opened the trap door, and climbed down. I had seen what I had come to see.

I made my way through the cackling women, each of whom wanted to touch me for good luck. Staggering out the front door, I was greeted by the male wedding guests. They were speculating wildly about how many new children the "kind-hearted tiger" had given the village during his brief visit.

Captain Fong asked me if the bride was "a good piece."

"Ample," I replied noncommittally.

"You are lucky to come out of there in one piece yourself," he said.

Colonel Lu added: "If one of us had gone in, they would have stripped us, mauled us, and perhaps emasculated us."

"What is that place? The local madhouse?" I asked.

[ 328 ]

"No," said Lu. "Those women are in a position of honor. They stay there for three days before the wedding. Only the bride may go out — in her enclosed chair. Did you notice that all the women in there — including the bride — are dressed alike?"

"No. I was too busy keeping *myself* dressed."

"They dress alike to confuse any intruder. It becomes impossible to identify the bride."

Now that the prenuptial entertainment was over, we drifted back to the chief's house. Light refreshments were served. Latecomers took their places at the tables in the courtyard. Like weddings the world over, this one started late — at two P.M.

The ceremony, before the altar in the open reception room, was simple but colorful. Several documents were read aloud and chanted. The participants signed papers by stamping them with a seal. Almost everyone there had a hand in the ceremony.

The bride wore a beautifully embroidered pink-and-white silk dress. Her matching hat was square and small; it contained little gold ornaments. Her face was plastered with thick coats of white powder and rouge.

The groom did not glance at her once during the ceremony.

When it was over, the chief took my arm, and said: "She is not handsome. But she will make a good first wife for my brother. He is not a very strong boy. She is big and strong. She can work hard. She will bear him many children. And, when my brother is old enough to be a man, he may choose other wives and concubines to suit himself."


The wedding feast began with cows' nostrils, elephant's trunk, Tibetan bear's paw, pigs' intestines, duck's tongue, and fish lips. Just name your taste and it was there.

I never attended a large Chinese dinner without encountering a brand-new delicacy. This time it was monkey-brain soup.

A live baby monkey was brought out and placed beneath a small table that had a hole in its center. The monkey's head was poked through the hole and a clamp was placed around its neck.

Then, with a mallet, the village chief hit the little ape on the head. It expired with a faint squeak.

[ 329 ]

One of the elders took a knife and quickly sliced off the top of the skull as if it were a soft-boiled egg.

The chief scooped out its brains with a spoon. He dipped the brains into a boiling hot bowl of clear soup and then offered the spoon to me. As guest of honor, I took a sip and then passed the spoon ceremoniously to the other dignitaries.

When the meal was over, I gave one final belch of contentment and my host said, *"Kan-pei!"* Our drinking bout was on.

Fortunately, courtesy dictates that one lets the host win — but I gave him a good battle. Everybody agreed that I had justified my seat of honor.

Around 4:30, an intermission was declared, enabling the celebrants to rest up and change for that night's Harvest Moon Festival.

Local hospitality toward me, however, was far from over. Before I could take my nap, the village chief, a few elders, my officers, and I retired to an inner room of the house. It was furnished with opium beds.

As guest of honor, I was obliged to smoke the first pipe. I was complimented upon my skill and then I fell asleep musing that Chan would have been proud of me.

Colonel Lu did not nap. He had been trained as an Intelligence officer. He kept his eyes closed and his ears open. He once told me: "When people are at their ease, the first thing they do is unbutton their lips. It is surprising what one hears."

At six P.M., a boy came in with hot towels and awakened us. On our way out, Lu took me aside and said: "Do not try again to win at *kan-pei.*"

"I couldn't if I wanted to."

"And look out for two strangers. They will want to kill you."

"You sound like a God damn fortuneteller, Lu."

"I have no crystal ball, just two good ears. But I heard the chief refer to you as 'Governor Lung's guest.' He said two men from Kunming would 'present their compliments.' The elders asked why and he said you once made a Yunnanese general lose face."

"So that's why the hell the chief invited me!"

"He likes you, but he says his relatives in Kunming do not. He will miss you, he says. Do you think we ought to go now?"

"No," I said. "We can handle any two gangsters Governor Lung might send. In the meantime, let's enjoy life while we may."

We walked with the others to a paddy that had been cleared, leveled, and smoothed for the celebration. Dozens of tables and hundreds of chairs were arranged at one end. From the seat of honor at the head table, I had an excellent view of all that went on.

Food seemed to grow on the tables. Wine flowed like tea. There was the inevitable *kan-pei* competition. I let the chief win again, although I prolonged the struggle with a few tricks I had learned long ago from Chan. I would stagger with my drink and spill some. During the toast, I would crash my cup against my opponent's and allow half the wine to drain discreetly. I would dispose of the rest in small trickles from the corners of my mouth and down my chin.

Darkness fell. The lanterns were lit. The air filled with aromas of candle wax and burning oil. Ancient instruments pierced the night with familiar folk tales set to music. In the field, villagers danced a dragon dance, a lantern dance, and the dance of the harvest moon. Somewhere offstage, a thousand firecrackers were exploded. They illuminated the silvery blue sky and dimmed the bright moon in whose honor the people of the land were rejoicing.

I thought I could feel the heartbeat of China — a culture thousands of years old and, here at least, unblemished by the madness of the outside world.

With this thought on my lips, I turned to my host. I found him deep in conversation with two young Chinese I had never seen before.

They were dressed like farmers, but their clothes looked all wrong on them. Their hatchetlike faces, sleek hair, and pallid skins reflected the city.

I caught Colonel Lu's eye. He nodded. By looks alone, these had to be Governor Lung's two assassins.

In a primitive setting of lavish hospitality, a trap had been sprung. My doom had been plotted a few miles away in another world.

Nobody paid us much heed any longer. The fuss over guests had given way to general merriment. I glanced at my watch. It was almost midnight.

The village chief, staggering from a day's drinking, made his way over to us. Would Colonel Stuart and Colonel Lu join him in a pipe of opium? We rose to our feet and tottered with feigned drunkenness.

The chief left us alone for a moment. The two strangers were nowhere to be seen. I briefed Captain Fong: "You and the others will follow us after we leave. If you see those two strangers, follow them everywhere."

A coolie boy brought five cups of wine, which my officers and I pretended to drink. Then Lu and I followed the chief and an elder to the main house. The courtyard was lit by paper lanterns and the harvest moon. We were led to the same inner room where we had smoked that afternoon. This time, three young girls handed us tea and hot towels. They offered to relieve us of our tunics, but Lu and I refused.

The chief was very irritable. Perhaps this was due to his discomfort at betraying us; perhaps to his impatient craving for the pipe. Whatever the reason, he settled onto the smoking bed with the elder beside him and immediately lost interest in everything around him except the opium. He and the elder were present, but no longer really there.

The girls prepared a pipe for Colonel Lu and me. "Keep them busy," I muttered to Lu. The girls were not hard to distract with jokes and flirtations. They had their minds on all the fun they were missing outside. During our half-hour of banter with the girls, the chief smoked four pipes.

As we ran out of material, the dour but happily married Colonel Lu began chasing two young girls around the room. He was trying desperately *not* to catch them.

I sat near the door. Suddenly, I heard whispered, conspiratorial voices just outside the building.

I nodded to Colonel Lu, who braked himself. He listened for a moment and then dismissed the girls. He insisted that they take the rest of the night off and join the festivities in the field. The girls departed in a flurry of giggles.

Lu and I jumped to our feet. We buttoned our tunics. I doused the oil lamps and candles. The two opium lamps, however, burned on. We could not disturb the chief and his elder. Both were dozing in another life where men do not lay traps for one another.

[ 332 ]

The dull yellow light of the opium lamps guided us to the door. We drew our guns and poised ourselves to spring out.

It was lucky we waited. Suddenly, a series of gunshots masked the firecracker sounds in the distance. Peering out the door, I saw the two strangers racing toward us. Both were carrying pistols. One was firing back at Captain Fong, who was giving chase. The other gangster was intent on reaching our room.

I threw a shoulder block as he entered. Then I brought my knee up into his groin. He snapped forward and I crashed my pistol butt down on his head.

Lu was fighting the other assassin, but his pistol was lighter than mine, and was having very little effect as a club. I handed Lu my officer's sword. He drove it through the man's heart.

Captain Fong finished off my man with one bullet. Then we carried the two corpses through the courtyard. We dumped them into a ditch near the now deserted house of the bride's women.

We rejoined the party briefly and said our farewells. All the way back to Black Dragon Temple, nobody spoke. We savored the simple pleasures of inhaling and exhaling for at least another night.

I never saw the chief again, but I did see his guilty conscience in action. Twice a month, Colonel Lu and I received a basket of eggs, a side of pork, a ham, or even live chickens from him. We donated his gifts to our cook, who never again had to cook dubious dog meat.

Every year I was in China, I was invited back to the village for the Festival of the Harvest Moon. Each time, I declined politely. The chief continued to send gifts. His kindness to us knew no bounds.

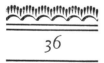

## 36

# Death of a Beggar

My headquarters in Yanglin were surrounded on three sides by rice paddies and on the fourth by rolling hills. A narrow road interlaced the three villages. The entire valley was rich with rice; it produced two or three cuttings a year. The houses were mostly mud brick. Some had tile roofs. Others were thatched.

The people were friendly enough, considering that we were anything but welcome guests. It was customary for a Chinese Army unit to commandeer the best houses in any town it selected for its base. I had chosen the home of the town's elder, but, in an effort to be humane, I used only the upper floor.

As my office, I selected a room above the stable, where water buffalo and other creatures spent the night. My bedroom was a cubicle separated from my office by a partition. Once I had cleaned up the place and exterminated the vermin, it was most comfortable.

The house was square. It surrounded an inner courtyard and was itself surrounded by a wall eight feet high. From my upstairs windows, I could gaze out at all three villages, and watch the passersby — villagers who worked in the paddies; beggars; an occasional peddler. There was also a small boy who came to play in our courtyard every afternoon. He wanted to be a soldier. He promptly became our unit's mascot. His name was Li, but I christened him "Looey." He could not have been more than eight years old.

The only times we ever chased him out of our courtyard were when we had prisoners to torture.

Our courtyard was also used for missions of mercy. There was no doctor for miles around. Whenever I had time, I would hold a "sick call" for civilians.

One afternoon, I finished my clinic hour by treating a six-month-old baby boy, whose mother had brought him to me a week earlier. His body had been covered with running sores. Guessing that he had been infected by bedbug bites, I had cleaned him off and sprinkled him with sulfa powder. Now, on his second visit, the sores were healing. I dusted the baby again with sulfa and sent him and his mother on their way.

As they left, a guard appeared at the gate with two more children — a boy and a girl in their early teens.

"Oh, God!" I moaned. "More patients!" But the two children looked healthy to me.

[ 334 ]

"They tell story," the guard said apologetically. "I think they should tell to you, sir."

"All right," I said resignedly. "We'll make this the story hour."

The story the children told was no fairy tale. While playing in the street of their village they had seen an old beggar sit down near the village well. He had taken a large red can out of his basket and poured a green powder into the well. When they asked him what he was doing, he chased them away. They fled to my headquarters.

I ordered the guard and my Officer of the Day to bring in the beggar and his basket. Ten minutes later, they returned — half-dragging, half-pushing the old man every inch of the way.

He was no stranger. I had seen him many times as he traveled among the villages in the valley and begged for food. He was originally from north China and stood six feet tall. He held himself erect. He was in his late sixties. His clothes were in tatters and his body was crawling with lice. When he stood before me, he met my gaze with a smile of recognition. Now, he must have thought, he was among friends.

I said nothing to him, but snatched the red can from his basket. It was about ten inches square and three inches deep. Its lid was unhinged. In the seams of the can were green powder and traces of white powder. I recognized Paris green, a lethal insecticide. The white powder, I suspected, was arsenic.

I told the Officer of the Day: "Put four men at every well in every village around here. Don't allow anyone to draw water. Also, have another man inquire in each village whether anyone has taken water from the well since the time this beggar was there. Spread the word that the wells are poisoned."

I also assigned a detail to bail water from each well. I wanted samples of the water and the sediment at the bottom.

In the courtyard, my sergeants were tying the beggar's hands behind him. He refused to utter a word. All he did was smile and bow. I shut the main gate of the courtyard after making sure that Looey was not around. For once, I was glad not to see Looey. Like all children, he hated to be chased away.

"Who gave you the poison?" I asked the beggar.

He stood mute and smiling.

"Who told you to dump it into the well?"

He remained mute and smiling.

At his feet lay all his belongings. Rummaging among them, I found a beggar's usual paraphernalia — chopsticks, rice bowl, dried orange peel, and scraps of paper — plus six brand-new Chinese five-dollar bills. It was far more than any beggar in Yunnan Province would hope to see in a whole year.

"This is payoff money," I said, renewing my interrogation. I explained to the old man what he had done. I told him that he would have wiped out a village if the children had not seen him at the well.

He only smiled. He did not seem to realize the seriousness of his crime.

"Someone has taken advantage of you," I said. "Tell us quickly who it is, old man, or we must kill you slowly."

After an hour of one-sided conversation, I dragged him to the middle of the courtyard, where there was a post as tall as a man.

"Nobody has left this post alive without telling us what we want to know," I told the beggar as my men tied him to it.

Age is venerated in China and I could see that my soldiers were not eager to proceed. I cursed the head sergeant and told him: "If you don't hurry, I'm going to break every bone in your idle hands. We have to find out what other wells this traitor has poisoned."

I stood before the beggar and repeated my questions. He said nothing. I struck him hard across the face. My blow erased his smile, but it did not unseal his lips.

"Hundreds of people may be cooking their evening rice with poisoned water right now," I told him. "If you answer my questions, I will see that you are set free. I will personally give you many times as much as you were paid to do this work."

My words had no effect. His expression was fixed in blankness. The skin of his face was drawn and gray. My blows had told him what lay ahead. The shock had numbed his brain. In his mind, he was already dead.

I had seen this happen before to other men. I suspected that the torture would elicit nothing.

Nevertheless, it had to be tried. I ordered my sergeants to work him over while I went upstairs to my office. There, I arranged for new wells to be dug near where old ones had been poisoned.

[ 336 ]

After half an hour, I returned to the courtyard with my green rawhide whip.

Some twenty soldiers were standing around the old man. All were shouting questions at him. Some stood with clenched fists. Others had their arms folded across their chests. Some wore nervous grins belied by the horror in their eyes. Some faces twitched with nervous tension. Some jaws would clench and then sag idiotically. One man was drooling. On every face was an ugly mixture of fear and delight.

All eyes were riveted on the old beggar. Nobody wanted to miss the crucial moment when man either submits to man or dies.

The head sergeant stood closest to the beggar. In the sergeant's hand was a long split bamboo pole, poised to strike.

The beggar's tattered rags had been stripped from his body by the sergeant's blows and his chest and stomach were red with blood and welts. The old man's eyes were glazed and uncomprehending. Saliva oozed from his mouth, but still no words came.

I handed the sergeant the whip and said: "Try this on him!"

The sergeant stood back and swung the whip in the air a few times. Then he brought it down across the old man's chest. It cut through the welts and sent a new gush of blood down his stomach.

The sergeant asked a question, then struck again, asked another question, then struck again. . . .

The sixth lash laid open the beggar's stomach. He sagged forward against the ropes that held him.

The sergeant stopped and I took the man's pulse. It was still beating strongly.

"He's unconscious," I said. "One of you men get a pail of water."

I intended to throw the water into the old man's face to revive him.

Just as a soldier handed me the pail of water, the old man's eyes opened. He saw me standing there with the pail and he smiled faintly. "Water," he said.

It was a supplication, but I said: "First, old man, you will answer my questions. Then you can have all the water you want. Now, who gave you the poison?"

His head rocked from side to side. His lips moved as he tried to form many words. The only one that came out however, was "water."

"Speak up and you'll get your water," I promised him. Now that his silence had been broken, I knew truth was near.

The sergeant leaned close and translated the old man's mumbles to me. Two other beggars, whom we knew well, were also carrying the poison. He told us where they could be found.

"Who gave you the money? The Japs?" I asked.

He hung his head with shame, but said no more except: "Water!"

"That's enough for now," I said to the sergeant. I took the beggar's rice bowl, filled it with water from the pail, and pressed it to his lips.

He regained some of his strength. I cut him loose and sat him down against the wall. Holding the rice bowl in trembling hands, he gulped the rest of the water and asked for more.

"You must wait," I said. "You must tell us everything you know and then you can have more water — much more water."

I sensed that he would tell us all. Men under torture were like that. Once they started talking, they held nothing back. In the meantime, I had to put out an alarm for the other two beggars. I returned to my office and left the old man to be interrogated by my soldiers.

A few minutes later, I heard a commotion outside the main gate. It sounded like wailing and chanting. I also heard the high-pitched screams of a woman. I sent my orderly to find out what was the matter.

"The woman has a very sick boy," he reported. "They all want you to see him."

"For God's sake, tell them to go away! We've got bigger problems right now."

"But they say it is the little boy who plays here all time."

"Looey!" I exclaimed, remembering that I hadn't seen him all day. "What's the matter with him?"

"They do not know, but they say it is very bad."

I grabbed my first-aid kit and rushed through the courtyard. Although several of the men were clustered around the beggar, I did not stop.

The entire male population of the village stood outside one hut. I pushed my way through. Inside were women, bewailing death amidst a pall of smoke cast by a cooking fire.

On a straw mat lay little Looey, but I barely recognized him. His body was arched like a bow. His mouth was open. His eyes stared emptily. His face had frozen in a mask of agony.

I felt for a pulse in his skinny little wrist. There was none.

[ 338 ]

Looey's father was kneeling in silent grief beside his dead son. I asked him if anyone had drawn water from the village well that afternoon.

Yes, he said. His oldest daughter had gone there early in the afternoon before our guards had been posted. And Looey had drunk from the water his sister had brought back.

For what it was worth to him now, I told the father what had happened. His daughter had already disposed of the pail of water. I told her to throw out the rice that was cooking over the fire.

In my car, I had a Chinese Army field jacket. I covered Looey's small body with it.

When I reached headquarters, I asked the head sergeant: "How is the beggar now?"

"He is dead, sir."

"What did you do to him?" I asked. I knew that the beggar had been strong enough to withstand the punishment he had absorbed.

"He did not die of the torture, sir. He died of his own poison."

I was furious: "Bring me the man who let him have the poison!"

"I cannot do that, sir," the sergeant said.

"Why not?" I demanded.

"You, sir, are the man who gave it to him."

"Have you gone out of your mind, sergeant?"

"No, sir. He had already poisoned the well that we use here. The bucket from which you gave him a drink was filled only a few minutes before we brought him in."

"Good God!" I said. In one afternoon, I had lost my mascot and killed his murderer.

"At least," said the sergeant, "the old man died by his own evil. We would only have had to shoot him anyway."

# 37

# In the Courtyard of a Special Purpose

I SOMETIMES guessed that half of Yunnan Province was in the opium trade. The rest seemed to be consumers. Often, business and pleasure overlapped.

General Tu Yu Ming did not concern himself with local sale and consumption, even though they were illegal. What bothered him was a flowering opium trade between Yunnanese and Japanese.

Tons of opium were being smuggled from Yunnan to south China and Indochina, where the Japs had control. The Japs paid for it with precious gems, plain rice, and U.S. dollars. Then they sold it to the Chinese in occupied areas. This kept the people under Japanese thumbs. Occasionally, it resulted in betrayal of our agents there by addicts who would do anything for their opium.

For this reason I looked upon opium smuggling as a personal threat to Nora, who might still be alive and working in Canton. On the roads leading to occupied China, my men made daily spot checks. They searched travelers and took prisoners. Not a day passed without a haul of five to fifty pounds of opium. On one occasion, we seized a truck carrying four tons.

Ordinarily, we burned the confiscated opium in our Courtyard of a Special Purpose at Yanglin. This courtyard was our place for formal inspections and the occasional execution of a smuggler. But, early in 1944, the Courtyard of a Special Purpose took on new meaning. General Tu Yu Ming acquired a new general, whom he appointed Chief of Staff, and a new colonel, who became Adjutant General. Both men were dope addicts.

The Adjutant summoned me on his third day in office. He knew I took orders only from General Tu, so he put it this way:

"There is a new policy. It comes from the Chief of Staff. Opium that is confiscated is to be turned over to me for safekeeping."

"Oh?" I said. "Is there any dissatisfaction with the way my men are burning it?"

"Certainly not! But the Chief of Staff wishes to put it to good use — as evidence. Then he will destroy it before an assembly of troops. He will lecture them that this is an evil menace to mankind. He will warn of the dangers. He is an excellent speaker."

This argument may have had some merit. Not, however, in the mouth of a man whose skin, eyes, and fingernails all looked jaundiced — the telltale sign of an addict.

Nevertheless, I had to say yes at this stage. When I did, the Adjutant gave a sigh of relief and invited me to lunch. He had not expected to effect the new "policy" this easily.

"But why did you consent?" Colonel Lu asked me later. "Don't you know that, whatever they can't use for themselves, they will sell right back to Governor Lung?"

"We'll have to catch them at it," I said. "If I'd refused, the Adjutant and the Chief of Staff would have to find another way to finance their opium buying." Lu and I both knew that they would then engage in a less detectable form of "squeeze," such as stealing rice or gasoline, which sold like liquid gold on the black market.

Opium ranges in color from dark brown (the best) to light amber. Lu and I worked cautiously at first. Whenever our men seized high-grade opium, we burned it furtively. Only the lighter shades were passed on to the Adjutant — after the packages had been weighed, measured, and secretly marked.

A friend of Colonel Lu's worked for the Adjutant. He kept us informed that some of the opium was being smoked by his boss and the Chief of Staff. Still more opium was not finding its way to the new dope-burning ceremonies.

Every Monday was Memorial Day in the Chinese Army. Some two thousand men would assemble on the parade grounds at Fifth Army Headquarters near Kunming. There, they paid homage to General Sun Yat-sen, father of the Chinese Republic. His party's principles were read aloud. The oath of allegiance was recited by all. The two-hour ceremony would conclude with a speech by an officer.

In 1944, the Monday-morning speaker was the Chief of Staff. He was tall, tough, and heroic-looking. He had received his military training in Germany and had stayed there much longer than most Chinese officers. Perhaps this was why he took so little interest in the war. Most of his directives concerned pomp and ceremony rather than tactics or improvements. Personally, he concentrated on being modern and living high.

He would conclude his impassioned speech on "The Evils of Opium" by flinging packages onto a fire. It does not take much opium to fill the air with fumes. The rest of the packages could be filled with less valuable materials that burned prettily.

To prove all this was another matter. Lu and I bided our time.

Our next major raid came when a party of Governor Lung's Yunnanese soldiers were reported advancing on Yanglin. Colonel Lu's reports indicated that they were carrying large quantities of opium.

"There are twenty-six soldiers," Lu said, "plus a woman who is being carried in a sedan chair. It will take a good-sized patrol."

The Yunnanese troops were approaching on foot from the north. My fifty men spread out on both sides of a narrow street just inside the north gate of the town.

Soon, we heard feet on the cobblestones. Then there were the grunts and puffs of men bearing heavy burdens.

They entered Yanglin in single file. As soon as the last man drew abreast of me, I blew a whistle and my men stepped out of doorways and side streets. Our weapons were pointed. The Yunnanese halted. The four soldiers bearing the sedan chair lowered it gently to the ground.

"Who is in charge here?" Colonel Lu barked.

A colonel in the Yunnanese green uniform stepped forward, bristling. "What right have you to detain us?" he demanded. "I am an official of the Yunnanese Government."

The air reeked of raw opium. Colonel Lu sniffed loudly and said: "That is one good reason why you are under arrest. Carrying opium is against the law of the Central Government in all provinces of China. Please surrender your weapons."

The twenty-six men, their burdens, the woman, and her sedan chair were transported by truck to the Courtyard of a Special Purpose.

The search began. In their luggage, we discovered flashlights with batteries hollowed out and stuffed with opium; Thermos bottles filled with opium; and tubes of toothpaste containing opium. When we examined their rifles and pistols, we found the barrels, breeches, and stocks crammed with opium. The cartridges were not filled with gunpowder. . . . Now I knew why the Yunnanese troops had offered us no physical resistance.

"Let's have a go at the sedan chair," I said.

I had never seen one so sturdily constructed. Its bamboo and its carrying poles were at least three times the usual diameters. And every inch of extra space was packed with small waxlike marbles of opium.

The male prisoners were stripped and searched in the Courtyard of a Special Purpose. Each bore several pounds of opium on his person: in pockets, under puttees, and around the waist.

"Do you want us to examine the wax in their ears?" Colonel Lu asked me.

"May I search the woman?" Captain Fong asked, licking his lips. The woman, who was the Yunnanese colonel's wife, was young and beautiful. She was sitting in my office and looking utterly disinterested.

"I'm beginning to think she's made of opium, too," I said. "But we already have more than a ton of the stuff. That should be enough evidence." The Yunnanese colonel had already told me, loudly and often, that his wife was the sister of a high Yunnanese official who had Governor Lung's ear. There would be repercussions if we laid hands on her.

My men weighed, counted, and photographed the opium while I reported our coup to the Adjutant General. I thought he would faint. He was, I suspected, a man who transacted a great deal of unofficial business with Governor Lung's bandits.

"You should never take such risks!" he screamed at me. "Suppose you had found nothing! There would be a civil war! As it is, there will be many complications. . . ."

"Don't worry. I have made the arrest. I will furnish the evidence."

"Then it is your responsibility," he said, brightening at the thought.

"Only partly. In a short while, I will deliver it to you for safekeeping. That is the policy nowadays, isn't it?"

"No, no!" he said frantically. "Not in big cases like this! You must keep the opium as evidence until the people come to trial. It is *your* responsibility, Stuart."

Instead of returning to the Courtyard of a Special Purpose, I reported to General Tu Yu Ming. He handed me an English cigarette as I told of the raid.

"I already know of it," the general said. "The Chief of Staff has phoned. He said he expects great problems as a result of your action. Henceforth, he said, you will please notify him in advance of all arrests you plan to make."

Seething, I said: "That can't be done, sir!"

"Have some tea," General Tu said, as an orderly placed cups before us. "I never thought I would hear you say that, Stuart. But you're right. I told the Chief of Staff that I saw no reason to alter your operating procedures."

I sipped my tea happily. Then I said: "I will need your advice, sir, on how to proceed with these prisoners. They should be executed, but that might start a war with Yunnan. And with your own Chief of Staff. And with your Adjutant General." Quickly, I sketched recent fluctuations in "policy" on confiscated opium. I told him I was sure only a tiny fraction was being destroyed.

General Tu Yu Ming frowned once or twice. Then he asked me: "Have you a full description of today's haul?"

"Yes, sir. I've cross-indexed it three different ways."

"Very well, Colonel Stuart. You will turn it over to the Adjutant General along with the twenty-seven prisoners. You will tell him that the opium is *his* responsibility."

"With pleasure, sir."

Weeks passed before our captives came to trial. General Tu Yu Ming took some time to negotiate a face-saving truce with the Yunnanese Government. Twenty-four of the prisoners received jail sentences. The colonel and his top sergeant were executed. Despite the colonel's high connections, an in-law often proves dispensable.

His widow never came to trial. She was turned over to her influential relatives. She would have no trouble finding a second husband.

After the trial, the Chief of Staff ordered a gala Memorial Day ceremony, with a huge bonfire on the parade ground. He made his lengthiest and most fervent speech ever on the sins of narcotics. As a grand finale, the ton of opium was brought forth with an honor guard headed by the Adjutant General himself.

As the opium came forward, so did Colonel Lu and I. We handed the Adjutant a paper from General Tu Yu Ming. It authorized us to seize, inspect, and evaluate the contents of the packages that were about to be burned. The Chief of Staff watched helplessly from the speaker's platform.

More than eighty per cent of the original opium had been replaced by harmless chemicals. Only the poorest grade of opium remained.

We reported our findings to General Tu Yu Ming. What ensued provided another eventful day in the history of our Courtyard of a Special Purpose. The remaining opium was destroyed by fire shortly before noon. The Chief of Staff and the Adjutant General were destroyed by a firing squad at sundown.

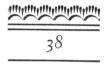

## 38

# Men of China

In any Western nation, corruption that led to the execution of a high-ranking Chief of Staff and an Adjutant General would make front-page headlines. The opium affair in the Chinese Fifth Army, however, created no great stir outside the Courtyard of a Special Purpose. The Chinese populace took military dishonesty for granted.

Soldiering was not a part of Chinese philosophy or the Chinese way of life. As late as 1944, at least two Chinese civilians spat at me contemptuously on the streets of Kunming. Why? Not because I was a foreigner, but because I had the "misfortune" of being a lieutenant colonel in the Chinese Army.

One of the difficulties I had in training Chinese troops was that they were conditioned by public contempt for soldiering. First, I had to train them to respect their officers. Then I had to train them to respect what they were fighting for. Hardest of all, I had to train them to respect themselves.

It was too late, however, to give the same training to the career officers of China. In some ways, the Chief of Staff and the Adjutant General personified the thin skin of the Chinese Army, while men like General Tu Yu Ming, Major Mar, and Colonel Lu were its backbone. The flesh was weak.

War-weary and penniless, the two disgraced officers had lost interest in the outcome of the war. After a decade of fighting, war was part of their everyday life. Soldiering became a business to them. If you were smart, you could live well and make money at it.

This attitude was easy to condemn. It could even be linked with the easy fall of China to the Communists after World War II. It was not, however, a peculiarly Chinese phenomenon. Had World War II lasted a few years longer, the attitude might not have been uncommon in England or America.

Early in 1945 Major John Hamlin, surgeon for the OSS Operational Groups, was ordered to select Chinese recruits to create a Second Commando Group. Major Hamlin requested me to accompany him on this recruiting mission. I personally had organized and trained the First Commando Group in China before the OSS arrived. In 1944 I had returned to Burma with my original motorized infantry group to fight in the Second Burma Campaign. During that time General Tu assigned my Commandos in Kunming to OSS for special training and operations. The Chinese-American cooperation was so successful in this effort that OSS decided to double its strength.

When General Tu Yu Ming dispatched me on my first and last recruiting mission, I asked Major John Hamlin, surgeon general for the OSS operational groups, to go along. This was also John's first encounter with Chinese recruiting. Neither of us had the vaguest idea of what we were getting into. Tu Yu Ming simply told us that the "candidates" were assembled in Chanyi on the Chungking road. His instructions were: "Pick only the two hundred best."

John was a clean-cut and kindly young American doctor. He and I drove the sixty miles to Chanyi on a hot, dusty morning. We arrived shortly before noon.

Following directions, we took a dirt road that skirted the old city wall. It cut its way through rice paddies to a large tent. There, a Chinese officer welcomed us and said he would take us to the recruits. We climbed into his jeep with him.

"How many recruits do you have?" I asked.

"Seventy-five thousand," he replied.

John and I were already staggered by his statistics. "How many trucks did it take?" John inquired.

"None," the officer said blandly. "They marched here. Some have marched more than a thousand miles."

John observed: "Then they'll either be in excellent condition or else more dead than alive."

Having witnessed thousands of living corpses trudging the road from Chungking, I sensed what we would find. Until then, I had seldom asked myself where on earth these wretches ended up. I had been blessed with the civilized Western gift for putting misery out of mind just as soon as it was out of sight.

The officer parked the jeep and we walked the rest of the way. The figure of seventy-five thousand suddenly seemed an underestimate. There were men and more men as far as the eye could see.

The rice paddy in which they waited had once been green and damp. Now it was trampled flat and packed into hard clay. From this soil rose the sour smell of human sweat. The "recruits" were massed together like sheep in this brown pasture. Men might faint, but there was no space for falling down.

Their bodies were covered with standard thin cotton khaki trousers and tunics. Some still had straw sandals. Most were without footgear. All were weak from marching and malnutrition. Many also had dysentery.

"I've seen more flesh on a three-month-old corpse," I said.

"I don't believe my eyes," said John Hamlin. "Is this some kind of a trick that's being played on us, Gil?"

"I think the dirtiest trick was played on them, John," I said, pointing to the recruits.

"Gil, we can't accept any of these men. They're dying on their feet. Even in trucks, I doubt if they'll last to Kunming. This is a crime against humanity."

"It is indeed," I agreed. "Nevertheless, this is the manpower of

China. Some may still have some life in them. They are young. Most of them were taken off the land. . . ."

"Speak bluntly, Gil! You mean they were shanghaied!"

"Kidnapped would be a better word. There is no other way to get men to join the Army in China. Now let's see what we can salvage from this graveyard!"

A small platform had been erected in a clearing. The recruits were to march past and be examined like sheep.

"It'll take a week just to move them up there," I told the Chinese officer. "Line them up in squads with a space in between lines for us to drive a jeep through. Before we do, though, I want you to make a little speech to them. Tell them who we are and why we're here. Tell them we want volunteers only!"

When the officer addressed the recruits, they made the first sound I had heard from their ranks. Until then, they had been too weak even to moan.

A faint murmur rolled from one end of the mob to another. The message was being relayed. It was answered by an excited rumble as the words penetrated numbed minds. *Somebody wanted them!* Their hopes lifted. We knew we would have seventy-five thousand volunteers.

As the officer drove us up one ragged line and down the next, John and I felt like slave buyers. Occasionally, we would stop and gaze into a man's mouth or pinch his skinny body. By sundown, we had seen most of the seventy-five thousand — and selected two hundred.

"I still think we're doing the wrong thing in taking any back to camp with us," said John.

"We've saved their lives," I said, "if they survive until they reach camp. You may be surprised what a few weeks of rice can do. These guys must have been tough to come this far."

We stood one last time on the reviewing stand. I gazed at the unending blanket of faces. Most would remain here until they died. This day, I had played God once again. John and I had judged who would live and who would die. Of the two hundred men we had rescued, how many would end up dead in battle?

I turned to John Hamlin with my unanswerable question. He was frozen in a stare of horror. He was not looking at the sea of men, but at the old city wall some three hundred feet behind us.

Over the ages, small bushes and trees had forced their way through the high stone wall. Ugly stunted little trees grew at its base. Draped across every bush and every tree were naked bodies.

These corpses had been flung over the wall from inside. Some had been impaled. Others were cradled by the nightmarish trees.

"What is this?" I asked the Chinese officer.

"The Army hospital is just on the other side of the wall," he said matter-of-factly — as if this explained everything.

"So what?" I shouted.

He looked at me curiously and then said: "Many recruits die of dysentery every day. But do not be concerned, sir. They will be buried at a later date."

A few hours after we reached Kunming the next day, I wandered over to John Hamlin's little OSS hospital. Our two hundred recruits had been delivered there by truck. They were disrobing in the courtyard.

As soon as the recruits' clothing fell to earth, John's GI's doused the little piles with gasoline, preparatory to burning.

"Every one of them has scurvy," John said. His men were opening twenty-pound drums of sulfa ointment. The recruits were ordered to smear their bodies with it.

They were issued new underwear and nothing else. In this informal garb, they were marched to their first real meal in months. Some of them had never eaten meat before.

They rested for three days with orders not to wash. The sulfa needed time to work on their bacteria. On the fourth day, they were given soap and taught to wash. Then they were issued new uniforms and other clothes.

For ten more days, they received ample rest and three meals a day. They were taught basketball and mild exercises.

Then they were assigned to my battalion for training. Their total weight had more than doubled since I had first seen them. They were almost all healthy.

"Seeing is believing," John Hamlin said modestly. "Now I can say that I've witnessed a miracle in my lifetime."

"I've seen several million miracles in my time," I told him. "The greatest miracle I know is the Chinese coolie and how he survives."

[ 349 ]

Back in 1943, I had mentioned to General Chennault that security was inadequate on several new air bases the Americans were building to the south and west of Kunming.

Chennault had replied testily that I shouldn't raise problems unless I had solutions.

"I think I have one, sir," I said. "I'd like to organize a Chinese unit of paratroop commandos. If the Japs ever attacked any of the fields, it could be defended. Each field could have a small permanent garrison of cars, tanks, and mortars from my armored car battalion. If the enemy drew near, we'd drop a few hundred paratroopers onto the base to help defend it."

"Draw me up a table of organization," said General Chennault.

With the help of Colonel "Rosie" Grubbs, the U. S. Air Force field commander in Kunming, I drew up a blueprint that met the most rigid specifications of the American military bureaucracy.

I submitted copies to Chennault and Tu Yu Ming. Each routed the idea to Chiang Kai-shek with a favorable recommendation. The Generalissimo approved the plan almost instantly.

I had picked five hundred good men from my unit and others. I had found a training site. I gave the would-be paratroopers special toughening-up drills there after hours. But I could not really move until I had jump equipment and instructors. I also needed airplanes.

I went to General Chennault.

"I simply don't have parachutes for you, Stuart. I'm sorry," he informed me. "But if you can get Stilwell to give them to you, I'll furnish planes for you to move them over the Hump from India."

Stilwell was somewhere in the jungle, preparing for his second Burma campaign. I went to General Frank "Pinky" Dorn, Stilwell's Chief of Staff in the Kunming area.

I had met Dorn many times. Like many of Stilwell's officers, he had spent years in Peking before the war. I am sure he was very fond of the Chinese. I don't think he particularly liked the British. I know he didn't like the idea of a Briton in Chinese clothing — particularly a colonel's uniform. Fundamentally, though, he just didn't like me.

I submitted my requisition to him and asked him to pass it on to Stilwell for approval.

Dorn asked me one question: "Did General Chennault help you with this plan, Stuart?"

When I said yes, Dorn assured me Stilwell would not go for it. He refused to "bother" his boss about it. I argued that Stilwell had once expressed some interest in such an organization. Dorn was adamant.

I knew that there was considerable rivalry between Chennault and Stilwell. I had not known until then that a subordinate would be so imbued with his chief's dislikes that he would veto a promising military operation. I turned on my heel and never set foot in Dorn's office again.

I remembered Stilwell's once saying to me wearily: "None of my staff officers are any good, Stuart. I feel let down. I can trust no one."

Whether or not he was right, his replacement by General Albert C. Wedemeyer in 1944 was inevitable. When a general cannot trust his own staff, he is sitting on a time bomb.

Begging, borrowing, stealing, and lying, I eventually pieced together my Paratroop Commandos with no help from Dorn. They were ready for the OSS. I was pleased.

Colonel Richard Heffner, who headed OSS operations in China, proved to be one of the finest men I have ever met. His aides trained my men with American weapons and parachutes. Most invaluable of all, they brought to Asia the commando tactics that had been successful behind enemy lines in Europe.

The OSS operational groups were the first American military men to achieve substantial success in training Asians. Every last OSS instructor knew his specialty from A to Z. Each had a record of success in his subject. Therefore, he was given considerable independence in his teaching.

Each commando soon reflected his teachers' personalities. And, oddly enough, these tough Yanks who came to teach the Chinese how to kill also brought with them more brotherly love than many do-gooders I have met on Asian soil.

The OSS believed in what I had been practicing and preaching for years: individual training. Where Stilwell's school in India had trained troops by the thousands, the OSS used more instructors and taught fewer pupils per class. Students learned new things only after truly mastering fundamentals. Later, the OSS men went into combat

[ 351 ]

with their trainees. But they did not give orders; they merely "advised" the Chinese squad leaders. In World War II, American "advisory" warfare worked very well in Asia. It has not proved highly successful since then.

I knew that whenever there was an American influx, there would be Sammy Yuan, a young Chinese businessman from Shanghai who had been my best friend in Rangoon.

Sammy was almost six feet tall and quite handsome. He always dressed expensively, and neatly. He was more American than Oriental, although he had never been west of Bombay. He was an expert on American philosophy, American women, American business, American history, and America. He even knew that Jefferson City was the capital of Missouri, which was more than many of the Americans in Rangoon could boast. Sammy's dream was to visit Jefferson City, Olympia, Helena, and all the other state capitals that nobody else knew about.

I began looking for my old Rangoon drinking companion on the streets of Kunming. Since Sammy was the most resourceful Chinese I have ever known, I almost expected him to turn up in an American uniform. Instead, late in 1943, Sammy appeared in the same uniform as mine — as an interpreter for General Tu Yu Ming's Army.

In early 1945, when I was sent on a mission to the Central Government in Chungking, Sammy went along as my interpreter. By then, I had been promoted to a full colonelcy.

I scarcely remember what the trip was about. Far more vividly, I remember a game that had become the new rage of Chungking's sophisticated international military set.

Some two dozen people would be invited to dinner. The guests were seated at one long, narrow table. Each guest dropped a twenty-dollar bill into a bowl on the table. Then he was issued a full bottle of liquor plus a small two-ounce shot glass.

Dinner was served. After the first course, each glass was filled to the brim with whiskey. Everybody would stand and face the host, who stood at the head of the table. He would propose a toast. Then every man there would drain his glass in one gulp, place it on the table, and refill it.

The host fell to his hands and knees. He crawled under the table from one end to the other. Each guest followed suit.

Upon arising, the men marched back to their assigned seats. This was done after each course and on into the evening. After a while, not everybody who crawled under the table emerged. Others were unable to lift themselves from their seats.

The winner of this game was the last man still standing at the table. He helped himself to the money in the bowl, from which the host's liquor expenses had been deducted.

I didn't win very often, but it was worth twenty dollars a throw to play the game with somebody I disliked. Under the table, my uniform spurs had a nasty habit of becoming caught in sensitive places.

I learned much later that this game did not originate in Chungking. It had been played in Moscow during the last days of the tsars.

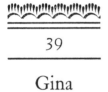

## 39

# Gina

IN 1945, about six weeks before the war ended, General William H. "Wild Bill" Donovan, head of the OSS, made a flying visit to London, Naples, Cairo, Karachi, Ceylon, New Delhi, and Kunming.

I didn't meet Donovan, but I reaped the harvest of his whirlwind tour.

A comely girl from Providence, Rhode Island, traveled with Donovan's official party. She had requested duty with OSS in China and Donvan had approved. Some twenty American women were already stationed at OSS headquarters in Kunming. Donovan would deliver her before returning to the States.

I met her on my way into OSS headquarters. I was on a routine errand. As I hurried up the steps, she came out of the building. A file of letters was in her hand. She didn't notice me, for she had to lower her eyes to watch the steps. I gave her a momentary glance, but every detail of her was etched in my memory.

She was slender. Even the WAC uniform (which she wore without insignia, as she was a civilian) looked feminine on her. Blonde hair embraced her shoulders. Her face, eyes, lips, and fair complexion sparkled in the clear blue sky of Kunming.

She radiated a certain joy of one newly arrived at her Shangri-La, but with a wistful awareness that enabled her to see the place as it really was. I knew the feeling well.

Everything about her made me vow: "I will meet her!"

I didn't have the nerve to accost her without being introduced. I started going to parties in the hope of meeting her. This was particularly risky for me if General Tu Yu Ming was giving or attending a party.

The general suffered from kidney trouble. He was not allowed to touch hard liquor. It was a Chinese custom, however, to appoint a deputy to do one's drinking in such circumstances. Whenever he could, General Tu deputized Sammy Yuan or me. We gave the general an excellent reputation for prodigious drinking.

As luck would have it, General Tu Yu Ming was everywhere I went in those lovesick, hopeful days. Several hangovers later, I concluded that, if I ever saw that girl again, I would be seeing double.

Ours was not a wartime romance. I didn't meet her until the day Japan surrendered — August 14, 1945. That date was a cherished milestone in many lives, particularly mine. My private war with Japan had raged in my soul since the early 1920's. Now it was over. And my courtship of Virginia Rathbun began.

General Tu Yu Ming's victory celebration was held in a dance hall overlooking the Flower Circle, a small cobblestoned park surrounded by stalls selling the finest blossoms of China.

The hall was jammed with American and Chinese military people. The orchestra was playing "Somewhere over the Rainbow" when I spotted the girl dancing with an OSS major. Luck was with me, for I knew her escort. His name was Paul Gale. I made my way over to them and was at their side when the music stopped.

"Gil, this is Virginia Rathbun. Her friends call her Gina [pronounced *Jinna*]. And Gina, this is the mythical Gilbert Stuart I've been telling you about," Paul said.

"Not the kind-hearted tiger!" she said in a warm voice that neither gushed nor mocked, but made me feel at home with her.

[ 354 ]

We looked into each other's eyes. Before I could speak my first words, a thousand firecrackers exploded. Kunming was celebrating peace with an impact worthy of an air raid.

Below us in the Flower Circle, people — clad in faded blue coolie clothes adorned with bright yellow chrysanthemums — were dancing. A tremendous paper dragon emerged from a side street and slithered into the Flower Circle. The excited crowd drew back to give it room. The Dance of the Dragon was on. It reared, twisted, and swayed. It dodged among streams of firecrackers and clouds of thick blue smoke.

We all watched from the dance hall balcony. I stole a glance at Gina. My gaze lingered and she caught me in the act. I blushed. She smiled reassuringly.

When my first words could be heard, I spoke to Gina and Paul. "This calls for a drink. What'll you have — red wine or green wine?"

Paul said: "I don't care if it's red, white, and blue. Let's drink to the victory."

Others joined in the toast. Soon, we were separated by the bedlam. But, at last, Gina and I had met, although only our eyes had conversed.

When we met again at a formal dinner party given by General Tu Yu Ming, we danced and exchanged a few words. I learned that Gina was twenty-four and had served the OSS in Italy, Cairo, and Washington. She learned that I was not the brutal soldier of fortune whom some of the paternal Americans had warned against.

Our conversation was very casual. Even after it ended, however, I could not keep my eyes off her.

Our hostess, Madame Tu Yu Ming, found me a little distracted. Her eyes followed mine to Gina and then made their way back to me. "Yes, she is beautiful," Madame Tu agreed with a smile and a nod.

Sammy Yuan caught me in the middle of an uncharacteristic sigh. "Is it love at first sight?" he asked.

I didn't answer. My thoughts were with Gina as she danced in and out of the shadows. Her fair hair, too, danced in the light, wound sinuously around her neck and shoulders, and swayed gently with the rhythm of the music. Her face beamed tenderly at all about her.

When I danced with her again, I asked if she would be interested in

[ 355 ]

driving with me to the West Mountain of Kunming on Sunday. She said she would love to.

There are people who pray for rain, but I wasn't one of them. On Sunday, *my* prayers were answered: It was a glorious day!

The canvas top of my jeep was down as Gina and I drove off. On our way up the mountain, we stopped at the Temple of the Five Hundred Gods. It overlooked Kunming Lake, the valley, and the city.

There was a man-made pond in the entranceway and I took Gina's hand as she studied the goldfish. Then I led her into the courtyard, where a Buddhist priest served us tea. While we sipped, we heard the deep boom of a gong and the jingle of many little bells.

Helping Gina to her feet, I said: "I'll take you into the main temple and introduce you to Buddha. You'll see all the priests and monks at prayer. And you'll see me make my own wish to Buddha with the prayer sticks!"

"I don't want to miss this for the world," she said, looking as rapt and observant as a little girl at a carnival.

The inside of the temple was filled with the light blue haze of burning joss sticks. Priests chanted prayers to the tunes of gongs and cymbals. The hundreds of ugly little carvings, representing Buddhist legends, were old friends today. I sensed their approval and Buddha's as I brought Gina before them.

The priests handed me the prayer sticks. Deftly, I shook one out onto the floor as I murmured inaudibly my only wish:

"Buddha, if you have brought Virginia Rathbun across the world to find me in China, let me spend the rest of my life with her — here, there, or anywhere."

I handed my prayer stick to the priest. He checked its number in an old, sacred book. Then he nodded slowly and read to me:

"It shall be as you wish."

On the way out, I handed the priest several dollars for Buddha's work well done. Then I offered to drive Gina to the very top of the West Mountain.

"I know of an old bullock trail that leaves just enough room for a jeep. I've taken one other person up there before."

"And who was she?" Gina asked.

"*He* was a British general. One of the top men in British Intelligence. I could think of no quieter place to talk with him. Nobody but bandits ever ventures up there."

Gina glanced at me uncertainly, but made no protest. I didn't tell her that the day before, I had dispatched a patrol of fifty men to make sure no suspicious persons were in the vicinity.

At the summit was Observation House. It was a small, venerable French mansion with windows opening out to encompass a breathtaking view of the lake and the valley.

I told Gina: "This is where I intend to come back and live. Right here in this house, if I can buy it."

She looked the place over anew — this time, possessively. Then she said: "I approve."

We strolled beneath the trees. Once, Gina stooped to pick some wildflowers. I watched her slender figure. All the beauty I had found here — in sky, mountains, lake, and valley — was embodied in her now. It would go wherever she went.

The mountain breeze played with the gentle wave in her blonde hair as she straightened up. Without a word, we kissed. Gina dropped her flowers and I whispered into her ear the secret wish I had made in the temple.

All she said was: "I know."

Word traveled fast in Kunming. Before we had descended the West Mountain, my Chinese Army friends seemed to know that the kindhearted tiger and the American girl wanted to be married.

We visited little coolie restaurants, the Black Dragon Pool, the Copper Temple, and other places around Kunming. And everywhere we went, the Chinese word *tai-tai* — meaning wife — followed us like a rustle of wind.

At Tu Yu Ming's headquarters, my friends told me they had never seen me happier.

A man in love is a pacifying sight. Even my enemies paused long enough to congratulate me on my "choice" — which was a strange word for the inevitable.

# 40

## Wedding in Shanghai

THE Japanese surrender terms were signed aboard the battleship *Missouri* on September 2, 1945 — V-J Day. General Tu Yu Ming's undeclared war with Governor Lung and the bandits of Yunnan Province raged for another month. Governor Lung was no political threat to us any longer; there didn't seem to be any enemy left to whom he could betray China.

At four A.M. on October 3, 1945, General Tu Yu Ming's troops — an infantry division, a mechanized division, the Special Battalion, and my Paratroop Commandos — laid siege to the city of Kunming. In the south of Yunnan Province, other Chinese Fifth Army troops intercepted and defeated two divisions of Governor Lung's troops in a full-scale battle.

The siege of Kunming lasted four days. I was on the go every minute of that time. I fought room-to-room gun battles with Governor Lung's high officials and their bodyguards. As I raced between command posts in my jeep, I was a frequent target for snipers.

On the fourth day, my paratroopers captured Governor Lung and the war was over.

We also captured hoards of gold bullion; millions of U.S. dollars' worth of stolen gasoline, jeeps, guns, and ammunition. We found stolen goods that nobody knew were missing.

Even in victory, the balance of power was so uneasy that Governor Lung had to be handled with care. He was exiled to Chungking. General Tu Yu Ming thought it would be good politics to give him a gala sendoff.

I was at the Kunming Airport for the occasion. Governor Lung looked even older than his portraits. He was bald, short, and very thin. One of his eyes was glazed and sightless. His other eye took everything in.

Above all, Governor Lung was a man of dignity. With dry charm, he thanked Tu Yu Ming for the generous sendoff. Two bands played.

An honor guard fired a rifle salute into the air. Tu Yu Ming shook the old man's hand as eight armed guards escorted him aboard a special plane for Chungking.

Even today in Kunming, I'm told, any reference to "the Revolution" means our overthrow of Governor Lung and not the Communist upheaval that was starting up then in the north of China. Governor Lung, incidentally, fared rather well under the Communists. They bled him of most of his wealth, but they let him return to Kunming and live in one of his palaces. There the ancient warlord lives out the rest of his life amidst delicate jade and antique furniture — himself a relic of China's past, twice removed.

It was a time of abrupt departures from Kunming. Ten days after Governor Lung's exit, most of the OSS personnel in Kunming were transferred to Shanghai. Gina was among them.

Before she left, we made a date for Shanghai — to be married there.

The Chinese Fifth Army left Kunming, too. Its official destination was Peking to the north. But everybody knew by late 1945 that the ultimate destination would be Manchuria, where the Russians and the Chinese Communists were operating at the time. General Tu Yu Ming was slated for Chiang Kai-shek's Northeast China Command.

For the Chinese people, World War II had been one of many preludes to the Chinese Civil War.

I was left behind in Kunming temporarily. My assignment was to hover like a vulture around the American base in Kunming. The Americans were liquidating their facilities there in a misguided effort to remain neutral toward Chinese politics. I was to take whatever they threw away or left behind.

Many Americans in China and Washington complained that Chiang Kai-shek had stored Lend-Lease equipment in warehouses instead of using it in the China Pacific war. They said he had been keeping it for the civil war to come.

I cannot say sweepingly whether or not this was true. I know for certain only that it was not true in Kunming. Everything that came to the Chinese Fifth Army was needed and used.

The Americans also insisted that only Chiang's stubbornness had kept Mao Tse-tung and his People's Army out of World War II. It is true that the Generalissimo refused to recognize the Communists as

[ 359 ]

a legal party. Even if he had, I don't think Mao's army would have fought the Japs any more than they did. Mao's Communist cadres attacked the Japs only when a guerrilla attack would provide urgently needed arms, equipment, or food. More than any others in China, the Reds were hoarding their strength for the war *after* World War II.

American neutrality took the form of not giving Chiang Kai-shek all the equipment they had to spare. Instead, surplus planes, sitting on the ground at Kunming Airport, were to be destroyed. Helplessly, I watched P–51's, L–5's, B–24 and B–25 bombers, and observation planes (some of them brand-new) become twisted, mangled wreckage — fleeting symbols of American policy in China. I saw American mechanics weep as they put sledgehammers and acetylene torches to planes they had tended like babies.

The American scorched-earth policy had become a grotesque caricature of itself.

When nothing more could be salvaged, I boarded an American plane for Shanghai — and Gina.

It was December of 1945. After long years in Japanese hands, Shanghai had come back to life. The city was a huge factory that had been shut down but kept oiled. Its heart beat to the rhythm of big business. Its night life throbbed with intrigue — international, interoffice, and domestic.

For years, the masses of China had been stirring uneasily in their long sleep. Now they were teeming with energy. Refugees from all over the land appeared in Shanghai like a plague of marching ants. In no time at all, they blanketed the city.

The horrors of war seemed forgotten overnight. There were immediate problems of starvation, unemployment, inflation and slums that sprang up overnight. The streets of Shankhai resembled Rangoon's. Like all the streets of urban China, they provided fertile soil for Communism.

The Shanghai climate was cold. Years had passed since I had felt the chill of winter in my bones. Now cold winds — trapped between the Gobi Desert and the Yellow Sea — whistled through my uniform.

Each night, my shivering frame climbed eight flights of stairs to Gina's apartment, which she shared with another American girl.

Shanghai did not yet have sufficient electric power to operate its elevators.

Our favorite rendezvous in Shanghai that winter was the Mandarin Club, a posh, romantic night spot. We would make our way past rickshaws and pedicabs (taxi versions of children's tricycles; a chauffeur pedals a seat built for two) to the entrance. We would walk down a passageway and then, stooping slightly, step into a dimly lit room that smelled faintly of sandalwood and Oriental perfume.

The cozy room was circular with blackwood and lacquer furnishings, small tables, a low ceiling, and three walls painted black, red, and gold. The back of the room was paneled with a decorative moon gate. Beneath it was an electric organ. The organist was a Filipino, who had only to brush the keys lightly to fill the room with music. Whenever we arrived, he played "If I Loved You," which promptly became "our" song.

I don't know how the organist spotted us at all. Small, exquisite Chinese lanterns cast the dimmest of lights. A shadow fell on each little table like an individual screen. One had the feeling of being alone in a Chinese courtyard designed for lovers.

I have a few other special memories of my brief two months in Shanghai: our favorite restaurant, the Yar, run by White Russians . . . the Hotel Metropole, where Gina and I lunched almost every day . . . riding home in a pedicab late on a rainy night.

Our engagement was announced officially shortly before Christmas. Sammy Yuan's mother held a formal reception for Virginia and me in the traditional style of old China. Aside from us, only members of the Yuan family were there. Sammy and his brother Jimmy came hundreds of miles to attend.

The matriarch received us in her bedroom, where the chairs had been decorated with embroidered red silk covers that were used only on holidays and special occasions. Afterwards, there were many toasts to *Tz'u-hsin Hu* and his *tai-tai*-to-be.

Most of Gina's fellow Americans in Shanghai wished her well, but a few of her superiors (and I use the word only with reference to rank) resented her marrying into the Chinese Army. At one stage of strained relations, I was barred from OSS headquarters on "suspicion of espionage."

A notice with my photo was posted outside the main gate. I took to meeting Gina there after work, while the Indian guards eyed me uneasily and passersby did double-takes as they saw me posing beside my portrait.

The notice was taken down at the request of U. S. Army C.I.D. and afterwards General Chow, Tu Yu Ming's deputy in Shanghai, officially commended me on the incident. At that time, any officer who was in the Americans' disfavor gained much face in the Chinese Army.

More than half of our twenty wedding guests were Americans. Gina and I were married on January 19, 1946 at Holy Trinity Cathedral, an Anglican church in the center of Shanghai. It had been built with bricks imported from England. The day was a gray, foggy, rainy Saturday. It was almost dark when we reached the church at four P.M.

Colonel Morris de Passe, the American military attaché in Chungking, gave Gina away. He was about her father's age and had three daughters back in the States. Dean A. C. Trivett performed the ceremony. Gina wore a gray satin suit and a small hat with a veil. To the veil was attached a tiny antique jeweled crown worn by Chinese brides. Her flowers were two white camellias — probably the last two in wintry Shanghai.

Dean Trivett apologized for the lack of heat in his church. He explained that the Japanese had taken away all the metal pipes for their final war effort. But, to this day, Gina and I insist that we didn't feel the least bit cold.

After a wedding reception (complete with flowers, champagne, and wedding cake) and a week's honeymoon in Shanghai, I reported to General Tu Yu Ming in Peking. Mrs. Gilbert Stuart went north with me to prolong our honeymoon.

We checked into the Peking Hotel and stayed there for a few days. The U.S. Army colonels and majors were billeted there. I don't know who was more embarrassed, Gina or I, when we entered the lobby and were greeted by a huge sign with black letters reading: "OFFICIAL U.S. ARMY PRO [for Prophylactic] STATION."

Even before registering, I ripped down the sign and grumbled to my bride: "They sure as hell wouldn't hang this out in the lobby of the Waldorf-Astoria, would they?"

"No," Gina admitted.

"I wonder if they call Peking 'the Rome of the Orient' because American tourists make asses of themselves here, too," I said.

Within a week, we moved out. I rented a small Chinese house on Nan Ho Yan in the shadow of the Forbidden City's wall. The Forbidden City was the part of Peking containing the Palace of the Chinese Emperors — magnificent buildings with tiled roofs and filled with artistic treasures. Within the wall were also a lake and trees. Once upon a time, the area was off limits to all but royalty. Now it was no longer forbidden, but open as a park and museum.

Our house and garden were surrounded by a high wall of our own. The large living room had French doors opening onto a terrace. Our bedroom opened onto the garden. An elderly houseboy was around to cater to and anticipate our every need. Our days in Peking were filled with happiness and love, but honeymoons — like peace in China — are not meant to last forever.

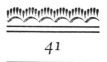

## 41

# At the Yamata Hotel

I LEFT Gina in Peking when General Tu Yu Ming dispatched me on a mission to Manchuria. The Russians were in control up there at the time. I was to look into the ugliest, wildest, and most contradictory rumors that Tu Yu Ming's Intelligence Service had ever assembled. I was also to gather what information I could about connections between the Russian Army and the Chinese Communist guerrillas. The latter were fighting a hit-and-run war of harassment against the Chinese Central Government.

The general sent me because he thought the presence of an Englishman in Chinese uniform would confuse everybody long enough for me to look around.

A few days after I arrived in Mukden, the industrial center of Manchuria, I sent word to Tu Yu Ming that the more improbable reports on his desk were true.

Manchuria had been in Japanese hands since 1932, when the Japs established the puppet state of Manchukuo under Emperor Henry Pu-Yi, the last of China's Manchu dynasty. Because of the long-term Japanese influence in Mukden, the Russians had trouble distinguishing between Japanese and Chinese civilians. When in doubt, they killed.

Hundreds of civilians had been lined up in the streets of Mukden. They had been mowed down by machine-gun fire. Russian tanks had then driven over the bodies until the gutters gushed with blood.

As late as 1946, the Russians were still engaging in wholesale slaughter of their Japanese prisoners-of-war. At least one whole Japanese division had taken to the hills. They had surrendered to Chinese troops, who gained admission to Manchuria themselves only after long negotiations.

There had been six thousand factories in Mukden alone when the Japs left. The Russians had seized all but eleven of them and stripped them bare. (The exceptions included the British-American Tobacco Company, and a few other foreign-owned properties.)

At each factory, the management and all the workers were placed under arrest. They were forced to dismantle their factory and load it — complete to the last bolt — on freight cars. Then managers and key mechanical personnel were shipped with their factory to Siberia or North Korea. There, they reassembled the machinery and trained new workers.

Some 750,000 Manchurians were "missing" in this manner when I arrived there in 1946. The Russians had not only industrialized their backward satellites, but they had also broken the spirit of the embattled Manchurian people.

I saw drunken Russian soldiers wandering the streets at night. They always traveled in pairs and seldom in packs of fewer than six. They fired bullets at random into the air, the ground, and the people. They raped women before their families' eyes. Then, when passion was spent, they choked their rape victims to death.

One evening in Mukden, I trailed a group of Russian soldiers enjoying a night on the town. They wandered into home after home — and found nobody there. The residents had fled as the soldiers approached.

The Russians entered a humble one-room Asian home with their hands clasped behind their backs. Their eyes roamed the room. When they had studied everything, they picked up every object — familiar or unfamiliar — and fingered it carefully. They replaced each item exactly where they found it. This examination went on for as long as an hour.

Suddenly, one of the soldiers would erupt in a frenzy and the others would join him. They smashed, ground, tore, and ripped everything in the house. This never took them more than ten minutes.

This orgiastic cycle was reenacted several times that night. At their last stop, the soldiers went to sleep in the debris they had created.

I didn't know what to think. Was this Communism's method of destroying property? Did these humble homes represent luxuries that Russians could never own? Or were these men exercising the instincts of victorious soldiers everywhere?

All I knew for certain was that new vistas of terror in Asia were still being opened by the white man. And I sensed that there was no depth to which man — white, yellow, or black — could not sink if he applied himself.


I stayed at the Yamata Hotel in Mukden. It was one of the few buildings left intact by the conquerors. Russian Army headquarters were in the Yamata.

The first night, I decided to drop in at the hotel's dining room. Almost all the tables were occupied by Russian staff officers. They were huddled over their plates. Hardly any conversation was audible over the clatter of silverware and dishes.

All four walls were covered with gigantic portraits of Josef Stalin. Below him were massed Russian flags — all brand-new and blood-red. The hammers and sickles looked as if they were poised to strike.

All eyes in the dining room were upon me — except those of two American civilians. I had met them in Kunming and Shanghai. I knew they represented an American secret intelligence agency. I decided to sit with them.

They almost choked on their caviar. Their eyes told me to go away. I thought I would put them at their ease by pretending not to know them.

"Hi there, boys!" I blustered loudly. "You don't look like Russkies

[ 365 ]

to me. Mind if I sit down with you? I hate to eat with Communists; they live too well for my taste."

As I sat down with the two mortified, speechless Yanks and ordered a bottle of vodka, I saw that my little speech — delivered with a British accent by a colonel in Chinese uniform — had thoroughly perplexed the rest of my audience.

At a table to my right sat a party of high Russian officers and one Russian civilian. He was a small, dark-haired little man. His hair was sleekly combed and so was his thin black mustache. He was trying to look dapper in a loud blue pencil-striped, double-breasted suit and several pounds of shoulder pads.

"Say," I said loudly to the two Americans, "doesn't that oily little man there look like a Russian version of that actor of yours — what's his name?"

"Clark Gable?" one of them tried diplomatically.

"I don't know," the other said.

I snapped my fingers and said: "Adolphe Menjou! That's it! Adolphe Menjou gone Communist."

I could see that the object of our discussion understood English. He was practically winking at me. After conferring with a general at his table, he stood up and smirked his way over to our table.

"Permit me to introduce myself," he said, clicking his heels and giving a name that was not Adolphe. "I am a correspondent for Tass."

"I don't read your newspapers," I said in my surliest manner. One of the Americans, however, invited him to join us. He was not a bad fellow, as it turned out. For the rest of the conversation, he bought the vodka.

When I stood up to leave I drew my .45 pistol and slammed it to the table with a thud that brought the entire room to dead silence.

My American friends blanched. The little man from Tass trembled. His mustache slithered as he licked his lips. I pointed an accusing finger at his previous table. Then I pointed to the portraits and flags. And then, speaking loudly and thickly, I addressed the Tass correspondent as he shrank in his seat:

"Tell the senior officer here that we are no longer at war. Tell him that the Russian Army's departure is long overdue. Tell him that Manchuria is part of China and under the protection of *all* Allied nations. And tell him that, as a Chinese officer, I demand that only one picture of Stalin and one Russian flag be displayed here. If there are any more than that, I will shoot Stalin off the wall myself the next time I come here."

The next morning, when I went into the dining room for breakfast, only one poster of Stalin survived. On the other walls were pictures of Chiang Kai-shek, Franklin D. Roosevelt, and Winston Churchill.

I didn't even register a complaint that Roosevelt and Churchill were out of office by then. The picture of Churchill was especially well mounted. It was opposite Stalin. While Roosevelt and the Generalissimo were smiling at each other across the room, Churchill was scowling at Stalin. This was one of many incidents that proved to me that the Russians were not invincible, that when their bluff was called, they would back down.

One drizzly afternoon, I saw two elderly Japanese civilians come running out of a tailor shop, with three Russian soldiers in pursuit. One of the Russians pounced on the old man and beat him to death with his submachine gun. Another took careful aim at the old lady and shot her down as she crossed the streetcar tracks. The third Russian brandished his tommygun menacingly at passersby until his companions were ready to leave.

I considered giving chase. Instead, I joined the crowd around both bodies. I stood with Chinese who wept for the two dead Japanese. Both civilians had come to Mukden in the 1930's and established their own tailor shop. They had become part of the Manchurian community — shopkeepers who kept their noses clean and stayed on when the Army left.

I gazed down at the dead Japanese tailor. In the rain, his back and face were wet with a fine mist. His blood mixed with the water and trickled slowly into the street. I thought of the three expressionless Russians who had murdered him.

I said to myself: "Stuart, those are the people who are finishing up what you came to Asia to do — to kill the Japanese."

What I had seen of Communism in action did nothing to convince me that it was where China's destiny lay. My sympathies were with the Western nations, but I realized that they shared one drawback with their Communist rivals: In battling for the Asian "masses," both preached a togetherness that inevitably would rob the Asian people of their own individuality.

Neither side was offering the Chinese people an independent blueprint for progress that would respect the variety of cultures, customs, and philosophies among half a billion people living on two million square miles of land.

I had often marveled at how well I fared in Asia despite my coming there for many wrong reasons — starting with passionate hatred for one nationality and blind devotion to another. And yet, as early as 1938 in the bowels of the Hong Kong Mines, hadn't I embodied an indigenous philosophy? The concept of the kind-hearted tiger — slapping with one hand and proffering a bowl of rice with the other, being cruel in order to be kind — was as paradoxical as all of Asia. Whether or not it was universal, it had improved the ways of life inside the Hong Kong Mines, along the Burma Road, and within the Chinese Army.

The path of the kind-hearted tiger had led to many personal rewards — ranging from sheer survival all the way up to my dearly beloved Gina. Along the way, it had brought me closer to myself.

Standing over the dead Japanese tailor in Mukden, I dimly remembered a callow youth talking earnestly to his girl at a boathouse in Hong Kong. The young man was insisting that killing his first Jap had been the beginning of wisdom.

Almost eight years later, however, the young man was still shedding the false skins of prejudice, hatred, contempt, and blindness with which he had armed himself against reality. All that had proved worthy of saving was the kind-hearted tiger, still pacing fiercely on the threshhold of wisdom and maturity.

# 42

# Last Flight to Mukden

I WAS thirty-six in 1948. My days in Asia were numbered. General **Tu** had become chronically ill since our arrival in Manchuria two years earlier and had returned to Shanghai. Each time I visited him, he looked worse; he was sick in heart as well as in body.

Relations between Chiang Kai-shek and the United States had deteriorated following the failure of the Marshall Mission, which had begun in 1946. The Marshall Mission was doomed at its inception by the impossible assignment given General Marshall: to effect a compromise between the Chinese Nationalists and Communists. The various truces ordered by the Marshall teams had served the purposes of the Communist armies in the north and provided them opportunity to regroup and grow strong with Russian aid. The Nationalist forces suffered from the enforced immobility during the truce periods and morale began to slip badly. With General Tu Yu Ming immobilized, among the officers of the Chinese Fifth Army, the more ambitious career soldiers had little trouble deciding on which side their futures lay; they defected and subverted.

Still, I continued to fight the Communist onslaught in Manchuria with every means at my disposal, including espionage and sabotage, and apparently not without some effect. The Communists had put a price on my head in 1946 and they had recently doubled it, so that my net worth to them was a quarter of a million dollars, dead or alive. Ironically, more than ever before, I was concerned with staying alive; Gina was in the States, we had one small daughter and another baby was on the way. General Tu sent for me and, in what was to be our last conversation, he told me that my military career in China was ended, that I had served well, but there was nothing more I could do. He saw that China was lost; the Communists would eventually kill me and my death would be no service. General Tu ordered me to leave China.

There were many times when I would have laid down my life for this heartsick invalid, but that was not one of them. I was thoughtful. I knew that General Tu was right; the end for the Nationalist Chinese was not far off, but I also knew equally well what he saw for my future — that the seeds of Communism sown throughout Asia had widened the horizons on which to fight for the freedom and dignity of men. This would be my last flight to Mukden . . . ironically it was nearly my last flight.

I arrived at the Peking airfield at ten A.M. The sky was clear. The Chinese Air Force C–47 I had requested was waiting for me. Pilot, copilot, and crew chief were standing by. They saluted snappily. Departures seldom began this smoothly.

One other officer and I boarded the plane. Cartons of parachutes were stacked along the length of the fuselage. The other passenger and I climbed over them to the front. We seated ourselves on cartons. The bulkhead, which divided the pilot's compartment from the rest of the plane, made a reasonably good back rest.

The pilot warmed up the engines. He checked out all his indicators. Then he took off like a veteran. He made a slow, gradual climb and brought the plane around on course for Mukden.

Having made several trips, I knew the flight plan and the terrain. I glanced out the window. All was well. I settled back with a book.

Flying time to Mukden was two and a half hours. After the first hour, the bright sun disappeared. Everything became gray. Through the window, I saw a severe rainstorm.

Below us, the mountains vanished from view. So did that famous but futile fifteen-hundred-mile long symbol, the Great Wall of China. It had never succeeded in protecting China from northern barbarians. Now it was hidden by dense, menacing clouds.

The plane's behavior was unpleasant, though no worse than was to be expected in a storm. I tried to keep my eyes glued to my book. An hour and a quarter later, I had turned exactly two pages. The plane was still battling the storm. But now — thank God — it was making its descent.

After a while, I noticed that our descent was taking unusually long. I assumed, however, that we had lost some of our forward speed in the storm.

The cabin door opened for the first time since takeoff. The crew

[ 370 ]

chief scurried out. Scrambling across the cartons, he traveled from window to window. He peered out anxiously as if in search.

I exclaimed aloud: "Jap planes!"

Then I burst out laughing. So did the other passenger, who was also a colonel. The war had been over for a year. The Chinese Communists did not have any planes in the air — *yet!*

With each lurch and roll of the plane, the crew chief grew more frantic. He began to bite his nails. He pushed his nose flat against each window. Whatever he was looking for, he wanted very badly to see it.

Eventually, he threw up his hands in despair. Stumbling back to the cabin, he slammed the door behind him.

I looked out. To my surprise, I saw land only three hundred feet below. It was still raining and we were passing through frequent low-lying clouds. But the plane was making some maneuvers that no pilot in his right mind would make at three hundred feet — even in perfect weather.

The plane would flip sharply to either side. Then it would flatten out — sometimes at high speed; sometimes at a speed slow enough to cause a near-stall.

I was about to go up to the cabin when the pilot came out.

He appeared calm. He gave me a reassuring smile as he looked out of a couple of windows.

Then he asked if I had a cigarette. I handed him a pack. After he had lit a cigarette, he inquired casually: "Do you happen to know the Mukden area, sir, from the air?"

"Why, yes," I said.

"Do you think you could spot the air base from up here, sir?"

I was taken slightly aback: "Is that why you're flying so low, lieutenant? Y' know, there are some pretty high mountains in this area."

"Well, sir. I figure that since I'm two and a half hours out of Peking, I ought to be over Mukden soon. I was told Mukden is on a river. I'm following that river you can see below. Maybe you can go up forward and tell us how far we are from Mukden."

In the cabin, I traced the pattern of the river three hundred feet below and announced: "You have the wrong river, lieutenant."

[ 371 ]

The pilot's mouth fell open. His copilot began to scream at the crew chief. But the pilot remained calm. He eased himself into his seat. Visibility ahead was no more than a thousand feet. The plane was bucking wildly.

Gazing at the compass and the scenery, I gathered we were too far northwest of Mukden. I asked the pilot what his course had been before letting down and finding the river.

His answer was the right one for fair weather. He had not allowed for drift and changed speed resulting from the storm. In fact, when I mentioned these factors, he didn't even know what I was talking about.

He had no charts of the area. His radio was out of order.

"How long have you been flying planes?" I asked.

"This," he said proudly, "is my first solo flight in a two-engine plane."

I looked at the fuel gauge. There was enough gas left for one and a half to two hours of flying.

"O.K.," I told pilot and copilot. "You've been following this river for half an hour. Turn this plane around. Fly back on exactly the opposite course at the same speed for half an hour. When you're just about where you let down and spotted the river, call me back up here."

I returned to my seat in the main compartment. There, the other passenger had unpacked a carton and laid out five brand-new parachutes.

I examined them. Then I looked at the labels on all the other cartons.

"Hundreds of parachutes," I told the other passenger, "but not one harness. They're useless."

Five minutes later, the plane swerved upward wildly. It was clearly out of control.

I climbed up to the door of the forward cabin. With great effort, I pushed it open. The crew chief was clinging to the other side. He had also been trying to open it. When he saw me, he tugged me inside. I jumped forward to the pilot's seat.

Both fliers were strapped in by their safety belts. The copilot was banging the pilot's head with one fist and clawing at his hair. The pilot was fending off the blows with one hand and trying to control the plane with the other.

I whipped out my .45 and brought it down on the copilot's head. He slumped over in his seat. I barely caught his head before it hit the instruments.

I unstrapped him. I told the crew chief to take him out, tie him up, and ask the other passenger to guard him.

I had never flown a plane, but I took the controls while the pilot patched up his wounds, smoked a cigarette, calmed down, and cursed his copilot: "That woman of a man. That God damn mother-f——er! . . ."

"You must have been trained to fly in the United States," I said.

"We both were," he said. Further questioning elicited the news that each of my youthful Lindberghs had some five hundred flying hours to his credit. And each had failed his tests!

Both men had been sent back to China in disgrace. They had expected at best to be given menial ground jobs. Instead, they had been appointed C-47 transport pilots. They had saved face, but at whose expense?

I had one last question: "Why did you keep failing your tests in the States?"

As he took over the controls, he said: "Landings. I made lousy landings."

Sweat was dripping from beneath my hatband as the C-47 meandered above the Mongolian plain.

Suddenly, to the east, I spotted a single-track railway line. I told the pilot: "Follow that track! It must be a branch of the main line to Mukden. If we're lucky . . ."

Fifteen minutes later, the track joined a double-track line. This had to be the main route! Calculating our position, I figured that we were an hour from Mukden. We had just about an hour's fuel supply.

I instructed the pilot: "Follow that track as if you're a railroad train. I'm going back to see if I can find you a copilot."

"I don't want that fool," the pilot whined.

"You'll need all the help you can get to make that landing," I assured him.

The copilot was propped up against the side of the fuselage. He looked sick and very sorry for himself. I cut him loose and gave him a ten-minute lecture on military rank and responsibility. I told him I would court-martial him unless he apologized to the pilot and resumed his job.

I went forward with the sheepish copilot. He begged most eloquently for forgiveness. After a tense five minutes, the pilot beckoned him to his seat. The pilot's face, however, had a stony expression.

I stayed on in the cabin. Rain was coming down in sheets again. The fuel supply was dwindling.

Then the clouds ahead opened up just long enough for me to glimpse a familiar bend in the river that swooped around Mukden. From above, the city lay like a corpse. Roofs of looted buildings stood open and gaping up at us. Chimneystacks were silent, clean, and naked. What one outside civilization had given to Mukden, another had taken away.

I gave the pilot directions until the nose of our plane was aligned with the runway of Mukden Air Base. There was no time for a dry run over the field. The fuel gauge read "Empty."

Clutching the roof of the plane, I said my prayers just as the pilot suddenly remembered to lower the wheels.

We zoomed in low and fast. There was a Chinese cemetery at the air base — a pile of dirt mounds, about four feet high, planted at the end of the airstrip. It whizzed by disconcertingly. On other approaches, the graves had been well below us. This time, they loomed like mountains.

Instead of goosing the gas and raising the plane a few precious feet, the pilot cut his engines. We came to earth with a wrenching jar. One of the graves ripped off the starboard wheel. The plane twisted, bounced, skidded, and then slipped along the ground on its left wing. I was thrown to the roof and back to the floor several times. The plane was still sliding on the wet ground when I picked myself up and tried to open the door to the main compartment.

All the parachutes had moved forward to jam the door. When the plane halted, the two "aviators" and I managed to crawl out through the front of the plane.

The passenger and the crew chief were standing outside. They were battered, but not badly hurt.

The wreckage of the plane was sprawled across the edge of the runway.

"You see, colonel," the pilot boasted. "I made the runway this time. I learn by experience."

He and the copilot threw their arms around each other. Round and round they went as they shouted fervent personal congratulations to each other. Now that they were back on the good earth, all their fright had vanished. One would never have guessed that, an hour earlier, one of these men was trying to kill the other in a frenzy of fear.

For them, the ending had been happy. True, one had lost face and the other had lost his plane. But from the way they danced on the wet runway, you might have thought they had performed the impossible.

Perhaps they had. They had survived another day — somehow.

By nightfall, another heroic story of bravery and skill in midair would be born. It would be embroidered with dragons of lightning and bellowing furies of thunder to cover the more blatant miscalculations. Their legend would be told and retold. Out of it all might come a medal or two — to be awarded posthumously if they ever laid hands on another airplane.

I left Mukden Air Base with a vivid recollection of two fools dancing madly around their wreckage of a flying machine.

I walked away, knowing that I had helped an indestructible people withstand the perils of progress. My contribution had been small, but, in making it, I had backed the nearest thing to a winner in the history of the earth: human endurance.